Tony Davies

Price reduced
to 9.99
as a result of
damage?

# LANDMINES

# TITLES OF RELATED INTEREST

*Landmines in El Salvador & Nicaragua*
*The Civilian Victims (1986)*
Americas Watch

*Landmines in Cambodia*
*The Coward's War (1991)*
Asia Watch & Physicians for Human Rights

*Hidden Death*
*Landmines and Civilian Casualties in Iraqi Kurdistan (1992)*
Middle East Watch

*Hidden Enemies*
*Landmines in Northern Somalia (1992)*
Physicians for Human Rights

*Landmines in Angola (1993)*
Africa Watch

# LANDMINES

## A Deadly Legacy

### The Arms Project of Human Rights Watch

### &

### Physicians for Human Rights

**Human Rights Watch**
New York · Washington · Los Angeles · London

Library of Congress Catalog Card Number: 93 80418
ISBN 1-56432-113-4

Cover photo shows a collection of antipersonnel and antitank landmines in Iraqi Kurdistan. Copyright ® R. Maro; courtesy of Medico International (Germany).

## THE ARMS PROJECT OF HUMAN RIGHTS WATCH

The Arms Project of Human Rights Watch was formed in 1992 with a grant from the Rockefeller Foundation for the purposes of monitoring and seeking to prevent arms transfers to governments or organizations that either grossly violate internationally recognized human rights or grossly violate the laws of war. It also seeks to promote freedom of information and expression about arms transfers worldwide. The Arms Project takes a special interest in weapons that are prominent in human rights abuse and the abuse of non-combatants. The director of the Arms Project is Kenneth Anderson and its Washington director is Stephen D. Goose. Barbara Baker and Cesar Bolaños are New York staff associates, and Kathleen Bleakley is the Washington staff associate. Monica Schurtman is counsel.

Members of the international advisory committee of the Arms Project are: Morton Abramowitz, Nicole Ball, Frank Blackaby, Frederick C. Cuny, Ahmed H. Esa, Jo Husbands, Frederick J. Knecht, Andrew J. Pierre, Gustavo Gorriti, Di Hua, Edward J. Laurance, Vincent McGee, Aryeh Neier, Janne E. Nolan, David Rieff, Kumar Rupesinghe, John Ryle, Mohamed Sahnoun, Gary Sick and Tom Winship.

# HUMAN RIGHTS WATCH

Human Rights Watch conducts regular, systematic investigations of human rights abuses in some sixty countries around the world. It addresses the human rights practices of governments of all political stripes, of all geopolitical alignments, and of all ethnic and religious persuasions. In internal wars it documents violations by both governments and rebel groups. Human Rights Watch defends freedom of thought and expression, due process of law and equal protection of the law; it documents and denounces murders, disappearances, torture, arbitrary imprisonment, exile, censorship and other abuses of internationally recognized human rights.

Human Rights Watch began in 1978 with the founding of Helsinki Watch by a group of publishers, lawyers and other activists and now maintains offices in New York, Washington, D.C., Los Angeles, London, Moscow, Belgrade, Bucharest and Hong Kong. Today, it includes Africa Watch, Americas Watch, Asia Watch, Helsinki Watch, Middle East Watch, and four collaborative projects, the Arms Project, Prison Project, Women's Rights Project, and the Fund for Free Expression. Human Rights Watch is an independent, nongovernmental organization, supported by contributions from private individuals and foundations. It accepts no government funds, directly or indirectly.

The executive committee includes Robert L. Bernstein, chair; Adrian W. DeWind, vice chair; Roland Algrant, Lisa Anderson, Peter D. Bell, Alice L. Brown, William Carmichael, Dorothy Cullman, Irene Diamond, Jonathan Fanton, Alan Finberg, Jack Greenberg, Alice H. Henkin, Stephen L. Kass, Marina Pinto Kaufman, Alexander MacGregor, Peter Osnos, Bruce Rabb, Orville Schell, Gary Sick, and Malcolm Smith.

The staff includes Kenneth Roth, executive director; Holly J. Burkhalter, Washington director; Gara LaMarche, associate director; Ellen Lutz, California director; Susan Osnos, press director; Jemera Rone, counsel; Michal Longfelder, Development director; Stephanie Steele, operations director; Allyson Collins, research associate; Joanna Weschler, Prison Project director; Kenneth Anderson, Arms Project director; Dorothy Q. Thomas, Women's Rights Project director; and Gara LaMarche, the Fund for Free Expression director.

The executive directors of the divisions of Human Rights Watch are Abdullahi An-Na'im, Africa Watch; Juan E. Méndez, Americas Watch; Sidney Jones, Asia Watch; Jeri Laber, Helsinki Watch; and Andrew Whitley, Middle East Watch.

*Addresses for Human Rights Watch*

485 Fifth Avenue
New York, NY 10017-6104
Tel: (212) 972-8400
Fax: (212) 972-0905
email: hrwatchnyu@igc.org

1522 K Street, N.W., #910
Washington, DC 20005
Tel: (202) 371-6592
Fax: (202) 371-0124
email: hrwatchdc@igc.org

10951 West Pico Blvd., #203
Los Angeles, CA 90064
Tel: (310) 475-3070
Fax: (310) 475-5613
email: hrwatchla@igc.org

90 Borough High Street
London, UK SE1 1LL
Tel: (071) 378-8008
Fax: (071) 378-8029
email: africawatch@gn.org

# PHYSICIANS FOR HUMAN RIGHTS

Physicians for Human Rights (PHR) is an organization of physicians and other health professionals that brings the knowledge and skills of the medical sciences to the investigation and prevention of violations of international human rights and humanitarian law. PHR works to apply the special skills of health professionals to stop torture, "disappearances" and political killings by governments and opposition groups; to report on conditions and protection of detainees in prisons and refugee camps; to investigate the physical and psychological consequences of violations of humanitarian law and medical ethics in internal and international conflicts; to defend the right of civilians and combatants to receive medical care during times of war; to protect health professionals who are victims of human rights abuses; and to prevent medical complicity in torture and other human rights abuses.

Since 1986, PHR has sent over forty fact-finding and emergency missions to over twenty-five countries. PHR bases its actions on the Universal Declaration of Human Rights and other international human rights and humanitarian agreements. The organization adheres to a policy of strict impartiality and is concerned with the medical consequences of human rights abuses regardless of the ideology of the offending government or group.

H. Jack Geiger, M.D. is President; Carola Eisenberg, M.D. is Vice President; Eric Stover is Executive Director; Susannah Sirkin is Deputy Director; Kari Hannibal is Membership and Education Coordinator; Gina VanderLoop is Development Director; Barbara Ayotte is Senior Program Associate; Shana Swiss, M.D. is Director of Women's Program; Vincent Iacopino, M.D. is Western Regional Representative; and Clyde C. Snow is Senior Forensic Consultant.

Physicians for Human Rights can be reached at 100 Boylston Street, Suite 702, Boston, MA 02116; Tel: (617) 695-0041; Fax: (617) 695-0307.

*To the mine clearers*

# CONTENTS

# PREFACE

As chairman of the Foreign Operations Subcommittee of the United States Senate, I have seen the terrible toll of antipersonnel landmines on innocent civilians. Hundreds of thousands—perhaps millions—of people, many of them children, have lost their lives, their legs and arms, or their eyesight from stepping on landmines. These insidious weapons, sometimes designed to look like toys to lure unsuspecting children, are strewn indiscriminately in fields, along jungle paths, and on main travel routes. From Cambodia to Nicaragua, tens of millions of landmines have rendered whole areas uninhabitable long after the conflicts end and the causes of war are forgotten.

Four years ago, I initiated a fund in the U.S. foreign aid budget to provide artificial limbs and other assistance to civilian victims of landmines. Last year, I sponsored legislation to impose a one year moratorium on the sale, transfer and export abroad by the United States of antipersonnel landmines, and to provide funds for demining efforts. This year, I successfully spearheaded the effort to extend the moratorium for three years and to provide additional demining funds. But these are only first steps. Much more needs to be done to stop the carnage caused by landmines.

The Arms Project of Human Rights Watch and Physicians for Human Rights have been instrumental in raising awareness of the urgent need to address the global landmines problem. Their on-site investigations and reports on the use of landmines in such places as Cambodia, Angola, Somalia, and Iraqi Kurdistan have revealed in gruesome detail the long-term effects of these weapons. Armed with these reports, these two organizations are at the forefront of a global campaign to ban the production, stockpiling, trade and use of antipersonnel landmines.

With this book on global landmines, the Arms Project of Human Rights Watch and Physicians for Human Rights have assembled the most comprehensive collection of information about the worldwide landmine crisis to date. It presents both a global overview and detailed country studies. It reviews and analyzes international law governing landmines, and examines what limited national measures exist to control landmines. It includes in-depth research on global production and trade in landmines, and describes the medical, social and economic consequences

xi

of landmines in chilling detail. Altogether, this report makes a convincing case for an international agreement to prohibit the production, stockpiling, trade and use of antipersonnel landmines.

This book will serve as an invaluable resource for policymakers, journalists, researchers, humanitarian and human rights organizations, experts and non-experts alike. However, what matters most is how we, as concerned citizens, use this book to counter the growing scourge of landmines. Governments, non-governmental organizations, and people everywhere must work together to put an end to this senseless slaughter of the innocent.

Senator Patrick J. Leahy
Washington, D.C.

# LANDMINES

# 1
# A WEAPON OF MASS
# DESTRUCTION IN SLOW MOTION

There is no doubt of the landmine crisis.[1]

Although many people believe that landmines are a tragic issue for only a few deeply infested places, the problem affects a wide range of countries including Afghanistan, Angola, Cambodia, El Salvador, Ethiopia, Iraq, Mozambique, Nicaragua, Northern Somalia, Vietnam, and former Yugoslavia. Experts estimate that at least 85 million and possibly more than 100 million unexploded landmines currently lie scattered through at least 62 countries.[2]

Unlike a bomb or artillery shell which explodes when it approaches or hits its target, a landmine lies dormant until a person, vehicle, or animal triggers its firing mechanism. Landmines are blind weapons that cannot distinguish between the footfall of a soldier and that of an old woman gathering firewood. They recognize no ceasefire and, long after the fighting has stopped, they can maim or kill the children and grandchildren of the soldiers who laid them.

---

[1] "Landmines" or "mines," as used in this report, refer to antipersonnel landmines, boobytraps, or similar explosive devices, rather than to antitank landmines or water mines. Where antitank mines are meant, then that term is used. This terminology is adopted strictly for convenience in this report and carries no substantive implications.

[2] A recent State Department report estimates that there are roughly 65-110 million antitank and antipersonnel landmines scattered in 62 countries. United States Department of State, *Hidden Killers: The Global Problem with Uncleared Landmines* (Washington, D.C.: United States Department of State, 1993), pp. i, 3, reproduced as Appendix 5. The United Nations believes that the figure is more than 100 million and perhaps as many as 200 million. Patrick Blagden, "Summary of United Nations demining" in ICRC, *Report of the Symposium on Antipersonnel Mines: Montreux 1993* (Geneva: ICRC), p. 117.

It is estimated that several hundred people fall victim to landmines each month.[3] The primary victims are unarmed civilians; children are particularly affected.[4] The presence of vast numbers of live mines also renders large areas of land inaccessible, prevents refugees and displaced people from returning home, precludes farmers and shepherds from working their fields, hampers humanitarian aid, and hinders development and rebuilding following the end of war.

The countries most contaminated by landmines are located in the developing world, and they lack the resources to respond to the medical, social, economic, and environmental consequences caused by mines. These countries are inhabited mainly by rural agricultural and pastoral populations who depend on working the land to survive. The danger created by landmines often makes such forms of subsistence impossible.

The effects of landmines are felt at all levels of society: individual, family, community, and nation. Survivors of mine explosions suffer extreme physical pain and, frequently, loss of livelihood. Families of mine victims must contend with severe financial strains due to the cost of treatment and rehabilitation, loss of the victim's earnings, and the need to support an unproductive relative. In areas with significant mine problems, villagers either must learn to co-exist with mines and work their fields as best they can, risking death every day, or else abandon their homes to live elsewhere. As a result, community life becomes strained or disintegrates altogether. For nations, the presence of mined regions can seriously cripple the ability to build a postwar economy through, for example, disabling the transport and communication systems, and preventing agricultural endeavors. In its recent report on landmines, the U.S. State Department underscores the problem, stating that uncleared mines "provide a continuing element of chaos in countries

---

[3] According to the State Department, landmines kill or wound more than 150 people per week worldwide. DOS, *Hidden Killers*, p. 2. The American Red Cross, has estimated that 800 people are killed and 450 are injured each month because of landmines. Statement of Elizabeth Dole on behalf of the American Red Cross, April 21, 1993, reproduced as Appendix 6.

[4] Statement of Sen. Patrick Leahy, *Congressional Record*, p. S11376, Sept. 10, 1993, reproduced as Appendix 8; DOS, *Hidden Killers*, p. 2; Statement of Elizabeth Dole, April 21, 1993.

striving for stability....The impact of uncleared landmines on a developing economy is tremendous."[5]

Originally designed to maim or kill enemy troops or slow their movement, and to defend territory, military installations, antitank minefields and personnel, landmines currently are used against civilians, both intentionally and indiscriminately, in violation of international law. Recent evidence from a number of countries shows that mines are increasingly used as part of deliberate military strategies to spread terror among civilians and keep them away from their homes and sources of food.

Two characteristics distinguish landmines from other weapons and cause them to be particularly insidious. First, they are delayed-action weapons. They are meant not for immediate effect, but rather are primed, concealed, and lie dormant until triggered. In theory, mines can be directed at legitimate military targets. However, because of the time lag between when mines are laid and when they explode, mines frequently strike civilians instead. Thus, landmines are indiscriminate weapons or, at least, are weapons indiscriminate in their effects. Senator Patrick Leahy, author of the Landmine Moratorium Act—a ban on the export of landmines enacted by the United States Congress in 1992—has drawn a parallel between mines and chemical and biological weapons:

> What do chemical and biological weapons have in common with landmines: They do not discriminate. A landmine will blow the leg or the arm off of whoever steps on it. It does not make any difference whether it is a combatant, a civilian, older person, or a child.[6]

The delayed-action function of landmines also causes serious long-term consequences unmatched by any other low-tech weapon. In Poland, for example, as late as 1977, 30–40 people were still being killed annually by mines laid during World War II, despite the fact that more

---

[5] DOS, *Hidden Killers*, p. 3.

[6] Statement of Sen. Patrick Leahy, *Congressional Record*, p. S9290, July 22, 1993, reproduced as Appendix 8.

than 25 million mines had already been cleared within Polish borders.[7] Large areas of land in other parts of Europe, North Africa and the Middle East remain impassable as a result of World War II minefields.[8]

The on-going threat created by live landmines can prevent civilians from living in their homes and using their fields, and can seriously threaten the ability of an entire country to re-build long after war has ended. The psychological pressure of living with such a threat also cannot be discounted.  As Senator Leahy has noted:

> Think of the horror of living day to day in a country
> where at any moment you could lose a leg, or your life,
> or your child's life, because of these hidden weapons.
> Where any open field, or patch of trees, or roadside ditch
> is a potential death trap.  That is a way of life for tens of
> millions of people around the world.[9]

The second distinguishing feature of landmine use is the particularly egregious nature of mine injuries. The majority of landmine explosions that do not cause death result in traumatic or surgical amputation. In Cambodia, for example, an estimated one out of every 236 people has lost at least one limb to an exploding mine.[10]  As reported in the *British Medical Journal*:

---

[7] Jody Williams, "Social Consequences of Widespread Use of Landmines" in ICRC, *Report of the Symposium of Anti-personnel Mines: Montreux 1993* (Geneva: ICRC, 1993), p. 69.

[8] Lt. Col. P.R. Courtney-Green, *Ammunition for the Land Battle*, (London: Brassey's [U.K.], 1991).

[9] Statement of Sen. Patrick Leahy, *Congressional Record*, p. S9290, July 22, 1993.

[10] This ratio was established by Asia Watch and Physicians for Human Rights in investigations for their 1991 report, *Landmines in Cambodia: The Coward's War* (New York: Human Rights Watch, 1991).  Further epidemiological research will refine this statistic, but it is the best currently available figure and remains correct to an order of magnitude.

> "Landmines...have ruinous effects on the human body: they drive dirt, bacteria, clothing and metal and plastic fragments into the tissue causing secondary infections. The shock wave from an exploding mine can destroy blood vessels well up the leg, causing surgeons to amputate much higher than the site of the primary wound."[11]

The result for the individual is not one but, typically, a series of painful operations, often followed by a life at the margins of a society heavily dependent on manual labor.

Mine clearance cannot effectively deal with the crisis; it is too little, too late. When undertaken at all, efforts are badly funded and poorly coordinated. Yet even if demining were given top priority, it would not be a solution. Mines are being laid worldwide far faster than they are being removed. The political will to undertake mine clearing efforts in societies already devastated by war is minimal. Clearance is slow, dangerous, and expensive. Technology for clearing mines is primitive. "Most mine-clearing tools are glorified farm implements," according to a recent analysis in *The Bulletin of the Atomic Scientists*, and "a man with a stick is still the most common instrument."[12] Few experts believe that any "silver bullets" can be developed to transform removal.

Moreover, while the average mine costs between $10 and $20, the average direct and indirect costs of removal range from $300 to $1,000 a mine—a ratio frightening in its implications for a world with roughly 100 million uncleared mines. Even if new technology and economies of scale brought mine removal costs down by a factor of ten, the cost of mine clearance would still be so prohibitive that clearance alone could not abate the crisis.

The Landmines Protocol, an international treaty intended to diminish landmine use against civilians, has also proved utterly ineffective in stemming the crisis. Although the Landmines Protocol does contain provisions to curb certain kinds of use, it does not address the

---

[11] Rae McGrath and Eric Stover, "Injuries from Landmines," 303 *British Medical Journal*, Dec. 14, 1991.

[12] Jim Wurst, "Ten Million Tragedies, One Step at a Time," *The Bulletin of the Atomic Scientists*, July/Aug. 1993, p. 20.

fundamental problem of temporal indiscriminateness inherent in mine warfare: the effects of mines that outlast their military utility and place civilians at risk, typically on a long-term basis. Landmines thus cannot distinguish civilians from combatants. In failing to take into account that mines will strike civilians and combatants without distinction, and that the effects of landmine use cannot be controlled, the Landmines Protocol fails to conform with existing customary international law, particularly as set forth in 1977 Additional Protocol I to the Geneva Conventions of 1949.[13]

Complex rules, discretionary language, and broad exceptions and qualifications further limit the utility of the Landmines Protocol. Moreover, its provisions do not generally apply to internal conflicts in which the vast majority of mines are used, and it contains no enforcement mechanisms. Finally, even its limited rules are rarely followed: armies both regularly use mines deliberately against non-combatants and fail to take even minimal precautions to safeguard against collateral harm to civilians.

The Landmines Protocol is eligible for review and revision following the tenth anniversary of its entry into force, on December 3, 1993. Several countries have indicated a desire to convene a review conference. The Arms Project and Physicians for Human Rights favor a review conference, provided that the agenda is broad enough to allow full consideration of a complete ban on production, stockpiling, transfer, and use of landmines, on the model of the 1972 Biological Weapons Convention, which combines humanitarian and disarmament law concerns into a single treaty. It is essential that a review conference avoid the difficulties of the conferences in the 1970s that brought about the current, deeply flawed Landmines Protocol, and that participants understand clearly how the Landmines Protocol has failed in concept and in fact.

There are six main reasons why the use of landmines has reached crisis proportions.

---

[13] See especially 1977 Additional Protocol I, art. 51(4). The egregious nature of mine injuries and the severe, long-term impact that mines have on civilian populations also renders landmine use in violation of Protocol I, art. 35(2) which prohibits weapons that cause unnecessary suffering—a problem not contemplated by the drafters of the Landmines Protocol.

First, an ever-growing number of nations, particularly from the developing world, are producing and exporting landmines.[14] During recent years, Singapore and Pakistan, for example, have become significant producers and aggressive exporters of landmines. China has also emerged during the past five years as a top exporter of landmines. More than 340 types of antipersonnel landmines have been produced in at least 48 countries. At least 29 countries have exported landmines. The increase in availability of landmines significantly contributes to the current crisis.

Second, mines are now used in armed conflict frequently as destabilizing weapons. They have shifted from being primarily a defensive, tactical battlefield weapon to an offensive, strategic weapon often aimed deliberately at civilians in order to empty territory, destroy food sources, create refugee flows, or simply spread terror.

Third, the nature of warfare has changed in recent decades: many wars are long-running, internal, and low intensity, often involving cash-starved militaries for whom low-technology, low-cost landmines are a weapon of choice. Such conflicts are rarely fought on conventional battlefields; rather, entire countries become theaters of war. In conventional wars mines are used by rapid-maneuver, armor-based armies primarily to hamper the movement of enemy troops, thereby buying time. In many modern insurgency-counterinsurgency conflicts, however, mines are used principally as area denial weapons, useful in overcoming the low force-to-space ratio typical of such conflicts. Consequently, in wars today, mines are frequently placed in areas of high civilian concentration rather than being confined to discrete battlefields of limited size. Mines are laid in vast quantities across whole zones, and are often aimed directly at civilians. They thus take on certain features of strategic weapons.

New forms of conflict, particularly ethnic conflict, give rise to new abuses. Ethnic warfare tends to alter the usual insurgency-counterinsurgency calculations that might otherwise constrain the use of landmines in internal wars; one side in an ethnic conflict, for example, may not care about permanently ruining the land of its ethnic enemy if it does not plan to occupy that land.

---

[14] See "Producers and Exporters of Anti-Personnel Landmines" Map and Tables I and II of Chapter 3. pp 103, 4

The outbreak of local and regional conflicts in the post-Cold War era has already led to the sowing of millions of new mines world-wide. Iraq's invasion of Kuwait resulted in the laying of an estimated seven million mines in Kuwait.  Iraq's offensive in Kurdistan during and after the Gulf War combined to flood Kurdistan with an estimated three to five million additional mines.  The splintering of Yugoslavia already has been accompanied by the deployment of approximately two million mines. It is possible that more mines are being laid there every day than anywhere else in the world.  The break-up of the Soviet Union has seen landmines spread by the tens of thousands throughout Nagorno-Karabakh, Tajikistan, and Georgia.

A fourth reason for the current landmine crisis is that mine technology has become more sophisticated, and those who can afford the more advanced mines use them.  Many technological developments have made mines more lethal.  Plastic construction, for example, with little or no metal, makes mines more difficult to detect and remove.  The manufacture of small mines similarly hinders clearance.  Sophisticated anti-handling devices, often with microchips or electronic sensors, increase the risk to demining personnel.

The development of remotely delivered mines, also known as "scatterables," which are delivered by aircraft, artillery, or rocket, allows mines to be laid far more rapidly and in far greater numbers than in the past.  What might have taken a World War II battalion all day to put in place can now be accomplished in minutes.  In addition, the ultimate location of where remotely delivered mines are placed is much more difficult to control than manually-emplaced mines.  Because of imprecise placement, and the large areas that can be covered with remotely delivered mines, it is also much harder to record their location. Consequently, it is much more difficult to locate and remove remotely delivered mines. These mines have been used primarily in Vietnam, Afghanistan, and the Falkland/Malvinas Islands.[15]

---

[15] In addition to landmines, which are deliberately designed to be a delayed-action weapon, so-called antipersonnel "submunitions"—including cluster bombs and bomblets—create many of the same hazards as landmines because a high percentage fail to explode when delivered. Submunitions are not covered by the Landmines Protocol, because they are not *designed* as a delayed-action weapon, but insofar as they fail to explode and remain live, they pose virtually the same risks.  Submunitions were used extensively in the Gulf War.

A fifth explanation for today's crisis is that, compared with other modern weapons, mines are relatively cheap. The U.S. Defense Intelligence Agency notes that mines are cost-effective for the following reasons:

1. When compared with its intended target, the price of a landmine can increase significantly before losing its cost-effectiveness;

2. the cost of technological improvements in landmines is generally less than the cost of the technologies needed to counter them;

3. recent developments in mine technology, such as rapid delivery systems, while resulting in a more expensive landmine, can also result in a more economical minefield.[16]

Finally, the current landmine crisis results from the sheer accumulation of mines throughout the world. This is due to the factors described above: the increase in landmine producers and exporters; wars fought by poor armies which rely heavily on landmines; wars in which the whole nation becomes the battlefield; long running wars; wars in which enormous quantities of scatterable mines are strewn from aircraft; the use of mines that are more difficult to detect; the cheap cost of using mines; and the inability of mine clearance efforts to respond adequately to the magnitude of the problem. The crisis shows no sign of abating.

The current crisis requires that landmines be reconceptualized. Because they traditionally have been seen as defensive weapons used primarily on the battlefield, landmines have not been high on arms control and disarmament agendas. Landmines today, however, are used in certain ways characteristic of weapons of mass destruction.

Indeed, it is useful in some respects to think of landmines as a weapon of mass destruction *in slow motion*—on a slow fuse. They work in slow motion because it is the gradual accumulation of mines that creates the potential for mass destruction; once there, however, the destruction

---

[16] U.S. Defense Intelligence Agency and U.S. Army Foreign Science and Technology Center, *Landmine Warfare — Trends and Projections*, December 1992, DST-11608-019-92, p. xvii. This document was obtained by the Arms Project through the Freedom of Information Act.

is akin to that of a weapon of mass destruction. It is easy to overstate this point, but it is worth making for comparison.

To those unfamiliar with their consequences, mines may not initially evoke the nightmarish visions of warfare conducted, for example, with chemical or biological weapons, traditionally thought of as weapons of mass destruction. However, in their inability to distinguish civilian and military targets, the numerous deaths and egregious injuries they cause, and their terrible potential for massive long-term devastation, landmines are not very different. Indeed, in some ways landmines are worse than chemical weapons, which at least rapidly dissipate.

The use, production, stockpiling, and transfer of biological and toxin weapons was banned by international treaty in 1972 as "repugnant to the conscience of mankind."[17] Mounting evidence of the destruction caused by landmines has led the Arms Project and Physicians for Human Rights, along with other human rights, humanitarian, and development organizations throughout the world, to call for a similar total ban on landmines. A total ban on production, stockpiling, transfer, and use of landmines is preferable to the existing restrictions contained in the Landmines Protocol for several reasons.

With regard to use, the Arms Project and Physicians for Human Rights believe that only a proscription against all use of landmines comports with customary humanitarian law, particularly as expressed in Protocol I. In addition, the experience of recent decades has been that if combatants have access to landmines, they will use them in abundance, typically without regard for the limited, but quite complex, rules prescribed by the Landmines Protocol. A complete ban would be easier to monitor and enforce than intricate regulations on use which will always engender debate as to whether a particular use is permissible or not.

Moreover, given the magnitude of the crisis, the only way to affect use is to attach to landmines the same stigma attached to chemical and biological weapons. But such a stigma cannot come about if some uses of landmines are legal and others illegal, with an interminable argument over particular cases. The stigma must be attached to the weapon itself. But it is not really possible to create universal revulsion

---

[17] Convention on the Prohibition of the Development, Production and Stockpiling of Bacteriological (Biological) and Toxin Weapons and on their Destruction.

against landmines without a simultaneous ban on production, stockpiling, and transfer.

The Arms Project and Physicians for Human Rights understand that this program for a total ban may be viewed as quixotic. However, seeking a total ban is not based on idealism but instead on a realistic assessment of the facts. Experience has shown again and again that if combatants have ready access to landmines, they will use them. Only a squeeze on supply can affect use.

A ban on production and export will surely not drive all suppliers from the field. Nevertheless, it is easier to create international revulsion against the weapon if the number of supplier countries were reduced from an estimated 48 currently to perhaps fewer than half a dozen. Forty-eight suppliers cannot all be treated as international pariahs. But a handful can.

It is possible that if the number of producers and exporters is sharply reduced, remaining suppliers will see landmines not as the relatively cheap commodity they are today, but as a weapon for which a premium can be charged. That premium would represent the monetized cost of breaking a political and legal ban on the weapon; hence, the greater the revulsion, the greater the premium. Of course, no one knows how far the number of producers and exporters must drop to cause an increase in the unit cost of landmines. Nor does anyone know how much the cost of landmines would have to be raised to affect combatant behavior and reduce landmine use. The combination of a flat ban, international stigmatization of users and suppliers, and the possibility that censure or sanctions against producers and exporters will raise the price of landmines makes the proposal for a complete proscription more viable than simply proposing further modest, and likely unenforceable, restrictions on use.

This book was undertaken by the Arms Project and Physicians for Human Rights in order to synthesize as much information as possible about landmines worldwide and, on the basis of this information, argue that an absolute ban on production, stockpiling, transfer and use of mines is the only appropriate response. Chapter 2 contains a history of landmine use, an explanation of how the principal types of mines operate and are deployed, and a discussion of changes in the uses of landmines. This background is essential to understand subsequent legal and technical arguments in support of a ban on landmines.

In order to consider future bans on landmine production and trade, up-to-date information is needed about these subjects.  The Arms Project has undertaken extensive research in this area and has assembled what is currently the most comprehensive collection of data publicly available in Chapter 3.  This research publicly identifies for the first time the production of over 340 types of antipersonnel mine products in at least 48 countries by almost 100 companies and government agencies. These figures are far higher than those previously available and indicate for the first time just how widespread the production and trade of landmines is.  Equally important, this research is beginning to cause other non-governmental organizations in various countries, and governments themselves, to research the issue and release previously nonpublic information.   The Arms Project and Physicians for Human Rights anticipate that the results of these efforts will cause these figures to go higher still.[18]

Adjunct to the need for information about producers, exporters, and purchasers is the need to make such information publicly available— "transparent," in the terminology of disarmament and arms control. Chapter 4 describes existing mechanisms of transparency and argues in particular that the new United Nations Register of Conventional Weapons ought to be expanded to cover landmines.

Chapter 5 gives an overview of the medical and social effects of landmines.  It describes what typically occurs when a victim steps on a landmine—death, or, assuming survival, amputation and several expensive, painful and difficult surgical operations, the fitting of a prosthesis, if the patient is lucky, and the difficulties in finding a productive life as an amputee in the developing world.  The direct and indirect social and economic costs of landmines are also discussed.

Chapter 6 offers a collection of country-specific case studies of landmine use.  These profiles, taken mainly from earlier reports of Human Rights Watch and Physicians for Human Rights, draw on every region of the world.  They illustrate the range of conflicts in which landmines are deployed, the different technologies utilized, varying patterns of mine warfare, and the consequences of mine use in particular

---

[18] The Arms Project serves as a clearinghouse for such information globally, and encourages anyone with information to forward it to the Arms Project, so that it can be included in master data bases and disseminated worldwide.

countries. This analysis also clearly demonstrates that the landmine crisis has now spread throughout the developing world.

Chapter 7 describes current mine clearance techniques and operations, and explains how limited expectations of them should be.

Chapter 8 describes the regulation of landmines in international law. This chapter argues that the existing legal regime, found in the Landmines Protocol, is inadequate to the task, and indeed is weaker than what customary law of war otherwise requires. This chapter is written for legal specialists and diplomats; it is an argument developed at considerable length and with the documentation necessary to be legally persuasive that international law already bans the use of landmines.

Certain states, notably the United States and France, have already taken unilateral measures to control the transfer of landmines. Chapter 9 reviews these and other similar initiatives adopted or under consideration by different countries and multilateral institutions.

Future technical developments and new military uses of landmines are considered in Chapter 10.

The book closes at Chapter 11 by reiterating the call to ban landmine production, stockpiling, transfer, and use. It argues that a ban is supported by the facts of landmine warfare, by humanitarian laws forbidding the use of weapons which cause indiscriminate and excessive injury to civilians, and by disarmament principles prohibiting the production, stockpiling, and transfer of weapons which cause unconscionable human harm. The chapter also discusses the political and practical feasibility of a total ban.

Ending the world landmine crisis requires that mines be reconceived as a wholly illegitimate weapon of mass destruction, with the same stigma that chemical and biological weapons carry. That stigma will only come about if there is a total ban on production, stockpiling, transfer, and use.

# 2
# THE DEVELOPMENT AND USE OF LANDMINES

Landmines today range from very simple devices improvised in the field by soldiers to high-technology, sensor-activated weapons. Indeed, the once humble landmine has been a major beneficiary of the latest developments in materials, electronics, and other technologies. Modern landmines are fabricated from sophisticated non-metallic materials and incorporate advanced electronics, making them increasingly "smart." Mines are readily available to any armed group.

## I.     From World War I to Vietnam

The earliest precursors to the modern landmine were developed during World War I, when German soldiers used buried artillery shells with exposed fuzes to block the advance of French and British tanks.[1] Just as the refinement of the internal combustion engine fostered the development of the tank as a counter to the stalemate of trench warfare, the invention in the 1920s of the easy-to-handle, powerful, and lightweight explosive trinitrotoluene (TNT) led to the development of the first reliable antitank pressure mines. During World War II, these flat steel cylinders, measuring about 30 centimeters in diameter and containing about 10 kilograms of TNT, were used extensively by all parties. According to the U.S. Defense Intelligence Agency (DIA), more than 300 million antitank landmines were used during World War II, including 220 million deployed by the Soviet Union, 80 million by Germany and 17 million by the United States.[2]

However, these antitank mines had one major weakness: they could be easily removed by enemy troops, who would re-plant them in their own minefields. To keep mine clearing soldiers at bay, both

---

[1] William Fowler, "The Devil's Seed," *Defence*, August 1992, pp. 11–19. See also Lt. Col. C.E.E. Sloan (RE), *Mine Warfare on Land* 1 (1986).

[2] U.S. Defense Intelligence Agency and U.S. Army Foreign Science and Technology Center (DIA/FSTC), *Landmine Warfare—Trends & Projections*, Dec. 1992, DST-1160S-019-92, p. 2-1. This document was obtained by the Arms Project through the Freedom of Information Act. Lt. Col. Sloan states that in the past 55 years over 650 million mines have been emplaced. *Mine Warfare*, p. 4.

16

German and Allied troops began seeding their antitank minefields with small metallic or glass containers containing a pound or less of explosive. These early antipersonnel mines were activated by the direct pressure of 15 to 40 pounds on pins projecting from the mine, or by a few pounds of pull on a tripwire. One of the most effective of these mines, a German-made bounding device dubbed the "Bouncing Betty," popped up from the ground to a height of seven feet before spraying hundreds of steel balls half the length of a football field.

Soldiers also booby-trapped antitank mines to prevent removal. In the early stages of the war, most of these devices were improvised with hand grenades or simple electric fuzes. Later, more complex machine-made fuzes were rigged to an explosive charge that would easily detonate when pressure was applied or when an electrical circuit was closed.

It was not long before improvised explosive devices and antipersonnel mines were being used as weapons in their own right, rather than merely to protect antitank mines. Both weapons were used to demoralize troops or terrorize civilians. Japanese soldiers, for instance, often booby-trapped harmless, everyday objects, such as pipes, flashlights, radios, and fruit cans. The practice of booby-trapping the bodies of dead or wounded soldiers, although officially denied, was also common.

Advances in mine technology, as in all areas of weaponry, accelerated in the decades following World War II, primarily in response to changing battlefield requirements and the development of new military technologies. In the early 1960s, the United States first introduced the use of a new and sophisticated class of contact antipersonnel mines, known as remotely delivered mines or "scatterables," to stop the flow of men and material from North to South Vietnam through Laos and Cambodia. The most commonly deployed were the BLU-43 and BLU-44, nicknamed "dragon tooth" because of their needlelike shape. American pilots dropped so many of these mines they referred to them as "garbage." They were scattered from the air and landed on the ground without detonating. When stepped on, the device, which weighed only 20 grams, could tear off a foot. (The BLU-43 and BLU-44 were the forerunners of the Soviet PFM-1, or "butterfly" mine, used extensively in Afghanistan.) Another remotely delivered mine widely deployed by the United States in Vietnam was the BLU-42, or "spider" mine, which sent out eight tripwires, like spider legs, after landing on the ground.

For all their tactical advantages, scatterable mines had drawbacks. Because of the hit-and-run nature of the Vietnam War, American ground forces often found themselves retreating through areas that their own pilots had previously saturated with mines—sometimes just days, or even hours, earlier. These areas were not "minefields" in any traditional military sense; they were simply zones randomly scattered with surface mines. The boundaries of these areas were therefore not precisely knowable.

Vietnamese forces, which used several dozen types of improvised or simply manufactured mines, proved that advanced technology was not needed to deploy landmines with deadly effectiveness. In 1965, one year for which detailed statistics are available, 65-70% of U.S. Marine Corps casualties were caused by mines and booby-traps.[3]

With the proliferation of low-intensity conflicts since the 1970s, the landmine, like the automatic rifle, has become a weapon of choice for many government and guerrilla armies around the world. They are not only durable and effective, but also readily available from governments as well as the vast global network of private arms suppliers. Mines are also easy and relatively cheap to manufacture locally.[4] As scientists invent new high-technology devices, older but equally lethal models are unloaded on the surplus arms market or supplied directly to armies or guerrilla groups, usually in developing countries.

## II. Types of Antipersonnel Mines

Antipersonnel mines, as the term implies, are weapons designed specifically to kill or incapacitate human beings, as distinguished from other weapons whose function is to destroy or render vehicles, equipment or material ineffective. Antipersonnel mines can be specific, as in a pressure-operated blast mine which will usually kill or injure only the

---

[3] DIA/FSTC, p. 2-1. See also U.S. Army Countermine Systems Directorate, Ft. Belvoir RD&E Center, *Worldwide Informational Mine Guide*, 1993, which identifies more than three dozen Vietnamese landmines, most of them field-improvised models developed during the conflict with the United States. This document was obtained by the Arms Project through the Freedom of Information Act.

[4] See discussion in Chapter 3.

person stepping on it, or general, such as fragmentation mines, which will kill or maim not only the victim initiating the mine but also anyone within its effective range.

Today, more than 340 antipersonnel landmine models have been produced in at least 48 nations around the world.[5] Antipersonnel mines can be divided into four basic categories: blast, fragmentation, directional, or bounding devices. Of these, the blast mine is the most common.

Blast mines are usually designed to activate when the victim steps directly on the mine. Some are quite small, have a plastic case, and are mass produced. Others are larger and may have a wooden, glass or concrete case, and in some cases are improvised in the field. The blast mine may be laid directly on the ground or buried with up to approximately 4 centimeters of covering. When the mine is detonated, the blast drives fragments of the mine, along with dirt, gravel, footwear, and surrounding vegetation, well up the victim's leg. Blast mines almost invariably kill, cause traumatic amputation or lead to surgical amputation of one or more limbs, as well as secondary injuries to the face and other parts of the body.

One of the most common blast mines is the Soviet-made PMN or PMN-2, sometimes referred to as the "black widow" because of its dark casing. These mines are either buried or placed on the ground or other surfaces and covered with natural camouflage. The PMN has a built-in, 20-minute delay after arming, and can be easily deactivated by specialists. In the case of the PMN-2, by contrast, the arming process is irreversible and there is no recognized neutralization technique. Both devices have a thermo-plastic outer casing.

Another popular pressure-activated blast mine is the U.S.-made M14. The device is extremely compact, measuring only 56 millimeters in diameter and 40 millimeters in height, and weighing less than 100 grams. When 9 to 16 kilograms of pressure are applied to a small pressure plate on top of the mine, the plate moves a key downwards to force a so-called Belleville spring disc to reverse its position in one sudden movement. The spring carries a striker pin that impacts upon a detonator, igniting the main charge.

Fragmentation mines are usually laid above ground, with the exception of bounding fragmentation mines. Most fragmentation mines are supported on stakes—hence the name "stake mine"—or are attached

---

[5] Ibid.

with mounting brackets to human-made structures, trees or undergrowth, and then camouflaged. They are usually activated by tripwire. When the victim walks into or brushes against the tripwire with enough force to generate a pull of about 1 kilogram, the mine detonates, causing fragmentation to be projected over the target area up to about 20 meters.

Directional fragmentation mines are also mounted above ground and contain pre-formed metal fragments located in front of an explosive charge. When activated, the mine scatters the fragments over a predetermined arc of about 50 meters. Directional mines have been described as the military equivalent of the sawed-off shotgun. One of the most popular and widely copied directional mines is the U.S.-made M18 and M18A1 Claymore mine. It was invented during the Korean War for use against "human wave" infantry attacks. The mine contains 700 steel balls packed in front of a powerful C-4 explosive. When activated, the steel balls are propelled in a 60 degree arc about two meters high and about 50 meters from the point of origin.

Bounding mines may combine blast and fragmentation, although most rely on fragments for their effectiveness. This mine is usually designed to be buried and concealed, often with only a small fuze mechanism protruding above ground. When a victim applies pressure to the tripwire or steps on the fuze, a small explosive charge projects the mine body upwards from a barrel assembly to a point above ground level where an anchor cable secured to the assembly pulls a pin from a fuze on the main body. When the mine reaches a height of approximately one meter or more, the main charge detonates, scattering fragments over a wide area.

Antipersonnel mines can be deployed either by hand or, in the case of scatterable mines, by artillery, rocket or mortar dispensers attached to helicopters, fixed-wing aircraft, or land vehicles. Scatterable mines usually lie on the ground where they land; however, they often become well-concealed in undergrowth, or by a light covering of dust.

Many landmines are equipped with anti-handling or anti-disturbance devices, making the dangerous job of mine clearance even more hazardous. A mercury tilt switch, for instance, can make any mine detonate immediately if it is moved. Though anti-disturbance and anti-handling devices were formerly found only in antitank mines, some of the most popular antipersonnel mines—including the widely distributed Italian SB-33 and the latest versions of the Chinese Type 72—now incorporate them, too. The SB-33, designed in Italy by Misar and licensed for production in Greece and Portugal, has been sold to Argentina, Holland, Iraq and many other nations.[6] The Type 72 is a small, plastic mine used extensively by both Cambodian government and Khmer Rouge forces in Cambodia. Its anti-disturbance mode is designed to prevent removal or deactivation by ensuring detonation when the device is handled or disturbed in any way. According to the DIA, some of the new Italian and Chinese mines pose a specially grave threat because they are identical in appearance to older models which lack anti-disturbance devices, and thus pose an added threat to mine clearance workers who "may wrongly assume that the mine poses little difficulty in removal."[7]

### III. Contemporary Military Uses of Mines

Modern conventional military tactics depend upon speed of movement and maneuver, coupled with firepower, to defeat an enemy. A defender will therefore see any time delay or physical hindrance that can be imposed upon an enemy as an advantage. In this regard, landmines—whether antitank or antipersonnel—can play a role in hindering the movement of an enemy and its access to large tracts of land, military bases, and key installations. Landmines can also be used to direct enemy troops towards an area where the defender is best able to defeat them.

Antipersonnel mines placed around approaches to an antitank minefield will make enemy troops more cautious, thereby causing delay. If a military commander wants his soldiers to enter a minefield, he has to accept that casualties will result unless he uses mine clearing techniques to breach the minefield, which require substantial time to carry out.

It is not certain, however, that the military benefits outweigh the military disadvantages (let alone the civilian costs). In Vietnam, for example, U.S. forces often found themselves travelling through areas they had previously mined. Deborah Shapley, in her biography of former Secretary of Defense Robert McNamara, describes a Pentagon study drawn from a database on actions in the ground war that "uncovered the alarming fact that, although the Army kept asking for more mines, *one*

---

[6] Fowler, "The Devil's Seed."

[7] DIA/FSTC, p. 3-35.

*fifth to one third of all U.S. deaths* were caused by these devices, while they killed relatively few enemy in exchange (emphasis added)."[8]

Some mines are carefully and deliberately designed to maim without killing in order to burden an enemy's medical organization and have a serious effect on troop morale. An injured soldier in a minefield crying for help can demoralize his comrades. Moreover, his commander will often be obliged to deploy other troops to rescue him and possibly slow down military operations. Weapons explicitly designed to blow off feet or inflict other debilitating but non-fatal wounds include the British Ranger scatterable mine, Pakistani P4 Mk.2, Spanish P-4-A, Swedish L1-11 and U.S. M14.[9]

Mines have been increasingly deployed as offensive weapons. For example, a conventional army might use scatterables as an offensive weapon to cut off an advancing adversary from its logistical base, interposing scatterable mines by aircraft or artillery between advancing armor and its supply depots. Alternatively, an advancing force might use either hand-emplaced or scatterable mines to support an offensive action by forcing the enemy to meet on tactically desirable ground. A force on the offensive as well as the defensive might use mines to protect its flanks, deny approach routes, reinforce a temporary defense, or break up a counter-attack.

The use of landmines as an offensive weapon, whether the low-tech hand-emplaced mine or sophisticated deep strike scatterables, alters the role of landmines from that of a limited utility, tactical weapon used on a particular battlefield in support of other weapons systems (especially antitank mines) to that of a strategic weapon. Landmines have become a weapon by which to overcome the low force-to-space ratio typical of insurgency-counterinsurgency and many internal wars, becoming a weapon for dominating whole theaters. They are, in effect, mechanical soldiers, or as Cambodian government and resistance soldiers have called

---

[8] Shapley, Deborah, *Promise and Power: The Life and Times of Robert McNamara* (Boston: Little Brown and Co., January 1993), p. 414. Shapley notes that factual information of this sort was published in *Southeast Asia Report*, a classified journal. The Arms Project is seeking to have this information released under the Freedom of Information Act.

[9] Fowler, "The Devil's Seed," p. 13. For descriptions of British, Pakistani and U.S. mines in this category, see also Chapter 3 and Appendix 17.

them, "eternal sentinels"—never sleeping, always ready to attack. With this fundamental shift in role from tactical, battlefield weapon to theater-wide strategic weapon, landmines take on certain characteristics of weapons of mass destruction: they blight the land practically forever, they pollute, they have particularly detrimental effects on civilians and civilian infrastructure, and there is no ready countermeasure.

Increasingly, and consistent with the "strategic" nature of contemporary landmine use, government and guerrilla armies (in flagrant violation of international humanitarian law) deliberately use mines for the purpose of terrorizing civilians and controlling their movements. They have been used for this purpose in many recent conflicts including Afghanistan, Angola, Cambodia, Somalia, Mozambique, Nicaragua, former Yugoslavia, and Iraqi Kurdistan.

Both manually-emplaced and remotely delivered mines are put to deliberate, offensive use. During the recent Cambodian conflict, government troops used mines offensively by placing them around the perimeters of enemy villages. They then bombarded the villages with artillery fire so that the "enemy"—mainly noncombatant civilians—was forced to flee into minefields. The Khmer Rouge, meanwhile, intentionally mined rice paddies and country paths to halt agriculture, keeping peasants from growing any food in an effort to force the Cambodian government to the bargaining table. According to a British demining specialist, both Chinese and British training of Khmer forces opposed to the Vietnamese-backed government in Phnom Penh stressed the use of mines (and improvised booby-traps) as anti-morale weapons targeted against the civilian infrastructure.[10]

Other examples of mines being used intentionally against civilian populations include Afghanistan, where, during the recent war, Soviet and Kabul forces mined grazing areas, agricultural land, and irrigation systems in an effort to undermine civilian support of the Mujahidin, and Northern Somalia, where Siad Barre's forces mined wells and grazing lands used by civilians. Barre's forces also placed mines and booby-traps in homes in Hargeisa which had been temporarily abandoned by civilians fleeing government bombing. In 1991, many people returned to their homes only to become victims of these hidden explosives.

---

[10] Asia Watch and Physicians for Human Rights, *Landmines in Cambodia: The Cowards' War* (New York: Human Rights Watch and Physicians for Human Rights, September 1991), pp. 40–42.

# PMN/PMN-2

These Soviet-made pressure-initiated devices are either buried or placed on the ground or other surfaces and covered with natural camouflage. The body of the PMN is black, olive green, or brown. It is sometimes called "the black widow." Both mines have been used in conjunction with other devices in stacked configurations. The PMN has a built-in, 15-20 minute delay after arming and can be easily defuzed by specialists. In the case of the PMN-2, the arming process is irreversible and there is no recognized neutralization technique. Because of the PMN's large explosive content (240 grams TNT), injuries from this mine can often be fatal. The PMN is one of the most commonly encountered antipersonnel mines in the world. (Drawing by Pamela Blotner for the Arms Project/PHR.)

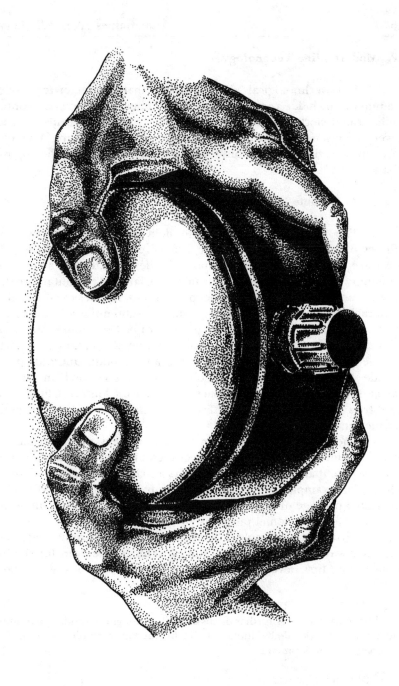

## IV. Modern Mine Technology

Key technological developments that characterize modern landmines include remote delivery systems, low metal content, sophisticated electronic sensors, and self-destruct mechanisms.[11] These developments do not mean that antipersonnel mines are now more "friendly" to civilian populations than earlier models; in fact, the opposite, is true.

### A. Remote Delivery

The development of remote delivery systems increases the efficacy of landmines as a strategic, offensive weapon, as opposed to a defensive, tactical, battlefield weapon. Modern scatterable systems are redefining the scope and nature of mine warfare. U.S. military analysts have stressed the importance of deep-strike systems, designed to deliver scatterable mines and other specialized "submunitions" to remote locations. Manufacturers known to produce or be developing deep-strike mine delivery systems designed to deliver antipersonnel mines (as part of a mine package which would probably also contain antitank mines) include Messerschmidt-Bolkow-Blohm (on its own and in separate partnerships with British Aerospace and France's Matra), China North Industries Corporation, and a French-German consortium including Dornier and Thompson Brandt.[12]

The growing emphasis on remote delivery of mines has also served to blur the already thin line between antitank and antipersonnel systems, potentially creating new dangers for civilians. U.S. development efforts, for example, center on the "Family of Scatterable Mines," an integrated package of antipersonnel and antitank landmines, often used in tandem for area denial purposes.

Virtually all technological advances in antitank mines eventually find their way into antipersonnel mines. This is true even for the "off-route" mine, first developed by France in the late 1960s as a kind of

---

[11] See Chapter 10 for further discussion of technological trends in landmines, and for a more detailed critique of the humanitarian implications of these technological developments.

[12] DIA/FSTC, p. 3-17.

automated warhead launcher system which would attack approaching or passing tanks from a distance with far greater force than the traditional antitank mine.[13] Over the past decade, off-route mines (often known as Wide Area Mines) have been the single most important focus of mine technology research and development. Though all known Western designs are designated as antitank devices, the former Soviet Union developed a fuze system, the MVZ-72, which transforms Claymore-type mines (such as the ex-Soviet MON series) into powerful off-route antipersonnel devices.[14]

Remotely delivered mines cause particular problems for civilians, and, in fact, were almost banned under the Landmines Protocol.[15] Air dispersion, in particular, leads to lack of accuracy in placement. Almost inevitably, a certain number of air delivered mines are dropped outside targeted areas. Similarly, with remotely delivered mines, it is virtually impossible to determine the parameters of the minefields, much less map the precise location of individual mines. During the Falkland/Malvinas War, for example, highly trained British troops kept detailed maps of the ostensible locations of remotely delivered mines. When mine clearance teams attempted to locate these mines, however, they were unable to do so. Consequently, large parts of the islands are now unusable. Remotely delivered mines also pose particular risks for civilians simply because they are capable of saturating vast areas in very little time.

### B. Minimum-Metal

Because many new mines are constructed almost entirely of plastic and have extremely low metallic signatures, they are often extremely difficult to detect and deactivate or destroy.[16] As a result, they remain a threat to civilians long after the cessation of hostilities. Mines with a high plastic content also create medical problems because

---

[13] DIA/FSTC, p. 3-41.

[14] DIA/FSTC, p. 3-48.

[15] See discussion in Chapter 8.

[16] See Chapter 7 on mine clearance. Apparently, some truly all-plastic mines are now being produced.

plastic fragments escape detection by x-ray.[17]  At least 18 countries
have produced low-metal or minimum-metal antipersonnel mines
(commonly, but usually inaccurately, advertised as "non-metallic"):
Argentina, Belgium, Brazil, China, Egypt, Germany, Greece, Hungary,
India, Italy, the Netherlands, Pakistan, Portugal, South Africa, Spain, the
United States, the former USSR and ex-Yugoslavia.[18]

### C.  Electronic Sensors

Electronics have played an increasing role in the development of
mine technology since the 1970s, providing new flexibility in arming,
target detection, detonation and self-destruction or deactivation.  Mine
fuzing sensors and their associated microprocessors, for instance, could be
used to discriminate between the movement of animals and humans, or
to count the number of passers-by before a mine will detonate.

As noted in the recent DIA study, the most advanced mine
systems "incorporate sophisticated fuze logic"—that uses magnetic, seismic,
acoustic and/or infrared sensors to identify targets—and include "improved
kill mechanisms [which when] coupled with sophisticated fuzing create a
formidable barrier that can destroy both clearance vehicles and
personnel."[19]     British, German, French and Chinese firms have
developed, or are developing, mine delivery systems in this class.

### D.  Self-Destructing and Self-Neutralizing Mines

The United States and several other nations are now producing
almost exclusively mines that contain self-destruct mechanisms for use in
remote delivery systems.  After a pre-set period of time, the mine
automatically explodes.  These mines were developed with a military
objective in mind—to lessen the danger of soldiers encountering their own

---

[17] Surgeons expert in mine amputations, however, note that a typical mine
explosion drives so much other non-metallic debris, such as dirt and vegetation,
up into the wound that plastic fragments are one additional difficulty in landmine
amputation surgery among the many that make it painful, risky, and expensive.

[18] See the Arms Project's mines database and DIA/FSTC, p. 3-19.

[19] DIA/FSTC, p. 3-12.

mines days, weeks, or months after they had been sown. Although these mines presumably would not pose the same long-term threat to civilians that non-self-destructing mines do, the dangers to civilians of the inherently indiscriminate fashion in which they are sown and of unpredictable explosions is apparent.[20] In addition, professional mine clearers are skeptical of manufacturers' claims about the failure rate of self-destructing mine mechanisms. Brigadier (Ret.) Patrick Blagden, a former British officer now working for the United Nations as its mine clearance expert, sometimes shows visitors to his office the "brain" of a self-destructing mine. "If they so successfully self-destruct," he says, "then how come I've got one?"[21] Mine clearance experts typically say that, whereas for military purposes 80% clearance is acceptable, successful humanitarian mine clearance requires at least 99% effective clearance.[22]

An alternative technology is "self-neutralization," whereby mines are designed to turn themselves off after a set period of time. In some cases, manufacturers propose a switch to indicate to the observer that the mine is deactivated. From the mine clearance perspective, however, even if a 99% rate of mechanism-effectiveness were achieved, the possibility of a mine remaining live means that each and every mine must be approached as if it were live. Therefore, from the standpoint of mine clearance, self-destructing mines—mines that actually explode and disappear—are preferable to self-neutralizing mines about which there are always doubts.

---

[20] Further discussion of the drawbacks of self-destruct and self-neutralizing mines is contained in Chapter 10 which addresses the future of landmines.

[21] Conversation with the Arms Project, February 17, 1993. See also James North, "War Without End," *In These Times*, Sept. 6, 1993, p. 18.

[22] The lower figure is considered satisfactory for military breaching because the military accepts a greater degree of risk. However, humanitarian clearance requires a much higher percentage so that civilians can resume normal activities. See Chapter 7 for a more detailed discussion of these issues.

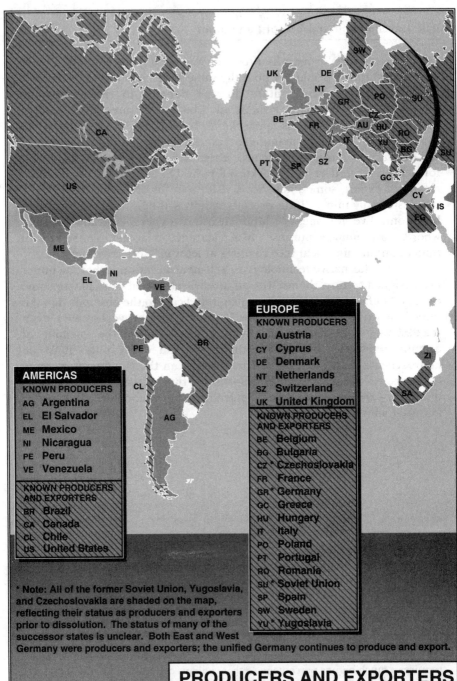

**AMERICAS**

KNOWN PRODUCERS

AG  Argentina
EL  El Salvador
ME  Mexico
NI  Nicaragua
PE  Peru
VE  Venezuela

KNOWN PRODUCERS
AND EXPORTERS

BR  Brazil
CA  Canada
CL  Chile
US  United States

**EUROPE**

KNOWN PRODUCERS

AU  Austria
CY  Cyprus
DE  Denmark
NT  Netherlands
SZ  Switzerland
UK  United Kingdom

KNOWN PRODUCERS
AND EXPORTERS

BE  Belgium
BG  Bulgaria
CZ * Czechoslovakia
FR  France
GR * Germany
GC  Greece
HU  Hungary
IT  Italy
PO  Poland
PT  Portugal
RO  Romania
SU * Soviet Union
SP  Spain
SW  Sweden
YU * Yugoslavia

* Note: All of the former Soviet Union, Yugoslavia, and Czechoslovakia are shaded on the map, reflecting their status as producers and exporters prior to dissolution. The status of many of the successor states is unclear. Both East and West Germany were producers and exporters; the unified Germany continues to produce and export.

# PRODUCERS AND EXPORTERS

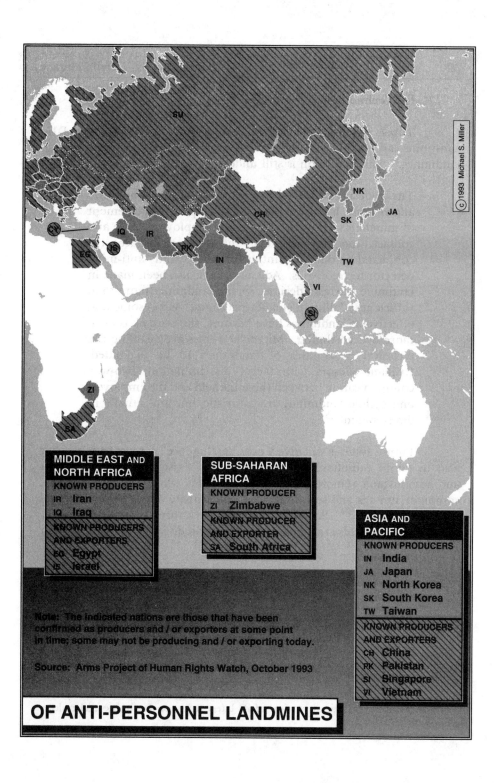

© 1993 Michael S. Miller

**MIDDLE EAST** AND
**NORTH AFRICA**

KNOWN PRODUCERS
IR   Iran
IQ   Iraq

KNOWN PRODUCERS
AND EXPORTERS
EG   Egypt
IS   Israel

**SUB-SAHARAN**
**AFRICA**

KNOWN PRODUCER
ZI   Zimbabwe

KNOWN PRODUCER
AND EXPORTER
SA   South Africa

**ASIA** AND
**PACIFIC**

KNOWN PRODUCERS
IN   India
JA   Japan
NK   North Korea
SK   South Korea
TW   Taiwan

KNOWN PRODUCERS
AND EXPORTERS
CH   China
PK   Pakistan
SI   Singapore
VI   Vietnam

Note: The indicated nations are those that have been
confirmed as producers and / or exporters at some point
in time; some may not be producing and / or exporting today.

Source: Arms Project of Human Rights Watch, October 1993

**OF ANTI-PERSONNEL LANDMINES**

### E. Technological Explosion

Taken together these developments, in the view of the DIA, constitute an "explosion," in the "technological sophistication in landmines." This explosion is still underway. The agency notes that:

> The widespread introduction of scatterable landmines allows a much more dynamic and responsive placement of minefields. Improved fuzes can employ pressure and contact, and also magnetic, infrared, seismic/acoustic, command-detonated, antidisturbance, and anti-mine detector technologies. Advances have also been made in landmine warhead designs, giving landmines more than sufficient lethality in smaller packages. As awesome and effective as landmines have become, the outlook is even more overwhelming. Microelectronics are enabling the technical capabilities of landmines to be expanded. Brilliant sensors with target discrimination, two-way communication between the minefield and the employer, and mobile landmines are futuristic, but are actually in development.[23]

Future systems will give a new "intelligence" not just to mines but also to entire minefields. Systems already exist for the creation of autonomous and remote-controlled minefields which will use complex computer systems and seismic sensors to detonate antipersonnel as well as antitank mines.[24] So far as civilians are concerned, these remote-controlled minefields create all of the risks of individual self-neutralizing mines.

---

[23] DIA/FSTC, p. xvii.

[24] DIA/FSTC, p. 3-55. Governments and producers appear to be closely guarding information on their plans for the next generation of "controlled" minefields. Almost all details on these new technologies were withheld by DIA when it released a sanitized version of its latest study on landmine technology trends.

### F. Mine Clearance Technology[25]

Mine clearance technology lags far behind these advances in destructive power. Despite mine clearance research and development efforts by many nations, the latest detection equipment is still no more than 60-90% effective in finding minimum-metal mines, according to one U.S. Army technical expert.[26] Even with the latest innovations, military experts believe that "recent and near-term advances in electronics and sensors are likely to favor the mine side" in the mine-versus-countermine equation.[27] While new methods are being developed to detect plastic mines, the next generation of "non-detectable" mines may incorporate even more sophisticated materials designed to thwart radar and infrared detection methods.[28]

Western manufacturers' successes in marketing mines to non-Western purchasers has led one commentator to conclude that modern mine technology "has come back to haunt the nations that developed it. In recent conflicts, Britain, France and the United States have found out how difficult it is to deal with modern landmines."[29]

### V.    Conclusion

Technological developments and changes in the strategies for using landmines have combined to put civilian populations at ever-greater risk from landmines. Increased "sophistication" has translated into an increased ability to kill and maim. Technological "advances" have

---

[25] See Chapter 7 for an in-depth discussion of mine clearance.

[26] Interview, U.S. Army Ft. Belvoir Research, Development and Engineering Center, April 23, 1993.

[27] Board on Army Science and Technology, Commission on Engineering and Technical Systems, National Research Council, *STAR 21: Strategic technologies for the army of the twenty-first century*, Washington: National Academy Press, 1992, p. 87.

[28] DIA/FSTC, p. 1-1.

[29] Forecast International, *World Weapons Review*, Sept. 23, 1992.

led to more landmines of greater lethality spread more quickly over larger areas of territory. Technological developments related to landmines or mine clearance have proceeded with virtually no consideration for their impact on civilians.

A requirement for self-destruct mechanisms on all landmines would lessen—but only marginally—the ongoing humanitarian disaster wrought by landmines. One reason is that expert mine clearers doubt that sufficient rates of self-destruction will be achieved—99% is generally regarded as essential—for effective humanitarian mine clearance. A second reason is that because self-destructing mines are more expensive than ordinary mines, developing-world and insurgency armies will not be able to afford them—at least not in the same quantities that they could afford ordinary mines. Worse still, countries in the developing world will not agree to a ban on weapons they can afford while permitting weapons they cannot; a meaningful ban would be politically dead from the beginning, on North-South lines. Finally, it is impossible to stigmatize landmines as a weapon and create a serious political disincentive to production, stockpiling, trade, and use if some landmines are legal while others are not. A major investment in humanitarian-oriented mine detection and mine clearance equipment and techniques could reap great benefits. But, as has been the case up to this point, it appears that most technological developments in the future will worsen, not improve, the landmine crisis.

# 3

# GLOBAL PRODUCTION AND TRADE IN LANDMINES

This chapter profiles the global landmine production and sales industry.[1] It summarizes the available information on companies and countries which produce and export landmines, the pricing of their products, the markets to which they sell, and the business and technological trends which will shape their future activities and earnings.

Until now, there has existed no reliable data on landmine production volume, pricing, and marketing. Military trade publications offered sketchy information and often inaccurate statistics. The publications of Stockholm International Peace Research Institute (SIPRI) and other independent research groups which track major weapons systems have been virtually silent on landmines. The most detailed reports on landmine production and trade are compiled by military and intelligence agencies, yet these organizations, too, expressed frustration at their inability to gather comprehensive information. Most past studies, the Arms Project discovered, drastically understated the size of the international landmine market.

Difficulty in tracking landmine production and sales was compounded by the fact that no company makes meaningful public disclosures of the financial results from its landmine business. Many of the world's landmine producing facilities are owned by governments or by closely held firms which release relatively little financial data of any kind. For publicly traded landmine producers—including such industrial giants as Daimler-Benz (Germany), the Fiat Group (Italy), Daewoo Corporation (South Korea) and RCA (United States)—landmines are usually a subsegment of a larger product line and are therefore not separately covered in annual reports or other corporate documents.

Despite these obstacles, the Arms Project has succeeded in compiling the first meaningful estimates of the size of the antipersonnel (A/P) landmine production industry, the value and volume of its output, and the extent of its penetration into markets throughout the world. It

---

[1] In the rest of this book, the word "landmine" refers to "antipersonnel landmine" unless otherwise specified. In this chapter only, the qualifying designations "antipersonnel (A/P)" and "antitank (A/T)" are frequently employed. However, where no qualification is given, "landmine" should be assumed to refer to both types of mine.

must be stressed, however, that our estimates are tentative, should be taken as a starting point for further research and analysis, and may require significant revision as more detailed information becomes available.

## I.      Summary of Key Findings

The Arms Project has identified almost 100 companies and government agencies in 48 countries which have manufactured more than 340 types of antipersonnel landmines in recent decades. (See Table I and Appendix 17). They include more than one dozen countries and more than 150 landmines not previously identified in published reports. Yet the Arms Project is certain that additional kinds of mines and additional producers will be found through further research.

The available evidence, though not conclusive, suggests that China, Italy, and the former Soviet Union have been probably the largest producers and the largest exporters of conventional A/P mines in recent years, though not necessarily in that order.  Our provisional estimates suggest that manufacturers have produced an average of between five and ten million A/P landmines per year in recent decades, roughly ten times the production volume previously reported in the trade press. Combined global production of A/P mines (excluding delivery systems and accessories) is probably worth at least $50 million-$200 million annually.  With respect to trade in landmines, the Arms Project has determined that at least 41 companies or government agencies in 29 nations have exported A/P landmines, though not all of them are currently involved in the trade. (See Table II.) We expect that further investigation will expand the list of past and present exporters.

These price and production figures do not include the vastly larger markets for integrated, scatterable mine systems: weapons packages which typically include both A/P and antitank (A/T) components together with sophisticated ground or air-based launching and delivery systems.  Nor do they include the market for A/T, anti-helicopter and other non-A/P mines, whose sophistication and cost have soared in recent years.

Though we have not tried to compile comprehensive revenue data for the landmine market as a whole, it is evident that individual A/P mines represent only a very small part of the total.  In the United States alone,  procurement of scatterable mine systems which include A/P components has averaged $168 million a year over the past decade.

Current stockpiles (including A/T) of the U.S. military's main current group of landmines, the Family of Scatterable Mines (FASCAM) now total $5 billion.[2] Expected future U.S. expenditure for a single product now being developed by Textron Defense Systems, the XM93 Wide Area Mine (A/T, anti-armor), totals $1.2 billion including delivery systems.[3]

Though far larger in sales and production volume than previously reported, the landmine business remains small in comparison with the market for most major weapons systems. However, landmine production is a changing, growing business. In some countries and for some companies, landmine production is assuming increased economic importance as part of the move toward increasingly sophisticated ground warfare technology. Moreover, producers are pursuing potentially profitable new markets for both scatterable mine systems and for more sophisticated variants of the conventional A/P landmine.

## II.    An Overview of the A/P Landmine Market

From a market perspective, there are three broad classes of A/P landmine products, considered here in the order of their emergence into world markets:

- Conventional A/P mines;
- Scatterable A/P mines;
- Improved conventional A/P mines.

Any discussion of A/P landmine markets must first consider the distinct mix of customers, producers, technology and business conditions shaping each of these three market segments.

---

[2] U.S. Army, *Information Paper - Anti-Personnel Landmine Procurement and Production*, 1992; and U.S. Army, Office of the Project Manager, Mines, Countermine and Demolitions, "Program Opportunities," presentation by Charles E. Digney, Deputy Project Manager, at American Defense Preparedness Association, *Mines, Countermine and Demolitions Symposium*, Asheville, North Carolina, Sept. 7-9, 1993 [ADPA Symposium].

[3] Forecast International, *Ordnance and Munitions Forecast*, "XM93 Wide Area Mine," December 1, 1992.

### A.  Conventional A/P Mines

Conventional A/P mines (and many of their A/T counterparts) have become commodity items.  Based on designs from the 1940s, 50s and early 60s, they have changed relatively little in the past quarter century.[4]  They are easily and typically produced in aging, often labor-intensive factories located in dozens of countries around the world.  Little technical sophistication is needed to produce these devices and little money is needed to purchase them.

The still-popular U.S.-designed M18A1 (the "Claymore"), discussed in more detail later, is a prime example.  The U.S. Army has been producing Claymores in their present form since 1960 and plans to keep making them into the 21st century; exact copies or minor variants on the Claymore have been produced in Africa, Asia, Europe, Latin America, and the Middle East.

Because many competing firms produce similar products using similar processes, it is unlikely that anyone other than the lowest cost producers can profit significantly from commercial sales of conventional A/P mines.  Though they are still produced in many developed nations — including the U.S. and many of its Western European allies — there is little evidence that developed world producers invest much money or efforts in upgrading, developing or marketing them.  During a recent trade conference, the Arms Project asked an official of a British firm which manufactures A/T mines, why his company produced no A/P products.  "Probably it's because the market is saturated," he said.  "If there was any money in it, I suppose we would make them, too."[5]

In general, private industry has a relatively small stake in the economic performance of conventional A/P products.  Private research and development costs, if any (many conventional landmines were developed at government expense in military facilities), were recouped decades ago.  Recent capital investment in production is low, because of both the age of production facilities and the tendency to produce conventional mines in government or quasi-government facilities. (In the U.S., for example, manufacture of older conventional A/P mines such as

---

[4] For descriptions of the "conventional" landmine and the early development of landmine warfare, see Lt. Col. P.R. Courtney-Green, *Ammunition for the Land Battle* (London: Brassey's, 1991).

[5] Conversation at the ADPA Symposium, Sept. 8, 1993.

the Claymore M18A1 takes place in government-owned factories operated by private firms under management contracts, while most newer models are manufactured in wholly private facilities.) There is no indication that any corporation, private or state-owned, anywhere in the world depends on conventional A/P mines for more than a small fraction of its annual revenue.

All identifiable recent export sales effort for conventional A/P landmines (as manifested, for example, through trade advertising, sales brochures and trade show exhibitions) involved non-Western manufacturers. Even among the more aggressive Third World producers, conventional A/P landmines are commonly advertised as one element in a larger line of ordnance, munitions and small arms products.

### B. Scatterable A/P Mines

Mines and mine systems have evolved rapidly in the past quarter century (trade literature sometimes speaks of "three generations" of modern mines, each more technically sophisticated than the previous) and are the focus of continuing research and development expenditure. A recent U.S. Defense Intelligence Agency (DIA) report notes that the "massive infusion of technology in the 1970s and 1980s has drastically altered landmine holdings the world over."[6]

Scatterable mine systems have been the principle focus of mine-related military procurement and government-financed research and development for at least 20 years, starting in the late 1960s, and remain the most important area of continuing A/P-related development and spending.[7] Rapid-dispensing scatterables were developed by the United

---

[6] U.S. Defense Intelligence Agency and U.S. Army Foreign Science and Technology Center, *Landmine Warfare — Trends & Projections*, December 1992, DST-1160S-019-92, xvii [DIA/FSTC]; this document was obtained by the Arms Project through the Freedom of Information Act.

[7] For descriptions of some of these systems, see *Jane's Military Vehicles and Logistics: 1992-93* (Surrey: Jane's Information Group Limited, 1992), pp. 214-220.

States in the 1960s for use in the the Vietnam War.[8] As the U.S. State
Department recently reported, Vietnam-era U.S. scatterables pose a
continuing threat to civilians in Southeast Asia decades after their
deployment.[9]

The proliferation of scatterable mines has served to blur the
already thin line between antipersonnel and antitank systems. Scatterable
mine systems commonly include sets of interchangeable A/P and A/T
mines along with mine launchers and mine-dispersing projectiles.
Ground vehicles, rockets, artillery shells, helicopters and planes can be
used to disperse them. At least 22 countries — including both developing
and developed nations — have manufactured scatterable mines and/or
mine scattering systems. Scatterable mine systems currently available
include the Chinese Type 74 minelaying rocket launcher, Egypt's
vehicular Mine Dispensing system, France's Minotaur, the German
Skorpion, the Italian Valsella Istrice, the Russian GMZ Tracked
Minelayer, and the various ground and airborne systems which comprise
the U.S. FASCAM. Other known producers of scatterable mines and/or
systems include: Belgium, Bulgaria, ex-Czechoslovakia, Great Britain,
Greece, Israel, Iraq, Poland, Portugal, South Africa, Spain and
Yugoslavia.[10] Some modern A/P mines — including the U.S. ADAM (a
member of FASCAM) and mines from two subsidiaries of the Italian Fiat
Group, the B.P.D. SB-33 and Valsella VS-50 — are designed to be
dispensed both by hand and through scatterable mine systems.

"Smart" and other hi-tech mines dispensed by some scatterable
systems can sell for 10 to 50 times the price of conventional mines; sale
of delivery systems further increases the profit potential for private
producers. Yet the cost of mines remains low compared with many other
implements of war. Some military strategists believe that scatterable
landmines are actually more cost-effective than their older, less

---

[8] *Armada International*, "Land Mines and Countermeasures — the Continuing
Duel," June 1990, pp. 42–49; see also ibid., p. 225 on the M56 Helicopter-
delivered Scatterable Mine System.

[9] U.S. Department of State, *Hidden Killers: The Global Problem with Uncleared
Landmines* (Washington: U.S. Department of State, July 1993), p. 37.

[10] All countries except Israel are listed in DIA/FSTC, p. 3-3. Israeli products
are listed in sales literature from Israel Aircraft Industries Ltd.

sophisticated counterparts because their rapid distribution makes it possible to create minefields much more quickly and cheaply.[11]

Data from Valsella provides evidence of the awesome destructive power of scatterable mines. Valsella's vehicle-mounted Istrice mine-scattering system dispenses up to 1,750 A/P mines per minute. The company also offers a helicopter-mounted scattering system designed to drop 2,080 A/P mines in three to 16 minutes.[12] This represents a ten-fold payload increase over the first helicopter scattering systems, fielded by the U.S. Army in the 1970s.[13]

Though Valsella's airborne mines scatter unpredictably if dropped from more than 200 meters, company literature explicitly notes that they are designed to be deployed from high altitudes "if dispersion is not important" (i.e. if users don't wish to record or control mine locations). Moreover, these high altitude scatterables include at least two models — the VS-50 and VS-MK2 — which boast "long field life" and lack any self-destruct or self-neutralization feature.[14] Use of such mines appears to violate Article 5 of the Landmines Protocol, which specifies that deployment of remotely delivered mines is banned unless "their location can be accurately recorded" or they contain "an effective neutralizing mechanism."[15] Surprisingly, Valsella asserts that both potentially convention-violating mines were developed in accord with "NATO standards."

---

[11] See DIA/FSTC, xvii, which argues that military planners should consider three issues when evaluating the cost-effectiveness of mines:

> First, when compared with its intended target, the cost of a landmine can still escalate considerably before becoming noncost effective. Second, the costs of incremental or even revolutionary improvements in a landmine are generally much less expensive than the technologies needed to counter them. And third, many of the improvements result in a more expensive landmine but a more economical minefield.

[12] Valsella Meccanotecnica SpA, product description brochure, 1990.

[13] *International Defense Review*, Aug. 1, 1986.

[14] Valsella brochure, 1990; see descriptions of VS-50 and VS-MK2.

[15] See Chapter 8 for a detailed analysis of the Landmines Protocol.

Many producers have invested considerable amounts in private research and development (that is, research and development not funded under government contracts) of scatterable mine systems. This demonstrates their belief in potential profitability, and gives them very strong incentive to aggressively promote the resulting products on the world market. The sometimes-fierce competition for market share among U.S. and Western European firms, and the involvement of cross-border, multi-firm consortia in some of the more important development efforts, provide further evidence that these new mines are viewed as potentially profitable products.

The mines dispensed in scatterable systems are increasingly designed to thwart detection and deactivation. They increasingly incorporate sophisticated electronic timing, remote control systems and advanced "target identification" systems using magnetic, seismic, acoustic and/or infra-red sensors.

"Deep strike" mine delivery platforms currently under development are expected to enhance greatly the ability of armed forces to deploy mines to distant locations in the late 1990s and beyond. In addition to U.S. firms, at least seven companies in five countries are currently developing deep-strike systems. Two companies are expected to field independently produced products in this category: China North Industries Corporation and Daimler-Benz's Messerschmitt-Bolkow-Blohm (MBB) subsidiary. MBB is also involved in two separate joint ventures in this field, with Matra (France) and British Aerospace. Another joint venture unites Germany's Dornier and France's Thompson Brandt.[16]

In recent years, technological and tactical developments have increasingly blurred the line between scatterable mines and the much broader range of rocket and aircraft-delivered bomblets, cluster bomb units (CBUs), and other submunitions, which are often antipersonnel in their deployment and effect.[17] The U.S. military itself has trouble

---

[16] DIA/FSTC, 3-12 through 3-17.

[17] For a detailed discussion of this issue, see William M. Arkin, "Military Technology and the Banning of Land Mines," paper presented at *Non-Governmental Organizations Conference on Antipersonnel Mines*, London, May 24, 1993.

drawing clear distinctions: some official listings of "landmines" also include bomblets and CBUs, while others do not.[18]

### C.  Improved Conventional A/P Mines

Sophisticated technologies initially developed for scatterable systems were quickly incorporated into tiny hand-implacable mines made almost entirely of plastic.  Deadliness, durability, and perhaps lower costs have fueled the seemingly irresistible market momentum toward plastic mines.  They are lightweight, easy to transport, almost impossible to detect and can be made fiendishly dangerous to deactivate.

The rise of the "undetectable" mine has ominous humanitarian implications.  Manufacturers have incorporated the once-costly anti-detection and anti-tampering features of advanced systems into low-cost, mass-produced, predominantly plastic A/P mines which can be hand-scattered by even the least technologically sophisticated army or guerrilla force.  These products—including some which consist of individual mine "modules" taken directly from scatterable systems and others which were specially designed for manual deployment—provide a potentially far more deadly replacement for the conventional A/P mine.

Global mass marketing of "undetectable" mines appears to have been initiated in the late 1970s by three Italian companies.  Italy's largest private manufacturing firm, Fiat, subsequently bought a 50% share in two of these firms.  Other companies around the world have since joined the ranks of significant producers and marketers.

Most of the mines advertised as "plastic" or "non-metallic" actually contain minute amounts of non-magnetic metal, though low metal concentrations and small mine size defeat existing metal detectors.  The Italian SB-33 and VS-50 mines weigh a mere 5-6 ounces each, including less than one-thirtieth of an ounce (0.86 grams) of non-magnetic

---

[18] Compare the U.S. Army Countermine Systems Directorate, Fort Belvoir Research, Development and Engineering Center, *Worldwide Informational Mine Guide*, 1993 (Army Database), which was released to the Arms Project under the Freedom of Information Act, with DIA/FSTC.

metal.[19]   Canada's C3A1 "non-metallic" mine is smaller still (weight 2 ounces, length 2 inches) and is designed to be undetectable unless the deploying force utilizes an optional add-on "detector ring."[20]   Recent tests by the U.S. Advanced Research Projects Agency (ARPA) revealed that even the best currently available hand-held and vehicle-mounted detection systems cannot consistently locate low-metal content mines under 6 inches in diameter.   "All the technology we have [for mine detection] is out of date," according to Dr. Thomas F. Hafer, Acting Assistant Director of ARPA.[21]

Truly "all-plastic" mines have entered the marketplace more recently, and they are even harder to find.  According to representatives from the U.S Countermine Systems Directorate, China, Italy, and perhaps others currently produce mines with no metal whatsoever, using chemical fuzes.[22]  All-plastic mines manufactured in the former Yugoslavia posed the greatest challenge during this year's demining operations in Kuwait, according to John C. Taffe of Explosive Ordnance Disposal World Services (EODWS), a subcontractor on the post-Gulf War demining of Kuwait's "American sector."[23]

Marketing of fuze upgrades for older existing mines provides an additional revenue source for some producers of "advanced conventional" mine products.  Fuze upgrades "have an international appeal" because

---

[19] See Valsella sales brochures and U.S. Army Engineer Center, *Desert Shield Mine Recognition and Warfare Handbook*, Fort Leonard Wood, November 1990, pp. 138-142.

[20] SNC Industrial Technologies Inc., *Mine, anti-personnel, non-metallic, C3A1*, (sales brochure), Le Gardeur Québec, Aug. 1991.

[21] U.S. Advanced Research Projects Agency, *ARPA Current and Future Tech Base Countermine Programs*, presentation by Dr. Thomas F. Hafer, Acting Assistant Director, Advanced Land Systems, Advanced Systems Technology Office, at ADPA Symposium, September 7-8, 1993.

[22] Interview with staff, U.S. Army Countermine Systems Directorate, Fort Belvoir Research, Development and Engineering  Center, April 23, 1993.

[23] Interview, September 7, 1993. In a subsequent meeting on September 30, 1993, Taffe maintained that there are more than two dozen different types of all-plastic mines (presumably both A/P and A/T) in existence today.

they reduce the cost of upgrading existing mine stocks.[24] Upgrades can add anti-disturbance devices, advanced target sensors, self-destructibility and sometimes even scatterability to existing conventional mines.

Swedish producers have been particularly successful in selling "after-market" and original equipment fuzes. German, South African, Italian, and Yugoslav producers have also been leaders in development of a new generation of specialty fuzes, viewed by the U.S. military as especially useful to "special operations type forces, insurgents, or terrorists." Perhaps the most advanced of these are the "Superquick" fuzes developed and marketed by the ex-Yugoslav Federal Directorate of Supply and Procurement in Belgrade. These electronic fuzes contain multipurpose sensors which can be triggered by vibration, sound, light or thermal sensors.[25]

### D. Future Market Trends

Military experts say that technological and strategic trends both point toward continued expansion in the use of landmines. Hand-emplaced A/P mines are cheap, deadly and—with the arrival of low-cost plastic mines—increasingly effective weapons for guerrilla forces and impoverished nations, especially since some of the cheapest mines on the market thwart the most sophisticated countermine technologies available to U.S. and Western European forces.

New technologies, notes the U.S. Defense Intelligence Agency, "boost the effectiveness of landmines, simplify laying minefields, and lower logistical burdens. Even with relatively costly new technologies," DIA says, "landmines are an affordable weapon for the entire range of military organizations, from terrorist groups to large, well-equipped armies" and "will continue to be a significant element in armed conflicts at all levels of intensity well into the foreseeable future."[26]

Sophisticated electronics and countermeasure resistance, highly valued in all landmines, will be especially important to future purchasers of scatterable mines. Mines employing fragmentation and shaped-charge

---

[24] DIA/FSTC, p. 3-26.

[25] DIA/FSTC, p. 3-38.

[26] DIA/FSTC, p. 5-1.

explosives are likely to gain market share relative to blast mines. While multiple rocket launchers will remain the most widely used scatterable mine delivery systems, aircraft and "specialized deep-strike weapon platforms" appear to be already gaining popularity.[27]   The U.S. is continuing to invest in development of specialized mines for use in urban and low intensity conflict and more powerful, lightweight antipersonnel mines for use by Special Operations Forces.[28]

DIA predicts that demand will continue to grow for integral and add-on fuzes which resist demining and incorporate anti-disturbance, delayed-arming, self-destruction and self-neutralization features. New fuzes reaching the market by the beginning of the 21st century will offer "improve[d] lethality" in smaller packages.

At present, advanced antitank systems—especially the Wide Area Mine and A/T-oriented "autonomous battlefield" technology—are the principle focus of Western mine research, development and procurement. By about 2005, the Defense Intelligence Agency has predicted, producers may be ready to market "smart and brilliant landmines ... which communicate with adjacent mines to establish their relative positions within a specifically located minefield" and electronically coordinate their attacks via a "base mine" which determines the "optimal time" for detonation.[29]

## III.    Landmine Production

### A.   Landmine Producers and Their Products

The Arms Project's database of A/P landmine producers and products (reproduced in summary form as Appendix 17) is the most comprehensive ever published; yet it remains incomplete.   The Arms Project has identified almost 100 companies or government agencies in

---

[27] DIA/FSTC, pp. 3–12 through 3–17.

[28] U.S. Army Special Operations Command Combat Development Division, presentation by Master Sergeant Mark C. Kuebler, Munitions and Demolitions Project Officer; John A. Rosamilia,Chief, Mines Division, Project Manager for Mines Countermine and Demolitions, at ADPA Symposium, Sept. 7-9, 1993.

[29] DIA/FSTC, p. 3-58.

48 countries which have produced or marketed more than 340 A/P mine products.

The database was compiled from sources including:

• the U.S. Army's *Worldwide Informational Mine Guide*, maintained by the Army's Countermine Systems Directorate, Ft. Belvoir, Virginia, obtained by the Arms Project under the Freedom of Information Act (FOIA);
• trade publications, including the most comprehensive previously published listings of landmine producers and products, those contained in *Jane's Military Vehicles and Logistics* and Forecast International's *Ordnance & Munitions Forecast*;
• previously classified U.S. Army Intelligence and Defense Intelligence Agency documents, also obtained under FOIA, including the DIA's 1992 *Landmine Warfare: Trends and Projections* study;
• sales literature from leading landmine producers;
• past Human Rights Watch and Physicians for Human Rights field research in Africa, Asia, Latin America and the Middle East, supplemented by recent interviews with military experts and mines industry officials;
• research materials provided by arms trade researchers in several key mine-producing countries.

All sources proved incomplete. The Army database, which includes more than 700 mines of all types and a total of more than 2,000 mine and fuze combinations, was the single best source. Yet, as its compilers stress, it is an unfinished draft which is viewed as neither "complete or 100% accurate."[30] The same warning applies equally to this report.

Though the Arms Project has identified many mines and producers not listed in any other publicly available study, it is clear that further research will uncover many gaps and some inaccuracies. A number of producing companies and countries are almost certainly missing; some listed producers have probably ceased production.

―――――――――――

[30] U.S. Army Countermine Systems Directorate, *Worldwide Informational Mine Guide*, Preface, p. i.

There are some countries for which further research is needed. For example, the Arms Project has received as-yet-unconfirmed reports of possible landmine production in Cuba, Guatemala, Nicaragua and several additional African nations. As will be indicated in the country and regional summaries below, the Arms Project is also aware of gaps in its information on the known producers.

The biggest information gaps lie in Eastern Europe and the former Soviet Union.   However, even the available information on the United States, the producer which provides the most detailed disclosures about its landmine production and trade, is incomplete and inconsistent.

Our count of 346 mine products covers only those which were manufactured solely or primarily for antipersonnel use. It thus excludes three classes of mines with significant antipersonnel implications:

> • Several dozen varieties of dual or multi-purpose mines which may have some antipersonnel applications;
> • Field-improvised A/P landmines, like those which were used with deadly effectiveness by both German and Allied soldiers during World War II and subsequently played a significant role in Vietnam, Cambodia and El Salvador, among other countries;[31]
> • The many A/T devices which can be jury-rigged to become A/P mines.  A particularly gruesome example has been identified in Somalia where some militia fighters remove the pressure plates from Pakistani P2 antitank mines, reducing the required detonation force from 200 pounds to under 20 pounds.  This simple act transforms them, in the words of a U.S. State

---

[31] The U.S. Army database (U.S. Army Countermine Systems Directorate, *Worldwide Informational Mine Guide*) lists about three dozen improvised mine types used in vietnam during the 1960s and 1970s.  On their role in other conflicts, see Asia Watch and Physicians for Human Rights, *Landmines in Cambodia: The Coward's War* (New York: Human Rights Watch and Physicians for Human Rights, 1991), pp. 5-6, 55; James S. Milling "Mines and Booby Traps," in *Infantry*, Jan-Feb. 1969.p. 39; Americas Watch, *Landmines in El Salvador and Nicaragua: The Civilian Victims* (New York: Americas Watch, 1986), pp. 24 and 42.

Department expert, into "perhaps the most horrible anti-personnel mines in the world."[32]

## B. Global Production Volume

### 1. Antipersonnel Landmines

The Arms Project estimates that manufacturers have probably produced an average of five to 10 million A/P mines per year over the past quarter century, about 10 times the production volume identified in past published reports. Because most landmine production lies, like an iceberg, beneath the visible surface of the arms industry, this is a provisional estimate which may have to be revised when new data becomes available. It would not be surprising if the actual number of landmines now produced annually is considerably higher.

Up to now, lack of information thwarted all attempts to accurately estimate production volumes or identify the largest producers. The Arms Project's global landmine production estimates are based primarily on worldwide deployment data, largely unavailable until this year. This approach was chosen after consulting a number of experts, including the arms trade analysts responsible for the two most recent published studies on the subject, issued by the U.S. Congressional Research Service (CRS) and the private Forecast International (FI). Those authors confirmed that their reports cover only the small fraction of landmine production which is openly acknowledged by producers or military purchasers.

The 1992 CRS survey, limited to A/P mines procured under "military contracts," offered a "conservative estimate" that 500,000 to one million such A/P mines are produced annually but acknowledged that "neither market analysts nor military intelligence agencies have devoted intensive, consistent efforts to record[ing] exact production and cost data."[33] FI reported global production averaging about 650,000 A/P mines per year, but likewise counted only the production needed to fill

---

[32] Interview, David Gowdey, U.S. State Department, Office of Politico-Military Affairs, April 29, 1993.

[33] Congressional Research Service, *Report to Sen. Patrick Leahy on Anti-Personnel Landmines*, Jan. 13, 1990, p. 3.

the small minority of landmine orders which could be verified from producer and purchaser disclosures or other public sources.[34]

Given the clandestine nature of the landmine trade and the failure of past reports to account for the number of landmines known to have been deployed around the world, the Arms Project concluded early in its research that publicly disclosed sales production data was incomplete to the point of uselessness. The Arms Project therefore based its production estimates on a combination of: data available from governments, non-governmental groups and mine clearance contractors regarding mines actually deployed around the world; a rough estimate of current stocks of previously acquired but as-yet-undeployed landmines; and some assumptions about the age of currently deployed and stockpiled landmines.

With regard to landmine deployments, the most comprehensive survey to date, conducted by the U.S. State Department, estimates that between 85 million and 90 million uncleared landmines are currently emplanted in the soil of at least 62 nations.[35] An earlier report by United Nations Under-Secretary General Jan Eliasson offered an even higher estimate of 200 million mines.[36] Since the beginning of World War II, about 400 million mines have been emplaced, according to Thomas S. Reeder, Senior Mine Warfare Analyst at U.S. Army Intelligence's Foreign Science and Technology Center.[37]

Based on conversations with many experts in the field, the Arms Project has provisionally assumed that the number of undeployed landmines still held in military or manufacturer stockpiles roughly equals the number emplanted around the world. In those countries for which

---

[34] Interviews with Forecast International analysts, April 21, 1993.

[35] DOS, *Hidden Killers*, p.3. The report makes clear that this is an uncertain estimate, and also gives a further range of 65 million to 110 million. The report's principal author has indicated that even this wider range could be off by a considerable factor.

[36] Jan Eliasson, Under-Secretary General, Department of Humanitarian Affairs, "Informal paper on the subject of land mines," April 7, 1993.

[37] Thomas Reeder at ADPA Symposium, Sept. 7-9, 1993.

information is available, the overwhelming majority of mines are antipersonnel.[38]

This would imply the existence of well over 100 million and perhaps more than 200 million deployed and stockpiled antipersonnel landmines worldwide. These figures closely parallel the range of estimates offered by participants in ICRC's April 1993 symposium on antipersonnel landmines, held in Montreux, Switzerland.

The Arms Project thinks it reasonable to assume that the vast majority of mines currently in existence were produced in the past 20 to 25 years. While some of the mines still in the ground may be more than 25 years old, the Arms Project assumes that an equal or greater number of mines produced during this period have already been cleared or expended.

Taken together, these assumptions lead to the conclusion that the average global production level of A/P landmines over the past several decades has been approximately five to 10 million units annually. It is likely that there have been great fluctuations in production volume due to fluctuations in demand. These are obviously very rough estimates. The Arms Project would not be surprised if actual production level figures are even higher. However, unlike previously-reported figures, this estimate is consistent with information available from a number of country-specific or company-specific reports, including the following:

> • A British military expert's estimate that 20 million mines may have been emplanted in Angola during that nation's civil war, which began in 1975;[39]
> • Estimates ranging from 10 million (International Committee of the Red Cross) to more than 30 million (U.S. Defense

---

[38] DIA/FSTC reports that 99.85% of landmines cleared in Nicaragua and 97.4% of the mines remaining were A/P as of the end of 1990 (pp. 2-29 through 2-21).

[39] Africa Watch, *Landmines in Angola* (New York: Africa Watch, 1993), p. 24. Note that the U.S. State Department offers a lower estimate for Angola of 9 million uncleared landmines. (DOS, *Hidden Killers*, p. 34.)

Intelligence Agency) of the number of landmines planted in Afghanistan during the 1980s;[40]
• Widely varying estimates, ranging upward from four million, of the number of mines planted in Cambodia since the late 1960s; and[41]
• Findings by an Italian court that one of Iraq's several landmine suppliers sold that nation nine million mines during a four year period in the 1980s.[42]

## 2. Submunitions

It is extremely important to note that none of these figures include the enormous number of submunitions with antipersonnel impact. Known producers of submunitions include China, France, Germany, Great Britain, Greece, Israel, Poland, Russia, South Africa, Spain, the United States, and former Yugoslavia.[43]

A recent study by William Arkin of Greenpeace estimates that the United States alone has manufactured 750 million submunitions since it started producing them in the 1970s—several times the total number of A/P and A/T landmines produced by all nations combined. The study further estimates that 24-30 million submunitions were expended during the Persian Gulf War alone.[44]

---

[40] Medical Educational Trust, *Indiscriminate Weapons - Landmines* (London: MET Reports, March 1993), p. 17; DIA/FSTC, p. 2-4.

[41] *Jane's Defense Weekly*, May 16, 1992. See also, Asia Watch and Physicians for Human Rights, *Landmines in Cambodia: The Coward's War* (New York: Human Rights Watch and Physicians for Human Rights, 1991).

[42] Middle East Watch, *Hidden Death: Land Mines and Civilian Casualties in Iraqi Kurdistan* (New York: Middle East Watch, October 1992), p. 3, p. 40. Note also that U.S. military officials have reported that Iraq deployed more than 3.5 million landmines in Saudi Arabia and along the Kuwaiti coastline. (DIA/FSTC, p.2-5.)

[43] Arkin, "Military Technology," p. 9-10.

[44] Ibid., p. 5.

These figures receive significant support from contractors involved in post-Gulf War demining. "I think we just emptied our depots of Rockeyes," says Major General (Ret.) Frank P. Ragano, president of CMS Incorporated. CMS, a subsidiary of Daimler-Benz, Germany's largest weapons manufacturer, was prime contractor for post-war demining in the "American sector" of Kuwait.[45] An official of Explosive Ordnance Disposal World Services Inc., CMS's main Kuwait subcontractor, told the Arms Project that unexploded U.S. Rockeye submunitions "duds" outnumbered post-war Kuwait's next most prevalent explosive hazard, Iraqi-deployed Chinese landmines. Officials of both companies agreed that unexploded Rockeyes are functionally identical to uncleared A/P landmines. Deminers also report that they found a quantity of failed U.S. GATOR mines—designed to self-destruct—though they could not provide information on precise quantities.[46]

### C. The Leading Producers

Estimating global output is difficult; allocating that output to particular producers is harder still. Lacking hard data, the Arms Project considered several methods for ranking producers.

One method, used by the Congressional Research Service in its 1992 study, simply ranks countries by the number of A/P mine models they produce.[47] Such a list undoubtedly underestimates the importance of those nations—including China, other Third World countries and some former Communist countries—which have tended to produce large quantities of a few landmine designs. However, it is useful as a rough index of national "commitment" to A/P landmine development on the part of companies which hope to profitably produce them and military officials preparing to deploy them. Applying this method to the Arms Project's

---

[45] Address to ADPA Symposium, Sept. 7-9, 1993.

[46] Interview with John Taffe at ADPA Symposium, September 7, 1993.

[47] Congressional Research Service, "Report to Sen. Patrick Leahy on Anti-Personnel Landmines," Jan. 13, 1990, p. 3. The following list uses the CRS method, but is based on the number of landmine models identified in the Arms Project Data Base.

findings on landmine producers and products, the leading developers of
A/P landmines in recent years have been:

- the United States (37 models)
- Italy (36)
- the former Soviet Union (31)
- Sweden (21)
- Vietnam (18)
- Germany [former East and West combined] (18)
- Austria (16)
- former Yugoslavia (15)
- France (14)
- China (12)
- United Kingdom (9)

A second, somewhat impressionistic, approach relies on a
combination of publicly reported transactions, declassified military
intelligence data and experts' observations of the deployment of A/P
landmines in civil wars and international conflicts.  (See Table III.)
Though this method may underestimate the importance of some
producing nations with exceptionally large stockpiles of undeployed
mines, the Arms Project believes it to be the least inaccurate technique
now available.  It also provides the best available indicator of a country's
relative significance as a producer of mines that raise serious
humanitarian concerns.

Most experts interviewed by the Arms Project believe that China,
Italy and the former Soviet Union were probably the largest producers
of A/P landmines in recent years, measured in number of units, though
not necessarily in that order.

Though official data would seem to place the U.S. behind these
market leaders, field reports from mine clearance groups suggest that the
U.S. must have been in the top ranks in the not-too-distant past.  (U.S.
government officials have sometimes asserted that the ubiquity of
American mines stems from foreign copying or past production under
foreign licenses.[48]  However, the same could hold true for other leading
producers.)  Additionally, if antipersonnel submunitions were included,

---

[48] Interviews, U.S. Departments of State and Defense, April-July 1993.

it is not unlikely that the United States would rank as the world's largest or second largest producer.

Beyond the top three or four producers, expert opinion diverges and reports of mine deployments must be augmented from other sources. Reviews of published literature and interviews with trade specialists, mine clearance professionals, and government experts produce a consensus suggesting that the following additional countries (not listed in ranked order) have probably also been among the world's larger A/P mine producers in recent years:

- In Western Europe: Belgium, and possibly also Austria, France, Greece, and Sweden.
- In Eastern Europe: former Czechoslovakia, former East Germany, and former Yugoslavia.
- In the developing world: Egypt, India, Israel, Pakistan, Singapore, South Africa, and possibly also Chile, Iran, Iraq, South Korea, and North Korea.

Experts interviewed by the Arms Project believe that the collapse of the Soviet Union left landmine producing facilities in at least three of the successor states—Russia, Ukraine, and Belarus. We have been unable to ascertain with confidence the current status of ex-Czechoslovak and ex-Yugoslav facilities. In addition to redividing old production capabilities, the dissolution of the Warsaw Pact has also "compelled some countries formerly supported by the Soviet arms industry to develop a domestic mine production capability," according to the Defense Intelligence Agency.[49]

## IV.    Landmine Prices and Expenditures

Landmine prices vary enormously.  The most technologically advanced "smart" mines can sell for 50 times the price of their "dumb" counterparts, yet some advanced conventional A/P mines incorporating modern anti-detection and anti-disturbance mechanisms are now priced very cheaply.  At all technology levels, A/P mines are considerably less expensive than comparable A/T products.

---

[49] DIA/FSTC, p. 3-59.

## A.  Conventional A/P Mines

The conventional A/P landmine can be a very low priced item. Reported unit prices paid in recent years for conventional antipersonnel landmines produced in Western nations range from $6.70 for Giat Industry's Belgian-made PRB NR 257[50] to $27.47 for the U.S. Army's most recent procurement of Claymore M18A1 mines.[51]  Producers can increase revenue by packaging their A/P mines with accessory kits.  For example, U.S. manufacturers export a Claymore and accessory package — test kit, detonator, detonator cable and carrying case — at an average unit price of $79.29.[52]

Non-western A/P mines often sell at or below the low end of this range.  China's widely distributed Type 72 A/P mines sometimes sell for less than $3 each, according to a U.S. State Department official.[53]  The cheapest mine for which the Arms Project has examined pricing data is the AP NM AE T1, sold for $5.80 by its Brazilian manufacturer, Quimica Tupan.[54]  The state-owned Pakistani Ordnance Factories' widely-used, aggressively-advertised P4 Mk.2 A/P mine sells for $6.75.[55]  Officials of

---

[50] Forecast International, *Ordnance and Munitions Survey - Landmines (Europe)*, March 1993, p. 1.

[51] U.S. Army, *Information Paper - Anti-Personnel Landmine Procurement and Production*, 1992.

[52] U.S. Department of Defense, Defense Security Assistance Administration, *Foreign Military Sales of Anti-Personnel Mines for the period FY 1983-1993 to date, JF171 as of 8/11/93*.  For accessory pack pictures and specifications, see Sherwood International brochure (undated).

[53] Interview, David Gowdey.  DOS, *Hidden Killers*, p. 3 also states, "Some Antipersonnel (AP) mines can be bought for less than $3 per mine, and some Antitank mines are available for less than $75 each."

[54] This mine is also produced in Mexico, according to the U.S. Army Countermine Systems Directorate, *Worldwide Informational Mine Guide*.

[55] Rae McGrath, "Collateral Damage: Anti-Personnel Mines — a Human Rights Perspective," Talk given at Handicap International, Brussels, 6 March 1992.

several landmine-producing companies and landmine clearing contractors have told the Arms Project that they believe Russia is now "dumping" landmines on the world market at unprecedented low prices; the Arms Project was not able to confirm these reports.[56]

Unit prices for the most sophisticated A/P mines can be much higher. The U.S. government, for example, paid a unit price of about $260 for 42,919 self-destructing M86 PDM mines ordered in 1988.[57] On the other hand some relatively advanced models sell very cheaply. Italy's Valsella has sold its plastic, "non-detectable" VS50 and VS50-AR mines—which can hand-emplanted or scattered—at unit prices ranging as low as $6.15.[58]

Low to moderate cost products—probably priced along the range between a $3 Chinese mine and a $27 Claymore—dominate trade in individual A/P mines.

Based on this assumption, it is possible to estimate the total annual value of worldwide A/P landmine sales. At an average cost of $10 per mine for 5-10 million mines sold annually, sales would total $50-100 million. At $20 per mine, they would total $100-200 million. While these figures are far from precise, the range given here, $50 to $200 million, represents a useful provisional estimate of the value of the global trade in A/P landmines, excluding accessories and mine scattering equipment.

---

[56] Interviews during ADPA Symposium, Sept. 7-9, 1993. Note that officials at the Russian Embassy in Washington have told the Arms Project that they are unable to comment on their country's current landmines export policies and practices.

[57] Though marketed as a hand-emplaced mine of particular value to Special Operations Forces, the PDM can also be deployed by helicopter for use both on land and in shallow-water. DIA/FSTC, p. 3-58.

[58] Italy, Ministero del Commerciacon l'Estero, "Elenco delle autorizzaioni rilasciate dal 1980 alla Valsella Meccanotecnica per esportazioni di materiale di armamento verso tutti i peasi (undated).

## B. Scatterable Landmine Products

Scatterable A/P mine systems are often in an entirely different price league from stand-alone mines. In some cases, the unit price of the "smart" A/P mines delivered in these systems range upward from 10 times the cost of their older "dumb" counterparts.[59] Countries purchasing American scatterable A/P mines under the Foreign Military Sales program pay unit prices ranging upward from $128.[60] Even when the mines themselves are cheap, as in the case of the Italian A/P products cited above, mine scattering units typically sell for several hundred thousand dollars each.[61]

U.S. figures provide an indication of the enormous price gap separating the low and high ends of the market. Spending for the U.S. Army's main scatterable A/P mine system—the Area Denial Artillery Munition, a 155 millimeter projectile which delivers 36 mines per round—has totalled $763.9 million over the past 10 years. This is more than 200 times the $3.5 million expenditure for all conventional A/P mines (M16A1 and M18A1) procured during the same period.[62] U.S. spending for scatterable mine systems peaked in 1987, when the government spent $450 million for landmines and landmine systems, including $246 million for systems containing substantial A/P elements.[63]

There is active competition for sales of scatterable mine systems in European, Asian and Middle Eastern markets. Competition from a growing number of new producers could cause some downward pressure on prices. South African firms, for example, displayed "smart" mines and

---

[59] *International Defense Review*, April 1991.

[60] US-DSAA, *Foreign Military Sales of Anti-Personnel Mines*, 1993.

[61] *Army Times*, Dec. 11, 1989, p. 26.

[62] Congressional Research Service, "Report to Sen. Patrick Leahy on Anti-Personnel Landmines," Jan. 13, 1990.

[63] Forecast International, Ordnance and Munitions Survey - Landmines (United States), March 1993, p. 6, and U.S. Army, *Information Paper*, 1992.

scatterable AP/AT mine delivery systems at a 1991 arms show.[64] Though India is not a traditional landmine exporter, it is worth noting that the Indian Department of Defense Research and Development has announced some advanced landmine products in recent years.[65]

## V.    Landmine Trade

Most landmine trade is cloaked in secrecy. Nonetheless, the Arms Project has found evidence that at least 41 companies or government organizations in 29 nations have exported A/P landmines. (See Table II.)

The obstacles to information gathering on landmine sales are formidable. Few countries release landmine import, export or procurement data. Recent inquiries by members of parliament in Britain and non-government organizations in West Germany were met with flat refusals to disclose information, on security grounds.[66] Though the U.S. government provides far greater public disclosure than any other government on procurement and some classes of landmine exports, it, too, keeps some critical facts hidden.[67]

In most other countries, specific landmine export transactions remain secret unless journalistic investigations, judicial inquiries,

---

[64] *International Defense Review*, December 1991, p. 1375.

[65] Government of India, Ministry of Defense, *Annual Report: 1990-91*, p. 56.

[66] United Kingdom, Foreign and Commonwealth Office, Letter from the Minister of State to Chris Mullin MP, Jan. 22, 1993, reproduced as Appendix 12; Angelika Beer, Medico International, Memorandum to the Arms Project, April 4, 1993.

[67] For example, the State Department's Office of Defense Trade Controls has failed to provide information first requested by the Arms Project in early May, for data on private, commercial exports which it licenses. The Defense Department—which monitors the majority of landmine sales through its Foreign Military Sales program—has been more forthcoming, but there are major discrepencies among the various disclosures provided by Defense Department offices in response to inquiries by the Arms Project and by the Senate Foreign Operations Subcommittee Chairman Patrick Leahy. Each time Defense Department officials have been questioned about A/P landmine sales, they have disclosed additional transactions which were omitted from earlier reports.

declassification of secret intelligence data or other unusual events thrust
information in the public arena, usually long after the transactions took
place.  For example:

> • Recent Paraguayan parliamentary investigations of covert arms
> transactions during the reign of former dictator Alfredo
> Stroessner uncovered new information on Greek and Italian
> landmine sales to South Africa.  In one previously unreported
> 1980s transaction, 90,000 mines, loaded onto a Danish ship in the
> Italian port of Ortobello ostensibly for delivery to the Paraguayan
> defense ministry, were actually diverted to South Africa.[68]  In
> another transaction, a Paraguayan general allegedly provided a
> false end use certificate for a secret sale of 45,000 "Booster M
> 125 C1" mines sold to South Africa by the Greek Powder and
> Cartridge Company.  It is not known if these were A/P or A/T
> mines since neither the Greek company's name nor the
> designation of the mines appears in any publicly available guides
> to landmines and their producers.[69]

> • A series of detailed studies compiled by U.S. Army Intelligence
> and the Defense Intelligence Agency have identified A/P mines
> from 10 countries—Belgium, Canada, China, India, Iran, Italy,
> Pakistan, the former Soviet Union, the United States and former
> Yugoslavia—held by Iraq at the time of the Persian Gulf war.
> Those reports also revealed that Iraq has produced local versions
> of  Italian,  Soviet  and  Yugoslav-designed  mines.[70]

---

[68] *Inter Press Service*, Mar. 17, 1993.

[69] *ABC Color*, Mar. 14, 1993, p. 16, as translated in Foreign Broadcast
Information Service .

[70] DIA/FSTC; U.S. Army Intelligence Agency — U.S. Army Foreign Science
and Technology Center, *Operation Desert Shield Special Report: Iraqi Combat Engineer
Capabilities*, 30 November 1990. AST-266OZ-131-90 (USAIA, *Desert Shield*, 1990);
and U.S. Army Engineer Center, *Desert Shield Mine Recognition and Warfare
Handbook*, Missiouri: Ft. Leonard Wood, November 1990, (USAEC, *Desert Shield*,
1990).  This document was obtained by the Arms Project through the Freedom
of Information Act.

Investigations in Italy have shed much light on one of Iraq's most important landmine trade relationships. (See below for details of Iraq's purchase of nine million Italian mines). In addition, one previously classified Defense Department document obtained under FOIA suggests that Iraqi authorities obtained some Chinese landmines through the Jordanian armed forces.[71]

## A. Exports of Conventional and Hand-Emplaced A/P Mines

As in the case of mine production, landmine deployment data is useful for identifying major exporters, in the absence of more direct sources of data. Wars in the developing world, and especially civil wars, have been the main arenas for use of low-tech antipersonnel mines. Published studies list at least 25 countries as the apparent points of origin for A/P mines encountered over the past decade in eight conflicts. (See Table III.) This chart should be viewed solely as an indicator of *possible* direct participation in exports to mine-recipient nations, as some mines may have been resold from third country stocks, and others may be third country copies of mine designs which originated in the listed countries.

China, Italy, and the former Soviet Union rank at the top of most experts' lists of exporters, though not necessarily in that order. A recent study by the U.S. Defense Intelligence Agency identifies ex-East Germany, Italy, the former Soviet Union and ex-Czechoslovakia as the sources for the majority of landmines obtained by third world countries in the past 10 to 15 years. The agency names China, Egypt, Pakistan, and South Africa as new "ambitious marketers of landmine munitions deeply involved in high technology proliferation."[72] Other countries identified by some sources as probable significant exporters of A/P mines in recent years included Belgium, Chile, Greece, Israel, Portugal, Singapore, Spain, and the former Yugoslavia.

There is contradictory evidence and testimony regarding the relative importance of U.S. A/P mine exports. The recent U.S. State Department report said, "The U.S. bears little blame for the global problem with uncleared landmines, having been a selective exporter of

---

[71] DIA/FSTC, p. 2-15.

[72] DIA/FSTC, p. 3-2.

limited numbers of landmines. Less than 15% of the landmines in countries with uncleared landmine problems originated in the U.S."[73] On the other hand, if 15%, or roughly one in seven, is an accurate figure, that could certainly be considered significant, and would probably rank the U.S. in the top five exporters. In fact, landmine clearance groups often place the U.S. alongside or immediately after China, Italy, and the ex-U.S.S.R. at the top of their lists of problem countries.

U.S. government data—though fragmentary and inconsistent—suggests that the U.S. was indeed a major exporter in the 1970s, but has not been a significant exporter of A/P mines since. (See U.S. case study below for details on U.S. exports.) Many of those older mines are probably still active, and being discovered by mine clearers. In addition, the prevalence of "U.S.-origin" mines noted by mine clearers could, at least partially, be the result of: copies of U.S. mines produced by other nations; U.S.-made mines that were re-sold by the original purchasing nation; and covert shipments of mines, unacknowledged by the U.S. government, to insurgent groups in such places as Afghanistan, Angola, Cambodia and Nicaragua.

## B. Advanced Systems

The world's ongoing wars give producers of lower priced A/P mines a steady supply of customers. Success in selling scatterable mine systems, on the other hand, depends upon a firm's ability to win the bidding for a few large contracts. Thus, U.S. manufacturers who profited from U.S. upgrading of scatterable mine systems in the late 1980s are now eager to sell similar systems abroad. European manufacturers are eager for the same contracts. European nations which have reportedly expressed interest in purchasing systems which combine A/T and A/P mines include Greece, the Netherlands, and Spain.[74] Industry officials have also been courting potential non-European purchasers, including India, Saudi Arabia, South Korea, and Taiwan. These markets—potentially worth upwards of $500 million over the next five years, according to

---

[73] DOS, *Hidden Killers*, p. 178.

[74] *International Defense Review*, Sept. 1991, Forecast International Ordnance and Munitions Forecast - Landmines (Europe), Mar. 1993; interview with industry officials.

Alliant Techsystems (formerly Honeywell Incorporated's Defense Systems Division)—have attracted sales efforts by U.S., Italian, French, and German companies.[75]

The largest recent or pending landmine sales do not, however, involve A/P mines. While the U.S. is continuing to procure some scatterable systems containing A/P mines, Anti-Helicopter and Wide Area (antitank) Mines are the main focuses of currently planned research, development and procurement.[76] Planned Western European expenditures include a potential $500 million joint expenditure for Wide Area A/T Mines by Britain, France and Germany and the planned British purchase of an A/T-only Vehicle Launched Scatterable Mines System.[77]

## VI.    Case Studies: Major Exporters and Producers

### A.  The United States

The U.S. was once a significant exporter and could—if business executives lobbying for relaxation of the current export moratorium are successful—become one again. This is largely because of the potential market for scatterable mines. In lobbying against current export restrictions, industry officials have said that eight producers of scatterable mines, systems and components could share in a market worth about $100 million a year if exports are allowed to resume. (For statistics on U.S. A/P landmine exports see Tables IV and V.)

In the past 10 years, it appears the U.S. has exported about 150,000 A/P mines, including both conventional and scatterable mines. The exact magnitude of past U.S. exports cannot be stated with certainty because government statistics are incomplete and internally inconsistent. Various agencies within the U.S. Defense Department, which controls the majority of landmine exports through its Foreign Military Sales program, have provided conflicting data. For example, U.S. Army figures released to the Arms Project under the Freedom of Information Act indicate that

---

[75] Alliant Techsystems, "Current Potential Fascam Overseas Markets," 1993.

[76] According to speakers at the ADPA Symposium, September 7-9, 1993.

[77] *International Defense Review*, Sep. 1992, p. 901; *Jane's Defense Weekly*, Sept. 14, 1991, p. 455 and Sept. 19, 1992 p. 28.

the U.S. exported at least 70,000 conventional A/P landmines during the past 10 years, more than twice the number included in an ostensibly complete report covering the same period provided to members of Congress by the Defense Security Assistance Agency.[78]

The State Department, which licenses "commercial exports" directly negotiated by U.S. firms, has thus far failed to respond to requests made by the Arms Project under the FOIA for details on the landmine sales which it monitors, though some summary data was available from disclosures made to Congress. The export data offered below thus must be viewed as provisional; we believe that it may understate the U.S. role.

### 1. Conventional A/P Mines

The U.S. was a leading exporter of conventional mines in the 1960s and 1970s but sharply curtailed exports in the 1980s, according to U.S. Army Ammunitions and Chemical Command (AMCCOM) statistics on Defense Department-administered "Foreign Military Sales" (FMS).

Data obtained under the Freedom of Information Act reveals that the United States has exported more than 4.3 million conventional A/P mines since 1969.[79] (See Table IV.)

U.S. exports of conventional A/P mines peaked in 1975 at more than 1.4 million. That year's shipments of mines to Cambodia, Chile, and Iran represent about one-third of all reported FMS exports of conventional landmines in the 24 years. Over the entire 24 year period covered by the AMCCOM data, the leading FMS purchasers of A/P mines

---

[78] U.S. Army, Armament, Munitions and Chemical Command (USAMCCOM), Letter to the Arms Project, August 25, 1993, and attached statistical tables; and U.S. Department of Defense, Defense Security Assistance Administration (US-DSAA), *Foreign Military Sales of Anti-Personnel Mines for the period FY 1983-1993 to date, JF171 as of 8/11/93*. This document was obtained by the Arms Project through the Freedom of Information Act.

[79] USAMCCOM, Letter to the Arms Project, August 25, 1993, and attached statistical tables on Foreign Military Sales of landmines 1969-92 and shipments of mines for use in Southwest Asia (Operation Desert Storm). USAMCCOM failed to provide any data for the first year covered by the Arms Project's request, 1968. Total U.S. mine exports, including antitank mines, exceeded 7.5 million.

were: Iran under the Shah (2.5 million); Cambodia (622,000); Thailand (437,000); Chile (300,000); El Salvador (102,000); Malaysia (88,000); and, Saudi Arabia (88,000). (See Table V.)

Other confirmed purchasers of U.S. A/P mines were Australia, Belize, Brunei, Canada, Colombia, Denmark, Ecuador, El Salvador, Ethiopia, Greece, Indonesia, Jordan, South Korea, Lebanon, Morocco, the Netherlands, New Zealand, Oman, Peru, the Philippines, Singapore, Somalia, Switzerland, Taiwan, Turkey, and the United Kingdom. A document provided to members of Congress last year also listed Kuwait as a purchaser of M14 A/P mines, but Kuwait was inexplicably omitted from subsequent disclosures.[80] Israel ranked second after Iran in total mines of all types purchased under FMS, with about 1.9 million mines, but most if not all Israeli purchases were antitank.

In contrast to the 1970s, over the past 10 years the U.S. has only exported about 70,000 conventional A/P mines under FMS. El Salvador was the largest recipient, accounting for about half the mines, followed by Lebanon and Thailand.

These figures do not include: licensed production of U.S.-designed mines in other nations; illegal or unauthorized copies of U.S. mines produced in other nations; possible covert shipments of U.S. landmines to rebels in Afghanistan, Angola, Cambodia, Nicaragua or elsewhere; and mines deployed with U.S. troops in conflict (as in Vietnam or the Persian Gulf). Each of these categories could involve significant numbers of landmines.

### a. The Claymore: America's Most Popular Conventional Mine

Over the past ten years, more than 80% of FMS exports involved the M18A1 Claymore bounding fragmentation mines. Internationally, the Claymore is one of the most widely-produced conventional A/P landmines. According to the U.S. Army, it is also the only mine still made in the U.S. which lacks a self-destruct mechanism.[81]

---

[80] US-DSAA, Land Mines Purchased under the Foreign Military Sales Program as of July 15, 1992.

[81] U.S. Army, *Information Paper*, 1992.

The U.S. Army developed the Claymore at Picatinny Arsenal and standardized it in its current form, the M18A1, in 1960.[82]  It is a durable, long-lasting, highly effective killing instrument. An estimated 70% of Claymores will remain effective for more than 20 years in any climate.[83]  The Claymore's 680 gram explosive charge propels 700 steel balls forward in a 60 degree arc. They can kill at a distance of up to 50 meters and may produce incapacitating wounds at up to 100 meters.[84]

Most U.S. Claymore mines are manufactured in government-owned, contractor-operated plants (GOCOs) managed by Thiokol Corporation, Mason and Hanger, and Day and Zimmerman, under the supervision of the U.S. Army Armament, Munition and Chemical Command (AMCCOM).[85]  In addition, Northridge, California-based Sherwood International, has marketed Claymores manufactured in Delaware by Mohawk Electrical Systems.[86]  U.S. production ranged between 5,000 and 20,000 units in recent years, but the Army plans to increase procurement to an average of 50,000 per year during the coming decade.[87]

The continued purchase of Claymores appears to contradict a recent U.S. Army statement that "all current production is designed to minimize hazard to innocent civilians" through the exclusive procurement

---

[82] J.I.H. Owen, *Brassey's Infantry Weapons of the World* (New York: Bonanza Books 1975), p. 262; U.S. Army, *Anti-Personnel Mine M18A1 and M18 (Claymore) - Department of the Army Field Manual* (Washington: Department of the Army, 1966), p. 2.

[83] *Defence Today*, no. 59-60, p. 158.

[84] Lt. Col. P.R. Courtney-Green, *Ammunition for the Land Battle* (London: Brassey's, 1991), pp. 176-7.

[85] U.S. Army, *Information Paper*, 1992; and USAMCCOM, *Louisiana Army Ammunition Plant*, August 1987 (brochure).

[86] Sherwood International, Undated sales brochure.

[87] Congressional Research Service, "Report to Sen. Patrick Leahy on Anti-Personnel Landmines," Jan. 13, 1990, p. 6 and U.S. Army, Information Paper, p. 2.

of self-destructing mines.[88]  In principle, current policy does say that Claymores may be used in "command-detonated" mode only, reducing the risk of inadvertent detonation by non-combatants.[89]  In practice, however, soldiers who want to protect their position can easily rig the mines for tripwire detonation.  "A [tripwire-rigged] Claymore is a very powerful device for stopping unseen enemies," noted a former logistics officer interviewed by the Arms Project.  In combat, he stressed, "no one is going to convince a soldier to use it other than in the most effective way he can."[90]

The Claymore remains the most widely distributed U.S.-origin landmine.  As of 1992, worldwide production of Claymores totalled about 180,000 units a year, at least nine times the U.S. level.[91]  Overseas copying has thus replaced direct export as the main route to the world market for Claymores and other U.S.-origin conventional A/P landmines.  Countries known to produce Claymores include Chile,  South Africa, South Korea, and Pakistan.  Mines closely modelled on the Claymore are produced in many other countries.

The existence of multiple production and distribution channels provides an element of deniability which may make purchase of this mine especially desirable for planners of covert military operations.  The Claymore is the only A/P mine which appears in a declassified U.S. National Security Council list of weapons purchased for the Nicaraguan contras by former National Security Council official Oliver L. North.[92]

---

[88] Congressional Research Service, "Report to Sen. Patrick Leahy on Anti-Personnel Landmines," Jan. 13, 1990, p. 5.

[89] U.S. Army, *Information Paper*, p. 1.

[90] Confidential interview, New York, June 25, 1993.

[91] Congressional Research Service, "Report to Sen. Patrick Leahy on Anti-Personnel Landmines," Jan. 13, 1990.

[92] Oliver R. North, "Memorandum for Robert C. McFarlane," National Security Council, May 1, 1985, Tab A.

Contra officials have publicly insisted that, during and after the period in which these mines were supplied, they were using no landmines.[93]

Experts have also identified U.S.-origin Claymores among the weapons used by such guerilla groups as the U.S.-backed UNITA rebels in Angola, and the resistance forces in Cambodia.[94] In addition, a 1990 U.S. Army intelligence report said that non-U.S. origin Claymores were found in Iraqi arsenals, and noted that similar Claymores were used in Afghanistan.[95] An Arms Project field researcher's report indicates that both U.S. and South African-origin Claymores have been used in Mozambique.[96]

Claymores remain an active part of U.S. arsenals. The U.S. Army units assigned to the Persian Gulf war were armed with 74,790 Claymores; Claymore "losses" in the war totalled 15,531.[97]

### b.  Other Conventional A/P Mine Exports

The only other conventional A/P mine purchased by the U.S. Army in recent years is the M16A1, last procured at a price of $23.80 each (for 79,800 units) in 1990.  Though the U.S. stopped buying plastic

---

[93] Americas Watch, *Landmines in El Salvador and Nicaragua: The Civilian Victims* (New York: Human Rights Watch, Dec. 1986), pp. 50-51.

[94] See Africa Watch, *Landmines in Angola*, p. 17; Asia Watch, *The Coward's War*, pp. 54-55; DOS, *Hidden Killers*.

[95] U.S. Army Intelligence Agency — U.S. Army Foreign Science and Technology Center, *Operation Desert Shield Special Report: Iraqi Combat Engineer Capabilities*, 1990, p. 35.  This document was provided to the Arms Project by Greenpeace, which obtained it under the Freedom of Information Act.

[96] Field research by Arms Project consultant Alex Vines, June-July 1993.

[97] USAMCCOM, Letter to the Arms Project, August 25, 1993, and attached statistical tables on Foreign Military Sales of landmines 1969-92 and shipments of mines for use in Southwest Asia (Operation Desert Storm).  Note: "losses" include all mines not returned from the theater of battle, whether or not they were actually deployed by combat forces.  See *U.S. News and World Report*, Mar. 11, 1993, p. 34 regarding the issuance of Claymore mines to members of U.S. Army Long Range Surveillance Detachments.

M14 A/P landmines more than a decade ago and has banned use of live M14s in U.S. Army training exercises because of the danger they pose to inexperienced users, the Defense Department shipped M14s from its stockpiles to El Salvador in 1986, and may have exported them even more recently.[98] The M14, "designed to incapacitate, rather than kill," has a plastic body which effectively defeats most detection and clearance measures.[99] The U.S. exported more of these mines (1.99 million) than any other in the 24 year period covered by AMCCOM's FMS data. Though the U.S. Army has stopped procuring M14 and M16 series mines, at least 227,376 M16A2s and 46,902 M14s were provided to U.S. troops for use in the Persian Gulf War.[100]

In addition to Defense Department-supervised FMS sales, the State Department reports that it has approved eight private commercial A/P mine export licenses with a combined value of $980,000 in the past 10 years. Though the government has withheld details on individual commercial transactions,[101] it has released aggregate data indicating that 98% of the commercial export approvals involved sales to Australia, New Zealand and South Korea. There were also much smaller approvals (averaging $4,000 per country) of sales to El Salvador, Norway, Portugal, Saudi Arabia, and the United Kingdom.

---

[98] US-DSAA, *Landmines Purchased Under the Foreign Military Sales Program as of July 15, 1992*, shows FMS exports of M14s to Kuwait as recently as 1991 and to El Salvador in 1989, but these sales are not included in subsequent, purportedly complete, listings of FMS landmine exports.

[99] Congressional Research Service, "Report to Sen. Patrick Leahy on Anti-Personnel Landmines," Jan. 13, 1990, p. 6; U.S. Army, *Information Paper*, 1992; *Armada International*, June 1990.

[100] USAMCCOM, Letter to the Arms Project, August 25, 1993 indicates that 227,376 M16A2 and 46,902 M14 mines were shipped to Southwest Asia. "Losses" totalled 21,200 and 600 respectively.

[101] U.S. Department of State, Letter to Vietnam Veterans of America Foundation, June 18, 1992.

# POMZ-2

The POMZ-2 antipersonnel mine was developed during World War II. Today, there are several variations of this mine, which has an olive green cast-iron fragmentation body. It is activated by a pull on the tripwire and has a lethal radius of four meters. The mine is often laid in clusters of four or more. It may be linked to other explosive devices, such as ball mines and grenades, to provide a wide killing area. Commonly referred to as the "stake mine," it has been used extensively in Cambodia. The POMZ-2M is a more modern version of the POMZ-2; the main difference is that it has five, rather than six, rows of fragmentation. Variations of the POMZ-2 have been manufactured in the former Soviet Union, former Czechoslovakia, former East Germany, former Yugoslavia, China, and North Korea. (Drawing by Pamela Blotner for the Arms Project/PHR.)

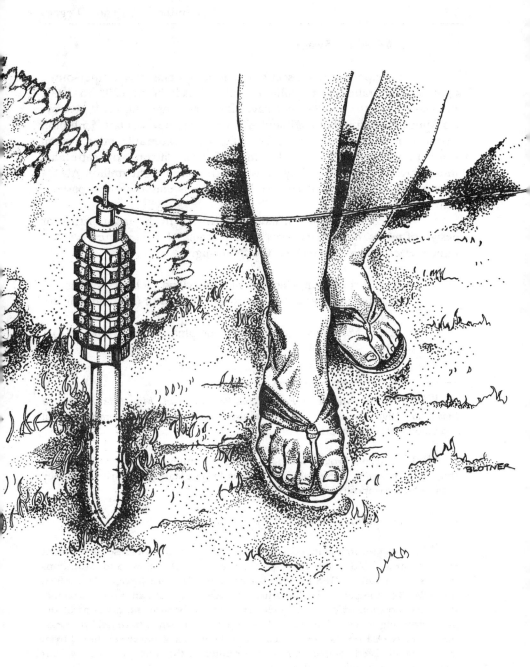

### 2.  Advanced Systems

U.S. expenditure for scatterable mine systems with antipersonnel applications totalled $1.68 billion in the decade from 1983 to 1992. Purchases peaked in 1987, and have since been tapering off.[102] Army stockpiles (including both A/P and A/T weapons) now contain $5 billion worth of FASCAM equipment, the main U.S. scatterable mine system since the mid-1970s.[103] The leading U.S. manufacturer of scatterable mine products, Alliant Techsystems, has produced eight million ADAM scatterable A/P mines for use in FASCAM systems over the past 15 years.[104]

U.S. companies which have participated in the manufacture or design of mines, delivery systems or components for integrated A/P-A/T mine-scattering systems include the following:[105]

- AAI Corporation, Cockeysville, Maryland (delivery systems)
- Accudyne Corporation, Janesville, Wisconsin (A/P and delivery systems)
- Action Manufacturing Co., Philadelphia, Pennsylvania (A/T)

---

[102] U.S. Army, *Information Paper - Anti-Personnel Land Mine Procurement and Production*, 1992.  Note that this figure also includes some A/T components of combined A/P-A/T systems.

[103] U.S. Army, Project Manager Mines, Countermine and Demolitions, *Program Opportunities*, presentation by Deputy Project Manager Charles E. Digney at the ADPA Symposium.

[104] Arkin, "Military Technology," p. 6.

[105] Companies are identified as producers based on U.S. Defense Department press releases, DMS 1989, Forecast International, Ordnance and Munitions Forecast - Landmines (U.S.), 1993, International Defense Review, Dec. 1992, Jane's MV&L, company sales literature, and Arms Project Landmines database. Bracketed notation—A/T, A/P or delivery system—refers to the portions of the mine-scattering system(s) for which the company is known to have held prime or sub-contracts. A/T only systems (such as the Wide Area Mine) are excluded from this listing; all listed companies have contributed to the construction of systems which are used to deliver A/P mines.

- Alliant Techsystems, Minneapolis, Minnesota (A/P, A/T and delivery systems)
- Brunswick Corporation, De Land Florida (Delivery systems)
- Gencorp (Aerojet Ordnance Division), Downey, California (A/P and A/T)
- EMCO Inc., East Gadsden, Alabama (A/P)
- ESD Corporation, San Jose, California (delivery systems)
- Ensign Bickford Aerospace Company, Simsbury, Connecticut (delivery systems)
- FMC Corporation, Santa Clara, California (delivery systems)
- Fort Belknap Industries, Harlan, Montana (A/P)
- Hamilton Technology, Lancaster, Pennsylvania (A/T)
- Ireco Incorporated, Port Ewen, New York (A/T)
- Lockheed Electronics Co., Denville, New Jersey (A/P & A/T)
- Loral Vought Systems (formerly LTV Missiles Division) Dallas, Texas (delivery systems)
- Magnavox Electronic Communications Systems Company, Ft. Wayne, Indiana (A/P)
- Quantic Industries, San Carlos, California (A/P & A/T)
- RCA, Somerville, New Jersey (A/P & A/T)
- Science Application International Corp., San Diego, California (A/T)

Other known past or present U.S. producers of advanced A/P landmines and components include:

- Hughes Aircraft Co. (MOPMS hand-emplaced A/P and A/T)
- Southern Ordnance Industries, Ft. Worth Texas (MOPMS spare parts)

The U.S. started exporting scatterable A/P mines in 1985, and has sold more than 78,000 mines (individual antipersonnel "rounds") to four nations: Greece (18,144 ADAM M692s for $2.56 million in 1988); South Korea (31,572 ADAM M692 and M731 mines for $4.07 million in 1986-88); the Netherlands (5,984 CBU89s for $14.58 million in 1991); and, Turkey (22,752 M692 and M731 mines for $3.48 million in 1988).[106]

---

[106] US-DSAA, *Foreign Military Sales of Anti-Personnel Mines for the period FY 1983-1993 to date, JF171 as of 8/11/93.*

The Arms Project has also seen unconfirmed reports of U.S. scatterable mine exports to Taiwan.

The advent of scatterable mine exports is notable not so much for the increase in the number of A/P mines exported as the dramatic increase in export revenue. The 1991 transaction with the Netherlands, which appears to have included mine-scattering equipment as well as individual mines, provides an indication of the comparative importance of conventional and scatterable A/P mines as market commodities. This one relatively modest-sized scatterable mine sale was worth more than twice all exports of hand-emplaced A/P mines over the past 10 years.[107]

### 3. Alliant Techsystems: U.S. Mine Industry leader

Minnesota-based Alliant Techsystems, the U.S. Army's largest munitions contractor, has emerged as the most active opponent of the current restrictions on U.S. A/P mine exports. In 1992 and 1993, Alliant lobbied for exemption of self-destructing and self-neutralizing mines from the U.S. export moratorium.[108]

Alliant was created in September 1990 as a spin-off of Honeywell's military production activities. In addition to mines, the company produces ammunition, artillery systems, cluster bombs, torpedoes and missiles. Though relatively small (sales about $1.1 billion per year) Alliant is popular with institutional investors and enjoys close working relations with larger weapons producers in the U.S. and abroad. The heavy use of Alliant products—including GATOR scatterable landmine systems—against Iraq in the Persian Gulf War gave the company's stock a significant boost on Wall Street at a time when investors were wary of larger weapons firms.

Ownership of Alliant stock is heavily concentrated in the hands of a few large investors. As of August 1993, eight major institutional investors controlled 53% of shares, led by the Oppenheimer Group (11%), Tweedy Browne Company (9%) and billionaire-philanthropist George

---

[107] Ibid.

[108] Alliant Techsystems, memorandum on "Moratorium on Sale of Anti-Personnel Mines," September 23, 1992 and "AP Mine Moratorium," April 1993.

Soros's Soros Fund Management (9%).[109]    Cooperative research, production and marketing agreements link Alliant to firms including Aerojet, IBM, Westinghouse, General Electric, AT&T, Giat Industries (France), Bofors (Sweden), Ferranti and British Aerospace (UK). Though formally separated from Honeywell, Alliant also maintains continuing business linkages with Honeywell Europe SA.[110]

Today, Alliant is the U.S. company with the biggest economic stake in scatterable mines.    Alliant officials contend that they, their subcontractors, and other U.S. producers could export $500-650 million worth of scatterable mines over the next five years if restrictions are eased to permit exports of self-destructing and self-neutralizing mines. The firm has told members of Congress that the ban has threatened potential exports to the United Kingdom, India, the Netherlands, Saudi Arabia, and Taiwan and forced cancellation of previously-approved exports to Greece and South Korea.[111]    However, some of Alliant's claims about the impact of the moratorium may be exaggerated. For example, U.S. State Department and South Korean military procurement officials say that—contrary to Alliant's claims—the moratorium actually had no effect on South Korea, as budget considerations had forced it to cancel a planned purchase of more than $150 million worth of mines in June 1991, long before the moratorium was imposed.[112]

Alliant augmented its own lobbying efforts by enlisting the efforts of other companies, including Accudyne, Day and Zimmerman, Mason

---

[109] Securities and Exchange Commission filings obtained through *Disclosure*.

[110] *Defense News*, April 30, 1990; *Barron's*, June 17, 1991; *Defense Daily*, June 19, 1991; *Forbes*, Oct. 14, 1991; *Financial World*, Jan. 19, 1993, and Alliant Techsystems literature.

[111] Alliant Techsystems, "Current Potential Fascam Overseas Markets," 1993.

[112] Interview with Lt. Col. Jong-Bun Jun, Foreign Military Sales officer, Embassy of the Republic of Korea, April 23, 1993; and U.S. Department of State, Undersecretary of State for Security Assistance Lynn E. Davis, response to "Question for the Record Submitted by Senator Leahy," Senate Appropriations Subcommittee on Foreign Operations, May 12, 1993.

and Hanger, Mohawk Electrical and Thiokol Company.[113]  Another
Alliant memo offers estimates of potential export sales income which
allegedly would be lost over the next five years if the moratorium is not
eased: Accudyne ($85 million), Aerojet ($20 million), Alliant ($235
million), Brunswick ($60 million), Day and Zimmerman ($80 million), Ft.
Belknap of Harlan, Montana ($60 million), Mason & Hanger ($10
million), and Thiokol ($100 million).[114]

### 4. Foreign Licensed Production

        Though the current U.S. export moratorium covers foreign
manufacturing licenses and technical assistance agreements as well as
direct exports, State and Defense Department officials disagree on the
effectiveness and enforceability of controls over foreign production of
U.S.-origin mines.[115]
        The State Department official responsible for enforcing the
moratorium told the Arms Project that all licenses expired long before its
enactment and that the last remaining technical assistance agreement,
involving an unnamed U.S. company's support for South Korean mine
production, was cancelled immediately after enactment of the
restrictions.[116]  However, a U.S. Army attorney argued that license
"expiration" is a meaningless term when applied to U.S. Army-designed
mines, including the Claymore.  Government-designed products, he
explained, are not patented.  "If the technical data [needed for production

---

[113] Alliant Techsystems, "Anti-personnel Mine Moratorium Bulletin," June
1993.

[114] Ibid.

[115] *Federal Register*, November 25, 1992, pp. 55614-55615.

[116] Telephone interview, Terry Davis, Compliance Division, Office of Defense
Trade Controls, May 3, 1993.

of a mine] were sold," he said, "the government would not have a basis for later directing a foreign company to stop producing."[117]

## B. Italy[118]

Italy's three landmine producing companies—Valsella, B.P.D. and Tecnovar—are probably the world's most aggressive exporters. Two of them, B.P.D. and Valsella, are 50% owned by Italy's largest private manufacturing firm, Fiat.[119]

The three Italian mine makers have much in common. Unlike producers elsewhere, they all specialize in landmine-related products. All three have been involved in both direct exports and licensed overseas production. They compete in the same markets with very similar product lines. According to the U.S. Defense Intelligence Agency, their licensing and coproduction agreements involve partners in at least five countries—Egypt, Greece, Portugal, Singapore, and Spain—making it difficult to determine where particular Italian-designed mines actually originated.[120] There also exist reports of sales through "dummy companies" in Nigeria and Spain,[121] production of Italian-designed

---

[117] U.S. Army, Donald Lappin, Director, Legal Department, U.S. Army Armament, Munitions and Chemical Command, telephone interview, July 16, 1993.

[118] Where not separately footnoted, facts on landmine products produced outside the United States are drawn from: Forecast International *Ordnance and Munitions Forecast*; Jane's *Military Vehicles and Logistics*, 1992-93; the U. S. Army Intelligence Agency's Desert Storm Special Reports; the U.S. Army *Worldwide Informational Mine Guide* and interviews with officials at the U.S. Army Countermine Systems Directorate, Ft. Belvoir, VA. Information on Italian mines is also drawn from *International Defense Review* May 1986 and April 1987.

[119] *Wall Street Journal*, Feb. 27, 1991; Valsella Meccanotecnica *Company Profile* (undated), p.1; and, Fiat Group, *1991 Annual Report*,p. 89.

[120] DIA/FSTC, 3-2.

[121] Alan Friedman, *Agnelli and the network of Italian power* (London: Harrap, 1988), p. 207.

landmines in Iraq,[122] Cyprus[123] and South Africa,[124] and mine smuggling via Jordan and Paraguay.

The relationship among these firms contains elements of both cooperation and competition. It is very hard for an outsider to gauge the balance between the two. Each company's scatterable mine units are designed to work in the others' systems, making their systems particularly attractive to foreign buyers. All three companies sold these interchangeably-deliverable systems to Iraq, serving as that country's most important source of advanced mine systems.

A number of deadly common features further enhance the Italian companies' market position. They provide mines in custom colors to blend into all terrains, were pioneers in the "booby-trapping" of A/P mines with anti-tampering devices, and the pathbreakers in marketing plastic "non-detectable" mines. U.S. Army intelligence analysts noted, on the eve of Desert Storm, that Iraq's Italian "blast resistant and magnetic influence-fuzed scatterable mines are state-of-the-art and are indicative of the seriousness of the mine threat."[125] They described Valsella's VS-50, a "first-generation" scatterable A/P mine sold to Iraq, as "very resistant to explosive countermeasures" and "survivable against both fuel-air explosive and bulk explosive countermeasures." Valsella's "second generation" VS-MK2 scatterable A/P mine comes with an electronic anti-disturbance device designed to explode if attempts are made to deactivate it.

### 1. Valsella S.p.A. (now Valsella Meccanotecnica S.p.A.)

Valsella was founded in 1970 as a specialist producer of mine warfare equipment. It merged in 1980 with the plastic components firm Meccanotecnica MT S.p.A. In 1984, Ferdinando Borletti's Borletti Group,

---

[122] DIA/FSTC, p. 2-16.

[123] U.S. Army Countermine Systems Directorate, *Worldwide Informational Mine Guide*.

[124] This is verified in the forthcoming Human Rights Watch report, *Landmines in Mozambique*.

[125] USAIA, *Operation Desert Shield Special Report*, 1990.

a leading fuze manufacturer, acquired the merged firm. In 1986, Borletti, a member of the Fiat board and long-time friend of Fiat Chairman Giovanni Agnelli, sold Fiat a 50% share in the company.[126]

According to a Valsella brochure, the company's sales fluctuate with the vagaries of "international policies concerning the export of defence material;" annual sales soar as high as $84 million in peak demand years and plummet as low as $10 million in "bad" years. The company offers a full line of A/P, A/T and antiship mines, ranging from "traditional models, up to now produced in large quantities" to "new, very advanced models, featuring top performances [sic] and sophisticated technology, as for example last-generation electronic mines." Valsella officials stress the capacity of their "fully-automatic high-output assembly lines" to satisfy large orders on a rush basis.[127]

Valsella also stresses its role as "official supplier to the Italian Army and to several European countries." However, the firm is best known for sales to developing nations. Seven Valsella officials were convicted in a 1991 Italian criminal proceeding for illegally selling $180 million worth of munitions to Iraq, including nine million A/P and A/T mines, the largest landmine sale (in units, though not dollar value) ever publicly reported.[128] One of the world's largest tobacco trading companies, Casalee Group S.A., appears to have served as an agent for Valsella in arranging the Iraqi deal.[129]

Italian government documents on Valsella exports in 1980-1986, provided to the Arms Project by the Geneva-based P.Network press agency, disclosed shipments of 100,000 A/P mines to Indonesia, 90,000 to Paraguay (for covert transhipment to South Africa) and smaller or unspecified quantities to Dubai, Finland, Gabon, Greece, Jordan, Kuwait,

---

[126] Alan Friedman, *Agnelli and the network of Italian power* (London: Harrap, 1988), p. 207; *Valsella meccanotecnica*, p. 1.

[127] Valsella Meccanotecnica, *Company Profile*, p. 4.

[128] *Wall Street Journal*, Feb. 27, 1991.

[129] For more information on Casalee's relationship with Valsella and its alleged role in other international arms transactions, see *Wall Street Journal*, "One Fiat Subsidiary Sold Mines to Iraq; Second Has Ties to U.S. Missile Maker," June 1, 1992 and *Intelligence Newsletter*, April 9, 1992.

Morocco, Nigeria, Pakistan, Singapore and Thailand. These Valsella customers paid unit prices ranging from $6.15 to $17.17 for scatterable A/P mines and $20 to $30 each for A/T mines. Chartered Industries of Singapore purchased parts and components for local assembly of at least seven million mines, including the Valmara 69 and scatterable VS-50 A/P mines, for prices as low as $3 to $4.50 per mine.[130]

## 2. B.P.D. Difesa e Spazio

B.P.D. Difesa e Spazio, Fiat's other mine-making subsidiary, was founded in 1977 under the name Misar by a group of former Valsella engineers. Formed as a specialist maker of underwater mines, the company soon developed a full range of A/P and A/T products, advertised under the slogan "Misar means mines."[131] The company has been especially active in foreign licensing and coproduction. Its most successful A/P product, the plastic-cased, helicopter-scatterable SB-33, has been sold directly to the Netherlands, Spain, and possibly other NATO countries, as well as Argentina and Iraq.

Reports from forces confronted by B.P.D. mines paint a particularly vivid picture of the features which make the SB-33 desirable to purchasers. British Royal Engineers assigned to clear Argentine minefields after the Falklands/Malvinas War considered this mine "particularly nasty," because its camouflage colors, small size and surface texture made it "hard to locate by even sight and touch."[132] A U.S. Army Intelligence report on landmines in Iraqi arsenals adds that:

> "Like many Italian landmines, the SB-33 series ... are described as effective against all countermeasures. It must be stressed that this type Italian pressure fuze is very resistant to explosive countermeasures. Indeed, Italian landmine developers have

---

[130] Italy, Ministero del Commerciacon l'Estero, "Elenco delle autorizzaioni rilasciate dal 1980 alla Valsella Meccanotecnica per esportazioni di materiale di armamento verso tutti i peasi," (undated).

[131] *Armada International*, 1/84; Fiat Group, *1991 Annual Report* (Turin: Fiat S.p.A., 1992).

[132] *Defence*, January 1989, p. 56.

consistently demonstrated their systems as survivable against both fuel-air explosive and bulk explosive countermeasures. This particular mine is also described by B.P.D. as being available in an infra-red detection resistant version with a special mine casing."[133]

Licensing and coproduction agreements have made B.P.D. an influential player in global production of detection-resistant small A/P mines. Many B.P.D. mines reach the global market via factories in Greece, Spain and Portugal. B.P.D. licensees have also produced for their domestic market. Under a mid-1980s agreement, Greece's ELVIEMEK SA manufactured at least 500,000 SB-33 mines for the Greek Army; B.P.D. supplied the accompanying SY-AT helicopter-mounting dispensers.

Deals involving water and anti-tank mines have further broadened B.P.D.'s network of international partners. In the mid-1980s the company developed a naval mines marketing agreement with the U.S. firm Aerojet. Under a 1987 co-production agreement, the company has also produced antitank mines in cooperation with two Australian firms and the Australian government's Office of Defence Production.

### 3. Tecnovar

Tecnovar officials believe that their early move toward plastic mines, starting in the 1960s, has been a key to market success. By the mid-1980s, their mine systems dominated the domestic Italian market, and had won export contracts in North Africa and the Middle East.

Tecnovar's helicopter-based DAT mine-scattering system, in use with the Italian armed forces, can dispense 1536 TS/50 A/P mines while flying over its target area at speeds up to 120 miles per hour.[134] Tecnovar has displayed this system for would-be purchasers in China, though it is not known if any orders resulted.[135] Tecnovar A/P mines have also been produced in Egypt and Singapore under licensing or co-production agreements.

---

[133] USAIA, *Operation Desert Shield Special Report*, p. 53.

[134] *International Defense Review*, "Italy's Mine Makers," May 1986, pp. 655–660.

[135] Ibid., March 1987, p. 333.

In 1986, Italy tightened arms export controls in response to embarrassing publicity about illegal exports to Iran and Iraq. Domestic critics of Italy's role in the global arms trade have argued that it would cost their country very little to halt all developing world weapons exports. Backers of a 1991 Parliamentary motion which would have banned all conventional arms transfers to the third world pointed out that such sales account for only 0.1% of Italy's Gross Domestic Product.[136]  However, the Italian Parliament, responding to exporter complaints about the resulting decline in exports, started to ease restrictions instead.  In September 1993, Italian Premier Carlo Ciampi called for further reforms to the country's export regulations that would cut through red tape in selling weapons systems abroad in order to help increase defense exports.[137]

## C.  Sweden: a leader in explosives and fuze technology

Though not one of the top A/P mine producers or exporters, Sweden's strength in explosives technology has helped it become a leader in mine fuze and explosives production. This section on Swedish exports, prepared with help from the Swedish Peace and Arbitration Society (SPAS), offers an example of the kinds of information which concerned groups around the world can and should compile on their countries' particular role in the global landmine trade.[138]

Swedish mine and mine component production—formerly divided among several firms—was consolidated under the control of Sweden's Celsius AB through a series of mergers in the early 1990s. In 1991, Nobel Industrier's mine-producing Bofors subsidiary merged with the

---

[136] *Inter Press Service*, April 12, 1991.

[137] *Defense News*, September 13-19, 1993, p.2.

[138] Information on Sweden is derived primarily from Lars Jederlund, "Svesnka minor - och dess offer," Svenska Freds (Swedish Peace and Arbitration Society), November 1992, and a memorandum Jederlund prepared in August 1993 at the request of the Arms Project. Additional information is drawn from *Jane's Military Vehicles and Logistics*, the publications of Forecast International, U.S. government documents obtained under FOIA and sales literature from Swedish mine and fuze manufacturers.

Swedish Ordnance/FFV unit of state-owned Celsius Industrier AB.  The following year, Nobel sold Celsius its share in the merged company. Other producers of landmine-related products which have merged into Celsius include Nobel Tech and Nobel Kemi.

The Swedish government partly privatized Celsius in mid-1993. Officials said they did so to improve the firm's competitive position in world arms markets—i.e. to increase exports.[139]  Landmines and mine fuzes rank among the products Celsius is most optimistic about selling internationally.  Company officials told SPAS in 1992: "Our judgement is that the potential for export of mines and modern fuzes for older mines are relatively large.  In times of decreasing numbers of troops there will be a need for [cheaper weapons like] mines that can compensate for the smaller number of divisions."[140]

Explosives have been the Swedish industry's most important contribution to global A/P mine production.  Bofors is known to have sold 573 tons of RDX directly to Valsella of Italy in 1981–1983; Valsella bought an additional 670 tons through the French Company SNPE in 1983–1987.   (This is enough explosive to produce 20-50 million of Valsella's light-weight scatterable A/P mines or 250,000-3 million A/T mines.)   Arms researchers believe that Valsella used these Swedish explosives to produce most or all of the A/P and A/T mines sold to Iran and Iraq in the 1980s.  Some of this explosive material, shipped to Chartered Industries of Singapore, was later found in Singapore-assembled mines deployed in Cambodia.  Swedish researchers believe that Bofors/Nobel Kemi mine explosives or other mine components may have been used by producers in Belgium, the Netherlands, Norway and former Yugoslavia.

Bofors' exports of mines date back at least to 1958, when the firm sold 33,000 Mina 5 A/P mines to Pakistan.  Some reports indicate that these mines, apparently resold by Pakistan many years later, were deployed by mujahadin guerrillas in Afghanistan in the 1980s.

Today, the Claymore-type FFV13 is Sweden's main A/P mine export.  It has been produced since 1978, offers command and tripwire detonation options, and is advertised as a "hard-hitting directional fragmentation mine" with "highly-lethal firepower and long range equal

---

[139] *Reuters*, July 28, 1992 and April 28, 1993.

[140] Bofors AB, letter to Swedish Peace and Arbitration Society, Nov. 18, 1992.

to that of a rifle company." In late 1991, the company agreed to sell more than 100 million Swedish kroners (about $17 million) worth of FFV13s to the Swiss Defence Technology and Procurement Agency.[141] Under an agreement signed the previous year, the firm sold SEK 30 million kroners (about $5 million) worth to Japan and licensed the product for Japanese production by Ishikawa Seisakusho Ltd. Norwegian, Irish and Swedish military forces have also bought the mines.[142] Austrian, Australian, Finnish and unspecified Asian military procurement officials considered the FFV13 for purchase in the late 1980s and early nineties, but we do not know which of these nations, if any, actually made purchases.[143]

### D. Other Western European Exporters

Comparatively little information is available on other Western European producers; there exists an urgent need for thorough country-by-country studies like those undertaken by the P. Network in Italy and SPAS in Sweden.

To date, most publicly reported Western European exports have involved A/T mines or mine scattering systems sold within the continent under competitively bid contracts. Published references to A/P mine sales—when they appear at all—usually list the destination as "undisclosed" (usually non-European) countries. The following brief survey of Western European exporters of A/P mines must therefore be viewed as representative, not comprehensive.

### 1. Belgium

Poudres Reunie de Belgue (PRB) went bankrupt in early 1990, but continued to produce A/P mines following its purchase by Giat Industries of France. Trade publications list PRB as an exporter of A/P

---

[141] Swedish Ordnance, "Swedish Ordnance Mine to Switzerland" (Press release, December 16, 1991).

[142] Jane's MV&L, 1992-93, p. 193.

[143] Forecast International, Ordnance and Munitions Forecast - Landmines (Europe), March 1993.

mines to Portugal, several African nations and "undisclosed" destinations. PRB mines have been deployed in Angola, Mozambique, Iraq and northern Somalia (Somaliland). There have been recent reports of a decision by the Belgian government to halt all production of antipersonnel landmines.[144]

## 2. Germany

East and West Germany both had significant track records as exporters of A/P mines, though little is known about the current status of former East German production.

Subsidiaries of the German automobile and arms giant, Daimler-Benz, have staked out key positions for themselves on the cutting edge of several very different landmine-related markets. Though not a known competitor for contracts to produce the current "generation" of mine scattering systems, Daimler-Benz—through its Messerschmitt-Bolkow-Blohm (MBB) subsidiary—is a leader in research and development for the "deep strike" landmine launching systems which military planners hope to deploy early in the next century. It is involved in joint development programs with British and French partners, as well as its own independent effort.[145] MBB is also one of the producers of the MU.S.A and MU.S.PA scatterable antipersonnel mines, developed in cooperation with Rheinmetall GmbH, which currently holds exclusive foreign marketing rights.[146]

MBB's role in the arms trade provoked some controversy when a U.S.-based MBB subsidiary, Conventional Munitions Systems Inc., moved into the "demining" business by winning the $100 million plus contract to remove the remnants of war from the American sector of Kuwait. A conservative U.S. think tank, the Center for Security Policy, attempted to convince Kuwait that it should refuse to consider the firm

---

[144] In addition, Belgium has reportedly announced that it will not permit the transit of antipersonnel mines within its territory. These actions were cited by U.S. Senator Patrick Leahy, *Congressional Record*, Sept. 10, 1993, p. S11392.

[145] DIA/FSTC, 3-12 through 3-17.

[146] Rheinmetall GmbH, *Mine Systems - Rheinmetall Defence Technology*, Düsseldorf, Germany, September 1990.

because it had allegedly sold arms to Iraq.[147] Conventional Munitions won the contract but, perhaps as a result of this controversy, was reorganized and renamed. The firm was restructured as a subsidiary of Daimler-Benz North America, cutting any direct tie to MBB. After winning the Kuwait contract, Conventional Munitions officials started soliciting mine-clearance business from foreign aid and international development agencies. After finding that its original name made development agencies wary, the firm formally truncated it to CMS Inc.[148]

### 3. Spain

Explosivos Alaveses exported to Argentina before the Falklands/Malvinas War. Production appears to have subsequently been localized in Argentina.

### 4. United Kingdom

Thorn EMI actively marketed its Ranger scatterable A/P mines to overseas customers in the 1980s and sold more than 1 million units to at least four unspecified nations. According to Lieutenant Colonel P.R. Courtney-Green of Britain's Royal Military College, the Ranger is a classic example of a mine deliberately designed to have "a limited effect for sinister reasons, because a wounded soldier will be a noisier and more morale-sapping distraction for his comrades than a dead soldier, and a burden to his own side's medical and logistic services."[149]

Britain appears, however, to have abandoned the A/P mine market in recent years. British A/T mine producers express little interest in production of A/P products.[150] The British defense ministry sees a

---

[147] Center for Security Policy, "Should Germany's M.B.B. be permitted to reap what it 'sowed' in the Gulf?, (1 page press release), July 31, 1991.

[148] Interviews with company officials at ADPA symposium, Asheville, North Carolina, September 7-9, 1993.

[149] Courtney-Green, *Ammunition for the Land Battle*, p. 172.

[150] Interviews at the ADPA symposium.

continuing requirement for A/P landmines, but is likely to rely on imports from the U.S. or other NATO nations in this area and in any purchases of mine-scattering systems with dual A/P-A/T capability.[151]

Many British firms remain active, however, in other aspects of the landmine trade.    British firms—including Ferranti International, Marconi Command & Control Systems Ltd., and the Royal Ordnance Division of British Aerospace—remain heavily involved in other landmine-related businesses, especially fuze production, but the extent of their involvement with A/P mine fuzes is unknown.  Ferranti is also one of the two finalists in the competition for a highly lucrative U.S. anti-helicopter mine contract.

In addition, there is strong and ongoing competition for sales within Europe to NATO nations for the current "generation" of scatterable mine technology.   Britain is reportedly interested in an exclusively antitank mine system, while others are reportedly interested in a combination A/P and A/T system.  Key competitors include:

- German Dynamit Nobel's DYNAMINE Family of Mines and its Scorpion Mine Launching System;
- The French Giat Minotaur Scatterable Mine Laying System (currently being evaluated, along with a competing system from U.S.-based Alliant Techsystems for possible use by the British armed forces);
- The Swedish Ordnance FFV minelaying system, designed for use with the firm's FFV 013 A/P and FFV 028 A/T mines;
- The Valsella Istrice landmine scattering system.

---

[151] Col. Alasdair A. Wilson (Royal Engineers) Land Systems Operational Requirements Office, Ministry of Defense, United Kingdom, speaking at the ADPA Symposium, Sept. 7-9, 1993.

### E.  The Former Soviet Union

Officials in Russia, Ukraine and Belarus—together heirs to 90-95% of former Soviet defense production capacity[152]—have all expressed interest in exporting landmines as part of a broader thrust into international markets for smaller conventional weapons systems. Advisors to President Boris Yeltsin have stressed the need to increase weapons exports, at least in the short term.[153]

With regard to landmines, the chairman of *Spetsveneshtekhnika*, which specializes in high-technology weapons, said in a March 1993 television interview that his company is seeking export markets for advanced mines like those deployed in Afghanistan. He made the reference while discussing the potential Turkish market for counterinsurgency weaponry.  Officials in Ukraine and Belarus have said that they have far larger stockpiles of landmines than are needed to meet domestic defense requirements, and have expressed interest in exporting some of the surplus.[154]  (It is interesting, though perhaps coincidental, that the Ukrainian defense ministry recently entered into a joint venture with U.S. landmine leader Alliant Techsystems for the recycling of surplus munitions and military supplies.[155])

Relatively little specific information is available on the current status of landmine exports.  For the most part, standard reference works still list "Commonwealth of Independent States 'state factories'" as the source for ex-Soviet mines, providing neither current exporter information nor details on the distribution of mine-producing factories

---

[152] U.S. Central Intelligence Agency, Directorate of Intelligence, *The Defense Industries of the Newly Independent States of Eurasia*, OSE 93-10001 (Springfield, VA: National Technical Information Service, January 1993); Grundmann, William, Director for Combat Support, Defense Intelligence Agency, *Statement for the Record to the Joint Economic Committee of Congress*, June 11, 1993.

[153] *Arms Trade News*, April 2, 1993.

[154] Interview, Dr. James Sherr, Lecturer, International Relations, Lincoln College, Oxford, telephone interview, July 21, 1993.

[155] *Reuters*, July 28, 1993.

among the various successor states to the Soviet Union.[156]  Some landmine producers report that they have seen evidence that Russia has started "dumping" conventional A/P mines on the world market at bargain basement prices.[157]

For the first time, the 1993-94 edition of *Jane's Military Vehicles and Logistics* listed a Moscow-based private export firm as agent for one landmine product: Moscow-based ELECTRONINTORG Ltd. is sales agent for one ex-Soviet A/P mine, the OZM-72. *Jane's* also newly listed a Polish firm, Cenzin Foreign Trade Export Enterprise, as sales agent for a Soviet-designed railway mine.[158]  In addition, an April 1993 report names Russia as the most probable source for a recent Iranian purchase of 1800 underwater mines designed to be laid by its 3 Kilo class submarines.[159]

How successful Russia and other ex-Soviet successor states will be in their efforts to export landmines is unknown and probably unknowable. It can, however, be said with certainty  that Russia sees small conventional arms as the one weaponry area offering the greatest hope for desired export growth.[160]  Experts on Soviet military industry say that the emphasis on small arms, including mines, is virtually inevitable, because the collapse of linkages which held together the old Soviet military-industrial complex has become a major barrier to continued production of some more sophisticated weapons systems.[161]

Controlling Russian exports could prove very difficult because many production facilities have fallen under the control of plant

---

[156] On Russia's general arms export goals, see *Jane's Intelligence Review*, November 1992, p. 490-91.

[157] Interviews at the ADPA Symposium, Sept. 7-9, 1993.

[158] *Jane's Military Vehicles and Logistics* 1993-94, p. 190.

[159] *Arms Transfer News*, Apr. 30, 1993.

[160] *Jane's Intelligence Review*, Nov. 1992, pp. 490-91; *Arms Transfers News*, April 2, 1993.

[161] Dr. James Sherr, Lecturer, International Relations, Lincoln College, Oxford, telephone interview, July 21, 1993.

managers or local government officials who face strong pressure to save jobs by selling any available product anywhere they can. President Yeltsin has gone so far as to grant some factories, industrial groups and municipal officials authority to export directly and even to issue their own end use certificates.[162] These actions create obvious opportunities for uncontrolled exports of landmines (and other weapons) to human rights-abusing governments or insurgent groups.

With regard to exports prior to the breakup of the Soviet Union, published sources tell much about the operational features of the Soviet Union's landmines, but little about their production and distribution. Soviet State Factories ranked third (after Italy and the U.S.) in the number of A/P models produced. Products ranged from wooden box mines unchanged since World War II to mine-scattering systems and relatively high-quality scatterable mines.[163] Russian A/P mines are known to have been used or deployed in Afghanistan, Angola, Cambodia, Iran, Iraq, Mozambique, North Korea, Syria, Vietnam, throughout the Warsaw Pact, and in many other parts of the world. Soviet-origin mines are locally manufactured in many Eastern European nations, as well as China and Vietnam. Judging from the general pattern of past Soviet conventional arms exports, it is likely that most landmines were delivered as grant aid or on a highly concessional basis.

The Arms Project has been unable to gather up-to-date information on landmine exports from other Eastern European nations. Preliminary inquiries addressed to defense officials in Bulgaria, Hungary and Romania have brought no response. Future research must also explore the state of A/P mine production industries in former Czechoslovakia and Poland.

### F. China

Most Chinese foreign sales are managed by the China North Industries Corporation (NORINCO), which markets at least four types of

---

[162] Galeotti, telephone interview, July 19, 1993; and, Grundmann, William, *Statement for the Record to the Joint Economic Committee of Congress*, June 11, 1992.

[163] See *Jane's Soviet Intelligence Review* May 1989 p. 213, June 1990 p. 258-9 and Mar. 1991 p. 128-130.

A/P mines. NORINCO also produces a Multiple Rocket Scatterable Minelaunching System, but there have not been reports of export sales.[164]

China's conventional A/P mines, many of them based on Soviet designs, are among the cheapest in the world. Chinese A/P mines have been deployed in Angola, Cambodia, Iraq, Mozambique, Nicaragua, Somalia and many other nations; whether these mines were sold, given away or both is unknown. However, one recent report provided current evidence of Chinese export activity. In late March, a landmine clearance expert working in Somaliland (northern Somalia) identified a shipment of Chinese landmines and cluster weapons in the East African port of Djibouti. The weapons appear to have been destined for Sudan, a nation whose landmine sources have not previously been publicly identified.[165]

China has also been an important export target for Western firms exporting mine-related technology. U.S.-based LTV and Italy's Valsella exhibited modern mine-scattering systems at Chinese trade shows in the mid-1980s. China reportedly also considered purchasing Japanese, French, Italian, or British mine-hunting sonars for use with mine-hunting vessels built in China in the 1980s under a technology-transfer agreement with Intermarine of Italy.[166]

### G. Other Developing Countries

There is a long history of landmine production in the developing world, sometimes by private firms, but more commonly in government-owned or government-linked facilities. In addition to China, at least seven developing nations in Asia, eight in Latin America, four in the Middle East and two in sub-Saharan Africa have engaged in industrial production of A/P landmines in recent years. This count excludes the

---

[164] *Jane's Intelligence Review*, "Chinese Multiple Rocket Systems," Sept. 1992, pp. 418–423.

[165] Interview with Maurice Brackenreed-Johnston, Rimfire International Ltd. April 8, 1993.

[166] *International Defense Review*, March 1987, p. 333.

many nations where there is evidence of locally improvised landmine-type devices.

Some third world producers already rank among the most active marketers of conventional landmines.   Notable exporters in the developing world include Egypt and Israel in the Middle East; Pakistan and Singapore in Asia; Brazil and Chile in Latin America; and South Africa.

The developing world's share of the market is likely to grow significantly, for several reasons.   The commodity nature of low-end landmine production means cheap labor is one of the keys to economic success.   In addition, the small size of domestic markets gives developing nations strong incentive to reduce unit costs by spreading overhead expense over a larger production run.   This motivation may be especially important for a nation like Pakistan, which ranks among the most active promoters of landmine exports.

Many developing world producers are moving toward production of more sophisticated landmine products—including both the advanced stand-alone mine designs and scatterable mine systems.

## 1.  Developing World Exporters

### a. Brazil

Brazil's Quimica Tupan SA pyrotechnics and grenade firm produces one of the world's cheapest mines, the AP NM AE T1, selling for just $5.80.   Forecast International reports that these have been exported to at least one (unspecified) Middle Eastern nation.   This mine has also been produced in Mexico, according to the U.S. Army's *Worldwide Informational Mine Guide*.   Founded in 1957 by a group of retired Brazilian military officers, Quimica is one of the nation's oldest pyrotechnics firms. Landmines, produced since 1978, are one element in a much larger line of products.   As of the mid-1980s, about 50% of the firm's output was exported.[167]

---

[167] *Military Technology*, October 1985, p. 112.

### b. Chile

Chilean mines are produced in both the public and private sectors. Carlos Cardoen's former Industrias Cardoen, now operating as Metalnor SA, is known to have produced mines which were sold to Iraq.[168] It is not known if the Chilean Ministry of Defense, which produces two A/P mine types in its FAMAE - Fabricaciones Militares facilities, is also an exporter.

### c. Egypt

Egypt produces landmines in at least three facilities, all of them run by the Ministry of War Production as part of its 10-plant Egyptian Military Factories (EMF) group.[169] They include licensed versions or close copies of Soviet, Italian and American mine designs. Egyptian mines are known to have been deployed in Afghanistan, Iraq and Nicaragua.

One of these firms, the Heliopolis Company for Chemical Industries (EMF Factory 81) has exported a small plastic A/P mine, the T/78, to a number of Middle Eastern countries. It is not known if EMF's other mine-producing facilities—the Kaha Company for Chemical Industries (Factory 270) and the Maasara Company for Engineering Industries (Factory 45)—also export mines.

### d. Israel

The antecedents of modern-day Israeli mine production can be traced to companies created in Palestine during World War II to manufacture antitank mine components under the direction of the British Middle East Supply Center. Post-independence landmine production by

---

[168] United States Army Intelligence Agency - U.S. Army Foreign Science and Technology Center, *Operation Desert Shield Special Report: Iraqi Combat Engineer Capabilities*, 1990 and Forecast International, Ordnance and Munitions Forecast - Landmines (International),1993.

[169] Information on Egypt is drawn from reference works by Jane's and Forecast International and from Nazir Hussain, *Defense Production in the Muslim World* (Karachi: Royal Book Company, 1989).

the highly export-oriented Israel Military Industries (IMI)—80% of its sales go to foreign customers—can be traced back to 1955, if not earlier.[170] Israel has been an exporter of A/P landmines at least since the early 1970s, when it provided some to South Africa.[171]

In recent years, reported Israeli landmine production has involved two A/P mines produced by IMI, based in Ramat Hasharon, and one from Tel Aviv-based Explosive Industries Ltd. (EIL). Nations listed in the trade press as acquiring IMI mines include Argentina, Ecuador, El Salvador, Guatemala, Nigeria and Zaire.

British mine clearance experts have identified EIL's No. 4 plastic A/P landmine among those deployed by Argentina in the Falkland/Malvinas War, but view them as posing fewer detection problems than other plastic mines.[172]

Israel's most visible mine-related marketing efforts, however, involve minefield breaching equipment. IMI has sold its Pomins II, portable A/P mine neutralization system to the U.S. Army.[173] Another firm, Israeli Aircraft Industries, has sold its RAMTA Mine Plow to the U.S. Army, U.S. Marine Corps and other NATO forces.[174]

There is some evidence of cooperation between Israel and South Africa in the development of countermine technologies.  For example, Armscor's mine-protected Buffel Armored Personnel Carrier (see below) uses armor plating provided by Israel in exchange for South African steel, according to some reports.[175]

---

[170] Stewart Reiser, *The Israeli Arms Industry: foreign policy, arms transfers and military doctrine of a small state* (New York: Holmes & Meier, 1989), pp. 6-7, 31; and Dr. Yoram Peri and Amnon Neubach, *The Military-Industrial Complex in Israel* (Tel Aviv: International Center for Peace in the Middle East, 1985).

[171] James Adams, *The Unnatural Alliance: Israel and South Africa* (London: Quartet, 1984), p. 93.

[172] *Defense News*, January 26, 1987.

[173] *Jane's Defense Weekly*, April 9, 1988.

[174] *Armada International*, June 6, 1990, p. 45.  (Advertisement).

[175] Landgren, *Embargo Disemplanted*, p. 97.

Though it could not be independently verified from other sources, one recent book asserts that Israel has produced nuclear landmines, which have allegedly been deployed in the Golan Heights.[176]

### e. Pakistan

Pakistan's state-owned Pakistan Ordnance Factories (POF) has earned a reputation as one of the most enthusiastic promoters of A/P landmines and a wide range of other ordnance, munitions and small arms products. The company was founded in 1951. As of the late 1980s, it maintained 14 factories in and around Wah with a workforce of 40,000, and combined capacity to produce $400-500 million worth of armaments per year.[177]

Sales literature for the firm's low cost (unit price $6.75) P4 Mk.2 stresses the careful calculation of the explosive charge to "make the man disabled and incapacitate him permanently" because "operating research has shown that it is better to disable the enemy than kill him."[178] According to one expert, Pakistan appears been the largest supplier, by a wide margin, of mines deployed in Somaliland,[179] but relatively little is currently known about other customers.

### f. South Africa

South Africa has produced landmines since the 1960s, if not earlier. By 1982, the South African government claimed that it had

---

[176] Andrew and Leslie Cockburn, *Dangerous Liaison* (New York: Harper Collins, 1991), p. 330.

[177] Hussain Nazir, *Defense Production in the Muslim World* (Karachi: Royal Book Company, 1989) and, Pakistan Ordnance Factories, *Provide Force to the Forces* (Sales brochure, undated, ca. 1988)

[178] Pakistan Ordnance Factories, Technical Specifications for Mine Anti-Personnel (P4 MK2).

[179] Interview, Maurice Brackenreed-Johnston, Rimfire International Ltd., April 8, 1993.

achieved self-sufficiency in a wide range of landmine-related products: including A/P and A/T mines, mine detectors and mine-resistant vehicles.[180]

Mines are produced by Naschem, a subsidiary of the Denel (Pty) Ltd. Group (formerly Armscor), at its factory in Potchefstroom.[181] Another subsidiary, Swartklip Products in Cape Town, produces a wide range of fuzes.[182]

Denel was formally launched on April 1, 1992, as the nominally privatized successor to Armscor, the state company under which South Africa's weapons production had been centralized since 1968. In practice, Denel remained a state company, with all shares owned by the government.[183] South African authorities asserted that Armscor was their country's largest exporter of manufactured goods, with exports accounting for 20% of the company's sales revenues.[184] In their first full year as Denel, company officials reported that exports to 37 countries worth Rand 480 million (about U.S.$160 million) accounted for 17% of sales.[185]

Naschem was founded in 1968, through the transfer of a plant run by African Explosives and Chemical Industries (a joint venture of South Africa's De Beers group and Britain's Imperial Chemical

---

[180] *International Defense Intelligence*, Oct. 4, 1992.

[181] James P. McWilliams, *Armscor: South Africa's Arms Merchant* (London: Brassey's (UK): 1989), p. 12. There is some evidence, however, that Armscor tended to overstate its export volume (See Landgren, *Embargo Disemplanted*, pp. 176-7, 183-6).

[182] Landgren, *Embargo Disemplanted*, p. 129.

[183] *The Argus* (Johannesburg), February 20, 1992, p. 14; *Business Day* (Johannesburg), Oct. 7. 1992, p. 12; *Pretoria Daily News*, May 25, 1992, p. 13. For a list of Denel divisions, see paid advertisement, "Denel. An industrial giant emerging from Southern Africa," *Weekly Mail* (Johannesburg), June 18-24, 1993.

[184] Helmoed-Römer Heitman, *South African Armed Forces* (Cape Town: Buffalo Publications, 1990), p. 122; *Sunday Star* (Johannesburg), Mar. 1, 1992, p. 16.

[185] *Reuters*, June 2, 1993.

Industries) to the newly created Armscor.[186] It has produced least two A/P landmine types, according to trade publications. Though Naschem appears to have originally operated the manufacturing facilities, a Naschem executive said in 1989 that the company was subcontracting all component manufacturing to private contractors. Naschem's own facilities, officials said, were used for filling and assembly, product testing and research and development. [187]

South Africa has advertised a number of landmine-related products for export, but very little is known about the quantity or destination of exports, beyond the fact that South African-made mines have been widely used against neighboring southern African governments, and—according to Forecast International—"may have been sold to Iran."

Little trade detail is available, because virtually all South African weapons trade has been conducted covertly since the imposition of a U.N. arms embargo in 1963. However, weapons trade documents leaked to journalists in 1991 reveal that at least one South African company, Nimrod International, included mines (type not specified) in a 1985 shipment of $600,000 worth of weaponry to Iraq. Mines were probably only a small part of the 200 carton-10 drum shipment to Iraq, which also included "bombs, grenades, torpedoes... guided weapons, and missiles and similar munitions of war and parts thereof."[188] Subsequent press reports have identified Nimrod as a covert arms export arm of Armscor

---

[186] Abdul Minty, *South Africa's Defense Strategy* (London: The Anti-Apartheid Movement, 1969), p. 4 (Pamphlet); Landgren, *Embargo Disemplanted*, pp. 124-5, and "Company of the Year: Armscor," a reprint of a special report from *Engineering Week* published in *Foreign Broadcast Information Service* (Sub-Saharan Africa Supplement), March 19, 1990, pp. 21-22.

[187] *Foreign Broadcast Information Service,* (Sub-Saharan Africa Supplement), Mar. 19 1990, p. 23.

[188] South African export documents examined by the Arms Project and reports in the *Boston Globe, Guardian* (London), and *Weekly Mail* (Johannesburg) of November 8, 1991.

which, in 1992, became involved in shipping small arms, ammunition and other weapons to Rwanda.[189]

By 1985, Armscor's export offerings included at least one non-metallic mine.[190] In 1991, Naschem and another Armscor affiliate, Silverton-based Mechem Consultants, displayed a range of sophisticated mine products for trade show audiences. These included an A/T-A/P mine-scattering system and an electronically automated off-route antitank mine. South Africa producers also advertise their mine-clearing line charge system, the Plofadder, as a lower-cost alternative to similar British and American products.[191] South Africa has also sold mine-resistant Buffel armored personnel carriers to Sri Lanka and sold or leased mine-resistant APCs to United Nations Transition Assistance Group (UNTAG) forces during the Namibian transition to independence.[192] Recent South African export efforts have focused heavily on the Middle East, but it is not known if South Africa's transactions in that region—including a Rand 1.7 billion deal with Saudi Arabia in 1992—have included landmines.[193]

Taken together, these products represented a demonstration of South Africa's ability to field advanced landmine-related products which, at least on paper, may have the potential to compete with some modern American and Western European designs.

### g. Singapore

Singapore's landmines are produced by Chartered Industries of Singapore, one of four groups of defense firms controlled by the state-

---

[189] *Reuter*, March 4, 1993. On Armscor, see also *The Observer* (London), April 26, 1992.

[190] Signe Landgren, *Embargo Disimplemented: South Africa's military industry* (Oxford: Oxford University Press, 1989), p. 127.

[191] *International Defense Review*, December 1991; and *Jane's Defence Weekly*, March 7, 1992.

[192] Heitman, *South African Armed Forces*, 1990, p. 125.

[193] *The Star* (Johannesburg), February 18, 1992.

owned Sheng-Li Holding Company, and through Sheng-Li by the Singapore ministry of defense. Sheng-Li's military subsidiaries have grown from a single plant opened in 1967 to a complex network of production, service and marketing companies.[194]    CIS's sales arm, Unicorn International, maintains offices in London, Dubai and Brunei.[195]    They produce and market two antipersonnel mines originated by Italy's Valsella. Press reports identified Singapore as one of the conduits for sales of Valsella-designed mines to Iraq and a partly-declassified U.S. Army Intelligence study confirms that the Singapore-made mines were found in Iraqi arsenals.[196]

### h. Former Yugoslavia

Former Yugoslavia was traditionally a leading exporter of both A/P and A/T landmines. Yugoslav plastic A/P mines rank among the most troublesome in the world, from a detection and clearance perspective.

Civil war and international embargoes have curtailed domestic production, and there are reports of mine imports over the past year, by Bosnia and possibly other successor states, from Singapore and Eastern Europe.

The current state of ex-Yugoslavia's mine-producing capacity is very hard to gauge. Before the country's disintegration, weapons production capacity, though scattered among the republics, was most heavily concentrated in Bosnia and Herzegovina. Subsequent fighting altered the balance of control. The former federal army moved a number of weapons facilities to Serbia, but Croatian Muslims reportedly

---

[194] Bilveer Singh and Kwa Chong Guan, "The Singapore Defence Industries: Motivations, Organization and Impact," pp. 96-124, in Chandran Jeshurun (ed.), *Arms and Defence in Southeast Asia* (Singapore: Institute of Southeast Asian Studies, 1989).

[195] Company Profiles (undated) for Unicorn International and Chartered Industries of Singapore.

[196] U.S. Army Intelligence Agency - U.S. Army Foreign Science and Technology Center, *Operation Desert Shield Special Report: Iraqi Combat Engineer Capabilities*, 1990. This document was provided to the Arms Project by Greenpeace, which obtained it under the Freedom of Information Act.

took control of at least one factory which produced mine fuzes, Slavko Rodic in Bugajno. Croatia is said to have maintained a significant mine-producing capacity, at least as of late 1992.[197]

## 2. Other Major Producers in the Developing World.

### a. India

India, unlike other large Third World arms producers, generally has not been an aggressive arms exporter.[198] The Indian munitions industry, in keeping with the traditional emphasis on domestic demand and import substitution, has no known history of landmine exports. However, about two years ago, India's largely state-controlled military industries began to actively search for foreign markets. It has been reported this year that India is attempting to double its arms exports from the 1992 level of approximately $40 million. If India chooses to export mine products, it could become a significant competitor.[199] In addition to its long experience producing two U.S.-designed A/P mines, India has made significant recent investments in antitank and submersible mine research through its Department of Defence Research and Development.[200]

### b. Iran

Iranian military and private experts believe that Iran produced significant quantities of A/P mines during the Iran-Iraq war of the 1980s. Yet no open source contains data on recent Iranian A/P mine production. (A U.S. Army study declassified under a Freedom of Information Act

---

[197] *Jane's Intelligence Review*, February and March 1993.

[198] Ralph Sanders, *Arms Industries: New Suppliers and Regional Security* (Washington: National Defense University, 1990), pp. 49-50.

[199] *Defense News*, July 26, 1993, p.1; *International Observer*, July 21, 1993, p. 881; *Times of India*, February 12, 1993; *Xinhua*, "India to enter far east arms market," Aug 12, 1991.

[200] Ministry of Defence, Government of India, *Annual Report 1990-91*, p. 56.

request by Human Rights Watch does show an Iranian variant on the U.S. Claymore M18A1, apparently produced during the reign of the Shah, but the Arms Project is still seeking data on post-Shah production.)[201]

### c. Iraq

Iraq has been involved since the 1970s in the development of domestic landmine production capacity. Though Iraq has deployed enormous quantities of mines in Kuwait and Iraqi Kurdistan, it appears that the overwhelming majority of mines used were imported. Known domestic A/P production includes at least one antipersonnel mine developed with Yugoslav assistance, one ex-Soviet model and two older Italian mine designs from Fiat's B.P.D. subsidiary.[202] In addition, an investigation by Middle East Watch revealed that Iraq has manufactured copies of another Italian mine, the Valsella Valmara 69 bounding A/P mine.[203]

---

[201] U.S. Army Engineer Center, *Mine Recognition and Warfare Handbook*, Ft. Leonard Wood, November 1990, p. 102-3 describes and provides a photograph of the Iranian Claymore, with markings in Farsi and an Iranian imperial crown.

[202] DIA/FSTC p. 2-16; U.S. Army Intelligence Agency—Foreign Science and Technology Center, *Operation Desert Shield Special Report: Iraqi Combat Engineer Capabilities, Supplement 2: Barriers and Fortification Protection*, 30 November 1990, AST-266OZ-131-90-SUP 2, p. 31.

[203] Middle East Watch, *Hidden Death: Land Mines and Civilian Casualties in Iraqi Kurdistan* (Human Rights Watch: New York, October 1992), pp. 40-41.

# Table I: Antipersonnel Landmine Producers

| Country | No. of models | Country | No. of models |
|---|---|---|---|
| Argentina | 3 | Mexico | 1 |
| Austria | 16 | Netherlands | 3 |
| Belgium | 8 | Nicaragua | 1 |
| Brazil | 2 | Pakistan | 4 |
| Bulgaria | 3 | Peru | 1 |
| Canada | 1 | Poland | 1 |
| Chile | 5 | Portugal | 8 |
| China | 12 | Romania | 3 |
| Cyprus | 1 | Singapore | 3 |
| Czechoslovakia (former) | 6 | South Africa | 5 |
| Denmark | 4 | Spain | 8 |
| Egypt | 5 | Sweden | 21 |
| El Salvador | 1 | Switzerland | 5 |
| France | 14 | Taiwan | 4 |
| Germany (combined) | 18 | United Kingdom | 9 |
| Greece | 2 | United States | 37 |
| Hungary | 7 | U.S.S.R. (ex), including: | 31 |
| India | 2 |   Russia | |
| Iran | 1 |   Belarus | |
| Iraq | 5 |   Ukraine | |
| Israel | 3 | Venezuela | 1 |
| Italy | 36 | Vietnam | 18 |
| Japan | 2 | Yugoslavia | 15 |
| Korea, North | 4 | Zimbabwe | 3 |
| Korea, South | 3 | | |
| | | **Total** | **346** |

Source:   Arms Project landmines database (compiled from press reports, industry directories, manufacturer's literature, declassified military documents and Human Rights Watch field research.)

Notes:    Mines produced in more than one country are counted as products of each country.
Mines produced by more than one manufacturer in a country are counted once for that country.
Antitank, multi-purpose, field-improvised and limpet mines sometimes adapted for A/P purposes are not included.
Figures represent minimum number of models known to have been produced in each country.

## Table II: Present & Past Exporters of Antipersonnel Mines

| Country | Company (parent) | Division or subsidiary |
|---|---|---|
| Belgium | Giat Industries | Poudres Reunie de Belgue (PRB SA) |
| Brazil | Quimica Tupan SA | |
| Bulgaria | Kintex (marketing agency) | |
| Canada | SNC Industrial Technologies Inc. | |
| Chile | FAMAE Fabricas y Maestranzas del Ejercito | |
| Chile | Metalnor SA | |
| China | China North Industries Corporation | |
| China | Chinese State Arsenals | |
| Czechoslovakia (ex) | Czechoslovak State Factories | |
| Egypt | Ministry of War Production | Heliopolis Company for Chemical Industries |
| France | Giat Industries | |
| France | Societe d'Armement et d'Etudes Alsetex | |
| Germany (ex-F.R.G.) | Rheinmetal GmbH | |
| Germany (ex-G.D.R.) | Former East German state factories | |
| Greece | ELVIEMEK SA | |
| Hungary | Hungarian State Factories | |
| Israel | Explosive Industries Ltd. | |
| Israel | Israel Military Industries (aka TAAS) | |
| Italy | Fiat Group | Valsella Meccanotecnica SpA |
| Italy | Fiat Group | BPD Difesa e Spazio srl (formerly Misar) |
| Italy | Tecnovar Italiana SpA | |
| Pakistan | Pakistan Ordnance Factories | |
| Poland | Not known | |
| Portugal | Sociedade Portuguesa de Explosivos, S.A.R.L. | |
| Romania | Romanian State Factories | |
| Singapore | Chartered Industries of Singapore | |
| South Africa | Denel (Pty) Ltd. (Successor to Armscor) | |
| Spain | Explosivos Alaveses SA | |
| Sweden | Celsius AB | Bofors |
| U.S.S.R. (ex) | ELECTRONINTORG Ltd. | |
| U.S.S.R. (ex) | Soviet State Factories | |
| United Kingdom | British Aerospace | Royal Ordnance |
| United Kingdom | Thorn/EMI Electronics | Defense Systems Division |
| United States | Alliant Techsystems | (Formerly Honeywell Defense Systems) |
| United States | International Signal and Control Group PLC | |
| United States | Lockheed Corporation | |
| United States | Loral Vought Systems (formerly LTV missiles div.) | |
| United States | Thiokol Corp. | Ordnance Marketing |
| Vietnam | State Factories | |
| Yugoslavia (ex) | Federal Directorate of Supply & Procurement (SDPR) | |

Source: Arms Project landmines database.
Note: Listed firms have exported A/P mines or scattering systems, or actively solicited export orders.

## Table III: Reported Countries of Origin for Antipersonnel Landmines Used in Selected Conflicts

| Producer | Reported Deployment |
|---|---|
| Belgium | Angola, Iraq (Kurdistan), Iraq**, Mozambique, Somalia |
| Brazil | Nicaragua |
| Bulgaria | Cambodia |
| Canada | Iraq* |
| Chile | Iraq (Kurdistan) |
| China | Afghanistan, Angola, Cambodia, Iraq (Kurdistan), Iraq**, Mozambique, Somalia |
| Czechoslovakia (ex) | Afghanistan, Angola, Cambodia, Mozambique, Nicaragua, Somalia |
| Egypt | Afghanistan, Nicaragua, Iraq* |
| France | Iraq (Kurdistan), Mozambique |
| Germany | Angola (former W. Germany), Cambodia (former E. Germany), Mozambique (former E. Germany), Somalia (former E. Germany) |
| Hungary | Cambodia |
| Italy | Angola, Iraq (Kurdistan), Iraq**, Mozambique, Somalia |
| Pakistan | Somalia |
| Romania | Iraq (Kurdistan) |
| Singapore | Iraq* |
| South Africa | Angola, Mozambique |
| Spain | Iraq* |
| United Kingdom | Afghanistan, Mozambique, Somalia |
| United States | Angola, Cambodia, Iraq (Kurdistan), Mozambique, Nicaragua, Somalia |
| U.S.S.R. (ex) | Afghanistan, Angola, Cambodia, Iraq (Kurdistan), Iraq**, Mozambique, Nicaragua, Somalia |
| Vietnam | Cambodia |
| Yugoslavia (ex) | Afghanistan, Cambodia, Mozambique |
| Zimbabwe (& pre-1980 Rhodesia) | Mozambique |

Sources: Human Rights Watch reports; U.S. Army reports summarized by the Congressional Research Service; USAIA and DIA documents obtained under the Freedom of Information Act. Iraq* means producers' antipersonnel mines have been identified by U.S. Army intelligence as held in Iraqi arsenals but may not have been deployed. Iraq** means identified by the U.S. Defense Intelligence Agency as emplaced by Iraqi forces in Kuwait or along borders with Kuwait and/or Saudi Arabia. Producing countries were not necessarily direct source of shipments to countries of deployment.

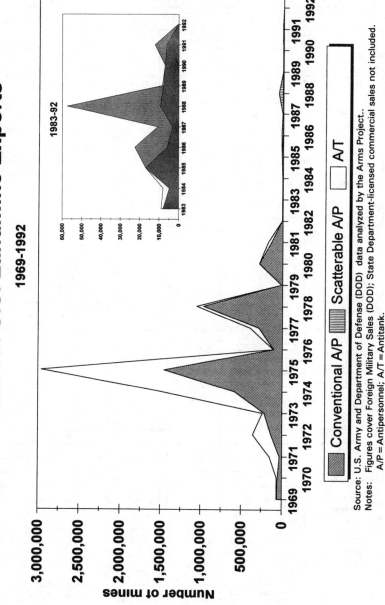

Table IV: U.S. Landmine Exports
1969-1992

Conventional A/P    Scatterable A/P    A/T

Source: U.S. Army and Department of Defense (DOD) data analyzed by the Arms Project..
Notes:    Figures cover Foreign Military Sales (DOD); State Department-licensed commercial sales not included.
          A/P = Antipersonnel; A/T = Antitank.

# Table V: U.S. Landmine Sales by Country

| | Last 10 years (1983-92) | | | All available years (1969-92) | | |
|---|---|---|---|---|---|---|
| | A/P | A/T | Total | A/P | A/T | Total |
| Australia | 0 | 0 | 0 | 38,000 | 2,915 | 40,915 |
| Belize | 1,414 | 0 | 1,414 | 1,414 | 0 | 1,414 |
| Brazil | 0 | 0 | 0 | 0 | 100 | 100 |
| Brunei | 600 | 0 | 600 | 600 | 0 | 600 |
| Cambodia | 0 | 0 | 0 | 622,458 | 208 | 622,666 |
| Canada | 3,932 | 0 | 3,932 | 13,540 | 0 | 13,540 |
| Chile | 0 | 0 | 0 | 300,000 | 100,000 | 400,000 |
| Colombia | 3,000 | 0 | 3,000 | 9,030 | 2,000 | 11,030 |
| Denmark | 952 | 0 | 952 | 976 | 0 | 976 |
| Ecuador | 1,248 | 0 | 1,248 | 1,248 | 0 | 1,248 |
| El Salvador | 36,924 | 0 | 36,924 | 102,246 | 0 | 102,246 |
| Ethiopia | 0 | 0 | 0 | 13,275 | 58,154 | 71,429 |
| Greece | 18,144 | 0 | 18,144 | 38,890 | 603,305 | 642,195 |
| Honduras | 0 | 708 | 708 | 0 | 708 | 708 |
| Indonesia | 102 | 0 | 102 | 102 | 0 | 102 |
| Iran | 0 | 0 | 0 | 2,522,391 | 98,300 | 2,620,691 |
| Israel | 0 | 0 | 0 | 0 | 1,900,015 | 1,900,015 |
| Jordan | 0 | 0 | 0 | 35,972 | 50,004 | 85,976 |
| S. Korea | 31,892 | 0 | 31,892 | 8,432 | 71,485 | 79,917 |
| Lebanon | 5,352 | 4,000 | 9,352 | 5,352 | 4,000 | 9,352 |
| Malaysia | 0 | 0 | 0 | 88,278 | 0 | 88,278 |
| Morocco | 0 | 0 | 0 | 1,998 | 0 | 1,998 |
| Netherlands | 6,614 | 0 | 6,614 | 630 | 0 | 630 |
| New Zealand | 3,948 | 0 | 3,948 | 5,634 | 5 | 5,639 |
| Norway | 0 | 0 | 0 | 0 | 2,100 | 2,100 |
| Oman | 0 | 0 | 0 | 802 | 0 | 802 |
| Peru | 252 | 0 | 252 | 10,252 | 0 | 10,252 |
| Philippines | 0 | 0 | 0 | 7,992 | 0 | 7,992 |
| Portugal | 0 | 0 | 0 | 0 | 250 | 250 |
| Saudi Arabia | 0 | 0 | 0 | 87,666 | 197,868 | 285,534 |
| Singapore | 0 | 0 | 0 | 3,853 | 36 | 3,889 |
| Somalia | 0 | 0 | 0 | 144 | 0 | 144 |
| Switzerland | 0 | 0 | 0 | 12 | 0 | 12 |
| Taiwan | 0 | 0 | 0 | 34,155 | 4,620 | 38,775 |
| Thailand | 5,118 | 0 | 5,118 | 437,166 | 66,863 | 504,029 |
| Tunisia | 0 | 0 | 0 | 0 | 250 | 250 |
| Turkey | 22,848 | 0 | 22,848 | 96 | 9 | 105 |
| U.K. | 5,514 | 0 | 5,514 | 5,604 | 0 | 5,604 |
| TOTALS | 147,854 | 4,708 | 152,562 | 4,398,208 | 3,163,195 | 7,561,403 |

Source: U.S. Defense Security Assistance Administration and U.S. Army Armament, Munitions
    and Chemical Command data, analyzed by the Arms Project.
Note: Includes sales under U.S. Department of Defense Foreign Military Sales program,
    but excludes commercial sales licensed by the U.S. Department of State.

# 4
# TRANSPARENCY IN THE PRODUCTION AND TRADE OF LANDMINES

It is evident from the foregoing that available information on worldwide production and trade of landmines is incomplete and of sometimes uncertain accuracy. Yet it is equally evident that any intelligent policy decision taken with respect to landmines by the international community requires reasonably accurate information as to who produces, who sells, who buys, what quantities, what types, how much is paid, and who actually uses landmines.

Even in the absence of stringent measures to restrict the use or supply of landmines, it is important to create mechanisms, both national and international, for collecting and disseminating this information. In the jargon of the arms control community, it is important to make transactions in landmines "transparent" to the public worldwide. These transactions today are cloaked in the usual secrecy surrounding arms transfers. Compounding this problem is the lack of concern about a less-than-major weapons system like the lowly landmine. As a result, it is difficult to track all the players participating in landmine manufacture and trade or to determine accurately the quantities of mines involved.

The purpose of this chapter is to review available mechanisms for creating transparency in landmines transactions, with an emphasis on the recently established United Nations Register on Conventional Arms.

## I.     National Transparency

Given that production and trade of landmines is truly global, with dozens of producing countries and scores of purchasers, a system of international transparency for reporting landmines transfers is strongly preferred.     Even in the absence of international transparency, however, unilateral national action to provide information about landmines transfers would be extremely valuable. The willingness of larger states and arms-producing countries to do so unilaterally would provide a foundation from which to press other countries to follow suit. Leadership by the permanent members of the Security Council, which together are the most prolific arms exporters in the world, is essential. Leadership by the United States toward greater transparency is

particularly important, given its position as the world's number one
military power and arms exporter.

Unfortunately, there appear to be, other than the United States,
virtually no countries with unilateral national mechanisms for obtaining
information on landmines transfers, because very few countries have
established mechanisms for revealing information concerning any type of
arms transfer all.[1]

### A.  The United States

There are a number of reasons why landmine transfers involving
the U.S. are more transparent than those involving other countries.
Perhaps most importantly, U.S. law allows private individuals greater
access to government information, including certain information on
landmine transfers, by means of the Freedom of Information Act
(FOIA).[2]  FOIA permits individuals to request documents and records
from any government agency on any topic; the agency may turn down
all or parts of the request that it believes would reveal information
exempted from disclosure by the statute.  These exemptions include,
unsurprisingly, matters affecting national security as well as the
protection of individual privacy and certain commercial secrecy
protections.

Moreover, U.S. law regulating both government-to-government
weapons transfers and private commercial military sales allows greater
public and Congressional scrutiny than the laws of other countries.[3]

---

[1] See generally, Ian Anthony (ed.), *Arms Export Regulations* (New York: Oxford
U. Press—SIPRI, 1991), for a catalogue of arms transfer and transparency
requirements on a country-by-country basis as of 1989.

[2] For a general, non-technical discussion of 5 U.S.C. Sec. 552, see C. Marwick,
*Your Right to Government Information*, An American Civil Liberties Handbook (NY:
Bantam, 1985).

[3] The two basic statutes governing U.S. arms exports are the Arms Export
Control Act (Pub. L. No. 90-629, as amended) and the Foreign Assistance Act of
1961 (Pub. L. No. 87-195, as amended).  Both impose certain conditions,

Other countries, like the U.S., frequently have licensing requirements for landmines as well as for other weapons exports. The U.S. differs, however, from virtually every other country in granting public access to aggregate information about commercial license approvals. Aggregate information about government-to-government foreign military sales is also available.

The U.S. does not, however, make information about individual commercial sales readily available to the public. It is typically withheld for proprietary reasons. Moreover, it is difficult to obtain information about sales—government or private—that fall below the Congressional reporting requirements of $14 million for major defense equipment (as defined by statute), and $50 million for other items. The net result is that although the U.S. makes available, by comparison to other countries, more information on landmine transfers, the data is insufficient to gain either a comprehensive understanding about this topic or knowledge about specific transfers.

There have been several specific studies produced by the U.S. government that contain significant information about landmines. In October 1992, Senator Leahy instructed the Congressional Research Service (CRS), a branch of the United States Library of Congress, to report on the antipersonnel landmine situation worldwide. In January 1993 and March 1993, the CRS issued non-classified responses.

In July 1993, the U.S. State Department released a major study of international landmine clearing needs and efforts. This study was produced in response to a legislative requirement contained in the same legislation that enacted a one year moratorium on landmines transfers.[4]

Another avenue for obtaining information on landmine trade and production is simply through the cooperation and goodwill of U.S. government officials, including State Department and Department of Defense personnel. The Arms Project and Physicians for Human Rights

---

restrictions, procedures, and public reporting requirements on arms exports. A useful guide is "U.S. Military Sales and Assistance Programs: Laws, Regulations, and Procedures," prepared for the U.S. House Committee on Foreign Affairs by the Congressional Research Service, July 23, 1985.

[4] Parts of the State Department study are reproduced as Appendix 5. The landmines moratorium is discussed in Chapter 9.

# PMD-6

The PMD-6 was developed by the Soviets before World War II and was first used in the Soviet/Finnish Winter War of 1939/40. This simple but effective pressure mine consists of a hinged wooden box containing a block of TNT and a detonator. Pressure on the lid of the mine forces the winged retaining pin from the striker and this detonates the mine. Variations of the mine can be locally manufactured without difficulty and may be tailored in size, initiation pressure, and explosive content to match a specific target. The mine is manufactured by many countries. (Drawing by Pamela Blotner for the Arms Project/PHR.)

have thus far been gratified by the interest on the part of members of Congress, the Clinton administration, and members of the U.S. military in dealing with the landmines problem.    One expression of this enthusiasm is a willingness to provide information on landmine production and transfer worldwide.

Nevertheless, the task of collating existing information, quite apart from collecting new information, remains daunting.  In the case of the United States, however, there is at least information to be collected and ways to find it.  The same cannot be said for the vast majority of other countries.  Still, the Arms Project and Physicians for Human Rights believe that U.S. should go further in increasing the transparency of production and trade of mines and other small weapons systems, so that, for example, information about small-scale transfers can be easily obtained.

### B.  Other Countries

The Arms Project and Physicians for Human Rights  are not aware that any other country has in place a unilateral, national mechanism for obtaining information on landmines production or transfers.

In some countries, such as Germany and the United Kingdom, governments have declined to provide any information at all. Particularly distressing in this regard is the response of the United Kingdom Ministry of Defence, refusing to provide information on landmines production and transfer requested by a member of Parliament.[5]  The Arms Project and Physicians for Human Rights urge all governments to provide such information, and encourage the U.S. to press other governments to provide information about the production and trade of mines.

### II.    International Transparency: The U.N. Register

The obvious mechanism for achieving multilateral and international transparency in landmine transfers is the United Nations Register of Conventional Arms (the U.N. Register), established by

---

[5] The text of the U.K. Ministry of Defence's refusal is reproduced as Appendix 12.

General Assembly Resolution 46/36L, "Transparency in Armaments."[6]
However, landmines currently are not covered by the U.N. Register.

## A. Description of the U.N. Register

The purpose of the U.N. Register, as stated in a report by the
Secretary-General in September 1991, is to promote "transparency so as
to encourage prudent restraint by states in their arms export and import
policies and to reduce the risks of misunderstanding, suspicion or tension
resulting from lack of information."[7] The fundamental policy, according
to a diplomat who played a key role in the negotiations, is to "establish
a universal and non-discriminatory repository of data and information ...
[including] ... data on international arms transfers as well as information
provided by members states on their relevant policies, military holdings
and arms procurement through national production."[8]

The mechanism by which the U.N. Register operates is relatively
simple.   Countries are requested voluntarily to submit data and, if
available, background information, by April 30 of each year on the
number of certain types of armaments exported to or imported from any
other country during the previous year.  The U.N. Register covers seven
major types of weapons:  tanks, armored combat vehicles, large-caliber
artillery, combat aircraft, attack helicopters, warships, and missiles and
missile systems.  The data base resulting from information submitted is
located at U.N. headquarters in New York.   This information is

------

[6] U.N. General Assembly Resolution 46/36L, "Transparency in Armaments,"
December 9, 1991, and "Annex--Register of Conventional Arms," U.N. Doc.
A/RES/46/36, December 9, 1991.

[7] Study on ways and means of promoting transparency in international
transfers of conventional arms:   Report of the Secretary-General, U.N. Doc.
A/46/301 (9 September 1991), p. 11.

[8] Hendrik Wagenmakers, "The UN Register of Conventional Arms: A New
Instrument for Cooperative Security," 23 *Arms Control Today* No. 3 (April 1993),
p. 16; see also Edward Laurance, "The U.N. Register of Conventional Arms, "16
*The Washington Quarterly* No. 2 (Spring 1993), p. 163.

eventually intended to be made available to the public, at least in aggregate form, through an annual report of the Secretary-General.[9]

The General Assembly vote on December 9, 1991 establishing the U.N. Register was 150-0, with two abstentions (Cuba and Iraq).[10] The vote was the result of intense lobbying and compromise in the First Committee of the General Assembly, which deals with disarmament issues. It remains to be seen how seriously countries will take their obligations under the U.N. Register, although the fact that a significant number of countries have participated seems to mark it as a success.[11] As of September 9, 1993, 77 countries had submitted information, including the top arms exporters (such as the U.S., Russia, U.K., France, Germany, and China). Those who have filed information include the 15 countries that the Stockholm International Peace Research Institute cites as the top suppliers of major conventional weaponry between 1988 and 1992, as well as 10 of the 15 largest importers during the same period.[12] (On the other hand, several top arms importers have not participated, including Saudi Arabia, Egypt, Iraq, and Iran.) Others yet to provide information include Syria, North Korea, and South Africa. In addition, there are questions about the accuracy of the data submitted by various countries.[13] The Secretary-General is expected to issue a report on the register, making its detailed information publicly available, sometime during fall 1993.[14]

After publication, the U.N. will designate a panel of experts to assess the register's progress and discuss its possible expansion. The panel will begin meeting in early 1994. Among the issues the panel is

---

[9] Ibid.

[10] See XIV *Disarmament Times*, No. 8, December 16, 1991, p. 1.

[11] British American Security Information Council, *BASIC Reports*, No. 33, Sept. 17, 1993, p. 1.

[12] Ibid.

[13] Ibid.

[14] See UPI wire story, August 9, 1993; AP wire story, July 29, 1993; and, *BASIC Reports*, No. 32, July 9, 1993, p. 4.

expected to consider are broadening the scope of the register beyond the current seven categories of weapons, and whether the register should deal with production and holdings in addition to transfers.[15]

### B. The U.N. Register and Landmines

The utility of the U.N. Register for increasing transparency of landmines transfers, of course, requires that landmines be included in the weapons systems to be reported. At present they are not. With respect to land battle systems, the seven categories of weapons to be reported under the existing registry system stop at the level of heavy artillery. The categories do not include small arms, light artillery, mortars, or landmines.

There are several reasons why the U.N. Register does not now include landmines and small arms. First, the first five categories correspond to the "descriptions developed for the weapons systems listed in the 1990 Conventional Armed Forces in Europe Treaty ... The focus is on weapons indispensable for surprise attacks and large-scale offensive military operations," rather than military operations generally.[16] As other chapters in this book have noted, landmines have not traditionally been regarded as offensive weapons. Second, these categories, unlike landmines (and other small arms), are "relatively easy to identify, define, record and monitor."[17] In addition, it should be noted that getting agreement on the existing list was not an easy achievement and resistance to expansion may be severe, at least until there is some indication that the original categories are being widely and accurately reported.

Notwithstanding these considerations, the reasons why the U.N. Register should be expanded are persuasive. First, the register should cover at least some of the weapons systems that cause the greatest devastation to civilians, especially in the developing world. It appears that the weapons systems now included in the U.N. Register are those believed to threaten cross-border peace and stability. The Arms Project

---

[15] *Basic Reports*, No. 33, p. 3.

[16] Wagenmakers, "The U.N. Register of Conventional Arms," p. 16.

[17] Ibid., p. 16.

and Physicians for Human Rights believe it should also include weapons—and landmines are chief among them—that cause internal and regional instability, particularly by devastating civilian populations. It is these smaller arms that pose major threats to international security today.

Second, even an incomplete record of transfers would be more useful than no record at all. As shown in the previous chapter, the paucity of information on international trade in landmines is striking.

Third, expanding the U.N. Register to cover additional weapons systems is already contemplated by existing diplomatic machinery. Specifically, General Assembly Resolution 46/32L calls upon the Secretary-General to establish a group of government experts to "prepare a report on the modalities for early expansion of the scope of the Register by the addition of further categories of equipment and inclusion of data on military holdings and procurement through national production."[18] The First Committee of the General Assembly is set to consider possible expansion of the register in its fall 1993 term.

The Arms Project and Physicians for Human Rights consider the inclusion of landmines to be an essential expansion of the U.N. Register, and call upon the General Assembly to add them to the covered categories of weapons during the next General Assembly term. More generally, it is critical that national governments and international bodies enact measures that will make transfers, production, and stockpiling of landmines more transparent. These efforts go hand-in-hand with the effort to impose a complete ban on landmines.[19]

---

[18] U.N. General Assembly Resolution 46/36L, "Transparency in Armaments," 9 December 1991, U.N. Document A/RES/46/36, point 8.

[19] The Arms Project has agreed to serve as a clearinghouse for information on landmines worldwide—especially trade, production, and transparency. Any information on these topics may be directed to the Arms Project's Washington, D.C. office.

# 5
# OVERVIEW OF THE MEDICAL AND SOCIAL CONSEQUENCES OF THE USE OF LANDMINES

Mines commonly kill or inflict ravaging wounds, usually resulting in traumatic or surgical amputation. Those who survive the initial blast require antibiotics, large amounts of blood, and extended hospital stays. After discharge from the hospital, mine amputees require physical therapy and prosthetic devices to lead normal and productive lives. Some are horribly disfigured and may need therapy to cope with their trauma. Many mine victims, however, will never receive these services.

Mines not only maim and kill, they also render large tracts of land uninhabitable, with a resulting loss of livelihood for millions. Once the fighting ends, refugees and the internally displaced often still fear returning to their farms or villages because of the presence of mines. As a result, they frequently gather in cities and large towns where they find little work and poor housing. In the meantime, mine clearing operations, particularly in hilly terrain, may take decades to complete.

Mines can be obstacles to post-war peacebuilding and economic development. For example, during World War II, almost 2.8 million hectares, or 87 percent, of Libya's rangelands were rendered unusable by mines or because herders feared they were mined.[1] By 1980 only 1.8 million, or 67 percent, could be declared safe. In Afghanistan, the United Nations currently maintains 31 demining teams and estimates that it will take 15 years to clear priority zones.[2] According to a U.N. official, mines strewn over huge areas of Cambodia constitute "one of the worst man-made environmental disasters of the century."[3]

---

[1] Khairi Sgaier, "Explosive Remnants of World War II in Libya: Impact on Agricultural Development," in Arthur H. Westing (ed.), *Explosive Remnants of War: Mitigating the Environmental Effects* (London: Taylor & Francis, 1985), pp. 33-37.

[2] ICRC, *Mines: A Perverse Use of Technology*, (Geneva, Switzerland, 1992), p. 14.

[3] F. Lewis, "Make a Misstep and You're Dead," *New York Times*, May 4, 1992, p. A17.

Mine victims who receive treatment are the lucky ones; many die in the fields from loss of blood or lack of transport to get medical help. Interviews with mine victims from several countries reveal that, before being injured by a mine, some victims were unaware that mines had been placed near their villages and homes.  Rarely, if ever, were the mined areas marked.  Some victims told of relatives or other villagers who also had been killed or injured by mines.  Others said that they could see the mines in the undergrowth along paths as they walked through the fields to work.  Many victims just assumed the risk, and went into mined areas because they needed to carry their crops to market, gather firewood or wild plants for food, or herd their animals.

The countries most contaminated today by landmines are in the developing world and lack sufficient resources to respond adequately to the medical, social, economic, and environmental problems caused by mines.  These countries are inhabited mainly by rural agricultural and pastoral populations who depend on working the land to survive.  The danger posed by live mines often makes such forms of subsistence impossible.  Thus, even able-bodied individuals can be deprived of their livelihoods by the presence of landmines.

For the rural poor in many war-torn countries, co-existing with mines has become a way of life.  The following accounts, drawn from interviews with mine victims carried out by researchers with Physicians for Human Rights and Human Rights Watch, illustrate this reality.

- Maria Angeles Cruz Arevalo, a 28-year-old single mother of three small children from the hamlet of Las Flores, El Salvador, stepped on a mine along a path on October 8, 1986.  She and her three companions were unaware that the area was mined, and there was no notice or warning. People frequently used the path while gathering wild plants or blue crabs in the mangroves.  After the mine exploded, several guerrillas appeared and told her friends to leave quickly because an army patrol was about to arrive.  The woman's friends wrapped her in a hammock and rushed her to a nearby military post where she was sent by helicopter to a civilian hospital.

- In February 1992, two doctors from Physicians for Human Rights examined a six-year-old boy at a hospital in Hargeisa,

Northern Somalia. Days earlier, the boy had picked up an object that looked like "the plastic top of a thermos bottle" on a road near his home. It turned out to be a small antipersonnel mine. The explosion blinded the boy in both eyes, destroyed his right hand which was subsequently amputated at the wrist, and left deep lesions on his face and knees. Years earlier, the boy had lost his father in the civil war. The boy's mother brought food to him at the hospital. She told the doctors that she had four other children at home and was destitute.

• At sunset on April 11, 1991, Praing Chhoeun, a 56-year-old Cambodian farmer, stepped on a mine as she was taking her cattle out to graze for the night. It was a trip she made every morning and evening. After the explosion, Praing Chhoeun apparently went into shock and recalled very little of what took place the rest of the day. Her husband took his injured wife by ox cart to the Sosphean district infirmary. The following day, he arranged for a truck to take them to Mongol Borei hospital. When asked if the countryside around her village was mined, Praing Chhoeun said that no one knew exactly where the mines were buried. "I had always worried about stepping on one," she said, "but then the cattle had to be grazed."

• Six-year old Chok Chuon lost her left leg when she jumped on a mine while playing near Cambodia's main railway line on the morning of April 6, 1991. Her mother heard the explosion and rushed to the railroad tracks and carried her home. According to Chok Chuon's mother, there were no markers warning of the presence of mines. Another relative fixed a tourniquet to Chok Chuon's left leg and, with the help of others, carried her in a sling to the main road, 15 kilometers, away where they flagged down a motorcycle. At 2:30 p.m., she arrived at the provincial hospital in Battambang and, two hours later, went into surgery, where doctors performed an above-the-knee amputation.

• Fifty-five year old Lach Pem and his wife are Cambodians who arrived at a displaced persons camp along the Thai border in March 1991. They are originally farmers from the Moung District in southern Battambang province. Several years earlier, Lach Pem had stepped on a landmine while gathering firewood in the forest. Five of his friends carried him in a hammock-sling to Moung District Hospital. The trip, on foot, took 20 hours. After his amputation, he developed a serious infection and had to remain in the hospital for three months. During that time, he spent 15,000 riels, or about $150, on medications. After leaving the hospital, he bought crutches and returned to work in the rice paddies. Soon after his arrival in the camp, Lach Pem learned that during his journey to Thailand, another son, also a noncombatant, had stepped on a mine and was in the Moung District hospital.

• Maria, a 32-year-old Angolan woman from Bengo Province, lost her leg in 1989 after stepping on a mine. Now, she operates a vegetable stall in the town market. "It is a difficult life, because I can't do all I need to do," she says. "The family members help me, but my husband found himself another woman. I am here to sell, to say "Amiga, amiga, buy this!' because it is necessary to earn something so that I and my children can live."

• J.D., a 20-year-old former Angolan soldier, stepped on a mine shortly after entering military service. He now views his future with despair. "Working with a hoe isn't possible for me any more," he says. "It has to be work writing...I've passed fourth grade, and I would like to work at a company, non-manual work, sitting at a chair, writing...I don't plan to marry; without a leg they won't accept me, as a woman wants a man who can work. Marry an amputated woman? That isn't possible either—how could we live?"

## I.     Mine Injuries

Mines damage the body either by blast or by driving dirt, bacteria, clothing, and metal and plastic fragments into the tissue and bone, often causing severe secondary infections.[4]   A victim's legs are most commonly affected.   However, damage is rarely confined to one leg; lesser, but still severe, damage is frequently caused to the second leg, other limbs, the genitals, chest, and face.   The shock wave from an exploding mine can destroy blood vessels well up the leg, forcing surgeons to amputate much higher than the site of the primary wound. In many cases amputation is required because those helping the victim fail to loosen tourniquets on the wounded limbs at regular intervals.

Surgery for mine injuries can be extremely problematic because the severity and degree of contamination are rarely seen in civilian practice, and few surgeons have experience and skill in dealing with such wounds.   The surgeon's task is to cut away all the dead and severely damaged tissue and remove debris and dirt, a process called debridement. In principle it is easy, but in practice it is not.   One doctor describes the difficulty of debridement with respect to mine injuries as follows: with an injury "caused by shrapnel from an artillery shell, you would do a simple debridement, clean it up, no problem.   But these mines drive dirt and bacteria as well as shrapnel up into the tissue.   So infection spreads fast."[5]   Surgeons who fail to remove all the dead tissue and leave debris lodged between muscles find that patients suffer from infection and protracted recovery, usually involving multiple operations.

An important determinant of infection and its severity in mine blast victims is the length of delay between the injury and access to

---

[4] For a general discussion of surgical techniques, see R. Coupland and A. Korver, "Injuries from antipersonnel mines: the experience of the International Committee of the Red Cross," 303 *British Medical Journal* 1509, Dec. 14, 1991. The ICRC Medical Division has also produced a useful video on amputation for training surgeons, available from the ICRC Geneva.

[5] Statement of Dr. Chris Giannou, a Canadian surgeon with the ICRC, in Asia Watch and Physicians for Human Rights, *Landmines in Cambodia: A Coward's War* (New York: Human Rights Watch, Sept. 1991), p. 67.

# Valsella VS-50

The Italian-made Valsella VS-50 is a plastic antipersonnel mine that is fitted with a pressure fuze and can be laid conventionally or scattered from ground vehicles, helicopters or low-flying aircraft. The VS-50 is non-magnetic, waterproof, and has a long storage and field life. The Valsella VS-50 is manufactured by Valsella Meccanotecnica SpA in Brescia, Italy. It is also produced by Chartered Industries of Singapore. (Drawing by Pamela Blotner for the Arms Project/PHR.)

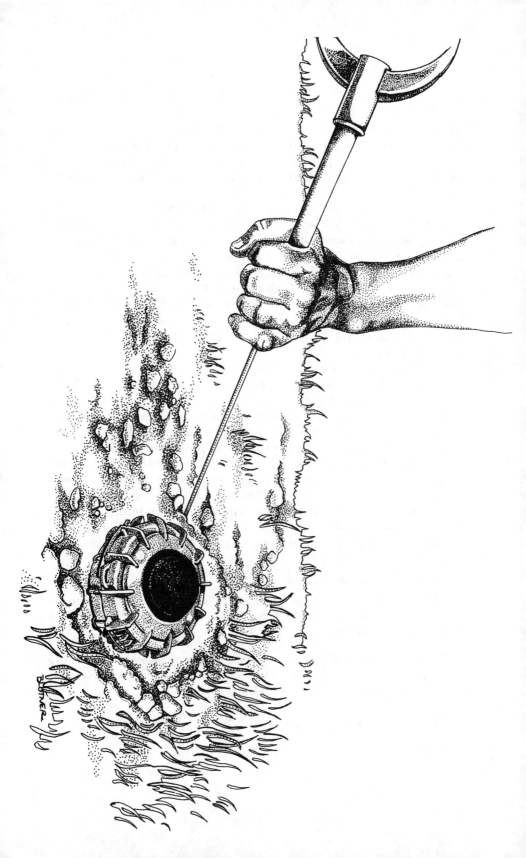

antibiotic treatment.[6]   Royal Army Corp surgeons estimate that an upper limit of six hours delay before antibiotic prophylaxis appears to be the "safety net." ICRC protocol for land mine injuries calls for pre-operative hydration and administration of antibiotics and delayed primary closure following surgery for several days.

Medical studies of combatants injured by mines indicate that early evacuation from the battlefield and prompt surgical care is crucial to saving lives and reducing disabilities.[7]   In Vietnam (1965-1973) and Lebanon (1982), medical facilities operated by the United States and Israeli militaries, respectively, achieved treatment results previously unsurpassed in war surgery.  This was due to the short transportation distances, the availability of helicopters, and well-equipped medical facilities.  In most conflicts, however, battlefield first aid, evacuation, and treatment facilities are far from ideal, and high rates of morbidity and mortality result.

Military personnel injured by antipersonnel mines stand a better chance of receiving prompt and appropriate medical care than civilians. Foot soldiers usually travel in groups and carry first aid equipment.  They can also radio to military bases or camps for transport and further medical assistance. In contrast, few, if any, civilians living in or near war zones in developing countries have access to rapid transport.

According to a 1991 study of landmine use in Afghanistan, mine victims in areas where mine injuries are common and where established evacuation procedures exist have a better chance of survival than those injured elsewhere.[8]  The study found that "communities in such localities understand the need for evacuation by the fastest method available and recognize that any mode of travel is preferable to delay."[9]  Modes of

---

[6] See Fiona King, "Landmine Injury in Cambodia:  A Case Study," London School of Hygiene and Tropical Medicine, London, U.K., September 1991, p. 14 [unpublished manuscript].

[7] See R.M. Hardaway, "Vietnam wound analysis," 18 *Journal of Trauma* 635 (1978); and L.D. Danon, E. Nili, El Dolev, "Primary treatment of battle casualties in the Lebanon war," *Israeli Journal of Medical Sciences*, 1978.

[8] Mines Advisory Group, *Report of the Afghanistan Mines Survey*, 1991, p. 48.

[9] Ibid.

initial transport for mine victims in these areas include animal, makeshift stretcher, or, if several rescuers are available, a standard first aid technique called "fireman's lift." Rapid evacuation of the mine injured is so critical for survival that the ICRC often offers local taxi drivers bonuses for each mine victim they bring to the hospital.

The manner in which rescuers initially approach a mine victim and administer first aid is also critical. Mine injured who are immobilized or unconscious may be killed by rescuers who detonate a mine near the victim. For this reason, the ICRC and mine clearance organizations, such as the Mines Advisory Group and Halo Trust, teach local deminers and other villagers in mined areas basic first aid and ways to safely approach mine victims.

## II.    Epidemiology

Accurate data on civilian mine deaths and injuries in war time is scant, in large part because hospitals and clinics often are overburdened and pay little attention to gathering reliable health information. In addition, until the late 1980s, most medical articles on mine injuries were written by military physicians and based almost solely on studies of injured combatants. Medical and relief organizations, such as the ICRC, Handicap International, Save the Children U.K., and Physicians for Human Rights, have only recently begun collecting systematic data on mine blast injuries and deaths.

The information that the ICRC has begun to collect on mine blast injuries at its field hospitals includes the patient's age, sex, time between injury and admission, and activity at the time of injury. The ICRC also documents the distribution of injuries (head, neck, chest, abdomen, genitals, limbs); whether there was traumatic amputation of limbs; and whether the patient sustained other injuries or underwent surgical amputation. Also recorded is the total number of times the patient went to the operating theater and the number of units of blood administered. The ICRC has not yet released most of this information.

Statistics on mine-related deaths and injuries currently remain estimates based on extrapolations from partial survey information. What is known, however, indicates that civilians are now being injured and killed in large numbers by landmines in many countries in the developing

world.[10]   In Cambodia, for example, approximately one out of every
236 people is an amputee due to a mine explosion.[11]   In 1991,
surgeons in Cambodia performed between 300 and 700 amputations a
month because of mine injuries.[12]   According to currently available
information, the approximate ratio of amputees due to mine explosions
to the general population in Angola is one to 470;[13] in northern
Somalia, one to 1,000;[14] and in Vietnam, one to 2,500.[15]   By
comparison, in 1989, surgeons in the U.S., which has a population of 220
million, performed no more than 10,000 amputations on patients who
had suffered traumatic injuries.   This means the amputation rate was one

---

[10] See, e.g., U.S. Department of State, *Hidden Killers: The Global Problem with
Uncleared Landmines* (Washington: U.S. Department of State, July 1993), pp. i,
1–3.  Countries with significant mine problems are indicated on the "Producers
and Exporters of Anti-Personnel Mines" map.

[11] Asia Watch and Physicians for Human Rights, *Landmines in Cambodia: The
Coward's War* (New York: Human Rights Watch, 1991), p. 59.  Because of the
difficulty in compiling complete statistics, this figure, like those cited below, is an
estimate based on initial research.  Further studies undoubtedly will refine the
numbers; the ratios given here are believed to be correct as orders of magnitude.

[12] Ibid.

[13] See Africa Watch, *Landmines in Angola* (New York: Human Rights Watch,
Jan. 1993), p. 26; Africa Watch, *Angola: Violations of the Laws of War by Both Sides*
(New York: Human Rights Watch, 1989), p. 11; Jody Williams, "Social
Consequences of Widespread Use of Landmines," in ICRC, *Report of the Symposium
on Anti-Personnel Mines: Montreux, 1993* (Geneva: ICRC, 1993), p. 74.

[14] See, e.g., Physicians for Human Rights, *Hidden Enemies: Land Mines in
Northern Somalia* (Boston: Physicians for Human Rights, 1992), p. 23.

[15] Dr. Robin Gray, "Humanitarian Consequences of Mine Usage" in ICRC,
*Report of the Montreux Symposium*, p. 63, citing the Medical Educational Trust,
*Indiscriminate Weapons: Landmines* (London: MET Reports, June, 1993).  See also
D. McClellan, "New Limbs for Viet amputees," *San Francisco Examiner*, May 12,
1991, p. A1.

per 22,000 Americans.[16] Of course, the rate for amputations of Americans due to landmine injuries sustained in the United States is virtually nil.

Those most likely to encounter mines are the rural poor. Peasants foraging for firewood and food, herding cattle, or tilling their fields are particularly at risk. Shepherds are especially vulnerable, because they often traverse wide tracts of land in search of fresh pastures. In addition, agriculturalists and pastoralists following familiar routes through their fields may be unaware that a military patrol passed through during the night and planted mines.

Children who play with mines may be killed or suffer traumatic amputations of the hands and injuries to the eyes, often resulting in blindness. In Afghanistan, the Soviet-made PFM-1 antipersonnel mine has killed or maimed thousands of children. Small, flat, light in weight, with light green polyethylene wings, the PFM-1—called the "green parrot" by Afghan tribesmen—is generally dropped by helicopters and spirals gently to the ground, where it lies until pressure is put on it. Children are frequently victims because the device looks more like a toy than a mine.

Many mine blast victims die from loss of blood while still in the fields or on the way to the hospital. An ICRC study of 757 patients being treated for mine injuries in two hospitals in an unspecified developing country found that most patients were admitted between six and 24 hours after injury.[17] In a 1991 study of civilian mine-injured in Cambodia, Physicians for Human Rights and Asia Watch, a division of Human Rights Watch, found that mine blast victims from rural areas spent an average of 12 hours from the moment of injury until they reached a hospital with surgical facilities. In Angola, civilian mine victims generally receive first-aid within a few hours, but, because of poor air evacuation services, must wait an average of thirty-six hours before arriving at a hospital.[18] Such delays can result in sepsis and severe shock.

---

[16] E. Stover and D. Charles, "The Killing Minefields of Cambodia," *New Scientist*, Oct. 19, 1991, p. 27.

[17] Coupland and Korver, "Injuries from antipersonnel mines."

[18] Africa Watch, *Landmines in Angola*, p. 36.

Dr. Johannes Schraknepper, a surgeon with the Swiss Red Cross in Cambodia, has explained that, in his experience, soldiers who are wounded by mines usually have better access to transport and thus arrive at hospitals much sooner than civilians. He characterized the situation for noncombatants as follows:

> For civilians, finding transportation is a big problem. If they're lucky, someone—most likely a relative or friend—will find them wounded in the field and will apply a tourniquet. It stops the bleeding, which is good, but too often they forget to loosen it, which causes problems later. So the wounded person will lie in the fields, or maybe in his house, while someone goes looking for transport, which is usually a horse or motorcycle taxi. Now, first they have to find one, which isn't always easy, as it may require riding a bicycle five miles away to another village. In the meantime, the family had better have enough money, because usually the rule is no cash, no transport. All of this may take 6 to 12 hours or even an entire day. They may take several more hours to get to the hospital.[19]

Even when civilians injured by mines reach medical facilities, they often fail to receive proper care because blood, surgical instruments, x-ray film, anesthesia and antibiotics are in short supply or unavailable. An ICRC study on the use of blood in its hospitals found that, on average, for every 100 wounded, 44.9 units of blood were required, while 103.2 units were required for every 100 mine-injured.[20] Inadequate or non-existent blood transfusion services add to the difficulties of providing for mine blast injured in developing countries.

Victims of mine blasts are also more likely to require amputation and remain in the hospital longer than those wounded by other

---

[19] Asia Watch and Physicians for Human Rights, *Landmines in Cambodia*, p. 69.

[20] Chauvin B. Eshaya and R.M. Coupland, "Transfusion requirements for the management of war wounded:  the experience of the International Committee of the Red Cross," 68 *B.J. Anaes* 221-223 (1992).

munitions. An ICRC study of 1,253 patients in field hospitals in Cambodia and Afghanistan found that 84 percent of the patients had received lower limb amputations because of mine blast injuries.[21] Hospitals in or near war zones are usually understaffed and have few, if any, orthopedic surgeons, let alone general surgeons with extensive experience treating blast-related injuries. For instance, in northern Somalia, the principal hospital has only a part-time volunteer staff of doctors and nurses, few antibiotics, and, according to its only orthopedic surgeon, an 80 percent wound infection rate.[22]

Once the mine-injured reach a hospital, they often find that there is little or no food, except what relatives bring. In some Cambodian hospitals, if meals are provided, war veterans are given first priority. Until recently, mine blast patients in government-run hospitals in Cambodia had to pay doctors and nurses for their services, medicines, and intravenous fluids. If blood was needed, the patient's family had to find donors and pay them. One Cambodian farmer who stepped on a landmine in 1987 and eventually fled to a refugee camp in Thailand, said that he wasn't even sure which was worse: losing a leg or knowing that his wife had gone to relatives and friends to beg for money to pay for his hospital care.[23]

## III.    Rehabilitation

There are few, if any, state-run rehabilitation facilities in most developing countries. Those that do exist focus on trying to fit mine amputees with prosthetic devices. Systematic physical therapy is uncommon.

---

[21] J. Rautio and P. Paavolainen, "Afghan war wounded: experience with 200 cases," 28 *J. Trauma* 523-525 (1988); and, D.E. Johnson, P. Panijayanond, S. Lumjiak, J.W. Crum, and P. Boonkrapu, "Epidemiology of combat casualties in Thailand," 21 *J. Trauma* 486-488 (1981).

[22] Alain Garachon, "ICRC Rehabilitation Programmes on Behalf of War Disabled," in ICRC, *Report of the Montreux Symposium*, p. 81.

[23] Asia Watch and Physicians for Human Rights, *Land Mines in Cambodia*, p. 70.

Soldiers usually receive limbs before civilians.  Even where prosthetics are available to civilians, they often opt to return to their villages rather than pay the extra expense.  Many are not even aware of the advantages of such devices.  Back home, a few will fashion limbs out of scraps of wood and metal.  But most amputees will grow accustomed to their crutches and, as time passes, simply keep postponing the trip to the workshop for financial or other reasons.

Another problem in some societies is a cultural bias against amputations.  This often results in poor stumps because families insist on surgeons cutting only a few centimeters above the site of the initial injury.  This may mean that an artificial limb cannot be properly fitted, when and if it becomes available.

For many mine amputees, the price of an artificial limb is far beyond reach.  According to the ICRC, a prosthesis for a child should be replaced every six months, and for an adult every three to five years.[24] A 10 year-old child with a life expectancy of another 40 or 50 years will need 25 prostheses.  At a cost of $125 per prosthesis, the child will spend $3,125 on artificial limbs in his or her lifetime.  In countries were average incomes are only $10–15 a month, it is easy to see why prostheses are considered a luxury.[25]

Several international humanitarian agencies, including the ICRC and Handicap International, are trying to produce prostheses for the world's mine-injured.  Since 1979, the ICRC has implemented 33 orthopedic programs for amputees and two for paraplegics in 17 countries.[26]  In 1991, ICRC workshops made artificial limbs for 7,979 amputees, the majority of whom were mine blast victims.  Despite these efforts, the number of artificial limbs produced by the ICRC and Handicap International fall far short of the demand.

Handicap International tries to contain the costs of producing artificial limbs and help the local economy by using local materials (wood,

---

[24] See N. Hirschhorn, L. Haviland, and J. Salvo, *Critical Needs Assessment in Cambodia:  The Humanitarian Issues*, a report to the U.S. Agency for International Development, April 1991, p. 8.

[25] See Alain Garachon, "ICRC Rehabilitation Programmes on Behalf of War Disabled," in ICRC, *Report of the Montreux Symposium*, p. 81.

[26] Ibid.

leather, and, where possible, locally processed rubber). It can produce a below-knee prosthetic device for $12, and above-knee for $20. Unlike other prosthetic manufacturing techniques, Handicap International produces without the need for power, crucial in wartorn countries where both electricity and diesel fuel for generators are in short supply.

The Handicap International system, however, has its drawbacks. Leather, which is used for the knee socket, gradually loses its shape as it gets wet, and must be replaced every two years. Some amputees complain that the device's rubber foot breaks within a year and that the rigid wooden limbs, particularly on the above-knee devices, are cumbersome and unsuitable for farm work, especially in rice paddies.

New techniques for constructing more flexible and easily fitted artificial limbs are being developed in a number of developing countries. One device called the "Jaipur foot," invented 12 years ago in Jaipur, India, is covered entirely in vulcanized rubber, and can be fabricated for less than $30. It requires no imported materials other than sheets of raw aluminum, is impervious to mud and water, and lasts up to five years. Another artificial limb, called the "Seattle Shapemaker" because it was pioneered at the Prosthetics Research Foundation in Seattle, Washington, uses a lifelike foot that is springy, enabling amputees to run, jump and walk without a limp.

## IV.    Social and Economic Consequences

Landmines are devastating to all levels of society: individual, family, community, and nation. Mine victims and their families suffer physical and psychological trauma caused by mine explosions. Relatives of the mine-injured often must assume the total burden of care. For people who live in infested areas or who are displaced because of severe mine contamination, the stress created by the constant danger or the inability to return home can erode family life.

In agrarian or pastoral societies, where muscle power means survival, an amputee is often viewed as unproductive and simply another mouth to feed. In Cambodia, for example, nearly every aspect of life is set to the rhythm of rice cultivation—the flooding, the planting, the replanting, and harvesting. It is very labor intensive, requiring the participation of every man, woman, and child. A person who is physically disabled can become a burden—someone who eats but produces nothing. Female amputees are often considered less desirable as wives because they cannot work in the fields or tend livestock. Male amputees may drift to the larger towns where they become beggars or petty criminals. Spouses of amputees may eventually abandon them, especially if they are poor, to seek more productive, able-bodied partners. In addition, where adults are injured or killed, their children frequently are left destitute.

In some postwar countries, amputee soldiers often band together to protect one another. They may hold protest vigils in front of government buildings, demanding food and shelter. They frequently set up makeshift encampments in market places or around tourist hotels and beg for food. Although they may eventually receive artificial limbs, they are rarely given government-sponsored training in new job skills applicable to civilian life. Abandoned by the government and society they fought to protect, many will grow resentful and turn to alcohol or drugs or become petty criminals. Like abandoned street children, they are in danger of being viewed by government officials and police as an unpleasant nuisance to society and arrested or, even worse, "disappeared."

War and famine can undermine the strong family ties that are typical of most peasant cultures, leaving mine victims in a terribly vulnerable position. Take for instance the plight of a young child who had become paraplegic after stepping on a mine near his house in Cambodia in 1991. Dr. Chris Giannou, the surgeon who attended to the child, related what happened:

> At first, the family didn't know what to do. So they abandoned him at the hospital because there was nothing left to expect from him. He stayed alone at the hospital for four months before they finally came back and got him. But the mere fact that they abandoned him...and we didn't know if they were going to come back or not. And they probably didn't know either! In a Third World society, in a peasant culture, that's a sacrilege, it's unthinkable...[27]

The effects on community life can be equally devastating. With peace, communities already shattered by war must rebuild their homes and villages, find new pastures and farmland, and seek out new markets

---

[27] Asia Watch and Physicians for Human Rights, *Landmines in Cambodia*, pp. 73–74.

A minefield in Iraqi Kurdistan.

An Italian Valmara-69 in Iraqi Kurdistan.

A de-miner using a metal prod to probe for buried landmines in Iraqi Kurdistan.

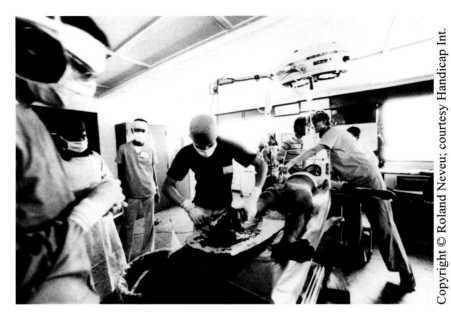

Surgical amputation of landmine victim in Cambodia.

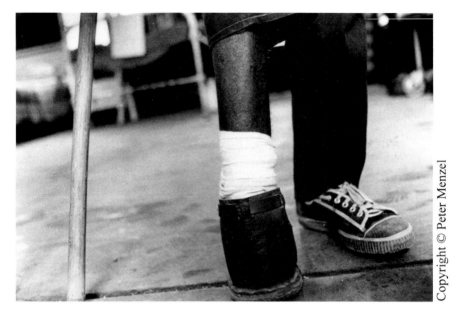

A landmine amputee in Somalia.

Mine clearance in Somalia.

A ten-year-old Cambodian boy putting on prosthesis.

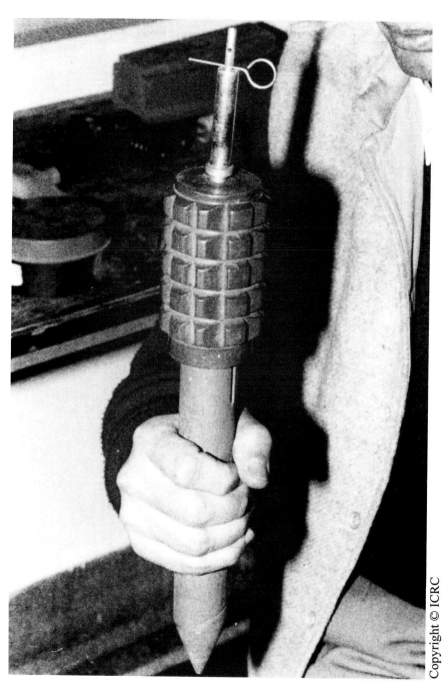

A stake mine, triggered by a tripwire.

A six-year-old Cambodian refugee girl.

for their goods—all with the ever present threat of landmines. Communities in areas where there are high casualty rates will often disintegrate, as villagers, fearful of encountering mines, abandon their farms to live with relatives in other villages or towns. Landmines can seriously hinder the ability of a country to rebuild its postwar economy. The U.S. State Department recently concluded:

> The impact of uncleared landmines on a developing economy is tremendous. During civil strife or regional conflict it is common to lay mines around key economic installations such as electric plants and powerlines, water treatment plants, key road nets, major market centers, warehouses and harbor installations, and government buildings. These are the key installations required to support a rebuilding economy. When the economic infrastructure has been isolated by landmines, it can not sustain economic development. As a consequence, economic reconstruction is delayed until the roads, the electric power system, and the water system, etc. can be cleared of landmines.[28]

The State Department also observed that:

> The disruption of the transportation system produced by even a few mines results in local scarcities of products, lessened exports and balances of the hard currency they bring, inflation, and sometimes famine.[29]

In addition, in underdeveloped, mainly rural countries where mine warfare is most common, the presence of live mines means that agriculture and pastoral endeavors will be significantly restricted. The aggregate negative effect on national economies, particularly in countries without a large industrial base, of a reduction in such activities can be quite significant.

---

[28] DOS, *Hidden Killers*, p. 3.

[29] DOS, *Hidden Killers*, p. i.

As one development official recently posed the problem with respect to Cambodia:  "Economic development in Cambodia is heavily dependent on the speed in which the mines can be cleared—and that could take not years, but decades."[30]

Clearly, most postwar countries in the developing world have neither the economic nor organizational infrastructure to support a large-scale mine clearance operation.  It must therefore fall to the international community, particularly to those countries who supplied mines to the combat factions, to provide the funding and organization for mine survey, marking, clearance, and destruction, thereby assisting the economic rebuilding of mine infested countries.

## V.  Repatriation and Resettlement

In several post-war countries, the existence of unexploded mines has been one of the principal factors preventing or delaying the return of refugees to their countries of origin.  This especially has been the case in Afghanistan, Angola, Cambodia, Kuwait, and northern Somalia where hundreds of thousands of refugees have lived in refugee camps in neighboring countries.  Mine awareness programs offered to refugees in the camps are helpful but of limited value and, in some cases, can give returnees a sense of false security.  Even when refugees understand the danger of mines, and are aware that their fields may be mined, they also know that they must work to survive.  Consequently, they often condition themselves to ignore the risks.  Mine awareness programs should never be a substitute for—rather they should be an integral part of—extensive and thorough mine eradication programs.

So far, no systematic, survey-based studies have been conducted on the medical and social consequences of mines for returning refugee populations, although a large number of refugees have recently been repatriated to heavily mined countries such as Cambodia, Kuwait, and Afghanistan.  The experience of these repatriation efforts suggests, however, that when refugees and the internally displaced return home spontaneously and not in organized groups with the assistance of aid organizations they are more at risk of being killed or maimed by mines.

In Cambodia, interviews with refugees, relief workers, and deminers by a Physicians for Human Rights team in June 1993 suggest

---

[30] Interview with Tony Stadler, Swiss official with CARE, June 1993.

that returnees have not been killed or injured by mines at a rate proportionately higher than the rest of the population. Most relief workers agreed that the organized manner in which the U.N. High Commissioner for Refugees handled the repatriation process, including the establishment of reception camps for refugees, has helped limit mine casualties among Cambodian returnees. They also suggested that the surveying and marking of known mined areas with "Danger!! Mines!!" signs, in English and Khmer, by non-governmental mine clearance groups and U.N.-trained demining teams has helped reduce mine casualties generally. However, Khmer and expatriate relief workers fear that when the last of the U.N. peacekeeping forces depart in November 1993, mine casualties may increase unless donor countries continue to fund—and substantially increase their donations to—mine clearance programs.

Refugees who leave camps spontaneously are at high risk of encountering mines because they tend to leave while hostilities continue and do not have the benefit of warnings, markings, or education about the location of mines. In 1992, for instance, doctors from Physicians for Human Rights collected and analyzed data on war-related injuries in several hospitals in northern Somalia.[31] Records at the hospital in the capital of Hargeisa showed that landmine injuries, especially of children between five and 15 years of age, had increased dramatically in early 1991, a period when thousands of Somali refugees spontaneously left camps in Ethiopia and returned to northern Somalia.

Repatriation always brings with it a multitude of problems. Refugees often return to their villages to find that their lands are being farmed by others. Prime farming land may be in short supply, so they must seek land in unfamiliar areas. There may be a shortage of draft animals, farm implements, and fertilizers, as well as a lack of means to transport crops to market. People who have acquired professionals skills in camps are likely to encounter resentment from locally trained professionals as they compete for jobs. Many of the new arrivals have no home, no village, and no immediate means of livelihood and may wander in search of work. All of these factors means there will be mass movement across the country, and with movement, the dangers posed by mines will increase.

---

[31] Physicians for Human Rights, *Land Mines in Northern Somalia*, p. 18.

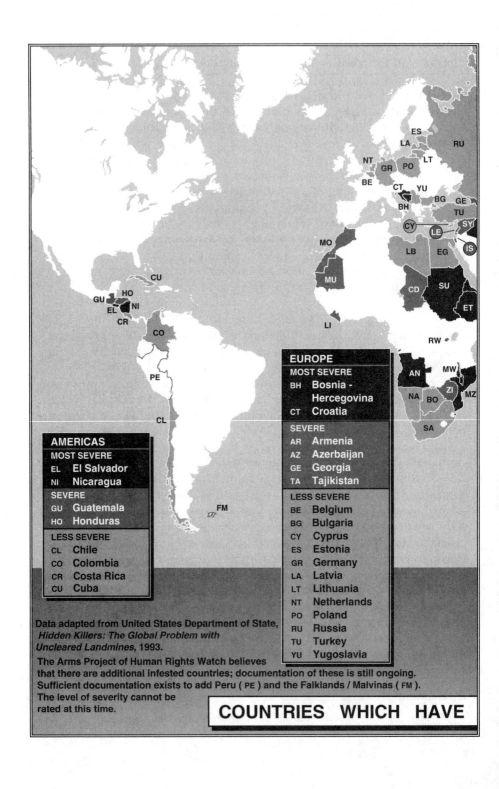

## AMERICAS

**MOST SEVERE**

EL  El Salvador
NI  Nicaragua

**SEVERE**

GU  Guatemala
HO  Honduras

**LESS SEVERE**

CL  Chile
CO  Colombia
CR  Costa Rica
CU  Cuba

## EUROPE

**MOST SEVERE**

BH  Bosnia -
    Hercegovina
CT  Croatia

**SEVERE**

AR  Armenia
AZ  Azerbaijan
GE  Georgia
TA  Tajikistan

**LESS SEVERE**

BE  Belgium
BG  Bulgaria
CY  Cyprus
ES  Estonia
GR  Germany
LA  Latvia
LT  Lithuania
NT  Netherlands
PO  Poland
RU  Russia
TU  Turkey
YU  Yugoslavia

Data adapted from United States Department of State,
*Hidden Killers: The Global Problem with
Uncleared Landmines*, 1993.

The Arms Project of Human Rights Watch believes
that there are additional infested countries; documentation of these is still ongoing.
Sufficient documentation exists to add Peru ( PE ) and the Falklands / Malvinas ( FM ).
The level of severity cannot be
rated at this time.

# COUNTRIES  WHICH  HAVE

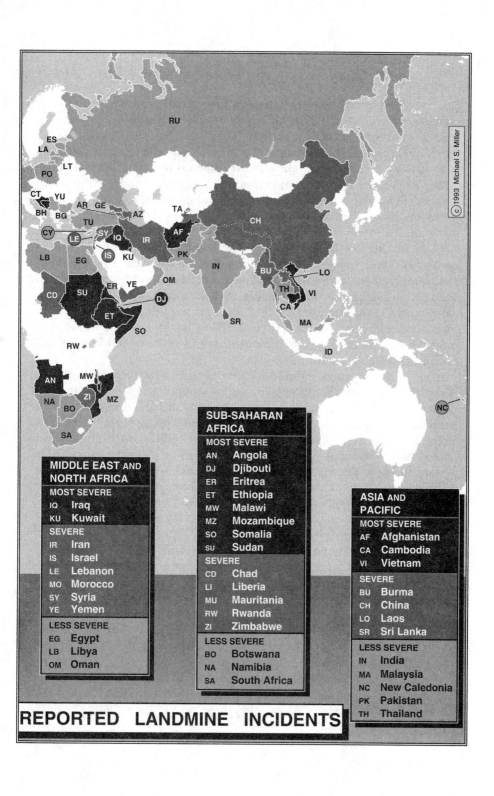

# REPORTED LANDMINE INCIDENTS

**MIDDLE EAST AND NORTH AFRICA**

MOST SEVERE
- IQ Iraq
- KU Kuwait

SEVERE
- IR Iran
- IS Israel
- LE Lebanon
- MO Morocco
- SY Syria
- YE Yemen

LESS SEVERE
- EG Egypt
- LB Libya
- OM Oman

**SUB-SAHARAN AFRICA**

MOST SEVERE
- AN Angola
- DJ Djibouti
- ER Eritrea
- ET Ethiopia
- MW Malawi
- MZ Mozambique
- SO Somalia
- SU Sudan

SEVERE
- CD Chad
- LI Liberia
- MU Mauritania
- RW Rwanda
- ZI Zimbabwe

LESS SEVERE
- BO Botswana
- NA Namibia
- SA South Africa

**ASIA AND PACIFIC**

MOST SEVERE
- AF Afghanistan
- CA Cambodia
- VI Vietnam

SEVERE
- BU Burma
- CH China
- LO Laos
- SR Sri Lanka

LESS SEVERE
- IN India
- MA Malaysia
- NC New Caledonia
- PK Pakistan
- TH Thailand

©1993 Michael S. Miller

Until quite recently, there was little consensus and considerable confusion within the United Nations about how to handle the problem of mines and repatriation of refugees. There was also reluctance in some circles to accept the humanitarian nature of the problem or its scale and seriousness. An example of the latter tendency is found in the September 1989 "Report for Repatriation Planning for Afghan Refugees," prepared by the U.N. High Commissioner for Refugees, which stated, quite incorrectly—as other reports show—that the problem of mines had been exaggerated.

In the last few years, however, there has been an increased awareness and acknowledgement of the menace of landmines to returning refugee populations. U.N. agencies and other international refugee organizations have begun to collaborate with medical and development organizations to find ways of resettling returnees in an organized and safe manner. They also have begun to recognize that in mined areas, successful repatriation programs require well-funded and extensive mine clearance initiatives.

Such programs should be based on three fundamental precepts. First, the program should be directed at stopping the loss of life and injury caused by landmines among non-combatants and livestock, as well as returning mined land to its peacetime use. Second, the program's aims should be strictly humanitarian and not military or political. No mines should be handed over to military units or any other party. To ensure absolute neutrality, the program should be administered by the United Nations, in collaboration with nonpartisan, private mine clearance organizations. Finally, all mines must either be destroyed *in situ* or, where this is impractical, removed, taken to a safe location, and destroyed.

An example of a successful program is one run by Tony Stadler, a Swiss relief official with CARE in northwestern Cambodia. Since August 1992, Stadler has worked with demining teams from Halo Trust, the Norwegian People's Aid, and the U.N. in an effort to return approximately 45,000 internally displaced persons to six villages. The villagers had fled during intensive fighting between government and rebel forces in 1989 and 1990, and had been unable to return because of mines along the roads and in rice paddies.

By June 1993, roughly 35,000 people had been resettled in their villages and demining teams had begun clearing mines from the surrounding farmlands. "Essentially, these people built their way back home," Stadler explains. "The deminers went first, lifting and destroying mines. Then the villagers followed, rebuilding the roads."

## VI. Mines and Humanitarian Activities

During and after hostilities, mines can hinder, or even prevent humanitarian activities. Relief workers obviously are less likely to enter areas heavily infested by mines. Mines can also be used to harm and terrorize peacekeeping forces, as happened in August 1993 when Somali militia used a landmine to ambush a U.S. military vehicle in Mogadishu, killing four soldiers.[32] In Bosnia, there have been incidents in which refugee convoys have been thwarted by mines on roads intended as evacuation routes. The presence of mines also increases the cost of delivering relief supplies. For example, in Angola in 1988, the cost of delivering one ton of relief supplies from Cobito to Municipio overland cost 106 Swiss francs. By air, the cost was 2,600 Swiss francs per ton, or 25 times the overland cost. This figure did not even include the extra cost of insuring planes against war risk. However, because air transport is much safer than ground delivery, relief supplies in Angola often were flown despite the expense.[33]

In a communique issued on February 9, 1993, the ICRC denounced three incidents in which staff of humanitarian organizations working in Africa had been killed or wounded by mines within a 10-day period:

- On 25 January, seven first aid workers of the Senegalese Red Cross were killed and four others injured when their vehicle hit a mine in Casamance.

- On 5 February, in Zambesia Province, Mozambique, a mine blast killed two Mozambicans, one of whom was an Oxfam

---

[32] "Somalia mine kills 4 US soldiers; U.N. blames attack on clan leader," *Boston Globe*, August 9, 1993, p. 1.

[33] Jean-Michel Monod, "Mines and Humanitarian Activities," in ICRC, *Report of the Montreux Symposium*, p. 3.

employee, during a mission in which ICRC
personnel were taking part.    Three other
people were wounded.

- On the same day, in Lasanod in northwestern
  Somalia, another mine incident cost five people
  their lives, three of them local ICRC staff.
  Three other Somali employees were injured
  and required hospitalization.[34]

In recent years, aid agencies have instituted programs on mine
awareness training for their foreign and local personnel. Similarly, relief
and mine clearance organizations have begun to collaborate formally in
mine awareness training and data collection on the location of heavily
mined areas.    Although helpful, these initiatives are unlikely to
dramatically reduce the problems of delivering relief supplies in mined
regions.

## VII.    Future Research

During recent years, the ICRC and other medical and
humanitarian organizations have begun a serious effort to document the
effects of landmines on civilian populations. These organizations have
established protocols and procedures for determining the number and
nature of mine casualties, collecting basic background information on
victims and their activities at the time of injury, and assessing their
immediate and long-term medical and rehabilitative needs. Little is
known, however, about the psychological after-effects of mine injuries
and therapeutic treatment needs in diverse cultural settings.
Furthermore, there is a need for long-term studies of how mines affect
economic development and the environment in post-war countries.
However, the need for such research should not detract from what is
readily evident to those familiar with the repercussions of mine warfare:
that mines cause tremendous and long-lasting hardships for civilian
populations throughout the world.

---

[34] Ibid., p. 4.

# 6
# COUNTRY CASE STUDIES OF THE LANDMINE PROBLEM

## Global Overview

This chapter consists of studies describing the landmine problem in seven different countries. These studies are intended to give the reader an awareness of the global scope of the current crisis and to illustrate the range of conflicts in which mines are used, the different technologies employed, varying patterns of mine warfare, and the consequences of mine use in various nations. They demonstrate just how devastating antipersonnel landmines can be for civilian populations, and how crucial it is for the international community to make immediate efforts to ban the production, trade and use of these indiscriminate weapons.

Six of the studies are adapted from previous reports published by Human Rights Watch and Physicians for Human Rights, on Angola, Cambodia, El Salvador, Iraqi Kurdistan, Nicaragua, and northern Somalia. The reader is referred to the original reports for additional details and footnotes. A seventh study, on Mozambique, is based on initial research by Human Rights Watch which will culminate in a comprehensive report later this year.

The studies of Angola, Cambodia, Iraqi Kurdistan, Mozambique, and northern Somalia detail perhaps the worst landmine disasters in the world, with the notable omission of Afghanistan. A full study on Afghanistan is not included simply because neither Human Rights Watch nor Physicians for Human Rights has yet had the opportunity to undertake a lengthy, on-the-ground investigation. However, a brief synopsis of the Afghan situation is given.

These are by no means the only nations adversely affected in a serious way. The scourge of landmines is a truly global phenomenon. The recent survey by the U.S. State Department indicates that landmines pose a threat to civilians in 62 nations, and that about two-thirds of those nations require assistance with demining efforts.[1] The State Department estimates that there are some 85-90 million landmines deployed

---

[1] U.S. Department of State, *Hidden Killers: The Global Problem with Uncleared Landmines* (Washington: U.S. Department of State, 1993). Excerpts from this report are reproduced as Appendix 5.

throughout the world, waiting to claim victims, and acknowledges that the number could be significantly higher.[2] "Landmines may be the most toxic and widespread pollution facing mankind," according to the State Department.[3]

The forces fighting in the seven countries detailed in this chapter have all employed methods of landmine use that violate both the international Landmines Protocol and customary international law;[4] most parties have used landmines deliberately against civilians, all have engaged in indiscriminate use in which the potential for severe harm to civilians was ignored, and few have ever taken precautions that could protect civilians. None of the seven countries is party to the Landmines Protocol; in any case, the wars are internal, and, therefore, not subject to the terms of the Protocol. However, all parties are bound by customary international law which unequivocally prohibits these practices.

While there is no way to know the precise number of landmine casualties during the last few decades, it is probably in the hundreds of thousands. The United Nations Working Group on Mines has estimated that worldwide, 800 people die from mines every month.[5] A much greater number of people are injured and maimed. The amputation rate due to mine injuries in some of the worst mine-affected nations is

---

[2] Ibid., p.3. State Department figures include both antipersonnel and antitank landmines. Experts inside and outside of the State Department believe that the vast majority, perhaps two-thirds or more, are antipersonnel.

[3] Ibid., p. 2.

[4] See Chapter 8 for an in-depth analysis of the Landmines Protocol and customary laws relevant to mine warfare. The chapter argues that because landmines are delayed-action weapons they cause indiscriminate *effects*, rendering them *per se* illegal under customary law, particularly as codified in certain provisions of 1977 Additional Protocol I to the Geneva Conventions of 1949. In addition, customary law prohibits certain *uses* of all weapons including deliberately or indiscriminately attacking civilians.

[5] Cited in Media Natura, "The deadly legacy: report on Western views on landmines and ways of restricting their indiscriminate use" in ICRC, *Report of the Symposium on Anti-personnel Mines: Montreux 1993*, p. 271. The U.S. State Department report estimates 150 people are killed or injured by landmines each week. DOS, *Hidden Killers*, p. i.

horrifying: Cambodia, 1 per 236 people; Angola, 1 per 470 people; northern Somalia, 1 per 1,000 people.[6]

It has been pointed out that for most of the affected countries, the devastation by landmines is felt at all levels: individual, family, community, and societal.[7]  A nation must respond not only to the immediate medical and rehabilitation needs of landmine victims, but also to the severe long-term effects of landmines on economic reconstruction and social reintegration.  Landmines in some cases make nearly impossible such basic tasks as planting crops, gathering firewood, gathering food, grazing livestock, and travelling between villages.

There are well over 20 nations where landmines pose a serious to severe threat to life, limb, and economic and social well-being. (See "Landmine Disasters" Chart and Appendix 5, "Countries Which Have Reported Landmine Incidents" Map).

### Regional Summaries

According to the State Department survey:

**Africa** is the most mined region of the world, with 18 to 30 million mines laid in 18 countries.  In addition to Angola, Somalia, and Mozambique, the other nations with very severe landmine problems are Ethiopia, Eritrea (which recently gained its independence from Ethiopia), and Sudan.  There are estimated to be as many as one million mines scattered in Ethiopia and Eritrea, and two million mines in Sudan.  The Western Sahara has been littered with more than 10,000 landmines during the Moroccan government's war with the Polisario. It is believed that hundreds, if not thousands, of landmines are scattered in or Chad, Rwanda, Liberia, and Zimbabwe.

The **Middle East** has 17 to 24 million mines in at least eight countries.  Kuwait, Iraq, and Iran face the biggest landmine problems.

---

[6] See Chapter 5.  Because of the difficulty in compiling complete statistics, these figures are estimates based on initial research.  Further studies are likely to refine the numbers.

[7] Jody Williams, "Social Consequences of Widespread Use of Landmines," in ICRC, *Report of the Symposium on Antipersonnel Landmines, Montreux, 1993* (Geneva: ICRC, 1993).

An estimated seven million landmines were laid in Kuwait during the Gulf War, less than half of which have been cleared.  Iraq laid an appalling three to five million mines in Iraqi Kurdistan alone, with perhaps that many again deployed elsewhere in the country.  There are many mines on the border between Iraq and Iran remaining from the eight year war between the two countries.  Significant numbers of mines have accumulated in Syria, Israel, and Lebanon as a result of years of hostilities involving those nations.

**East Asia** has 15 to 23 million mines, located mostly in Southeast Asia; eight nations in the region have landmine problems.  In addition to Cambodia, Vietnam continues to suffer greatly from landmines, and serious problems exist in Laos and Burma.  Thailand's borders with Cambodia and Burma are heavily mined, as is the Chinese-Vietnamese border.

**South Asia** has 13 to 25 million mines, mostly in Afghanistan and along the Afghanistan/Pakistan/India/China borders. The disputed area of Kashmir is reported to be heavily mined.  Sri Lanka is also plagued by mines.

**Europe** has three to seven million mines laid in 13 countries; it is the region experiencing the most rapid increase in the number of landmines.  The former Yugoslavia is obviously the most worrisome spot in Europe.  More than three million landmines may have already been deployed in Croatia, Bosnia-Hercegovina, and Serbia, and reportedly no minefield maps are being made.  Some observers believe that thousands of new mines are being laid each day, even as many as 50,000 per week.[8]

More than 50,000 landmines have reportedly been laid in the disputed Nagorno-Karabakh region.  It also appears that tens of thousands of landmines have been used in Tajikistan and Georgia.

**Latin America** has 300,000 to 1,000,000 mines in eight countries, mostly in Central America.  Nicaragua, El Salvador, and the Falkland/Malvinas Islands are the main trouble spots for landmines.

---

[8] Several experts at the ICRC Symposium in Montreux in April 1993 cited these numbers.

## Afghanistan Survey

By virtually all accounts, Afghanistan is the most heavily mined nation in the world. Some estimates of the number of landmines in Afghanistan run as high as 40 million, but 10 million may be a more accurate figure.[9] The vast majority of these mines were laid by the Soviet Union in its war with the mujahidin. The Russians claim that maps were kept of landmine deployments, but, to the extent they exist, such maps would be of little value today. Many of the mines have been moved from their original locations by people and by nature.

Even more importantly, many of the mines were delivered remotely, by aircraft, in a fashion that precludes accurate or meaningful recording and marking of minefields. Soviet-made "butterfly" mines rained down all over Afghanistan. They gained notoriety for their bright colors which attracted children. The indiscriminate use of landmines throughout the country makes maps largely irrelevant. A U.S. Defense Intelligence Agency study states that "Soviet landmine emplacement evolved to such an extent that they employed scatterable landmines in support of offensive operations."[10] The study further states, "The large-scale use of landmines proved invaluable to Soviet forces...and provided combined arms commanders with a useful (and often otherwise unavailable) tactical option. Future scenarios involving the operation of traditionally heavy forces in low-intensity conflicts will no doubt include the employment of landmines for similar tactical and operational advantages."[11]

---

[9] The U.S. State Department's report cites the United Nations estimate of nine to 10 million, while acknowledging that the number is "possibly as high as 35 million;" DOS, *Hidden Killers*, p. 42. On the other hand, the U.S. Defense Intelligence Agency report notes that "Soviet forces found it necessary to employ more than 30 million landmines against the lightly armed rebel forces." U.S. Defense Intelligence Agency and U.S. Army Foreign Science and Technology Center (DIA/FSTC), *Landmine Warfare—Trends & Projections*, Dec. 1992, DST-11605-019-92, p. 2–4. This document was obtained by the Arms Project through the Freedom of Information Act.

[10] Ibid.

[11] Ibid., p. 2-5.

Certainly, the Russians are not solely to blame. The Afghan government laid mines, as did the mujahidin. Landmines, either antitank or antipersonnel, manufactured by Italy, China, the United States, Pakistan, Egypt, Britain, and Czechoslovakia have been found in Afghanistan. According to the State Department report and the DIA report, the following antipersonnel mines have been found in Afghanistan:[12]

- Soviet Union— PMN; PMN-2; POMZ; POMZ-2; POMZ-2M; PMD-6; PMD-6M; PFM-1; PFM-1S; PMN-2; PGMDM; OZM-3; OZM-72; OZM-4; MON-50; MON-90; MON-100; MON-200; PMP; POM-2S
- Czechoslovakia— PP-MI-SR; PP-MI-SR II
- United States— M18A1
- China— Type 72; Type 69
- Italy— Valmara 59; SB-33; TS-50; VS-50
- Egypt— T/79

More than one observer has commented that, in effect, all of Afghanistan is a minefield. Nearly all of the national infrastructure has been mined, and much of the arable land. According to the State Department, "There are mines everywhere—on arable land and lowland grazing terrain, on footpaths, on all classes of roads, on the hillsides and mountainous grazing land, on hilltops and mountaintops, and in irrigation channels and canals in both urban and rural settings. The majority of mines are believed to have been laid in the provinces along the Afghan/Pakistan and Afghan/Iran border, but every region has some problem with uncleared landmines."[13]

The omnipresence of landmines makes repatriation of refugees extremely dangerous and greatly undermines postwar reconstruction. The human cost of landmines in Afghanistan is staggering; hundreds of thousands of people have been maimed and killed. Some estimates put the death toll from mine explosions as high as 200,000 and the wounded tally at 400,000. According to the ICRC, in 1992 some 1,400 mine victims were admitted to receiving centers for treatment in Kabul,

---

[12] DIA/FSTC, p. 2-6; DOS, *Hidden Killers*, p. 42.

[13] Ibid.

Peshawar, and Quetta. This represents a 130% increase over 1989, 1990, and 1991. If the political situation stabilizes, many more refugees will return (more than 600,000 are expected to return in 1993), thereby increasing the rate of death and injury due to landmines.[14]

In the face of this horrific situation, it is some comfort that Afghanistan has developed what is considered by some to be the most successful demining team system in the world. At the end of 1992, there were 31 teams consisting of 32 specialists each, operating with about 90 mine detection dogs and two mine flails. The demining program is administered by Afghan personnel with U.N. supervision and technical advice through the United Nations Organization for Coordinating Humanitarian Assistance for Afghanistan (UNOCHA). The U.N. estimates that it can clear a priority 60 square kilometers in Afghanistan within six years at a cost of $60 million.[15]

As in most locations, money is a problem. The Afghan government, such as it is, is unable to contribute any significant funding for demining. UNOCHA requested $15 million in FY1993, but, according to the U.S. State Department, is likely to receive less than half that amount. The U.S. Agency for International Development has an ongoing $2 million program to train dog teams.[16] Progress will also depend, of course, on the degree of political stability. Another outbreak of fighting could rapidly overwhelm all that has been accomplished so far.

---

[14] Ibid., p. 30.

[15] DOS, *Hidden Killers*, p. 28.

[16] Ibid., p. 42.

## LANDMINE DISASTERS

**Country      Number of Uncleared Mines**

| Country | Number of Uncleared Mines |
|---|---|
| Afghanistan | 9-10 million |
| Angola | 9 million |
| Iraq | 5-10 million |
| Kuwait | 5-7 million |
| Cambodia | 4-7 million |
| Mozambique | 2 million |
| Bosnia | 1-1.7 million |
| Somalia | 1-1.5 million |
| Croatia | 1 million |
| Sudan | .5-2 million |
| Serbia | .5-1 million |
| Ethiopia/Eritrea | .3-1 million |
| Iran | unknown |

Source:  U.S. Department of State, *Hidden Killers*, July 1993. The State Department considers the landmine problem in these nations "extremely severe."  Those considered "severe" include Burma, Chad, El Salvador, Falkland/Malvinas, Morocco/Western Sahara, Nicaragua, Thailand, and Vietnam.  See "Countries Which Have Reported Landmine Incidents" Map.

## Angola[17]

Landmines have claimed tens of thousands of victims in Angola. Even during the relative peace that prevailed between the signing of the ceasefire in May 1991 and the elections in September 1992, much of Angola remained uninhabitable or dangerous, in large part due to the vast number of landmines scattered throughout the nation.

Estimates of the number of landmines planted in Angola run as high as 20 million, but a more likely total is nine million.[18] Only Afghanistan is more heavily mined.

The future of Angola looks bleak. A return to fighting has resulted in many deaths already. Mines are again being laid in great numbers every day. The widespread and indiscriminate use of antipersonnel landmines—in violation of international law—will likely continue to be a significant feature of the war, as it has been in the past. The warring parties deserve international opprobrium if they return to their former tactics of landmine usage and do not clear mines already laid.

Angola itself does not manufacture mines; all the devices found in the country have been supplied by foreign manufacturers, governments, and arms dealers. Africa Watch has confirmed that 37 types of mines have been used in Angola, including 21 antipersonnel mines. The actual number is probably greater. While minelaying was practiced in Angola from 1961 onwards until 1991, the great majority of mines were laid in the period between 1975 and 1988.

Mines have been laid for a variety of military purposes, such as protecting key installations and denying the use of roads and bridges to the enemy. Few of these minefields have been recorded or marked; there have rarely been any attempts to protect civilians from the dangers they pose. Perhaps the most common use of mines has been their random dissemination in and around villages. While there may have been a slender military rationale for this use, its main impact has been to render paths, fields and villages unusable to civilians except at great personal

---

[17] The following is adapted from Africa Watch, *Land Mines in Angola*, (New York: Africa Watch, January 1993). Unless otherwise noted, all information is from that report.

[18] DOS, *Hidden Killers*, p. 45, cites nine million as the best estimate.

danger, thereby terrorizing the community. It is evident that the great majority of landmines in Angola have been deployed in flagrant disregard of the rules set forth in the Landmines Protocol.

Angola suffers from one of the highest per capita ratios of landmine victims in the world, second in all probability only to Cambodia. At least 15,000 Angolans are amputees as a consequence of stepping on landmines; about half of these are soldiers and half civilians. Children are also frequent victims. Civilians are injured in their fields, on paths, roads, riverbanks, and inside built-up areas. The medical care and physical and social rehabilitation of these people is a challenge and a burden to Angola. Evacuation and medical facilities are inadequate. At least 5,000 prostheses will be needed each year for the foreseeable future for the amputees, far more than are currently manufactured.

Even if peace returns, civilian casualties due to landmines will continue. As Angolans try to reclaim the use of their land, casualties will mount. Mines have rendered large areas of arable land and pasture, many roads, bridges, riverbanks and villages, and some important economic installations, off-limits to people. The presence of live mines represents a formidable obstacle to commerce and free movement, to economic reconstruction, and to the effective delivery of relief and other forms of aid. In particular, mines will prevent the rapid and safe return of refugees.

The resumption of war has put an end to initial demining efforts. The major program to clear landmines consisted of joint clearance efforts by the two armies. Some roads, railways, key economic installations and towns were cleared. However, the teams lacked much basic equipment and had no effective central coordination. In addition, a number of foreign governments, private companies and humanitarian organizations were involved in mine clearance operations. Some of these programs were seriously flawed, such as the British "training" program discussed in detail later in this section. Other governments and companies were notable by their absence or small-scale involvement—for example, the United States. A more concerted attempt to eradicate landmines in Angola will be needed in the future.

## I.      Technical Assessment

### A. Assessments of the Total Landmine Threat

No one knows the true extent of the landmine crisis in Angola. Brigadier Fann Grobbelaar, a mines expert with the South African Defense Force (SADF), noting that some mines in Angola date back to the independence struggle against Portugal, said, "The whole of Angola must be considered a mined area." The U.S. State Department has declared Angola's landmine problem "extremely severe," and stated that "the natural resources with which Angola abounds have been rendered inaccessible by mines. In addition, mining of the national road network has made any travel by vehicle extremely dangerous...the land surrounding any city, airport, village, farm, bridge, etc. is potentially hazardous, as well as all major roads."[19]

Some estimates have been made of the number of landmines in Angolan soil, and the size of the operations needed to clear certain sectors. As part of its July 1993 global survey, the U.S. State Department cited nine million landmines as the best estimate.[20]   Colonel Bob Griffiths of the British Army Royal Engineers and chief of the British Military Mission in Angola, told Africa Watch that there "are twenty million mines in Angola spread over one third of the land mass." He claimed that this figure was extrapolated from known supplies of landmines to Angola and other intelligence.  Colonel Griffiths further estimated that, of the twenty million mines, "four million are recorded and still in the ground, six million have been lifted or have functioned and eight million are unaccounted for." He could not give any details or explanation for his arithmetic, nor how these figures were arrived at, nor where the four million "recorded" mines were laid.  He also estimated that 52,000 kilometers of roads had been mined, though he also claimed that most of these roads had been cleared—a highly contestable claim.

Griffiths went on to say that 100 different mine types had been used in Angola, of which 46 had been recorded.  He was unable to explain on what basis the initial figure was estimated, but said that mines:

---

[19] DOS, *Hidden Killers*, p. 45.

[20] Ibid.

were supplied by twelve different countries, of which
Portugal, Russia, Cuba, South Africa and East Germany
were the prime suppliers. There are also British and US
mines and devices from many eastern bloc countries.
Many mines are thought to have been supplied through
individual commercial deals rather than as government
to government support.

According to the Joint Mine Clearance Committee, between June
and September 1991, a total of 22,124 mines were cleared.   Major-
General Helder Cruz, the senior Angolan army officer responsible for
mine clearance, claims that 50,000 mines were cleared by joint Angolan
army/UNITA teams in the year after May 1991.

### B.  Mine Types and Sources

Below is Africa Watch's list of 21 types of antipersonnel mines
that have been deployed in Angola.[21]   This count is based on physical
inspection of the mines themselves or detailed descriptions of them.   It
is likely that some additional types have been used.

1.  M409 blast mine, manufactured by PRB of Belgium.
2.  Type 72 mine, a small plastic mine, manufactured by China.
3.  Type 72b mine, a similar mine with a metal tilt
    mechanism, manufactured by China.
4.  Valmara VS-69 bounding, manufactured by Valsella of
    Italy.
5.  VS Mk-2 scatterable, manufactured by Valsella of Italy.
6.  USK, manufactured in South Africa.
7/8.  M16A1 and M16A2 bounding mine, manufactured in the
    U.S.A.
9.  M14 mine, a small plastic blast mine, manufactured in the
    U.S.A.

---

[21] The U.S. State Department's list of mines found in Angola includes 18 of
these 21 mines.   Not included are the U.S. M14, Belgian M409, and South
African USK.   In addition to those mines cited by Africa Watch, the State
Department's list includes the PPM-2 (made by China and the former East
Germany).  DOS, *Hidden Killers*, p. 45.

10. PMN blast mine, a very common mine, manufactured by Soviet State Arsenals.

11. PMN-2 blast mine, an advanced version of the PMN, manufactured in the former U.S.S.R.

12. PMD-6 blast mine, a widely copied design, manufactured by Soviet State Arsenals.

13/14. POMZ-2 and POMZ-2M fragmentation mines, mounted on a wooden stake, with a tripwire, manufactured by Soviet State Arsenals.

15. PP-MI-SR bounding mine, manufactured in former Czechoslovakia.

16. DM-11 mine, manufactured by DIEHL Ordnance Division, Rothenbach, (West) Germany.

17. DM-31 mine, manufactured in Germany.

18. MIM-25-ANO8 mine, (no reliable information available).

19. M18A1 directional ambush mine (Claymore), can be fired remotely or tripwire initiated, manufactured by Thiokol Corp. and others in U.S.A., and also widely copied in different countries.

20. MON-50 directional ambush mine, a virtually identical Soviet derivative of the Claymore, manufactured by Soviet State Arsenals.

21. MON-100 directional ambush mine, a larger version of the MON-50, manufactured by Soviet State Arsenals.

## C. Landmine Records

Existing records on the locations of landmines are extremely scanty. The Angolan army (FAPLA) appears to have kept records of the defensive minefields laid around economic installations and important military bases, but not those randomly disseminated in the countryside. However, the FAPLA maps remain secret.

The South African Defense Forces (SADF) are known to have mapped some of the minefields they laid on their incursions into Angola, and may have used these records in their clearance operations in the south of the country.

UNITA appears to have recorded very few of the mines that its forces (known as FALA) laid. British Army Major M.G. Cox, who conducted a 1991 survey of landmines in Angola wrote:

In general, UNITA mines were laid randomly and without record. Their minefields were of the nuisance type designed to deny key routes and industrial mining facilities to the MPLA (Popular Movement for the Liberation of Angola). Their most extensive mining operations were along major roads and all of the railways. In order to prevent easy clearance of these mines, UNITA extensively used anti-handling/booby trap devices.

The Cuban forces were also responsible for laying landmines. There are varying accounts of the practices used by the Cubans, some claiming that most Cuban minefields were accurately recorded, and others claiming that the Cubans kept no records at all.

The United States government was a significant though inconsistent supporter of UNITA, providing financial and military support. At least seven types of U.S.-manufactured mines are present in Angolan soil. Major Cox of the British army noted that "the mines laid by UNITA forces were mainly from the U.S.A." He did not, however, say who was the immediate supplier of mines to UNITA. His fellow British officer, Colonel Griffiths also declined to characterize the U.S. as a major direct supplier of mines. The United States government has not accepted that it bears any responsibility for the large number of U.S.-made mines in Angola.

## II.    The Human Dimension

Angola has one of the highest rates of landmine injuries per capita in the world. Out of a population of about nine million, it has many thousands of amputees, the great majority of them injured by landmines. The government claims that there are 55,000 amputees in the country. The International Committee of the Red Cross (ICRC) has a more conservative figure of 15,000, but that refers to lower-limb amputees only, excluding those who have lost an arm or their sight, or who have been otherwise maimed or disfigured by landmines. Even the extremely conservative figure of 20,000 victims seriously maimed by landmine injuries implies a rate of injury that would be equivalent to 500,000 people in a country the size of the United States.

The government has produced figures only for mine fatalities among FAPLA soldiers: between 1975 and 1991, 6,728 were killed by mine explosions. In reality, however, there are no reliable estimates for the total number of people killed by landmines. Because of the scarcity of medical care for the civilian population, the true figure probably is very high.

It appears that the provinces of Bie and Huambo have suffered a disproportionate share of landmine injuries. However, the landmine problem is also very severe in the south and east, particularly in Moxico Province. About half of those admitted to the ICRC center for amputees at Bomba Alto, near Huambo, are soldiers, and half are civilians.

The great majority of the soldiers are, of course, young men. This means that overall, a disproportionate number of those disabled by landmines in Angola are young men, a fact which has contributed to the militancy of many amputees in demanding their rights.

Among the civilians, there is a wide spread of casualties. Men and women of all ages are affected. Children are an important minority of those affected by landmines. For example, a 1990 survey of 113 landmine victims by the ICRC found that 29 were children.[22]

## A. Where the Mines are Planted

The great majority of mine victims interviewed had been injured by antipersonnel mines. Africa Watch's 1992 survey of 45 landmine victims found that only two were injured by antivehicle mines. The 1990 ICRC survey found that 96 of 113 victims had been injured by antipersonnel mines (84%). However, antivehicle mines typically caused many more deaths; for example one mine that had been set off by a truck killed five and injured 10 passengers.

---

[22] The surveys used in this chapter were done in 1990 and 1992 by Africa Watch and in 1990 by the ICRC. In 1990, Africa Watch collected information on 47 landmine incidents from interviews, including specific information on 26 victims. The 1992 Africa Watch Survey was based on interviews with 45 victims, in Kuito-Bíe, Huambo, and Viana in Luanda Province and Luanda City. The 1990 ICRC Survey was based on interviews with 113 landmine victims from eight provinces. See Africa Watch, *Landmines in Angola* (New York: Human Rights Watch, January 1993), pp. 26–36.

The ICRC survey distinguished three categories of places where mines were laid: paths, roads, and villages or towns. It found 69% of victims injured on paths, 15% on roads and 16% in inhabited areas.

The Africa Watch 1990 and 1992 surveys combined found that, out of a sample of 57 cases of civilian injuries, 35 occurred on paths, making these the most common sites of civilian mine injury. The victims were walking to fields, schools, markets, or medical centers.

Roads and roadsides are the second most frequent sites of landmine injuries. Both antivehicle and antipersonnel mines are common. Eleven out of the Africa Watch sample of 57 civilian victims had been injured on roads, nine of them by antipersonnel mines. Eleven of the 17 people in the ICRC survey injured on roads had been injured by antipersonnel mines. The risk of injury from roadside antipersonnel mines is particularly high, affecting people who left the road to follow a short-cut, to rest, or to urinate.

Many mines have been laid in built-up areas. Five of the 57 civilian victims studied by Africa Watch involved people injured inside towns and villages. The ICRC survey of 113 mine victims included 18 who were injured in this way. On occasion, villages have suffered a spate of landmine casualties within a short space of time—usually after a UNITA attack, or after a military presence in the area. Fear of landmines has led to the wholesale desertion of villages. About two-thirds of all mine accidents occur less than five kilometers from the village or town, giving the lie to the notion that there is a "safe zone" close to habitations.

In addition, many mines have been planted on riverbanks, especially around bridges. As bridges and their approaches are a well-known location for mines, civilians tend to be very careful. Some mines are left on or in the vicinity of railroad tracks. These are intended to disable trains, or to catch people who use the tracks and the embankments as footpaths. Only three out of the 57 civilian victims identified by Africa Watch were injured in fields.

## B. Who Laid the Mines

The majority of mines are attributed to UNITA. In Africa Watch's 1990 survey of 47 cases, 20 injuries and five deaths were attributed to UNITA, and 20 injuries and two deaths to "unknown persons." It may be that in some of those "unknown" cases, people knew the responsible parties but declined to identify them. This would be especially the case if the perpetrator was FAPLA, as most interviews were conducted in FAPLA-controlled territory. In many cases, however, the situation was genuinely too ambiguous to identify who was responsible.

In Africa Watch's 1992 survey of 45 mine victims, six said that FAPLA was to blame (including one soldier blown up by a mine his colleagues had planted earlier), 27 said UNITA, and 12 said that they did not know. Many of the "don't knows", particularly the six who were interviewed in Luanda, may have been reluctant to mention FAPLA.

In very few cases were civilians warned that mines had been planted in a certain area. Residents relied solely on observing military activity and on the incidence of mine injuries to discover which areas were safe and which were not.

### C. Emergency Care for the Injured

For most civilians injured by landmines, first-aid was available within a few hours. For soldiers, assistance was usually more rapid, with immediate evacuation often by helicopter or vehicle. The first-aid was usually extremely rudimentary, consisting of no more than bandaging the wound and providing comfort and perhaps some painkilling drugs. For civilians, transport to the nearest first-aid post usually involved being carried manually or by cart; onward transport to a hospital was usually by car or sometimes by airplane.

Civilians had to wait on average for about thirty-six hours before arriving at a hospital. One man interviewed by Africa Watch believed that it had been six days before he received hospital treatment.

### D. Medical Care and Rehabilitation

Care and rehabilitation for FAPLA soldiers is the responsibility of the Serviço de Ajuda Médica-Militar (SAMM) of FAPLA. It functions well, in part because the government and military attract good people by offering benefits and access to goods.

Civilians receive treatment in civilian hospitals. Adequate treatment is scarce. Drugs are often in short supply, and the staff are less qualified and motivated than in government-run hospitals. The variable quality of medical care means that hospitals can be dangerous for amputees. Wounds may become infected and secondary or even tertiary amputations often are needed. There has also been a high incidence of osteomyelitis, a bone-wasting disease, which may set in after a poorly-done amputation.

The existing facilities for rehabilitating landmine victims are grossly inadequate.  The ICRC has run its center at Bomba Alto, near Huambo, since 1980.  This includes 11 technicians working solely on the manufacture of artificial limbs and 78 workers in all.

Injured people come for a five week period to Huambo and are lodged there at the Red Cross shelter.  Ironically, those working and receiving limbs and therapy at the shelter cannot freely travel between Huambo and Bomba Alto, 10 kilometers away, because of the threat of landmines on the road.  At the center they are fitted with a prosthesis.

Some Angolan students are trained to become technicians at Bomba Alto; others study at the orthopaedic school in Huambo.  Artificial feet and limbs are made from wood.  Though there are woods nearby, it is not safe to enter the forests to cut the wood, because of landmines. Hence, the wood used has been brought in from Cabinda.  Other raw materials such as resin and nails are hard to find because of the economic situation of the country.

From January to November of 1990, 631 new civilian and military patients were fitted with prostheses at the center.  In total, 1,127 prostheses were manufactured in 1990, and 1,039 major repairs to prostheses were made during the same period.

The ICRC also has a center at Kuito, in the UNITA-controlled areas of the southeast which produces nearly two-thirds as many prostheses.  The Swedish Red Cross runs an orthopaedic center at Neves Bendinha and the Dutch Red Cross has one at Viana, Luanda Province. In its Jamba headquarters, UNITA's Special Department for War Wounded was set up in 1989.  It has at least three units caring for war amputees.  One of these is said to produce twenty artificial legs per month.

A prosthesis can only be expected to last two to three years, and children require new ones at least every year, as they outgrow the ones they have.  This means that a total of over 5,000 new prostheses is required every year, merely to cope with the existing number of amputees.  This is more than twice the number currently being manufactured.

### E. Social Rehabilitation

Angola remains a desperately poor country in which few facilities are available for the physically disabled. Most amputees are reluctant to leave the relative comfort of rehabilitation centers. Their future will consist of being cared for by their families, or attempting to earn a living in one of the few occupations open to them, such as street trading or—for those with education—secretarial work. The majority who come from farming backgrounds are likely to remain a burden on their families for the foreseeable future. Many have been reduced to begging; amputee beggars are already a common sight in Angolan towns. Angola will have to live with the human cost of the landmines war for many years to come.

### F. The Social and Economic Impact

Landmines have a significant impact on most areas of Angola's society and economy. There are tens of thousands of handicapped people. Thousands of acres of farmland, pasture and forest, and thousands of miles of riverbanks are unusable. For example, the fertile Mavinga valley in Cuando Cubango Province of southeast Angola is largely abandoned because of the vast quantities of mines laid there by UNITA and SADF. Roads and paths cannot be travelled, rivers cannot be crossed, either by bridge or ford. The return of refugees is particularly hazardous. Commerce and movement is obstructed, and relief supplies can only be delivered with great difficulty. The eradication of landmines is an essential prerequisite for peace and economic development.

The nature of the war in Angola has made the social and economic impact of landmines particularly severe. For the most part, it was not a positional war, with fighting confined to specific heavily militarized areas. At one time or another, almost every part of the country was affected, as the foci of battle shifted rapidly. Because of this mobility, the disruption of land communication and transport was a major aim of UNITA, and the mining of roads, paths and bridges was consequently an important strategy. UNITA's strategy aimed at destabilizing the government by making any semblance of normal life impossible in as many parts of the country as it could. Outside its base area of the southeast, it consolidated and administered few areas. Instead, it sought to deny the government free use of these areas. The wide dissemination of landmines was a central part of this strategy. Meanwhile, FAPLA laid mines to try to prevent UNITA forces operating throughout the country.

Landmines were therefore generally planted as part of a deliberate military strategy aimed at causing social and economic disruption. They will continue to have this effect long after the end of hostilities.

### III.    Mine Clearance Initiatives

There is a remarkable contrast between the widespread recognition that landmines present an extremely serious threat to Angola, and the actual response to the challenge of eradicating the mines during the period prior to the elections in September 1992, when relative peace prevailed and clearance initiatives were possible.

There has been no systematic assessment of the extent of the landmines problem, nor any serious attempt to coordinate eradication in an organized fashion. The clearance attempts by FAPLA and FALA teams were inadequately supported in technical, financial and logistical terms. In addition, there is at least one example of an initiative cynically based on potential profit and future business opportunities. If future mine clearing efforts are conducted in the same inadequate manner, then not only will there be needless casualties during the clearance operations, but there will be continuing large scale casualties among the civilian population.

#### A. FAPLA/FALA Teams

Several separate initiatives to clear landmines in Angola were underway prior to the resumption of hostilities. The intensity of the civil war has brought these efforts to a halt.

FAPLA/FALA teams consisted of soldiers from both armies. During the pre-election period, they were working throughout the country with varying success. FAPLA/FALA teams were using manual clearance methods, partly because of the lack of heavy equipment, and partly because they considered it the most effective. The priorities were to demine the major roads and railways, and the interiors of towns and villages. However, questions have been asked about how systematically the major roads were cleared.

There is general recognition of the limited impact of the Angolan demining effort. This is largely attributed to lack of organization, resources, and support. At a meeting on March 4, 1992, the Joint Mine Clearing Commission identified the following problems: serious command, control and communication problems at all levels; none of the mine clearing teams or regional mine clearing commissions had a radio or a vehicle; mine clearance teams lacked basic demining equipment such as helmets, flak vests, mine markers, engineer tape and demolition materials, as well as adequate, properly functioning detection equipment.

These problems persisted despite the involvement of British military teams in assisting FAPLA/FALA efforts.

### B. SADF Efforts

The South African Defense Forces were active in providing technical assistance and training to FAPLA/FALA clearance teams in the south of the country. In mid-1992, most sources agreed that the South African contribution was a well-motivated project based on a good knowledge of the general problems and the specific devices (many of which were laid by the SADF itself). All the Angolan parties responded positively to the South African initiative. A military representative of the U.S. Liaison Office in Luanda was more skeptical, however. He told Africa Watch that there was insufficient coordination and planning. This was the only significant criticism of the South African effort that Africa Watch was able to obtain.

### C. British Army Initiatives

British support to the Angolan mine-clearing operation consisted of two two-man Royal Engineer teams dispatched to instruct members of the integrated New Angolan Army (FAA) in minefield clearance techniques. The first mission was in December 1991, the second in March 1992. This training appears to have been of very low priority. In fact, most specialists would question whether the training had any practical value at all, particularly since the trainees had a more intimate knowledge of live mines than their trainers.

A restricted cable from the U.S. Liaison Office to the U.S. State Department shown to Africa Watch was very frank regarding the British training program. It said that although the British had obtained good public relations from their exercise, "effectively all they had done was give the Angolans thirty-six sets of Austrian detecting equipment."

A second aspect of British involvement also deserves mention.  The British policy was described by Colonel Griffiths and his colleagues as solely providing "neutral advice" to the Angolans, but it appears that it was motivated at least in part by the desire to bring commercial advantage to British firms.  Griffiths said that "the whole clearance initiative will be under the control of a joint Angolan-U.K. national coordination body which will be funded by donors such as the EEC."  He then went on to explain that the "major work" would be undertaken by a U.K. company and the South Africans.  He said that he could not reveal the name of the U.K. company because it was "commercial-in-confidence."  Further sub-contracts would be awarded to independent companies.

One of Griffiths' colleagues later confirmed to Africa Watch that the U.K. company involved was Royal Ordnance, and Africa Watch was later introduced to a Royal Ordnance representative who said he could be contacted through the British Embassy.  Royal Ordnance is the recently-privatized British arms manufacturer that is the major supplier of the British army, as well as an aggressive promoter of arms exports.

### D.  United States Involvement

When Africa Watch requested a clarification of planned U.S. involvement in mine eradication, the response indicated that the U.S. did not plan to assist with mine clearance.  The U.S. continues to refuse to confirm whether it supplied landmines to UNITA, but the extent of its military and political support to UNITA means that it bears a share of the responsibility for UNITA's use of landmines, and should aid mine clearance efforts.

### IV.    Conclusion

There is a very serious landmine problem throughout Angola, with certain parts of the country, such as Huambo, Bíe, Moxico and Cuando Cubango, being particularly severely affected.  All combatant forces, including FAPLA, FALA, the Cubans, and SADF, have been responsible for laying large numbers of landmines, especially antipersonnel landmines.  A variety of countries, such as the United

States and Italy, have manufactured landmines that have been used in Angola and will continue to be used in the present fighting.

Most of the mines have been laid without markings or warnings to the civilian population, and a large proportion have been laid in such a way that their victims are almost guaranteed to be civilians. As a result, a minimum of 15,000, and probably more than 20,000, Angolans are currently amputees as a result of landmine accidents, and many thousands more have been killed.

If and when a lasting peace is established, the human impact of the landmines is likely to increase in the short term, with the return home of refugees and displaced people and attempts by civilians to reclaim their villages, fields and pastures, and to travel along roads and paths still littered with active mines.

In peacetime, landmines will continue to present severe obstacles to the economic development of the country, the implementation of relief programs, and the return of refugees. Large areas of Angola will remain out-of-bounds for civilians until landmines are cleared and the community regains confidence in the land.

Facilities for the evacuation, emergency treatment, hospital treatment, and physical and social rehabilitation of landmine victims are inadequate. Hospital facilities are poor. More than 5,000 prostheses are required each year; current production is well under one-half of that number. The social needs of landmine victims are not attended to adequately.

Initiatives to clear landmines have been inadequate. Efforts by the Angolan government have suffered from lack of equipment, finance and coordination, and the international community does not appear to have made demining programs in Angola a high priority. Ironically, in view of its highly destructive military interventions in Angola, the South African clearance efforts appear to have been the best recent foreign initiative.

It is clear that in their use of landmines, all parties to the conflict in Angola have routinely violated the Landmines Protocol. There appear to have been no serious or systematic attempts to minimize civilian casualties from mines. Indeed, the strategies used for deployment of anti-personnel mines—such as random dissemination in inhabited areas, causing excessive civilian casualties and thereby terrorizing the population—clearly constitute a breach of international standards regulating means and methods of warfare.

The experience of Angola shows that antipersonnel landmines present a serious and long-term threat to civilians, far in excess of any short-term military advantage that may be gained.  Therefore, under international law, all parties to the current conflict should immediately suspend their use.  At a minimum, the Angolan government should sign and ratify the Landmines Protocol and abide by its provisions in any future internal or international conflicts.

The Angolan government should take steps to set up a systematic and coordinated mine clearance program that will eradicate mines in all areas that are used by civilians.  The Angolan government should launch an international appeal to solicit funds and expertise for this program to be carried out.

All combatant groups should provide expert personnel to assist future demining efforts in Angola.  All combatant groups should provide all available information about the types of mines they have used in Angola, the strategies of dissemination (including methods for preventing mine clearance) and the location of mines (including, wherever possible, minefield maps) to assist in clearance efforts.

The United Nations should take the lead in coordinating with the Angolan government, drawing up a national mine eradication program, and soliciting assistance for clearance.  All countries that have provided landmines to the parties that fought in Angola or manufactured landmines used there should contribute to the cost of the national mine eradication program.

## Cambodia[23]

Few countries exemplify humankind's capacity to inflict cruelty upon itself more than Cambodia. In the last 20 years, Cambodia's people have suffered a seemingly relentless series of man-made disasters—from the massive aerial bombardment by the United States in the early 1970s, to the rule of the murderous Khmer Rouge between 1975 and 1979, to the widespread famine which followed, and finally to a savage civil war.

Landmines have clearly been the weapon of choice of all parties in Cambodia since the Vietnamese invasion in 1979, but they were also used in the war at least a decade earlier. Cambodians are thus facing the task not just of clearing mines laid last year or the year before, but of finding and destroying mines laid regularly by different groups during the last two decades. Many of those mines are now overgrown by vegetation, immersed in water, or simply forgotten, but they may be no less lethal as a result.

In its recent global landmine survey, the U.S. State Department concludes, "In no country in the world have uncleared landmines had such an enormous adverse impact as in Cambodia." The report says that there are still no reliable estimates of the total number of uncleared landmines, but that estimates range from four to seven million.[24]

The menacing presence of these millions of landmines is a very real problem for Cambodia that affects most every aspect of the country's existence. Roughly half of the country contains sizeable concentrations of landmines.[25] Mines in Cambodia's interior and especially along its 700-kilometer border with Thailand are so widespread, they now rank as

---

[23] The following is adapted from *Land Mines In Cambodia: The Coward's War*, a report by Asia Watch and Physicians for Human Rights, dated September 1991. It also includes information collected by Physicians for Human Rights researchers in Cambodia in June 1993. Unless otherwise noted, all information is from the Asia Watch and Physicians for Human Rights report and the June 1993 mission.

[24] DOS, *Hidden Killers*, July 1993, p. 64.

[25] Heaviest concentrations are in Kampong Thom, Siem Reap, Kompong Chang, Kampong Speu, and Koh Kong provinces, and in Northwest Cambodia in Oddar Meanchey, Banteay Meanchey, Battambang, and Pursat provinces. Ibid., p. 65.

one of the country's greatest deterrents to economic development. The State Department calls Cambodia "a textbook case of a country crippled by uncleared landmines."[26] It notes that large amounts of agricultural land have been rendered unusable, that the road network is so infested in some areas that civilians can only travel on the smallest footpaths, and that rural populations displaced from their fields because of landmines have moved to Phnom Penh, more than doubling its population and placing grave strains on its limited infrastructure.[27]

Even today, government soldiers and Khmer Rouge guerrillas continue to lay landmines along footpaths, rice paddies, riverbeds, and around villages. Cambodian soldiers refer to landmines as their "eternal sentinels," never sleeping, always ready to attack. They see mines as a way of avoiding direct contact with the enemy and so have saturated contested areas with them on a scale unrelated to the actual military need or objective. Unless the mines are cleared and destroyed, they will kill or maim Cambodians well into the next century.

Renewed fighting between the Phnom Penh government and the Khmer Rouge in the summer of 1993, coupled with the eventual departure of U.N. demining training teams, will surely slow down efforts at mine clearance and begin another round of extensive mine laying, compounding today's tragic situation even further.

Cambodia, with a population of eight and a half million, already has the highest percentage of physically disabled inhabitants of any country in the world. There are now over 30,000 amputees in Cambodia. In 1990 alone, at least 6,000 Cambodians suffered amputations as a result of a mine injury. Most of the casualties were civilians—peasants who stepped on mines while gathering firewood, harvesting rice, herding animals, or fishing.

These grim statistics mean that the Cambodian conflict may be the first war in history in which landmines have claimed more victims—combatants and noncombatants alike—than any other weapon. The pervasive and indiscriminate use of landmines by the four warring factions in Cambodia has had significant medical, social, and psychological effects on Cambodia's civilian population, and will have long-term negative effects on future rehabilitation.

---

[26] Ibid., p. 37.

[27] Ibid.

## I.      Methods of Mine Warfare

Most of the mines in Cambodia were laid between December 1979 and October 1991, when Cambodia's warring factions signed the Agreements on a Comprehensive Political Settlement of the Cambodian Conflict in Paris. During this period, those responsible for laying mines throughout the country were military forces belonging to the Vietnamese government, which invaded Cambodia in December 1978; the Vietnamese-backed government of Hun Sen, known as the People's Republic of Kampuchea (PRK); and the three resistance forces: the Khmer Rouge; the Khmer People's National Liberation Front (KPNLF), headed by former prime minister Son Sann; and Prince Sihanouk's United Front for an Independent, Neutral, Peaceful and Cooperative Cambodia (FUNCINPEC), whose military wing was known as the Sihanouk National Army (ANS).

For all parties to the Cambodian conflict from 1979-1991, the main purpose of laying landmines was to limit military operations by enemy forces: to deny opponents access to bridges, roads or strategic installations or to protect one's own forces from attack. In addition, all forces used mines as offensive weapons. Government troops, for example, placed mines around the perimeters of enemy villages and then bombarded them with artillery fire so that the "enemy" was forced to flee into minefields. The Khmer Rouge used mines to channel and control the movement of people in the areas they control. Thai and Khmer black marketeers, often with the blessing of resistance forces, used mines to secure their trade routes.

One particularly deadly improvisation used by all factions was the multiple stacking of mines. This was done to hinder their removal by enemy forces or to increase the explosive effect and range of the mines. In its most extreme form, a tactic employed by Phnom Penh, an antitank mine called the TM-46 was placed above a standard pressure mine called the PMN with a Type 69 bounding mine at the bottom of the stack. The combination could be initiated in three ways. First, it could be detonated by a tank or heavy vehicle. Second, a person, exerting only .23 kilograms of pressure could detonate the stack; thus, even a child could easily initiate the combination. This turned the TM-46 into an antipersonnel mine with an explosive content of more than five kilograms of TNT. Finally, the Type 69 mine could be remotely detonated by a buried pull-wire attached to a hidden firing position.

The sheer number of landmines and their indiscriminate use by all sides in the conflict resulted in tens of thousands of civilian deaths and injuries. Exacerbating the problem is the fact that, by all accounts, none of the forces kept systematic records of mined areas. In 1991, a Red Cross worker in Battambang, Cambodia, put it this way:

> The problem with mines here in Cambodia, in comparison to other areas, is that they are the most important weapon. They are used as offensive weapons, as aggressive weapons....Here there is not a lot of direct confrontation. What you have is a concentration of soldiers in one place, the resistance will circle the area with mines then retreat and shell the area so the soldiers flee through the mined area....There are no maps because mines are given to soldiers like bullets.

### A. The Phnom Penh Government and Vietnamese Forces

Both the government PRK army and the Vietnamese forces employed a landmine strategy which incorporated the following elements: the mass dissemination of mines, primarily to secure Cambodia's borders from incursions by resistance forces; the selective defense of key military and civilian installations and strong points; and, the laying of mines to curtail contact between villagers and insurgents. Because of where and how these mines were placed, they have posed an unacceptably high risk to the civilian population, in contravention of the terms of the Landmines Protocol.

The Vietnamese laid mines in Cambodia in mid-1979, as they pushed the fleeing Khmer Rouge across the border into Thailand. It appears, however, that no attempt was ever made to record the location of these minefields, and Phnom Penh military sources claim that no maps have been handed over to the government by the Vietnamese Army. One key strategy used by the Vietnamese forces was to saturate the roads, trails and ground surrounding their bases and forward posts with mines. Antipersonnel mines were also used to channel and slow down resistance forces, often using inter-linked tripwire devices such as the POMZ-2, a Soviet-made antipersonnel mine. But the most damaging strategy introduced by the Vietnamese was the use of mines to isolate insurgents from their civilian supporters in the villages by mining rice paddies and the margins of forests. The Phnom Penh forces have continued to use these strategies since the Vietnamese withdrawal in 1989.

Although there are no reliable maps of minefields or individual mines placed along Cambodia's border with Thailand, both the incidence and the geographic spread of landmine casualties would suggest that there are hundreds of thousands—perhaps millions—of mines in the area.

Government troops used mines to protect key installations, especially bridges, from sabotage. Government troops also used mines to limit contact between insurgents and villagers. This objective was usually achieved through the random deployment of antipersonnel devices, such as the PMN-2 and POMZ-2, on the edges of forests close to towns and villages and in other areas where clandestine meetings were likely to take place. Strong points under siege or threat of attack were also heavily mined, leaving only key access routes clear.[28] To this day, such mine concentrations make agricultural and surrounding lands inaccessible.

## B.  Resistance Forces

Like the Phnom Penh government, the three resistance forces were heavily influenced by foreign military training. Khmer Rouge mine strategy tended to mirror Chinese doctrine, while the strategy of the KPNLF and the ANS—the two non-communist resistance forces—reflected British special forces training.  Chinese training of the Khmer Rouge, and the British/Thai Junior Commander Course attended by KPNLF and ANS officers until 1989 devoted considerable sections of the curriculum to the use of improvised explosive devices and booby-traps.

These Junior Commander courses, each lasting six months, were conducted from 1986 to 1989 at a Thai military facility believed to be near the Burmese border. At least six courses are known to have taken place. Instruction was carried out by a uniformed British Army team drawn from the Special Air Service(SAS) and the Royal Thai Army. Each course consisted of 50 students, 25 each from the ANS and KPNLF, who were selected on the basis of their physical fitness and weapons knowledge.

---

[28] Even these were routinely mined during hours of darkness; at daybreak mines would be removed, and the access routes reopened.

The Chinese provided training to all the resistance factions but, as would be expected, given their political stance, the most comprehensive instruction was reserved for Khmer Rouge forces. A Chinese military manual used in the training of both KPNLF and Khmer Rouge fighters emphasizes the use of improvised booby-traps, often employing "over-kill" quantities of explosives for maximum physical and anti-morale effect.

Resistance fighters told a joint Asia Watch and Physicians for Human Rights team visiting Cambodia and the Thai border camps in February and March 1991 that they often bombarded villages with mortars or artillery shells until the occupying troops or civilians retreated into the forest. The resistance fighters then advanced into the village and laid mines before withdrawing. Several resistance fighters and noncombatants said that water sources, access routes, and surrounding farmland were heavily mined, a statement supported by evidence of casualties among those who tried to return to villages. They also said that all sides booby-trapped dwellings and common buildings.

The Khmer Rouge seemed to use mines in a somewhat more sophisticated manner, but no less indiscriminately, than the KPNLF and ANS. The Khmer Rouge often used mines to channel and control population movements. This suggests that they may have kept some records of minefields. However, there is also evidence that the Khmer Rouge randomly deployed mines in the same way as other factions in areas not under their control; this is particularly evident in Kampong Speu province.

All resistance factions converted grenades into mines by a simple tripwire device. They were used in jungle areas and close to river banks, normally hung from, or fastened to, tree branches several feet from the ground.

Resistance forces routinely booby-trapped mines to prevent their removal by placing a pressure-release device below the primary mine or linking it to another device, often a hand-grenade, by a hidden tripwire. The Khmer Rouge have relied heavily on booby traps. Their training programs place considerable emphasis on fairly complex traps, often adaptable to use with large quantities of explosive.

## II. Types of Landmines and Other Devices in Use in Cambodia

Given the extraordinary number of types of mines in use in Cambodia, it is impossible to give a comprehensive picture of all the mines used by both government and resistance forces. The following information, however, is thought to be indicative of the current situation and a realistic overview of mass mine-laying strategy, particularly in the border "belt," used by the Phnom Penh government and resistance forces.

### A. The Phnom Penh Government

The types of antipersonnel mines used by Phnom Penh's PRK forces included:

1. PMN/PMN-2, manufactured by Soviet State Arsenals, used extensively throughout the Thai border belt.
2. POMZ-2/POMZ-2M, manufactured by Soviet State Arsenals.
3. Ball-Mine (P40), manufactured by Vietnam State Factories.
4. Type 72, a small, plastic antipersonnel mine used by both government and Khmer Rouge forces, manufactured in China. Devices set in the anti-disturbance role are often referred to as "72B."
5. "Duen" mine, supplied by Vietnam; little is known about this Vietnamese device reportedly widely used by government troops. Some sources say it is locally improvised and varies in size.
6. OZM-3, manufactured by Soviet State Arsenals, a bounding fragmentation mine frequently referred to as a Type 72, causing some confusion. These were used in large numbers in some heavily forested areas of Cambodia. They were also used by resistance factions, particularly the Khmer Rouge.
7. MON-50/MON-100, manufactured by Soviet State Arsenals, directional fragmentation mines used on the border primarily as ambush and position-defense weapons. The MON-50 is a copy of the U.S.-manufactured M18A1 Claymore mine.

### B. The Resistance Forces

The type of mines used by the resistance forces included:

1. M16A1/M16A2, provided by the U.S.A., Greece & India, manufactured in the U.S.A., in Greece (Hellenic Arms Industry SA), and India (Ordnance Factory Board, Calcutta), a bounding antipersonnel mine, of American origin, used by both Khmer Rouge and KPNLF forces.

2. Type 72, manufactured by China, reportedly used by the Khmer Rouge, although there is no available information on whether the mines were captured from government forces or supplied by other sources.

3. Type 69, manufactured by China North Industries, a bounding mine widely used by all factions in conjunction with other devices.

4. PMN-2, the most common mine in use in Cambodia, was heavily deployed by government troops. Resistance forces, however, also referred to it as their own mine, calling it the "Singapore Mine." The Khmer Rouge have also been reported to use the PMN-2 as a standard weapon.

5. MD-82B, probably provided by Vietnam, used infrequently, by all three resistance factions.

6. Valsella Valmara 69, provided by Italy and Singapore, manufactured by Valsella Meccanotecnica SpA and Chartered Industries of Singapore, a bounding mine.

7. M14, provided by the U.S.A. and India (Ordnance Factory Board, Calcutta), a non-metallic, blast mine used by the KPNLF and ANS forces, and possibly the Khmer Rouge.

8. PMD-6, provided by China, USSR and others, easily produced locally, this simple but effective pressure mine consists of a hinged wooden box containing a block of TNT and a detonator.

9. Type-59, a Chinese-supplied version of the POMZ-2. It has been used primarily by the Khmer Rouge.

10. M2A4, provided by the USA, a bounding fragmentation mine, used by the KPNLF.

11. M18A1 "Claymore," the most common U.S.-produced mine, often subject to unlicensed production and copies by many countries, it is a directional fragmentation mine manufactured at the Thiokol/U.S. Army facility in Louisiana. It is known to have been deployed by the KPNLF.

Information contained in a recent U.S. Defense Intelligence Agency report on landmines largely corresponds to this list which is based on field work by Asia Watch and Physicians for Human Rights.[29] The DIA report states that all mines identified have been manually laid and activated by pressure, pressure release, or tripwire, including blast, fragmentation, and heavy directional fragmentation mines. "Of particular concern," according to the DIA, "is the increased employment of boobytrapped mines or the use of mines incorporating their own anti-disturbance features."[30]

### III.    Medical Care

Cambodia today has the highest percentage of mine amputees of any country in the world. In 1991, surgeons in Cambodia performed between 300 and 700 amputations a month because of mine injuries. Experts estimate that one out of every 236 Cambodians has lost one or more limbs after stepping on a landmine. By comparison, approximately one out of every 2,500 Vietnamese is handicapped as a result of a mine explosion. Recent reports by the U.S. government note that there are reportedly over 30,000 amputees currently in Cambodia, with some 5,000-6,000 amputees in Thailand waiting to be repatriated.[31] The DIA study also states that during 1990, at least 6,000 Cambodians suffered shattered limbs and amputations as a result of exploding mines.[32]

According to Khmer and foreign surgeons working in Cambodia, for every mine victim who makes it to hospital another will die in the fields or on the way to hospital. No one, however, knows exactly how

---

[29] DIA/FSTC, p. 2-28. The DIA does not list the Italian Valmara 69, Chinese Type 59, Soviet MON-50, or Vietnamese "Duen" mines. Mines listed by the DIA, but not Human Rights Watch and Physicians for Human Rights include the Hungarian M-62; Yugoslav PMA-2 and PMA-3; Bulgarian PSM-1; Chinese Type 58 and Type 66; Czechoslovak PP-Mi-Sr; East German PPM-2; and Vietnamese MN-79, NOMZ 2B, MIN, MBV 78A2, POMZ-2B, MDH, MDH-2/-3/-4/-5/-7/-8/-10.

[30] DIA/FSTC, p.2-24.

[31] DIA/FSTC, p. 2-23; *Hidden Killers*, pp. 30-31.

[32] DIA/FSTC, p. 2-23.

many have died, nor is it likely that anyone ever will, since no institution has kept records of war-related deaths among civilians.

## A. The Health Care System

In early 1979, when the Vietnamese ousted the Khmer Rouge from power and installed a puppet government headed by Hun Sen, Cambodia had one of the most underdeveloped health care systems in the world. Only 25 doctors remained after the Vietnamese invasion. There were virtually no nurses and a severe shortage of medicines.

From 1979 to 1991, in spite of the civil war and a paucity of international aid, the Phnom Penh government made some progress in reconstructing and rehabilitating the health delivery system in Cambodia. As of mid-1991, Cambodia had 10,000 hospital beds—a 10-fold increase since the Khmer Rouge period—and more than 500 Khmer physicians. However, international health assessment teams routinely found them to be poorly trained, and isolated from primary care developments in other parts of the world.

The Asia Watch and Physicians for Human Rights team which visited Cambodia in 1991 found that blood was in critically short supply in nearly every hospital. For landmine victims, the availability of blood can often mean life or death. The team also found that hospitals in or near conflict areas were in serious need of x-ray film, anesthetics, antibiotics, latex gloves, and surgical supplies.

Cambodian hospitals were poorly equipped to deal with war injuries. In 1991, they were so overcrowded that many patients slept outside on cots. Most of the patients in surgical wards were victims of mine blasts. They laid on bamboo mats or propped themselves up against soot-black walls, as flies swarmed about their bandaged stumps.

In June 1993, a Physicians for Human Rights team travelled to Cambodia and revisited many of the hospitals that the Asia Watch and Physicians for Human Rights team had visited in 1991. In two years, conditions in most of the hospitals had improved largely as a result of the efforts of the ICRC and other international medical relief agencies, such as Medecins du Monde, World Vision, and Medecins sans Frontieres. Some hospitals appeared in better physical condition, with freshly painted walls and new operating rooms. Development agencies had built new sanitation facilities and installed water wells. The ICRC had held a training workshop on treating patients with mine injuries for Cambodian surgeons in Phnom Penh. Blood was in greater supply in many hospitals thanks to the revival of the National Blood Transfusion Center by the ICRC and the Ministry of Health in Phnom Penh, and the presence of blood banks in five provinces. Overcrowding in many of the hospitals appeared to have dissipated.

Most importantly, the Physicians for Human Rights team found that the number of patients admitted to hospital with mine injuries had declined since the signing of the peace accords in Paris in October 1991. Admissions records in three major hospitals located in northwestern Cambodia showed that the rate had dropped by almost half. Most Cambodian and foreign doctors attributed this decline to decreased fighting, the marking of mined areas by mines clearance teams with the United Nations and non-governmental organizations such as the Mines Advisory Group and Halo Trust, and a greater awareness among the Khmer of the location of mined areas and alternate routes around them.

### B.  Treatment and Rehabilitation

Most Cambodian amputees leave the hospital with little hope for the future. There are no rehabilitation centers, and Cambodia has no laws to protect amputees against discrimination or exploitation. Female amputees are less desirable as wives because they cannot work in the fields. In some cases, women have abandoned their disabled husbands as they have become more impoverished. Many amputees have drifted to Phnom Penh or larger towns and become beggars or petty criminals.

Amputees often find that they cannot compete with the able-bodied for farm land, even though they can still supervise the farming or actually till the fields themselves. In 1988, the Phnom Penh government formally abandoned its policy of collective farms and began a program of land reform. Land was divided based on the number of active adults in the family. As a result, families with amputees received less land or less valuable land than families without amputees.

According to Benoit Denise, Handicap International's representative in Cambodia, only half of Cambodia's amputees have artificial limbs. He says that many amputees may wait up to 10 years before they approach his organization for a prosthesis. By then it may be too difficult to fit the amputee with an artificial limb.

Cambodia has a very limited institutional ability to deal with the disabled. By its own laws, the past Hun Sen government was supposed to provide the disabled with a monthly pension, but relief agencies reported that these payments were often paid in a single lump sum soon after the accident or never paid at all. Until October 1991, the lion's share of care for the disabled was done by administrators and technicians with Handicap International and the American Friends Service Committee. Despite their valiant efforts, the number of artificial limbs they turned out (1,300 a year) fell far short of the demand. In 1991, only one in eight amputees received an artificial limb, and most of them were soldiers. At that rate it would have taken over 25 years to handle the existing waiting list of mine victims.

By law, the Ministry of Social Action has been required to fit soldiers with artificial limbs before civilians. After discharge from hospital, soldiers, especially higher ranking officers, are often transported individually or in groups to the prosthetic workshops. Civilians, on the other hand, are discharged from hospital and left to fend for themselves. Even though they may have heard about the workshops from fellow patients or hospital staff, they often opt to return directly to their villages rather than pay the extra expense. Many are not even aware of the advantages of prosthetic devices.

Today, there are 12 workshops in Cambodia that produce artificial limbs for amputees. Most of the centers are operated jointly by Handicap International and the Ministry of Social Action. Four other organizations also manufacture prosthetic devices in Cambodia: American Friends Service Committee, International Committee of the Red Cross, Vietnam Veterans of America Foundation, and Cambodia Trust. In October 1991, Handicap International entered into an agreement with the ICRC to replace their largely wooden and leather prosthetics for a polypropylene model developed by the Red Cross. Handicap International also agreed to turn over its workshop in Battambang Province, which is one of Cambodia's most heavily mined provinces, to the ICRC.

These arrangements appear to have helped increase both the quality and quantity of prosthetics available for Cambodian amputees. The ICRC reports that it started out producing 76 artificial limbs per month when it took over the workshop in Battambang but is now running an average of 130 per month. This yearly output from one workshop alone exceeds the production for all the prosthetic workshops in 1991. The ICRC reports that the Battambang center has filled over 1,150 requests for artificial limbs since it opened in August 1991.[33]

The ICRC has also introduced an incentive program for village leaders that encourages them to seek out amputees and to notify the workshop staff, who will send transport to bring them to the workshop. (At the Mongol Borei hospital, about two hours drive north of Battambang, the ICRC also pays taxi and mototaxi drivers a bonus for bringing in people with mine injuries.) Once the mine injured arrive at the ICRC workshop, they are given free housing and meals while they await their new artificial limbs—a process which can take two to three weeks.

## IV.    Mine Eradication

Of course, finding and clearing mines before they maim or kill would be far better than the best prosthesis or system of medical care for victims. But by 1991, there was little consensus and considerable confusion in the international community as to how the problem of mine eradication could best be handled, or whether it could be handled at all. Some officials, while professing ignorance of the technicalities of mine eradication, nonetheless had strong opinions regarding the practicality, or even possibility, of instituting a mine eradication program in Cambodia. "Mines will be cleared by people walking on them," one official with the U.N. High Commissioner for Refugees told the Asia Watch and Physicians for Human Rights delegation in Phnom Penh in April 1991.

In contrast, doctors and relief workers who worked daily with victims of mine blasts believed that something had to be done immediately to remove the mines. ICRC delegates considered mines one of Cambodia's most serious public health problems.

The cost of removing landmines in Cambodia will undoubtedly exceed the cost of supplying mines to the combat factions. To carry the eradication program through to completion will require political will and the investment of many millions of dollars. Clearly, Cambodia has neither the economic nor organizational infrastructure to support such a large-scale undertaking in the immediate or foreseeable future. It must

---

[33] *Hidden Killers*, p. 30.

therefore fall to the international community to provide the funding and organization for the demining operations.

During Cambodia's 12-year civil war, several countries provided military support to the four combatant factions; particularly, China, the U.S., Russia, Vietnam, the U.K., and the ASEAN nations. The countries claimed to have had the future of Cambodia and the rights of the Khmers at heart. It thus should not require any change in policy by those countries to fund a demining program so clearly beneficial to all Khmers, regardless of their politics. Such a commitment by the nations most heavily involved in arming and training the combatant factions, would likely ensure sufficient funds to institute a realistic large-scale mine eradication program.

## V.    Recent Developments

In March 1992—five months after the signing of the Paris accords—the first troops with the United Nations Transitional Authority in Cambodia (UNTAC) arrived in Phnom Penh. The Paris accords[34] authorized UNTAC to verify withdrawal of foreign forces, supervise and monitor the cease-fire, canton and disarm forces of the four parties, organize and conduct elections, and supervise mine marking and demining. The Cambodian Mine Action Centre (CMAC) was established in 1992 by the United Nations and Cambodia's interim government, the Supreme National Council, to coordinate demining activities in Cambodia. However, U.N. trained and supervised demining teams, comprised mostly of active and former Cambodian soldiers, did not actually begin clearing mines until August, and were not fully operational in many areas until early 1993. Among the countries providing mine clearing instructors were Bangladesh, Brazil, France, India, Netherlands, New Zealand, Pakistan, and the United Kingdom.

In the meantime, two non-governmental mine clearance organizations—the Halo Trust and the Norwegian People's Aid—had already deployed teams in northwestern Cambodia. And a third private organization—the Mines Advisory Group—became operational in the same area by late 1992. These organizations, though staffed mostly by former military ordnance specialists, are dedicated to humanitarian, as opposed

---

[34] *Agreements on a Comprehensive Political Settlement of the Cambodian Conflict,* United Nations, DPI/1180-92077-January 1992-10M, New York, 1992.

to military, mine clearance. Humanitarian clearance work is often slow as the aim is usually to clear and destroy every mine on a given site. Halo Trust and private demining groups usually select sites which will benefit as many people as possible. Thus the clearance of a mined path leading to a village well would be considered a higher priority than, say, a hectare of rice paddy (which would take a long time to clear and benefit only one family). Other priorities might include the clearance of land around schools and hospitals, sites prior to construction work, and of vital access routes and bridges.

The first project undertaken by Halo Trust was a mine survey for the United Nations High Commissioner for Refugees (UNHCR) of four northwestern provinces in March 1992. The aim of the survey was to locate heavily mined areas unsuitable for settlement of refugees from the Thai border camps. This information was compared with records kept by Handicap International on the reported location of mine injuries between May 1989 to March 1992 in northwestern Cambodia, and with similar records kept by Medecins Sans Frontieres in 1991. The survey, though rudimentary, provided the first glimpse of the mammoth task that lay ahead for the mine clearance effort. (In the first six months of 1993, CMAC conducted a more extensive survey, gathering information on mined areas in almost all of Cambodia's 21 provinces.)

By June 1993, CMAC officials and their non-governmental counterparts were highly pessimistic about the rate and extent to which Cambodia could be cleared of mines and other unexploded ordnance in the foreseeable future. "It will take 100 years to lift all the mines in Cambodia," said a Dutch military engineer working for the U.N. in Battambang. He continued, "The problem isn't the amount of mines, it's that the whole area must be cleared. You see, it doesn't matter if there is one mine or 100 mines in a given area—it can still take the same amount of time to clear it. Cambodians—and the world, for that matter—have to understand that mines will continue to be a way of life here for decades to come."

In Phnom Penh, a CMAC official[35] told Physicians for Human Rights researchers that his agency estimated there were 6 million mines in place throughout Cambodia. Of these, he guessed that 2 million mines were probably still active and had to be destroyed. He cautioned,

---

[35] Interview on June 5, 1992 with Major John Flanagan, Chief Information Officer for the Cambodian Mine Action Centre, Phnom Penh.

however, that when examining these figures it was necessary to consider that many mined areas had been conflict zones and thus were heavily saturated with unexploded mortar and rocket shells; they, too, had to be destroyed. In some areas, he said, demining teams had found a ratio of about 1 UXO, or unexploded ordnance, for every mine located.[36] Moreover, from the perspective of a farmer or herder, the CMAC official said, the fear that even one mine remained in a field could serve to inhibit them from putting it to productive use.

The reasons for the slow progress in demining are complex. First of all, demining teams often work in areas where there is a high security risk. James Brown, a deminer who works for Halo Trust in Pursat Province, told Physicians for Human Rights, "If the security would improve, it would make this work a hell of a lot easier."[37] Ironically, the day after the interview, Brown's co-worker, Chris Moon, and several Khmer deminers were abducted by Khmer Rouge guerrillas as they were leaving a demining site for the day.[38] Although Moon and his colleagues were released unharmed two days later, he said on several occasions during the ordeal he thought they were going to be killed. The guerrillas also took the team's two vehicles and most of their equipment.

Mine clearance has also been hampered by political obstacles. For instance, the Cambodian government has prohibited U.N.-supervised demining teams from clearing mines in some areas because they claim the mines are needed for security reasons.

Mine clearance is a slow and painstaking process. Since many mines in Cambodia were laid up to twenty years ago, they are now covered with thick undergrowth which must be carefully removed. Heavy demining equipment, such as flails, can be used along roads, but are useless in rice paddies and forests. Specially trained dogs, usually Alsatians or Labradors, are now trained in Cambodia to locate minefield perimeters. The dogs sniff out the mine's explosive, so they can find a plastic mine that a metal detector misses, and ignore metal objects (such

---

[36] Halo Trust, for instance, destroyed 150 mines at 5 sites between December 1992 and June 1993. At the same sites, they also discovered 1,000 UXOs, which were also destroyed.

[37] Interview on June 9, 1993 with James Brown, Halo Trust, Pursat.

[38] Interview on June 13, 1993 with Chris Moon, Halo Trust, Pursat.

as spent artillery shells) that the detector senses. The problem is that once the dogs are in the field they can only work for a few hours each day and must have a quiet environment with no distractions.

Virtually all of the mine clearance teams in Cambodia use metal detectors to locate mines. Once a mine is pinpointed, it is gently uncovered using a steel prod, then marked, and later destroyed. It is tedious and time-consuming work. "Imagine putting a pencil in the ground to a depth of 6 centimeters 400 times in just one square meter. That's what it is like," says a deminer with the Norwegian People's Aid in Sisophon.

Without maps of minefields, clearance teams have to interview villagers about the whereabouts of mined areas or rely on the memories of local commanders. "It's frustrating work," says Brown. "For instance, we worked in one area for six weeks and only found two mines, even though the [Cambodian] army had assured us there were hundreds of mines there. So, sure, it's slow going. But there are no prizes for clearing mines quickly."

Clearance teams have also found that areas they have cleared have been remined months later. In one instance a U.N. team, working without a minefield map, cleared several hectares of mines in Kampot Province near territory in the control of the Khmer Rouge. Two months later, the Cambodian army mined the area again—only this time they kept a map.

Foreign relief workers and even some U.N. deminers have characterized UNTAC's mine clearance program as having been "poorly conceived and organized" and "lacking central coordination." They say that too much money was spent in the beginning on "high-tech approaches," such as setting up an expensive computer system for collecting and analyzing information on mined areas and not enough on actually clearing mines. Although UNTAC eventually changed its mandate, permitting U.N.-supervised teams to clear mines, it was already too late for the teams to have any real effect.

According to a CMAC official, UNTAC had trained 2,200 Cambodians in mine clearance as of June 5, 1993. However, he warned that the "measure of success was not how many Khmer were trained but how many mines were lifted and how much land was cleared." He went on to say that since August 1992, U.N. teams had cleared 10,360 antipersonnel mines and 31 antitank mines from 220 hectares, or a little

less than 100 acres.[39]   "This means, with an estimated 20,000 hectares
left to clear," he said, "we have only dealt with 1 percent of the mines
problem so far."[40]

Today, Khmer and foreign relief workers fear that once the last
of the U.N. troops depart Cambodia in November 1993, the level of
funding for mine marking and clearance efforts will eventually dry up
and mine-related injuries and deaths could begin to rise.  Their fears are
shared by many U.N. and non-governmental organization deminers.
According to a CMAC official, CMAC now needs approximately $10
million per year for the next five to 10 years to cover the costs for the
administration of the center and to keep 10 mine marking and 40
demining teams in operation.[41]   In addition, he says a further $2
million per year will be needed to support the work of private demining
organizations.[42]  By June 1993, CMAC had received pledges of support
for only $790,000.

---

[39] Exact figures on the number mines destroyed by non-governmental
organization teams were unavailable at the time.  However, they would not have
amounted to more than 1,000 to 2,000.

[40] At the American Defense Preparedness Association Landmine Symposium,
Sept. 7, 1993, Ashville, NC, French Lt. Colonel Jean Francois Gros of the French
Army Corps of Engineers stated that from April 1992 to July 1993 UNTAC
removed 14,413 antipersonnel and 115 antitank mines, while French MCTU
removed 12,284 antipersonnel and 78 antitank mines.  He estimated that three
to four million mines remained.

[41] In a report issued on May 19, 1993, CMAC warned that "[it] will not be
able to fulfill its intended role as Cambodia's national demining body
independent from [the U.N.'s] financial and institutional support unless
international funding is made available as a matter or urgency."  See Cambodian
Mine Action Centre, "Progress Report on the Implementation and Funding
Situation of the Short-Term Plan of Operations," November 1992 to June 1993,
p. 9.

[42] For instance, Halo Trust, a British-based private mines clearance
organization, estimates the cost of operating one demining team in Cambodia at
$250,000 a year.

## VI.    Conclusion

In violation of international legal standards, all sides in the Cambodian conflict used landmines without regard for their effects on the civilian population. None of the warring parties routinely kept records or maps of the location of mines, nor did they warn civilians of mines laid in areas frequented by noncombatants. In some cases, the various forces, especially the Khmer Rouge, knowingly placed landmines in civilian areas to terrorize the local population or to control their movement. Moreover, both government and resistance forces often failed to remove mines once their military objective had been fulfilled. This was particularly the case along pathways frequented by civilians.

This blatantly indiscriminate use of mines has taken its toll. Statistics on war casualties from hospitals in Cambodia and the Thai border camps show that during 1990 and the first three months of 1991 landmines injured more combatants and noncombatants than any other weapon. Of the injured, half were civilians, including a significant number of women and children. In addition, Khmer and foreign surgeons reported that this had been the trend for several years. These statistics, coupled with accounts from government soldiers and resistance fighters, clearly indicate that all sides flagrantly disregarded the rule of proportionality, which holds that civilian casualties and damage to civilian objects should not be out of proportion to the military advantages anticipated.

The September 1991 Asia Watch and Physicians for Human Rights report, *Land Mines in Cambodia*, stated, "The widespread presence and density of landmines in Cambodia must be considered a humanitarian emergency, separate from, and regardless of, the other crises facing the Khmer people." The report urged the international community, under the auspices of the United Nations, to underwrite a mine eradication program in Cambodia, and called on nations that have supplied mines to Cambodia's warring parties to share the costs of landmine eradication. Finally, the report recommended that measures should be taken to prevent combat units or other groups from removing mines and stockpiling them for possible later use. All existing stockpiles should be turned over to the United Nations team and destroyed, the report said. These recommendations are still valid, and even more urgent, today.

## El Salvador[43]

Landmines were used extensively in El Salvador by rebel forces and government troops.  Mines not only claimed hundreds if not thousands of civilian casualties during the war, but also continue to plague Salvadoran citizens today; an estimated 20,000 landmines remain uncleared.[44]  According to a recent State Department report, "These landmines pose a significant public safety threat in heavily populated El Salvador, and are delaying the return of land back to agricultural production in some areas."[45]   Mines placed by both sides have been a factor in slowing and preventing repopulation of territory by people who had fled the fighting.

Mines were placed by both government troops and the opposition Faribundo Marti Front for National Liberation (FMLN) forces in areas known to be used by civilians, often without effective markings or other types of warnings.  Many mines were not removed, and it is doubtful that any have the capacity to self-destruct or self-neutralize once its military purpose is served.

It does not appear that either side to the conflict deliberately used mines against civilians, but both sides used mines in an indiscriminate manner, thereby violating international law.  Careless and negligent practices, particularly the failure to warn adequately the civilian population that a given area was mined, resulted in many civilian casualties.  Government forces used landmines sporadically; rebel forces used them extensively.  The U.S. government vigorously condemned the use of landmines by the FMLN, but not by the Salvadoran government troops.

Landmine use increased sharply during the course of the war in El Salvador, with a corresponding increase in the number of civilians killed and wounded by mines.  Many of the casualties took place in remote rural areas, so casualty figures vary.

---

[43] This section is adapted from, *Land Mines in El Salvador and Nicaragua: The Civilian Victims*, an Americas Watch report, dated December 1986.   Unless otherwise noted, all information is from that report.

[44] DOS, *Hidden Killers*, p. 85.

[45] Ibid.

## I.    Use by the FMLN

For the guerrillas in El Salvador, as for guerrillas elsewhere, landmines were a logical response to classic counterinsurgency doctrine, which prescribes incessant army foot patrols to wear the guerrillas down. The guerrillas anticipated the path of advancing patrols and sowed mines designed to injure on contact, disrupting the patrols and demoralizing the troops, who then hesitated to patrol aggressively.

Salvadoran guerrillas also used mines in ambushes and, more rarely, in booby-traps. They often employed mines to block entry to the zones they controlled, to protect their supply lines, and to protect their rear guard. In such cases, the guerrillas declared the mined areas off limits to the civilian population. This provided a warning, but also had the effect of displacing more people. Despite these precautions, the majority of civilian casualties resulted from mines placed by the FMLN. In some instances this was because the FMLN did not provide adequate warnings or did not remove mines after they served their military objectives. In others cases, warnings were given but desperately poor peasants took the risk anyway, venturing into mined areas because they needed food or firewood.

## II.    Use by the Government

The Armed Forces of El Salvador found mines less to their advantage militarily and their use was correspondingly more limited. Government forces mainly used mines defensively, to protect fixed installations and camp perimeters. But Americas Watch received compelling information in 1986 that mines were also used offensively in ambushes and in areas where FMLN forces were expected to pass through or camp.

The Armed Forces used both hand-detonated and contact mines, as well as grenades and "homemade" mines of the same type the FMLN used. A grenade would be converted into a contact mine by removing the pin and inserting a branch or other stopper; then, when a passer-by hit the branch, the grenade would explode. Recent information indicates that the United States supplied the Salvadoran Army with about 37,000 antipersonnel landmines between 1981 and 1990. It is not known how many of these were actually deployed. The vast majority of the mines were M18A1 Claymore mines. Others were M14s and M26s. The M14 is a plastic mine that is very difficult to detect and to clear and therefore can pose particular risk for civilians.[46]

## III.    Mine Types and Locations

According to Americas Watch, the FMLN used a wide variety of mines, but most were variations of three basic types: *mina de chuchito* (clothespin mine); *mina abanico* (fan mine); and *mina de pateo* (or *quita pata*, literally, kicked mine or mine that removes feet). The *mina de chuchito* is triggered by a wire stretched across a path. The *mina abanico* is detonated by hand and is intended for use in ambushing convoys. The *mina de pateo* is triggered by contact or pressure, such as a footstep.

According to the U.S. State Department, the following kinds of antipersonnel mines have been found in El Salvador:

- United States: M18A1 Claymore, M14;
- El Salvador: Atlacatl, Morazan, Atonal, Chucito;
- Improvised: Tepesquintle, Catapultas, Rampas;

The heaviest concentrations of mines are in the Guazapa volcano area, the San Miguel volcano area, and the Chalatenango Province.[47]

## IV.    Casualties

While it is not possible to have complete confidence in the precision of the numbers, it is clear that the number of civilians injured by mines was reprehensibly high. According to statistics compiled by the U.S. and Salvadoran governments, which focused on civilian mine victims attributed to the FMLN, in 1986 the civilian injury rate ran from 19 to 25 incidents per month, and the military rate was between 64 and 125 per month. It appears that the percentage of military injuries caused by

---

[46] U.S. Army Armament, Munitions, and Chemical Command, Letter to the Arms Project, August 25, 1993, and attached statistical tables on Foreign Military Sales of landmines 1969-92. This information was provided to the Arms Project in response to a Freedom of Information Act request.

[47] DOS, *Hidden Killers*, p. 85.

landmines increased from approximately 45% in 1985, to about 65% in 1986, to as much as 80% in 1987.

## V.     Mine Clearance

It is estimated that there are 20,000 uncleared mines in El Salvador. It is possible that many of the mines are already neutralized, since many are of the homemade variety that rely on regular batteries for fuzing, and the batteries will no longer have sufficient charge to trigger the mine. The government of El Salvador decided against participating in the regional demining program supervised by the Organization of American States (OAS), although it has received some assistance with mine clearance from the OAS, the Inter-American Defense Board, and UNICEF. The government has instead signed a $4.8 million contract with a private Belgian company, International Danger and Disaster Assistance, to clear all mines within two years.[48] According to the U.S. State Department, "Some irregularities in the manner in which this contract was awarded have caused reluctance in the U.S. and the E.C. to fund this program. As consequence, the future of this contract is in question."[49]

---

[48] Ibid.

[49] Ibid., p. 40.

**Iraqi Kurdistan[50]**

The Iraqi army sowed an estimated three to five million landmines[51] in northern Iraq (Iraqi Kurdistan) that were unrecorded and unmarked. These mines do not self-destruct.

These unmarked, unrecorded, nondegradable and unremoved landmines are an ongoing threat to the lives, limbs, and well-being of the Iraqi Kurdish population in northern Iraq. Thousands of civilians have suffered landmine injuries since mid-1991. Reports as of August 1992 indicated that landmine casualties continued at a rate of 12-20 a week.

Part of the problem lies in the fact that, since vast quantities of landmines were readily available, vast quantities were sown, far in excess of the needs of military strategy. The inevitable landmine injuries to civilians began to occur following the Iraqi army withdrawal from northern Iraq in April 1991. Kurdish farmers returned to the lands from which they had been forcibly ejected by the army, joined by homeless Kurdish refugees fleeing government repression in government-controlled areas like Kirkuk. They found their good farming and pastureland heavily salted with landmines.

It is a reasonable conclusion that the Iraqi army laid and abandoned these millions of mines to make large areas of Kurdistan unusable for all time. Such a deliberate practice, as well as the failure to take measures to protect civilians from mines, constitute violations of the Landmines Protocol. Though several mined areas were fenced, warning markings were only employed in isolated cases. The omission of warnings is unconscionable as they would not have vitiated any legitimate military purpose of the mine fields in the slightest. Further exacerbating the difficulty of future clearance, no maps of the minefields are known to have been kept by the Iraqi army.

The creation and abandonment of these minefields in Kurdish areas traditionally dedicated to farm and pastureland reflects Iraqi

---

[50] This section is adapted from *Hidden Death: Landmines and Civilians Casualties in Iraqi Kurdistan*, a Middle East Watch report, dated October 1992. Unless otherwise noted, all information is from that report.

[51] DOS, *Hidden Killers*, p. 36. The report estimates a total of five to 10 million landmines in all of Iraq, and notes the Save the Children estimate of five million mines in Dahuk governate alone. Ibid., p. 104.

government hostility to the Kurds on ethnic grounds. These practices continue the long Iraqi policy of driving the Kurds from their lands and punishing them collectively.

Moreover, the types of landmines used by the Iraqi army make clearance particularly difficult and dangerous. The manufacturers and distributors share a moral responsibility for the situation in Iraqi Kurdistan. The collusion of other governments is a central factor. The devices used in Iraqi Kurdistan were mostly of Italian-manufacture or design. The devastation that they have caused is attributable, in part, to Italy's careless and venal approach to the export of landmines. Thus, the fault for the terrible number of civilian injuries and deaths now resulting from these landmines lies not only with the irresponsible manner in which they were laid and then not cleared by the Iraqi army, but also with the designers, producers, and distributors of landmines, and those who facilitated this trade.

## I.    Background

Mine-related civilian casualties have only become a major issue since mid-1991, when the Iraqi Army withdrew from most of Kurdistan. Kurds who had been forcibly displaced by that army years earlier were finally free to return to their farms. They found their homes and villages destroyed by the army which had left landmines in many areas where the Kurds had formerly grown crops and grazed their sheep and goats.

The Kurdish demand for autonomy from the central government has been part of Iraqi history since the creation of the Iraqi state after World War I. Saddam Hussein's Ba'ath Party, which came to power in a 1968 coup, has engaged in several campaigns of forced displacement and destruction of villages. The army and militia has bombed, shelled, looted and burned villages to punish villagers for allegedly harboring Kurdish guerrillas, known as *pesh merga*.

In March 1991, in the wake of the allied coalition's ouster of Iraq from Kuwait, and with apparent encouragement from United States President George Bush, the vast majority of the nearly four million Iraqi Kurds rebelled against the Iraqi government. For a time it seemed that the uprising would succeed, but the expected allied military support never came, and the world community watched from the sidelines as Saddam Hussein's forces mowed down the Iraqi Kurds. The *pesh merga* withdrew to the Iraqi, Turkish, and Iranian mountains. At the same time, frightened Kurds from the cities and the sprawling complexes fled the advance of the feared Republican Guard.   Over one million Kurds reached Iran and more than 450,000 escaped to Turkey.

Media attention and public pressure in the West on the desperate plight of the Kurdish refugees starving in the snow-covered mountains in Turkey shamed the allies into a belated reaction.   A safe haven was created in Iraqi Kurdistan by 30,000 U.S., French and British troops who accompanied the refugees back into Iraq from Turkey.   The allies prohibited armed Iraqis from entering the safe haven. Additional protection for the Kurds against Saddam Hussein's reprisals was provided by the allies' prohibition of Iraqi fixed wing or helicopter flights over Iraqi territory above the 36th parallel.

Taking advantage of the safety provided by these various forms of protection, thousands of Kurds began returning in 1991 to their villages and towns from which the Iraqi army had expelled them years earlier.   Many went to inspect what remained, finding only rubble.

Kurds encountered landmines en route home from refuge in Turkey and Iran.   Farmers returning to their destroyed villages found landmines in the pastures. Kurds from government-controlled areas like Kirkuk, who had been afraid to go home after fleeing the crushing of the uprising in March 1991, ventured into farmland and encountered unmarked landmines.

Although international aid has diminished, the Kurds continue to return to the rural areas, including mined areas, because of their attachment to their traditional homes and for lack of any realistic economic alternative. The widespread dissemination of landmines creates more havoc for the Kurdish people as they return to lands from which they had been driven by Iraqi troops attempting to destroy their communities, their ethnic identity, and their very lives.

## II.      Sample Minefields

Research by Middle East Watch focused on those cases where the civilian population was significantly endangered and mine practices violated the Landmines Protocol.  These include situations in which the original military purpose of a minefield was no longer valid, and cases where landmines presented an ongoing or potential threat to the civilian population as a result of:  absence of, or inadequate, warning signs; absence of, inadequate, or incorrectly sighted perimeter fencing; random dissemination of devices in areas regularly used by civilians; placement of landmines in, or close to, land required by the civilian population for planting, livestock grazing or other essential purposes regardless of any restrictions which existed prior to Iraqi army withdrawal from the area in mid-1991.

Middle East Watch surveyed a limited sample of 15 minefields. Even in this limited sample, however, there were five minefields where a total of 30 persons, mostly refugees fleeing the Iraqi army, had been killed in the space of five months. All the minefields surveyed were heavily mined with a variety of sophisticated devices, many booby-trapped to prevent easy clearance. Details from some of the minefields follow.

### A. Shirawash

In Shirawash, Middle East Watch found small children playing within five meters of antipersonnel pressure- and tripwire-initiated antipersonnel mines. One mine was discovered within inches of a well-trodden path to the main community water source. Though adults take considerable care to protect their children from the mines, the children themselves have become inured to mines and pay them scant attention.

The Shirawash settlement and the area immediately surrounding it is a large and ill-defined defensive minefield consisting primarily of surface-emplaced antipersonnel devices. The area to the south of, and immediately adjacent to, the main concentration of refugees appears also to have been used as a dump for unused mines, probably when Iraqi forces withdrew from the frontier post in 1991. In the southern areas it appears that the mines, in most cases, were armed but deployed in a random and careless manner. This is particularly true of the many Valmara 69s which were not buried but linked in series on single tripwires. In the same area, many VS-50 and other pressure devices have been scattered at random—sometimes in groups of twenty or more.

The area to the north of the main cross-border road from Hajorma is a defensive minefield consisting predominantly of antipersonnel mines—Valsella 69, VS-50 and PMN-HGE, some buried, others surface laid, over a wide ill-defined and unmarked area.

### B.  Sardekan Hill

Sardekan Hill is a mountain meadow above Zinway, a traditional grazing area.   Most of this pasture was mined during the Iran-Iraq conflict and has a high density of antipersonnel devices.   The local population is aware of the landmines, yet the residents are faced with the need to graze their livestock.  New returnees with additional animals add to the pressure on this land and encourage attempts to make use of mined pasture. Middle East Watch met two young shepherds, ages 14 and 8, setting out to burn part of the Sardekan minefield so that they could use it to graze their flock.   This method of attempting to demine is widespread in Kurdistan. It is not effective.

Devices recorded in this area included the Valmara 69 and the VS-50, both surface laid in considerable quantities. Middle East Watch obtained reports of the presence in this minefield of an all-plastic Iranian pressure mine similar in appearance to the wooden Soviet PMD-7, although probably smaller.

### C.  Derband Gorge

During much of the Iran-Iraq war, the Derband Gorge was the frontline between the opposing forces, and was the scene of some of the most violent engagements of the war.  The result of the gorge's strategic importance is a significant concentration of mines and a high incidence of particularly hazardous napalm devices.

Landmine accidents are commonplace, especially among refugees and new returnees, most commonly while searching for firewood or grazing livestock. There is evidence that loss of life and injuries have become increasingly common since March 1991 and no improvement can be expected until the minefield is cleared.

The most disturbing aspect of the Derband minefield is the presence of booby-traps consisting of 20-liter steel drums of napalm connected on tripwire circuits. The drums have an explosive charge and are linked by fuze to pull switches. It would appear from those samples examined by Middle East Watch that the tripwires which form part of the initiation circuit are also connected to bounding mines. The napalm containers are, in most cases, buried, leaving the upper 25 percent of the drum exposed. In several instances, however, the drum is totally buried leaving only the top exposed at ground level. The potential for injury from such a combination of burning napalm and shrapnel needs no elaboration.

As far as could be ascertained, devices present include Valmara 69, PMN-HGE and VS-50. The ground surrounding the prominent water tower is heavily mined with Valmara 69 and various antipersonnel pressure devices (not positively identified by type).

### D.  Konyarasukosa

Although the Konyarasukosa minefield probably does not exceed two square kilometers, its impact on the local community has been considerable. It is completely unmarked. On April 21, 1991, a family of eight refugees was killed by multiple mine detonations, presumably while looking for shelter near a rock outcrop in the minefield. At least eleven returnees to the village of Nowpredam have been killed or injured since March 1991, four of them young children.

This minefield was laid by Iraqi troops to protect the flanks of a fire-base and observation post overlooking the Choman-Sadiq road from assault by *pesh merga*. Valmara 69 and VS-50 antipersonnel mines were identified.

### E.  Nowpredam

A large area of high grassland above the Nowpredam village settlement is heavily mined with antipersonnel devices. There have been four fatal mine incidents here since April 1991, all Nowpredam returnees. The strategic reasons for this minefield are not clear, although it is probable that the field was laid by the Iraqi forces during the war with Iran.

The mined area covers most of an extensive traditional grazing ground and the local herders have attempted to clear the mines in some locations by burning. This has led to the destruction of some mines but the majority of devices were unaffected or only partly melted and rendered unstable. Livestock are still being grazed on the limited tracts of land which are not mined, tended by young boys who appear to have little regard for the great danger that surrounds them.

Two devices have been used in great quantities in this minefield. Both are of Italian origin: the Valmara 69 and the SB-33. Middle East Watch recorded over sixty SB-33s in one area approximately 10 meters by 15 meters. The deployment of Valmara 69s, in lesser numbers than SB-33s, is widespread. In most cases they were buried to the top of the outer casing with just the fuze prongs exposed. Some are inter-linked by tripwires; others appear to be deployed so as to explode under direct pressure.

### F. Eenay

In Eenay, four villagers were killed and nine suffered amputations from March to September 1991, out of an estimated population of 480. There are two extensive minefields close to Eenay. The whole expanse of the first minefield is a mixture of well irrigated arable land and good pasture. It forms a major portion of the farmland which supported Eenay's population prior to the Iran-Iraq war and the expulsion of the Kurdish zone by the Iraqi government. Devices evident at the first field were surface-laid and buried Valmara 69s and scattered VS-50s. A large number of 20-liter drums identical in appearance and deployment to the napalm containers examined at Derband are also visible.

The second minefield in the area of Eenay village is located in good grazing and agricultural land. Laid during the Iran-Iraq war, this minefield formed a defense for the Iraqi artillery firebase at Goribasta which still remains as it was left by the soldiers, only the guns themselves having been removed by the Iraqi army at the end of the Iran-Iraq war. The initial military purpose for the minefield, protection of the firebase, has long since ceased.

Some VS-50 and PMN-HGE were identified but local information indicates that many other types of devices are present. As with so many other minefields, the mines could have been cleared at the end of the war, when the Iraqi army removed the guns from the firebase, but that was not done.

### G. Pirdi Kashan

The Pirdi Kashan minefield is situated above the bridge where the Dolbeshk to Mawat road marked the front line between Iranian and Iraqi positions. Casualties are very common among people who are not aware of the hazard, usually from stepping on devices laid close to the verge. There is an abundance of devices extremely close to a busy route and surrounding settlements.

Pirdi Kashan was the most densely laid minefield surveyed on this trip and, in places, mines were located only inches from the edge of the road. The most common device in the eastern section of the minefield is the PMN-HGE; literally thousands can be seen stretching up the hill. Some of these devices are buried, leaving only the pressure diagram exposed, but most are scattered randomly over the surface. Valmara 69s are also present in considerable quantities, buried so as to be set off either by tripwire or by direct pressure. No marking or fencing has been attempted.

### H. Chapazra

There have been no casualties in the Chapazra minefield, primarily because of clear marking and good local knowledge. However, the land is prime pasture which is urgently needed by the people of Daramyana. While this site clearly illustrates how responsible use of perimeter marking can reduce the risk to the civilian population, the loss of such large areas of pasture should not be allowed to continue indefinitely. Experience in similar situations in Afghanistan has shown that even good marking has its limitations; when land is at a premium, farmers and herders will eventually begin to encroach onto mined land, with inevitable consequences.

Chapazra is atypical of the minefields surveyed by Middle East Watch for two reasons other than its absence of casualties: the variety of device types deployed and the presence of at least one standard mine warning sign. Chapazra has clearly delineated boundaries adjacent to the road marked by barbed wire entanglement. One standard mine marker was visible and others may be present.

Two models of Italian antitank mines are used here and are protected against removal by Valsella 69 and VS-50 antipersonnel mines, both of which are also disseminated widely in an independent role.

Middle East Watch found two, as yet unidentified, antipersonnel devices, believed to be of Iranian origin: one is a "stake" mine, probably of the fragmentation-type set off by tripwire; the other is a small box-shaped mine of plastic construction which may be the Iranian pressure-release device described by local sources in other areas. Local reports also indicate the presence of SB-33 and POMZ-2 mines or their derivatives.

### I. Zakho

Detailed technical information on the extensive Zakho minefield, laid in 1990 to act as a barrier to an expected coalition attack from Turkey during the Gulf War, was given to Middle East Watch by two sources who had been directly involved in the operation. Their testimony demonstrates the total lack of responsibility displayed by the military authorities involved in laying the minefield.

The scale and density of this 32-kilometer minefield is such that it clearly exposes civilians to an unjustifiable level of danger. Large tracts of this good agricultural land were expropriated for military purposes from the farmers. Its location prevents safe access to the river from other farming areas which makes resettlement and reconstruction of villages in this area virtually impossible. Casualties are reported to be frequent among *pesh merga* who have bases along this stretch of the border. Young boys grazing livestock also account for a large percentage of mine victims from this sector.

The two devices most in evidence in this minefield are PMD-HGE and Valmara 69, in some sections laid in dense concentrations. Some VS-50 and antitank devices are also present. An estimated 15 to 20 percent of the mines are unarmed. Most of the perimeter of the Zakho field is delineated by barbed wire, but no warning signs were in evidence. In one location there was a fenced safe path to a forward observation/listening post in the minefield; others may exist.

### III.    Iraq's Mine Distribution and Mapping Strategies

Interviews with former Iraqi army officers illustrate the cynical political and military strategies that created the minefields described above. An officer and a soldier involved in the 1990 large-scale landmine laying campaign in Zakho made it clear that mines were laid without any mapping and in a hasty and careless manner.

The Iraqi government claims that minefield maps were kept but destroyed during the March 1991 Kurdish uprising. This is contradicted not only by these two witnesses but also by Middle East Watch's research.

It is clear that the Iraqi military retained no records of their mine-laying or, if they did, that it was not retained by the local military command.

According to an Iraqi military intelligence officer attached to a Divisional Engineer Unit with responsibility for a section of the defenses along the Iraqi-Turkish border:

> For four months before the coalition invasion, from September [1990] I think, we were involved in building a defensive barrier in the triangle formed by the Syrian and Turkish borders. It was an extremely large-scale operation—eight divisions were moved into the front and each began preparing minefields to protect its positions....for four months we laid mines throughout the front, every day—there simply weren't enough military trucks to bring them from the stores in Mosul so civilian vehicles were used as well.

When asked if each division or unit kept a record or maps of the minefields it laid, he responded, "I never saw any maps. We, the officers, knew where the mines were meant to be laid and those instructions were passed down to the sappers. No, I don't think any maps were made."

A section commander of a divisional sapper unit of the Iraqi army involved in defensive mine-laying operations in the period following the invasion of Kuwait and prior to the invasion by coalition forces indicated that there were more than 2,500 soldiers laying mines at a rate of about 5,000 each day. He said that his section alone laid between eighty and one hundred thousand mines, mostly antipersonnel, in the Zakho area, and that his was just one of many such sections.

He indicated that the most common mine used was the Italian Valmara 69 bounding A/P mine, which he called the "Broom," as well as Soviet-style PMN and POMZ-2 mines. He believed that the PMN was manufactured in Iraqi factories.

When asked if anyone kept records, maps or sketches of the minefields, he replied, "No, we were too busy, we just kept a count of the number of mines we laid. That was the only record anyone was interested in."

## IV.    Sources of Landmines

The most common mines Middle East Watch encountered during this mission were the Valmara 69 and the VS-50. The SB-33 and PMN-HGE were also extremely common. The first three of these mines are of Italian design, while the PMN-HGE is a derivative of the Soviet PMN. French, American, and Chinese landmines are also to be found in Kurdistan, as well as mines apparently manufactured in Belgium, Chile, Romania, and possibly Iran.

Two of the mines, the Valmara 69 and the VS-50, are designed and manufactured by an Italian company, Valsella Meccanotecnica SpA of Brescia, one of the world's leading manufacturers and exporters of landmines. Because Valsella could not obtain an export license for Iraq it formed a new company in Singapore, which was not subject to an export ban, and obtained a license from the Italian government for export to that company. The mines were then re-exported to Iraq. In February 1991, seven executives of Valsella were convicted of illegally exporting nine million landmines to Iraq between 1982 and 1985.

At the trial, the company's defense was that the Italian government was fully informed of the arms sales to Iraq. This was not the first time that Valsella had been cited in connection with alleged illegal export of landmines through shell or foreign companies. (In September 1987, a Tuscan magistrate, Augusto Lama, told journalists that he had issued warrants against Valsella's chairman and three executives of the company because he had documentary evidence that Valsella had illegally exported mines to Iran through Spanish, Turkish and Nigerian companies.)

Iraq had meanwhile begun to manufacture mines that were clones of the Valsella mines. In May 1989, at the Baghdad Arms Fair, the Iraqi stand displayed Valmara 69 bounding mines identical to those manufactured by Valsella but apparently manufactured in Iraq.

A Singapore-based company, Chartered Industries, partly owned and controlled by the Singapore government, also advertises devices identical to the Valmara 69 and the VS-50 as its own products; they are designated as VS-69 and VS-50 by Chartered Industries.

The SB-33 is described by its Italian manufacturers, BPD Difesa e Spazio of Rome, Italy as a general purpose local action mine ". . . complying with Italian Army and NATO technical and operational specifications." A recent U.S. Defense Intelligence Agency report notes that the mine is "designed to thwart detection and disarming.... the Italian SB-series of scatterable mines features anti-handling devices, is blast-resistant, and is nearly nondetectable by metallic or ferrous mine detectors."[52] Some mines identified as SB-33s could be the identical EM-20 marketed by the Greek company Elviemek S.A., Hellenic Explosives & Ammunition Industry of Athens.

The PMN is a Soviet-designed and manufactured antipersonnel blast mine used in many regional conflicts but especially in Afghanistan, where it is was widely disseminated by Soviet and Afghan government forces. The mine of the same design found in Kurdistan is a copy of the original, manufactured in Iraq.

This mine was displayed as an Iraqi-manufactured device at the Baghdad Arms Fair in May 1989. It is not known whether the Iraqi PMN-HGE is manufactured under license from the former Soviet Union, but it can be assumed that the Soviets supplied PMNs to the Iraqis before the local version was produced.

The DIA study and a U.S. Army Intelligence Agency report contain information about the Iraqi landmine arsenal. In addition to Iraq's domestically produced mines, they list more than twenty-three types of antipersonnel mines from at least ten nations. While Iraq probably did not deploy all of these in Kurdistan, the list is instructive as to the range of mines available to Baghdad.[53]

* Belgium: PRB M409;
* Canada: C3A1;
* China: Type 72, PMN;
* East Germany: PPM-2;
* Egypt: Claymore;
* Iraq: PMN, P-25, P-40;

---

[52] DIA/FSTC, pp. 2-9, 2-16.

[53] DIA/FSTC, pp. 2-16, 2-17; U.S. Army Intelligence Agency, U.S. Army Foreign Science and Technology Center, *Operation Desert Shield Special Report: Iraqi Combat Engineer Capabilities*, 30 November 1990, p.25. Both of these documents were obtained by the Arms Project under the Freedom of Information Act. At least three antipersonnel mines are blacked out as classified. The documents also list a large number of antitank mines, many manufactured by the same nations, as well as the United Kingdom, Chile, Yugoslavia, Singapore, and Romania.

- Italy: P-25, P-40, Valmara 69, Valmara 59, SB-33, VS-50, VS-MK2, SB-81;
- Singapore: VS-MK2;
- Soviet Union: PMD-6, MON-50, MON-100, MON-200, PMN;
- Spain: SB-33, SB-81;
- United States: M14.

## V.    The Threat to Non-Combatants

When landmines are laid in an irresponsible or deliberate manner, as in northern Iraq, the risk to noncombatants of course increases considerably. In rural agricultural communities, civilian casualties can reach alarming levels as the need to rehabilitate farmland and re-establish life-supporting activities becomes paramount.

As in other countries where extensive mining of agricultural areas has occurred, farmers and their families in Kurdistan face the deadly dilemma of either accepting the risk presented by landmines or abandoning the land they need to survive. Experience in Afghanistan, Cambodia, and other countries has shown that farmers and herders will take greater risks as their personal economic circumstances become increasingly critical and their familiarity with the presence of mines overcomes their fear.  This familiarity is rarely accompanied by an increased knowledge of the true risk element involved in straying into mined areas.

It is obvious that certain occupations expose people to extreme danger. These occupations are firewood collection, livestock herding, often done by children, and mine clearance. In addition, many people are injured by landmines when they return to reconstruct their homes in areas that were previously destroyed by the Iraqis as part of their scorched-earth counterinsurgency campaign, suggesting that mines were left there precisely to discourage civilians from returning to their lands.

Casualties from landmines continue to demand emergency and long-term rehabilitation efforts from a severely strained medical system. Middle East Watch visited five medical facilities during September 1991, and found that they treated 1,652 landmine casualties in Sulemaniya and 475 in eastern Erbil during a five month period alone.

## VI.     Control, Eradication, Marking and Awareness Initiatives

### A.  Community Initiatives

Many groups and individuals have taken on the task of clearing mines to allow land to be returned to use. One of the most remarkable initiatives examined by Middle East Watch was the work of Borhan Hussein and his team in Penjwin. This team has disarmed and collected enormous quantities of landmines and unexploded ordnance and, lacking the explosives and knowledge to destroy their haul, have established two guarded dumps near the Kommitee Bala headquarters in Penjwin. Ironically these dumps now contain such a huge amount of ordnance that they place the local community at considerable risk. It is estimated that one of the two dumps contained more than 5,000 mines at the time of Middle East Watch's visit. It is situated within 50 meters of the nearest dwellings.

One disturbing practice which is increasingly common within Kurdistan is burning of minefields in the belief that this will destroy the mines. The strategy is usually employed on mined grazing land, particularly mountain pasture, and, to a lesser extent, on arable land. Middle East Watch examined several minefields which had been burned and found that, while some devices were detonated by heat or rendered inoperable by burning, many were either made unstable or sustained no damage at all. The obvious danger of this practice is that people may be encouraged to believe that the ground is safe for use after burning.

### B.  Organized Clearance Initiatives

In 1991, prior to the Iraqi administrative pullout from Kurdistan, three Iraqi army teams working under the scrutiny and control of the Military Coordination Center (MCC) based in Zakho were engaged in organized landmine clearance in the Dohuk governorate, in the Zakho, Kanimasi, and Mangish areas. Middle East Watch did not observe these operations directly but was able to interview MCC staff to obtain details. Colonel Reynolds of the U.S. Armed Forces, serving with MCC, said that the teams "had their limitations and their equipment and skills are not all that could be wished for. The Iraqi officers were unable to read maps and there are problems of operational discipline." However, Colonel Reynolds considered the mines issue so important that any realistic initiative should be supported.

In June 1992, the Mines Advisory Group (MAG), funded by the European Community (EC) Emergency Office, began work training 160 Kurds in the skills required to survey, mark, record, and eradicate minefields in Kurdistan. The minefields targeted for the program are those where there is a specific risk to noncombatants and where low income and refugee communities are disadvantaged by the presence of mines. The recent State Department report indicates that, in addition to MAG, the Disaster Aid Committee and the United Kingdom are currently conducting mine clearing operations in northern Iraq.[54]

### C.  Mine Marking Projects

Both the Military Coordinating Center in Zakho and the United Nations High Commissioner for Refugees (UNHCR) in Penjwin initiated pilot marking projects. The MCC project aimed to mark minefield perimeters with skull and crossbone warning signs. The project began in mid-September 1991.

The UNHCR project in Penjwin was said by Amin Awad, their senior UNHCR representative, to have a budget of U.S. $45,000 and was to be implemented in conjunction with the local Kurdistan Front Committee. Some large signs had already been erected beside the Nowpires-Penjwin road at the time of the Middle East Watch mission giving a general warning.

### D.  Mine Awareness Projects

The Kurdistan Front initiated a mine awareness project in 1991 that involved radio broadcasts giving simple community warnings. This project ran its first broadcast in September 1991. There were also plans to launch a poster campaign throughout high risk areas.

Since June 1992, the Mines Advisory Group, with funding from Christian Aid U.K. and the Kurdish community in London, has conducted community awareness projects among the Kurdish villages in mined areas, targeting the most vulnerable groups through poster campaigns

---

[54] DOS, *Hidden Killers*, p. 104.

and employing the traditional verbal and play-acting tradition to ensure that children and illiterate villagers benefit fully from the campaign.

## VII.    Conclusion

The need for coordinated clearance of landmines from Iraqi Kurdistan is a humanitarian imperative. The Italian government should be a major donor to such an initiative because such a large majority of the devices in Kurdistan are either of Italian design or manufacture. Other landmine producing and exporting nations should also contribute to the demining effort. In particular, Iraq should be held responsible for funding eradication initiatives.

There is an urgent need to educate Kurdish refugees and returnees so that they have a full understanding of the landmine hazard. In those areas where there is perimeter fencing around minefields, or where the boundaries are well known to some local people, a program of affixing minefield warning signs should be initiated immediately.

Maximum technical and financial support should be made available to Kurdish-run medical facilities. Though emergency facilities established by international humanitarian agencies are essential in the short term, the landmines hazard is a long-term problem which will require an effective indigenous medical service.

## Mozambique[55]

Mozambique was at war almost continuously from the 1960s, when the nationalist struggle erupted against the colonial Portuguese, until October 1992 when the Mozambican government and the Renamo rebels signed a ceasefire accord. Throughout this period combatants on all sides used landmines, often directly against civilians or in an indiscriminate fashion, in clear violation of the Landmines Protocol. Mines have already claimed thousands of victims, and continue to do so even though the war has ended.

The United Nations estimates that there are about two million mines in Mozambique. Although Human Rights Watch's investigation leads it to believe that this figure is high, it is also certain that clearance will take many years—probably decades. So far, little has been done.

Human Rights Watch has confirmed 28 types of antipersonnel mines in Mozambique, but the number is probably greater. Few mined areas have been recorded or marked, and rarely have other measures been attempted to protect civilians. The main impact of mine usage has been to render paths and fields unusable by civilians except at great personal danger.

Mines have taken a terrible human toll in Mozambique. There are an estimated 8,000 amputees who have received some form of medical treatment; medical facilities, however, are quite primitive, and rehabilitation services inadequate. Landmines also constitute one of the most immediate obstacles to postwar redevelopment. They affect delivery of relief aid, repatriation of refugees, and agricultural and commercial reconstruction.

## I.    Background

Mozambique has been ruled since its independence in 1975 by the Front for the Liberation of Mozambique (Frelimo), the victorious nationalist movement. For a number of years, Frelimo ruled ruthlessly

---

[55]The following is adapted from a paper by Alex Vines, a consultant to Human Rights Watch, based on his research in Mozambique. He is writing a comprehensive report on landmines in Mozambique to be published jointly by the Arms Project and Africa Watch later this year.

as a Marxist-Leninist party which tolerated little opposition domestically, and which developed close links with communist and socialist countries.

In 1977, a long-running war began with the Mozambique National Resistance (Renamo or MNR), which was created in 1977 by the Rhodesian Central Intelligence Office (CIO) in retaliation for Mozambique's support for Zimbabwe nationalist guerrillas. Just before Zimbabwe gained independence in 1980, the management of Renamo was transferred to South Africa and run by South Africa's Military Intelligence Directorate (MID).

In 1983, Frelimo began to change its policies, moving toward free market capitalism, pursuing non-alignment internationally, and developing increasingly good relations with many Western nations. However, it could not introduce large-scale reforms because of the war. At the same time, Renamo began operating with greater autonomy from South Africa, expanding its operations, and becoming increasingly brutal, killing thousands of civilians as it carved out territory for itself. MID continued to support Renamo with arms and intelligence until President de Klerk took over the South African government in late 1989. By late 1988 it had become clear that there could be no military solution to the war. After several failed diplomatic initiatives and false starts, direct peace talks began in July 1990 and culminated in the General Peace Accord, signed on October 4, 1992. Under the terms of the accord, demobilized Renamo forces and government troops are to form a 30,000-strong joint army. A 7,500-strong United Nations Operation in Mozambique (ONUMOZ) force will oversee the transition period. Multiparty elections are to follow when demobilization is complete and voters have registered. Elections will be held in late 1994 at the earliest. One of the U.N.'s tasks is to coordinate the clearance of landmines.

## II.    The Mines

While minelaying occurred from 1964 until 1992, most mines were laid by Frelimo and Renamo between 1978 and 1990. In the absence of a comprehensive survey, no one knows the true extent of the landmine problem in Mozambique. The most commonly accepted estimate is the December 1992 United Nations estimate of 2 million mines. However, this figure has no scientific basis; it was reached by simply taking the average of estimates being circulated at the time. Human Rights Watch was unable to conduct a comprehensive assessment of landmine numbers, but its recent study indicates that the U.N. total is an over-estimate. U.N. mines expert Patrick Blagden has admitted to Human Rights Watch, "It is likely that our initial figures were over-pessimistic. However, Mozambique has a serious mines problem and we are concerned to improve this situation."[56]

## A. Types and Sources

The mines found in the greatest quantity are former Soviet PMN, POMZ-2, and POMZ-2M antipersonnel mines as well as mines of East European origin. Renamo's mines were initially supplied by the Rhodesians, and later by South Africa. Smaller quantities of mines from a variety of nations have also been discovered.

Human Rights Watch has confirmed that the following 28 types of antipersonnel mines have been deployed in Mozambique:[57]

- Soviet: PMN, PMN-2, POMZ-2, POMZ-2M, PMD-6, OZM-3, OZM-4, OZM-72, MON-50, MON-100;
- Czechoslovak: PP MI SR II;
- East German: PPM-2;
- Yugoslav: PROM-1;
- Chinese: Type 69, Type 72A;
- Italian: VAR-40, VAR-100, Valmara V-69;
- Belgian: PRB M409;
- French: M59;
- British: No. 6;
- Portuguese: M/969;
- United States: M18A1, M14;
- South African: M2A2, No.69, Claymore-type, Mini-Claymore;
- Rhodesian: Ploughshare;
- Zimbabwean: RAP-1, RAP-2.

---

[56]Telephone interview, New York, July 26, 1993.

[57] This information is based on physical inspection of the mines or detailed descriptions or photographs of them.

Human Rights Watch also identified 19 types of antitank mines, including Soviet, British, U.S., Chinese, Czechoslovak, Brazilian, Austrian, Belgian, South African, and Rhodesian types.

## B. Landmine Use and Strategies

Landmines were deployed by the parties in a variety of ways. Frelimo and Renamo frequently disseminated landmines in a random fashion. In many other cases it appears that civilians were the main target and that the mines were used deliberately to terrorize civilian communities and to deny them access to fields, water sources and fishing points. In the southern provinces, Human Rights Watch found that Renamo was largely responsible for laying mines specifically to discourage or make impossible the return of displaced persons to their homes. These uses of landmines violate the Landmines Protocol.

Renamo's war against the government involved the devastation of the economy and the isolation of government forces to garrisons and towns. As part of this campaign Renamo used landmines extensively. Rhodesian military officials began training Renamo combatants in landmine use in 1977. Renamo often undertook mining to achieve route denial, mining major roads, supply routes, and rural tracks. Airstrips were also an important target of Renamo mining. Ambush mining, particularly on roads and tracks, was extensively employed by Renamo.

Government forces began using mines to protect border installations against Rhodesian incursions in 1977. Many of the technicians had received training in mine laying years before when they trained as nationalist guerrillas, in Tanzania, China, and Algeria, as part of the struggle against Portuguese domination.

Government forces primarily used defensive mining, for the protection of key economic installations and strategic locations. Frelimo laid large defensive minefields along the border with South Africa in the early 1980s. In addition, government patrols laid mines around their positions when they stopped at night. Many of these mines were left behind when patrols moved on, posing a lethal danger to civilians.

Portuguese forces also used landmines in Mozambique. Rhodesian forces planted mines in cross-border raids in the late 1970s. Tanzanian troops laid defensive minefields around their bases in Zambezia province. Malawian and Zimbabwean officials deny that their forces used mines when stationed in Mozambique.

### III.    Social and Economic Impact

The human costs of the landmine problem in Mozambique have been high.  There are an estimated 8,000 amputees who have received some type of medical treatment, but neither the government nor Renamo has kept detailed records of the numbers of people killed or injured.

Many of the landmines laid by Renamo in particular were deliberately intended to cause maximum social and economic disruption, including random dissemination of mines in fields and along their access paths to stop peasants from producing food.  In some areas, farmland, pastures, forests and riverbanks remain dangerous because of mine infestations.

Mines are also a particular hazard to returning refugees.  Alice Simbane's story is typical.  She returned home after three years in a refugee camp in Zimbabwe.  In December 1992 she told Africa Watch in a Maputo hospital:

> I was excited by the peace. I and my family hoped to
> return to peace. We wanted no memories of war.
> However, my brother on the long walk home stepped on
> a landmine and has lost his foot. What have I done to
> deserve this? They told me we had peace.

Facilities for the evacuation, emergency treatment, hospital treatment and physical and social rehabilitation of landmine victims are poor.  This situation is often exacerbated by Renamo's failure to allow mine victims to travel freely to obtain medical care.

While the eradication of the landmine threat is crucial for future economic development, the response of the international community and the Mozambican authorities should not be focused only on mine clearance.  They should also take urgent steps to improve the situation of existing mine victims, get them better medical attention in the short and long-run, and  help them adapt to their handicap and rebuild their lives.

## IV.    Mine Clearing Initiatives

### A.  Gurkha Security Guards Pilot Project

In their first joint attempt to deal with the landmine problem, the Mozambican government and Renamo agreed at the December 31, 1992 meeting of the Supervisory and Control Commission (CSC) to hire a British company, Gurkha Security Guards Ltd. (GSG), to remove mines in central Mozambique. The agreement ended a dispute over who should be contracted; Renamo wanted to hire a South African security company and the government favored having the Zimbabwe army clear mines.

GSG is a privately owned company specializing in security and explosive ordnance disposal throughout the world. It mainly recruits former British and Indian Army Gurkha soldiers and officers. GSG has operated in Mozambique since its creation in 1990. Its initial work concentrated in protecting Lonrho de Mocambique (Lomaco) commercial interests against Renamo attack. During these operations their technicians were frequently required to clear areas and roads which had been mined or booby-trapped.

At the end of January 1993, GSG began a formal mine clearance operation in Mozambique in cooperation with Lomaco. The program is directed by the ICRC and is funded by the European Community. The aim is to clear roads of mines and unexploded ordnance, in order to allow relief vehicles carrying food and other forms of aid to reach more remote regions. GSG's clearance efforts initially concentrated on roads north of Beira. Its contract was extended in July 1993 for five months so that additional roads could be cleared.

### B.  The United Nations Program

In January 1993, the U.N.'s Patrick Blagden unveiled the ONUMOZ's mine clearance plan for Mozambique. The plan's long-term objective is for Mozambique to carry out its own demining operations and serve as a source of expertise for other mine clearance operations in Africa. The first stage called for identifying some 2,000 kilometers of road as priority for clearance. The priority roads were to be those necessary for the humanitarian transport of food to feeding centers in the areas most seriously affected by drought; the establishment and administration of transit centers for refugees; and access to assembly areas for demobilized soldiers.  Subsequently, the ICRC and the U.N. World Food Program (WFP) identified 28 roads as priorities for demining, and the CSC agreed.  Eighty per cent of these roads are in the central provinces of Manica and Sofala.

The second stage of the U.N. plan calls for identifying and clearing routes necessary for the return of refugees to Mozambique from neighboring states and routes necessary for the economic development of Mozambique.  The third stage calls for establishing a school in Mozambique to train mine clearers who will then complete the clearance of the remaining mines.

According to the original time frame, contractors were to be on the ground in Mozambique at the end of May 1993 to begin road clearance.  During June and July the mine clearing school was to be established, and the first group of students were expected to complete their eight-week course in August. Under the plan, 140 Mozambicans were to be trained in 1993, with a total of 570 students certified as mine clearers by 1994.

However, with the exception of the GSG pilot project, no professional demining has taken place because of delays by both Renamo and the government on matters largely unrelated to demining.

## C.  Mine Clearance Delays

U.N. plans for demining have to be approved by both parties in the CSC but little of substance has been agreed to since December 1992. All subsequent U.N. initiatives have been blocked or delayed by either the government or Renamo. The original U.N. "Mine Clearance Plan for Mozambique" failed to get government approval.  U.N. demining expert Patrick Blagden and the U.N. Demining Project Manager Andre Millorit have subsequently been redrafting the proposal.  Government officials told Human Rights Watch that they had disagreed with the text because it suggested that the government had been as responsible as Renamo for laying mines. In the CSC discussions, however, the government claimed it disapproved of the plan because it did not offer sufficient mine clearance training.

Following U.N. lobbying, both sides have agreed that individual mine clearance initiatives can go ahead before the overall Mine Clearance Plan is approved by the CSC. However, all individual initiatives still require CSC clearance. Although badly delayed, the U.N. is continuing to follow the plan.

Since March, the government has been increasingly cooperative towards the U.N. with respect to mine clearance, perhaps recognizing that open roads are to its advantage, and also seeing the political advantages if only Renamo could be blamed for hampering clearance efforts. In contrast, Renamo has become less enthusiastic and is increasingly responsible for serious delays and the postponement of decisions in the CSC.

Some progress was achieved in late August 1993 following a visit to Mozambique by Patrick Blagden. Blagden issued both sides an ultimatum and threatened to withdraw U.N. support for mine clearance if some headway was not made. This appears to have produced results. Both sides agreed to a nation-wide survey of the mines problem by Halo Trust.

The problems with the CSC have forced the U.N. to adhere rigidly to clearance of the 28 roads already approved by the CSC. U.N. officials admit that with the end of the drought and further information about needs, the priority of roads has changed, but fearing that any change would cause further delays, they believe it better to get a core of projects underway before any new agenda is pushed.

### D. Funding for Mine Clearing

Seven million dollars from the ONUMOZ budget and a further $7 million from the U.N. Department of Humanitarian Assistance (DHA) Trust Fund have been earmarked for mine clearance in Mozambique. The U.N.'s Humanitarian Assistance Coordination office (UNOHAC) announced on February 19, 1993 that Norway, the Netherlands, and Sweden will contribute funds towards the first phase of a national demining program. Sweden will provide $4.3 million and Holland $2.7 million. Italy has also announced it will provide funds. Norway will provide $1.1 million for mine clearance in Tete province. A Norwegian non-governmental organization, Norwegian People's Aid (NPA), trained an initial group of 64 Mozambican staff in July-August, and will employ them in two teams to clear mines from rural roads in Mutarara district (Tete).

According to U.N. minutes, UNOHAC has short-listed five companies for mine clearance contracts. The United Nations

Development Progamme Operations Department in New York will decide which company receives a contract for additional road clearance. Any contract signed with a foreign company must include a Mozambican training component.

As the demining plan progresses, the U.N. aims to replace the foreign companies with Mozambicans. Aldo Ajello, the U.N. Special Representative in Mozambique, estimates that the demining plan could provide employment for up to 2,000 people. These jobs would be designated for demobilized soldiers.

### E.  Uncoordinated Mine Clearance

Although both the government and Renamo have been responsible for delaying mine clearance initiatives in the CSC, uncoordinated mine clearance by both sides is underway across the country. The government has been clearing roads through its areas since November. The government's mines expert for Manica/Sofala provinces, Captain Boaventure Chupica Gavalho, told Human Rights Watch that the government has made Manica/Sofala a priority area for its own clearance. Government soldiers have also been active in mine clearance in many other areas.  The government has also been pressing for certain strategically important roads to be cleared in the ICRC pilot project with Gurkha Security Guards. Significant pressure was put on GSG to clear the road between Vunduzi and Casa Banana, although there was no humanitarian need. Casa Banana, which has a military garrison, was the location of Renamo's headquarters from 1983 until captured by the government in 1985.  This road, however, remains uncleared.

Renamo is also reluctant to see some roads opened through its areas as it fears that the government could then move armored units through the areas it controls.  Particularly sensitive is the Macossa–Maringue–Canxixe stretch of road: Maringue is Renamo's current headquarters.

The Direccao Nacional de Estradas e Pontes (DNEP) is also active in mine clearance. Under pressure from commercial entrepreneurs to re-open lucrative trade routes quickly, the DNEP has been using demobilized soldiers on short contracts.

Although Renamo is also active clearing mines along certain roads in its areas, the international agencies have found evidence that Renamo's clearance is particularly poor. Renamo denies this, claiming that the government has continued to lay mines in an attempt to denigrate Renamo's reputation.

### F. Other Mine Clearance Initiatives

Halo Trust, a London-based humanitarian non-profit mine clearance consultancy has obtained a U.N. contract to conduct a nationwide assessment of the landmines situation. Renamo and Mozambican government agreement for this project was eventually reached in late August, after months of paralysis; a contract is now being drawn up by the U.N.. Six teams will be sent with questionnaires to every district and municipality in an attempt to draw up a more scientific assessment of the worst areas for landmines. The British Overseas Development Administration has allocated some £700,000 in support of the plans of Oxfam U.K., Save the Children Fund U.K., and Action Aid to contract three Halo demining teams in Zambezia. Halo's mine clearance plans in Zambezia still require CSC approval as do all of the independent initiatives.

The Mines Advisory Group (MAG), a British-based mine clearance non-governmental organization, sent an assessment mission to Mozambique in March–April 1993, which visited Maputo, Tete and Inhambane provinces. MAG is seeking funding from the European Community to conduct a six month pilot project in Inhambane province. MAG also aims to send six expatriates to Mozambique. They will select and train 40 local staff in three months to conduct mine surveys and clearance. MAG will also link up with Handicap International in a mines awareness project.

From March 21 through March 30, 1993, the U.S. Department of Defense sent a mission to Mozambique to assess whether U.S. Army engineering teams could contribute to the rebuilding of roads and infrastructure. The team's conclusion was that direct U.S. Army involvement would be too costly and that funds channeled through private sector tender would be more cost effective.

The U.S. Agency for International Development (AID) intends to contract the clearance of some of the outstanding 2,170 kilometers of ICRC/WFP priority designated roads in Manica, Sofala and Zambezia provinces. It has earmarked $4 million for this demining. Some of the roads will also be chosen to complement AID's Rural Access Road Project. At least a dozen U.S.-based demining companies bid for the AID mine clearance contract in Mozambique. RONCO Consulting Corporation was awarded a contract in late September.

Companies from Zimbabwe and South Africa are also attempting to win contracts for demining in Mozambique from the U.N., non-governmental organizations, and various donor governments.

## VI.    Conclusion

Mozambique has a serious landmine problem, with certain parts of the country, such as Manica, Sofala, Maputo and Gaza provinces, particularly affected. Most combatant forces, including the government, Renamo, Rhodesian and South African covert forces, and the Tanzanian army have been responsible for laying landmines, especially antipersonnel mines. A variety of countries, including the former Soviet Union and Italy, have manufactured mines used in the Mozambican conflict.

Most of the mines were laid without markings or warnings to the civilian population.   No serious or systematic attempts to minimize civilian casualties from mines appear to have been made.  In fact, a large proportion were laid in such a way that their victims could not be other than civilians. One of the purposes of the random dissemination of mines in inhabited areas was precisely to cause excessive civilian casualties and thereby terrorize the population. The human impact of the landmines is likely to increase in the short term, with the return of refugees and displaced people to homes, fields and paths which could have been mined in their absence.

Facilities for the evacuation, emergency and hospital treatment, and physical and social rehabilitation of landmine victims are inadequate and not improving. Hospital facilities are poor.

Since the October 1992 ceasefire, little professional mine clearance has taken place.   Although the U.N. is responsible for coordinating initiatives, its plans have been postponed by government and Renamo politics, and by U.N. bureaucracy. Meanwhile, the government and Renamo themselves clear roads they want opened, without informing the U.N.. The U.N. has also over-focused on road clearance because of pressure from the humanitarian agencies, when the bush paths are consistently causing the greatest human suffering. Unfortunately, clearance of these paths is not commercially attractive.

The Mozambican government should take immediate steps to assist the U.N. in setting up a systematic and coordinated mine clearance program which will eradicate mines from all areas used by civilians.

Renamo should provide expert personnel to assist mine clearance efforts, and offer all available information about the location of mines to the U.N. Demining Projects Office or any CSC approved mine clearance operations or survey. Renamo must immediately allow landmine victims to travel freely in order to seek adequate treatment in line with Protocol 3, Article 3a of the October, 4, 1992 General Peace Accord.

The U.N. should see that those responsible for causing delays or blocking mine clearance initiatives are made publicly accountable. It should further ensure that mine clearance is not just focused on roads; bush paths and other badly mined rural areas should also be a priority.

All countries which have directly or indirectly provided landmines used in Mozambique should contribute to the cost of the national mine eradication program.

# Nicaragua[58]

An estimated 132,000 landmines were emplanted in Nicaragua during the 1980s.[59]  Many were placed in areas known to be used by civilians without effective markings, warnings or other measures to diminish harm to civilians, and some appear to have been used directly against civilians.  Such uses violate international law.

Mining by the rebels popularly known as the "contras" caused the great majority of civilian casualties.  The contras undeniably used mines indiscriminately, failing to take precautions to protect civilians.  Some evidence also points to deliberate use against civilians.  The particular placement of mines, the use of contact mines on highways traversed by civilian vehicles, the failure to provide any warnings, and an episode in which the contras fired on injured survivors of a mine explosion suggest that killing civilians was probably one of the purposes of contra mining.  The U.S. government was silent about the practices of the Nicaraguan rebels, or attempted to cast doubt on reports of civilian casualties attributable to those practices.

In December 1986, Americas Watch reported that it was aware of just one mining incident involving civilians within Nicaragua attributable to government mining.  However, additional civilian casualties occurred across the border in Honduras as a result of Nicaraguan government mining.  It does not appear that the Nicaraguan government used mines deliberately against civilians, but the lack of warnings indicates that mines were used indiscriminately, particularly in Honduras.

The landmines that caused civilian casualties in Nicaragua were planted primarily on roads in the north.  These roads were used by civilian as well as military vehicles, and served as the only means of travel and commerce between the towns of the area.  The most affected zone was Region 6 (Matagalpa and Jinotega).

Few statistics are available on wartime landmine casualties in Nicaragua.  The Nicaraguan government's human rights commission

---

[58] The following is adapted from *Land Mines in El Salvador and Nicaragua: The Civilian Victims*, an Americas Watch report, dated December 1986.  Unless otherwise noted, all information is from that report.

[59] DOS, *Hidden Killers*, p. 132.

reported 49 civilian deaths and 20 civilian woundings due to landmines in 1986, along with 22 Sandinista soldiers killed and 38 wounded. Americas Watch noted that the number of civilian deaths seemed consistent with the number reported by foreign journalists, but that the number of civilian woundings, and the number of soldiers killed and wounded seemed understated.

## I.     Use by the contras

There is no real debate on the fact that the contras laid the majority of mines that killed and injured civilians in Nicaragua. The contras made no effort to warn the civilian population of the placement of mines. Even if the mines were intended for military targets, they often struck civilians because they were contact mines placed on main highways that served as essential routes for civilians, and civilians used the mined roads more frequently than the military.

The New York Times reported on July 19, 1986, "According to diplomats who see Western intelligence data, the rebels, known as contras, began buying large numbers of mines in the second half of 1985." It is not known from whom the mines were purchased.

## II.    Use by the Sandinistas

The Sandinista People's Army (EPS) conducted an extensive program of defensive mining throughout the interior and along the borders of Nicaragua. According to a recent U.S. Defense Intelligence Agency study, "These activities were viewed as a necessary defense against the activities of contra forces," but, "ultimately, the minelaying activities of the Sandinista government and the EPS created havoc with farming and light industry as well as destroying confidence in the government."[60]

The Sandinista government mined access to bridges throughout the country. The bridges were clearly marked, and mined areas were fenced off with barbed wire. Americas Watch reported one incident in 1986 in which a mine near a bridge was inadequately marked and civilian casualties resulted.

---

[60] DIA/FSTC, p. 2-18.

The Sandinista government admitted to mining stretches of the Honduran border, where the civilian population was relocated by the government. The mines were placed in spots of possible contra incursions from Honduras. U.S. officials claimed that several dozen civilians were maimed or killed by these mines during a six month period in 1986.

Two American journalists were killed in Honduras in 1983 by a mine that was probably planted by the Sandinistas. Their car passed over a mine at a point where the road passes some 20 to 30 yards from the Nicaraguan border. It does not appear that there were warnings of any type.

### III.    Mine Types and Locations

In its 1986 report, Americas Watch identified two types of antipersonnel mines used by the contras. One was the M18A1 Claymore, the same kind provided by the United States to the Salvadoran Army. The Claymore was introduced by the contras in 1983, but Sandinista officials stated that it was not widely used.

The second was a Brazilian antipersonnel mine, first used by the contras in 1986. A small contact mine that requires only three pounds of pressure to explode, it was nicknamed "quitadedos," or "removes toes." Neither of these mines are included in U.S. government lists of mines in Nicaragua.

According to the recent U.S. State Department and Defense Intelligence Agency reports, the following antipersonnel mines have been found in Nicaragua:

- Soviet Union: OZM-4, PDM-1M, PMD-6, PMD-6M, PMN, PMN-2, POMZ-2, POMZ-2M, MON-50, MON-100;
- East Germany: POMZ-2, PMFM-1;
- Czechoslovakia: PP MI SR II;
- Egypt: PMFC-1, PMFH-1, PMM-1;
- Nicaragua: TAP-4.[61]

The State Department report notes that some 48,000 mines are located along the border with Honduras in 393 separate minefields, 5,000

---

[61] DOS, *Hidden Killers*, p. 132; DIA/FSTC p. 2-18.

on the border with Costa Rica, and 65,000 in 277 locations in the interior.[62]    With respect to the interior locations, the Defense Intelligence Agency estimates that 481 potential "targets" were protected by minefields in Nicaragua, the most prevalent being power pylons (369), bridges (52), and rural agricultural cooperatives (26), with others including military installations, warehouses, telecommunications relay stations, electrical sub-stations, and radio complexes.[63]

## IV.    Mine Clearance

The Sandinista government began clearing mines in 1990,[64] but approximately 113,000 antipersonnel and 3,000 antitank mines remained as of October 1991, according to a survey by the Inter-American Defense Board (IADB).[65]

There is now an international effort underway to clear mines in Nicaragua, as part of a Central America regional demining program being carried out under the supervision of the Organization of American States, in cooperation with the IADB and the multilateral Partnership for Democracy and Development in Central America (PDD).    France, Germany, Japan, the Netherlands, Spain, Sweden, and the United States together have contributed something less than $2 million for demining in Nicaragua under this program.[66]

---

[62] DOS, *Hidden Killers*, p. 132.  The DIA study states: "As of the end of 1991, approximately 120,000 landmines remain in 817 identified minefields." DIA/FSTC, p. 2-18.

[63] DIA/FSTC, p. 2-19.

[64] The Defense Intelligence Agency notes that according to EPS reports, almost 11,000 mines were removed during the first year, all but 16 antipersonnel, from 131 locations. DIA/FSTC, pp. 218-219.

[65] DOS, *Hidden Killers*, p. 132.

[66] Col. William C. McDonough, Chief, Intelligence Division, Inter-American Defense Board, Presentation at ADPA Symposium, Sept. 7, 1993.  The U.S. has given or pledged $755,000.  *U.S. Department of State Dispatch*, Vol. 4, No. 12, March 22, 1993, p. 171.

In the first phase of the program, 15 individuals from Argentina, Chile, Colombia, Guatemala, Costa Rica, Peru, and Brazil received demining training from the U.S. Army at Fort Benning starting on March 8, 1993, then proceeded to Nicaragua to begin training Nicaraguan demining personnel on April 15, 1993. Demining operations began in early summer of 1993. As of August 1993, according to an IADB official, 691 mines had been destroyed. The same official has noted that about 20% of areas known to be mined have no mapping, 30% have partial mapping, and 50% have detailed mapping.[67] The goal of the Central American Demining Plan is to remove 60,000 mines from Nicaragua, roughly half of the existing mines, in the first phase of the program from March 1993 to August 1994.[68]

---

[67] William McDonough, Presentation at ADPA Symposium, Sept. 7, 1993.

[68] *U.S. Department of State Dispatch*, Vol. 4, No. 12, March 22, 1993, p. 171; *Hidden Killers*, pp. 40, 41, 132.

## Northern Somalia[69]

In February 1992, Physicians for Human Rights sent a medical team to northern Somalia—which had seceded to form Somaliland in June 1991—to assess the magnitude of the problem of landmines left over from the 1988-1991 civil war.

While the catastrophic famine, political chaos and violence have riveted the world's attention, the devastating legacy of landmines cannot be ignored and must be examined for its own tragic consequences. The fact that the first U.S., French, Belgian, and Canadian fatalities in Operation Provide Comfort were attributed to landmines has focused some attention on the problem. But beyond the immediate loss of life, mines have added significantly to the economic devastation in the country and are one of the principal obstacles standing in the way of the repatriation of more than 800,000 Somali now encamped in neighboring countries.

Today, much of northern Somalia, as well as of the rest of the country, remains infested with landmines. Most of the mines lie scattered across pastoral lands or hidden near water holes or on secondary roads and former military installations. They are most prevalent in the countryside surrounding two of Somaliland's principal cities, Hargeisa and Burao, and in the pastoral and agricultural lands west of Burao. Now that the civil war has ended, the victims of mines have been principally civilians, many of whom are women and children.

No one knows exactly how many mines have been laid throughout Somalia. The U.S. State Department has estimated that approximately 1.2 million to two million mines were planted in Somalia between 1977 and 1992, primarily in the northern region bordering on Ethiopia.[70] The *Somalia Handbook* for U.S. armed forces states that "at least 300,000 mines have been emplaced in Somalia during the last few

---

[69] The following is adapted from *Hidden Enemies: Land Mines in Northern Somalia*, a Physicians for Human Rights report, dated November 1992. Unless otherwise noted, all information is from that report.

[70] DOS, *Hidden Killers*, p. 153. The report estimates the number of mines now in the ground at 1 to 1.5 million. U.N. officials have estimated as many as 2 million mines are strewn throughout the country. *Defense Week*, "Land Mines May Be Somali Conflict's Most Lethal Legacy," September 13, 1993, p. 1.

years."  It notes that "the landmine problem in Somalia can be described
as a general problem in the southern sectors of Somalia and a very
serious problem in the northern sectors."[71]   Unless the mines are
cleared and destroyed, they will kill or maim Somalis well into the next
century.

In the past two years, there has been some success in clearing
mines in Hargeisa and certain other cities, and the number of injuries has
decreased.  But serious problems remain, especially in the surrounding
countryside.[72]   Somaliland officials and international relief workers
fear mine-related injuries and deaths will increase significantly if
hundreds of thousands of Somali refugees suddenly return from camps
across the border in Ethiopia.  Refugees could return spontaneously to
northern Somalia, as they have in the past, or as a result of a decision by
the United Nations High Commissioner for Refugees (UNHCR) and
other U.N. agencies to close down the camps.

The menace of landmines in Somaliland transcends the tragedy
of the loss of life and limb.  Northern Somalia is a largely pastoral
society, dependent on the grazing of sheep, goats, camels, and, to a
limited extent, cattle.  While some nomads have returned to Somaliland,
many are afraid to reoccupy their traditional grazing lands because of
mines and now congregate in cities and towns where they become
alienated from their traditional way of life.

The future is bleak for Somaliland's mine amputees.  Like other
war-wounded, they have limited access to hospital care and rehabilitative
services.  For the most part, Somaliland's hospitals are poorly equipped
and staffed, and essential medicines are scarce or unavailable except to
a wealthy few.  There are no psychiatrists or clinical psychologists to
attend to the psychological consequences of mine injuries.  And while
volunteer medical staff struggle to provide basic services, they are unable
to give adequate care to the seriously injured.

---

[71] *Somalia Handbook: Foreign Ground Weapons and Health Issues*, U.S. Army
Foreign Science and Technology Center, December 1992, DST-1100H-107-92, p.
8.  This document was provided to the Arms Project by Greenpeace, which
obtained it under the Freedom of Information Act.

[72] The *Somalia Handbook* states, "Large patterned minefields, exceeding
100,000 mines have been emplaced in sections surrounding the city.  Extensive
boobytrap activity has also been reported from Hargeysa." p. 8.

Unless a large-scale mine clearance program is initiated soon, Somali refugees will encounter mines as they trek across large tracts of territory on their return home and when they resume farming and grazing their animals. Many of them will succumb to their wounds because little transport is available to get them to medical help. Those who survive will find a health care system so overwhelmed it will be unable to deal properly with their injuries.

## I.    Mines Types and Locations

Most of the landmines in northern Somalia are antipersonnel devices left by Siad Barre's forces and, to a lesser extent, by the Somali National Movement (SNM). Although the SNM forces placed mines on roads and grazing lands, they laid most of their mines along the Ethiopian-Somalian border to protect their own bases. During the Ogaden War, Barre's troops heavily mined the border to discourage incursions by the Ethiopian Army. According to the U.S. State Department survey, 70 percent of landmines in Somalia are planted in some 76 to 96 barrier minefields all along the mountainous terrain on the Somali-Ethiopian border.[73] From 1984 on, Barre's troops mined large tracts of land to prevent SNM attacks from Ethiopia. Until the cessation of hostilities in February 1991, mines had been placed around wells, the perimeters of military camps and installations, and across the network of many of the primary and secondary roads between cities and villages. The city of Hargeisa was also heavily mined and booby-trapped.

SNM officers claim that the mines were mostly planted by troops under the command of "Morgan", Siad Barre's son-in-law, who is known locally as "the butcher of Hargeisa." According to a former SNM officer, "When Siad Barre's troops controlled the capital and its surroundings from 1988 to 1990, they put mines in farm after farm, without keeping any record of where the mines were placed."

One of the cruelest—and clearly unlawful—tactics used by Siad Barre's troops was the deliberate mining of civilian homes. In 1988, government forces shelled and bombed the capital of Hargeisa. Before fleeing, many residents buried their valuables in holes dug in the floors or courtyards of their homes. Upon discovering these stashes, soldiers

---

[73] DOS, *Hidden Killers*, p. 154. The report has a lengthy list of areas, roads, and towns infested with mines.

removed the jewelry and other valuables and placed booby-traps or mines in these hiding places. After the fighting ceased, many of those who had fled returned to their homes in the first months of 1991 only to be injured or killed by these hidden explosives. While most of these booby-traps are thought to have been removed, some are still in place. Some families were said to be squatting outside their houses because they were afraid to enter. No precise accounting has been made of the number injured in this manner.

In 1991, Physicians for Human Rights noted one large minefield east of Hargeisa's airport that formed a giant arc from the south end of the runway to the Berbera road. Along the perimeter of the field, there were remnants from sandals of people who had stepped on mines.

Siad Barre's forces deliberately mined wells and grazing lands in an effort to kill and terrorize nomadic herders whom the army viewed as protectors of the SNM. While direct evidence is not available, most observers agree that Siad Barre's forces undertook this extensive mining to prevent resettlement by the predominantly Isaak nomads and agriculturalists.

At the time of the Physicians for Human Rights visit, many of Somaliland's principal and secondary roads were closed because of mines. On some roads, detours had been set up, especially for motorized transport, resulting in lengthy delays to get to markets or other destinations.

Rimfire, the British mineclearing firm contracted by the UNHCR, has reportedly identified landmines from some 24 different countries in Somalia. Some are World War II-vintage mines from the U.S. and U.K., but the majority are of Czech, Soviet, Pakistani, and Belgian origin. About 60% are thought to be antipersonnel mines.[74]

According to one report, the U.N. has positively identified at least 30 different types of mines from nine to 10 different countries, including the former Soviet Union, Pakistan, Belgium, China, Italy, and the U.S.[75]

The recent State Department report and the U.S. Army's *Somalia Handbook*, taken together, list more than 40 different mines from at least 10 nations. Twenty-four mines are antipersonnel:

---

[74] DOS, *Hidden Killers*, p. 153.

[75] *Defense Week*, September 13, 1993, p. 1.

- Belgium: PRB M409, PRB M35;
- China: Type 72, Type 72B;
- Czechoslovakia: PP-MI-SR, PP-MI-SR II;
- East Germany: PMP-71, PPM-2;
- Egypt: M/78, Claymore-type;
- Italy: V, Valmara 69, Valmara 59;[76]
- Pakistan: P2 Mk 2, P4 Mk 1;
- Soviet Union: PMD-6, PMD-6M, PMN, POMZ-2, POMZ-2M, MON-50;
- United States: M16A2, M14;
- United Kingdom: Mk 2.

## II.     The Consequences of Mines

### A.  The Injured

Somaliland's minister of health, Dr. Suleiman Abdi, formerly a practicing surgeon at the Hargeisa Hospital, has said that before the war ended in February 1991, about two-thirds of landmine-injured were military and one-third civilian.   But since liberation, more than 90 percent have been civilians.  Physicians for Human Rights found that in the first five months of 1991, after thousands of refugees spontaneously left the camps in Ethiopia, there was a sudden surge in civilians injured by landmines.  According to the medical staff at Hargeisa Hospital, the hospital was admitting two to three landmine-injured patients daily between November 1990 and April 1991.   They also said that an unknown number died before reaching the hospital.

Of the mine-injured people Physicians for Human Rights examined in Berbera, Hargeisa, and Borama, most were children under the age of 16.  Data from the Hargeisa Hospital shows that 74.6 percent of landmine-injured treated at that hospital from February 1991 through February 1992 were children between five and 15 years of age.

Physical disabilities are difficult to accept psychologically in any society.  But in a pastoral one, where muscle power means survival, the loss of a limb can be particularly cruel.  Among nomads, amputees may become a burden to their families.  Male amputees may eventually marry,

---

[76] DOS, *Hidden Killers*, p. 153; *Somalia Handbook*, pp. 11-49.

but marriage is less likely for female amputees, according to health officials in Hargeisa.

Children who play with mines, mine detonators, and grenades suffer from amputations of the hands and injuries to the eyes, often resulting in blindness.  One six-year-old boy Physicians for Human Rights examined at the Hargeisa Hospital had picked up an object that looked like "the plastic top of a thermos bottle" on a road near his home.  (This description fits that of an antipersonnel mine.)  The explosion blinded him in both eyes, scarred his face, destroyed his right hand which was subsequently amputated at the wrist, and left both knees disabled with presumed shrapnel injuries.  This young boy's situation is particularly tragic as his father died in the civil war.

Physicians for Human Rights found it difficult to determine how many Somalis were amputees as a result of mine blast injuries.  Virtually no such statistics exist in Somaliland, as the government has no capacity to collect them.  As a result, they developed an estimate of the total, drawing on the limited hospital data available and the tallies of the total number of physically disabled in the country collected by the various branches of the Somali Red Crescent Society (SRCS).  They estimated conservatively that of the more than 9,000 physically disabled persons in Somaliland about 1,500 to 2,000 are amputees.  Of this total, they estimated roughly half are landmine-injured.  Physicians for Human Rights also estimated that by February 1991, about 35 percent of these amputees were civilians and that the proportion was growing.

### B.  Health Care in Somaliland

Health care in Somaliland is a testimony to years of neglect, the looting of health care facilities during the civil war, persecution of the Isaak population, and the incapacity of the new government to function properly without revenues.  Physicians for Human Rights found that Somaliland's health infrastructure was woefully inadequate.  With the exception of the ICRC hospital in Berbera, nearly all hospital staff were volunteers, as the government was incapable of paying salaries. Furthermore, because of the absence of salaries, qualified staff often left for Ethiopia, Yemen, and elsewhere.  The doctors in Hargeisa complained of a shortage of surgical instruments, general anesthesia, and other drugs. Laboratory services were limited to urinalyses, stool examinations, and hemoglobin determinations. No chemistries, bacteriology or white cell counts were available.

At the time of its investigation, Physicians for Human Rights found seven hospitals in Somaliland where general surgery was practiced with a minimum of personnel and equipment. The numbers were largely insufficient to meet the needs. All hospitals could perform amputations, with the exception of Erigavo, but limited X-ray facilities existed only in Borama, Hargeisa, Burao, and Berbera. Only one antiquated X-ray machine was functioning in Hargeisa, where most trauma surgery was performed. Crossmatching for transfusions could be performed in Boroma, Hargeisa, and Burao, but the ICRC/SRCS hospital in Berbera was the only one with a functioning blood bank capable of screening donated blood for transmissible diseases. This latter hospital was described by the Minister of Health as the only fully functioning hospital in the entire country.

There were only three orthopedic and eight general surgeons in Somaliland. There was no ambulance service; the transportation of the sick and wounded was by any private vehicle available or by camels or donkeys. Except for the ICRC/SRCS hospital in Berbera, there was not a regular supply of anesthesia or antibiotics as the Ministry of Health, organized in June 1991, did not have a budget.

A number of non-governmental organizations have been attempting to help. The ICRC and Red Crescent Society were running the Berbera hospital and distributing food for inpatients and drugs to the hospitals in Las Anod and Borama. The ICRC planned to turn these activities over to the Norwegian Red Cross. Until April 1992, the German Emergency Doctors aided the Hargeisa Hospital with drugs, in-patient food, renovation and maintenance of the buildings, and water and fuel for an electric generator. The U.K.-based Somali Relief Agency (SOMRA) supplied medicines to the Sheikh Hospital. Doctors without Borders/Holland operated a maternal and child health service in Hargeisa but had to close down its surgical activities in Burao due to an outbreak of fighting in the city in January 1992. Save the Children/U.K. provided laboratory and administrative consultants to the Ministry of Health. Cooperazioni Internazionale, an Italian non-governmental organization, was helping to renovate and prepare for opening the Berbera District Hospital. Cooperazioni Internazionale also provided an orthopedic surgeon for the Berbera Hospital.

Transportation has always been difficult in northern Somalia. Physicians for Human Rights determined through interviews that the average delay in transportation to the hospital in Hargeisa was six to eight hours. Some of the mine-injured, however, took days to arrive at a hospital. The Minister of Health told of one instance of a 15-year-old girl who arrived at the Hargeisa hospital 15 days after stepping on a mine. Other occasional cases have arrived after two- or three-day delays due to lack of transportation.

Landmine victims in Somaliland suffer from a high rate of post-operative infections. Because of poor surgical procedures at the Hargeisa Hospital, surgeons there estimated an infection rate of 80 percent for amputees. In contrast, the rate of infection at the Berbera Hospital managed by the ICRC was four to five percent. Another serious problem is a cultural bias against amputations which, more often than not, results in poor stumps because families insist on the surgeon cutting only a few centimeters above the wound. Often this means that an artificial limb cannot be properly fitted, when and if it becomes available. Physicians for Human Rights saw several amputees who may have to undergo reamputation before they can be fitted with prostheses.

With the exception of the surgeons operating at the hospital in Berbera, it did not appear as if the surgical staff elsewhere had received training in trauma surgery from the ICRC or others outside of the country. Nor were there medical texts or journals available to them.

## C. Rehabilitation

Throughout northern Somalia, especially on the streets of Hargeisa, it is commonplace to see amputees shuffling along the road on one leg with the aid of crutches and canes. Somaliland had been without a formal rehabilitation program until the arrival of Handicap International in late 1991. Physicians for Human Rights found that there were no prostheses available in the country other than what local carpenters made from wood and metal. Such locally made prostheses are heavy and cumbersome, and thus rarely used. Physicians for Human Rights saw only one artificial limb during its two week stay in the country, and it was being repaired.

Besides physical rehabilitation and prosthetics, the severe psychological problems of amputees have gone unattended. Adaptation by the nomads to hospital life is not easy. The inability of amputees to tend livestock and to maintain a nomadic way of life is equivalent to a total disability and represents a severe economic and psychological loss to a Somali family.

Mine amputees usually do not go back to a nomadic area but to a village nearby. Children may be sent to a Koranic school if possible; regardless, they may be separated from their parents. Many of them are under the age of twelve and this loss is profound and with unknown consequences.

There have been a number of cases of children with bilateral limb amputations. Others have suffered from both blindness and the loss of either upper or both upper and lower extremities. For all of these patients, psychiatric help or psychological counseling is greatly needed. However, at the time of the Physicians for Human Rights visit, there were no psychiatrists or clinical psychologists in northern Somalia.

## III.  Mine Eradication

When the guerrilla forces of the SNM reoccupied northern Somalia in early 1991, they were well aware that though they had defeated one enemy, Siad Barre, they still faced another monumental adversary—hundreds of thousands of landmines, covering much of their national territory. The SNM promptly began demining operations under the leadership of Abdullahi Behi Obey. Behi, a professional soldier, first trained in Egypt in demolition and demining. He served with Somalia's military forces and finally with the SNM. Behi began mine clearance for the SNM with a force of 60 men, of whom 40 percent were killed or injured by mines in the first six months of 1991.

It took little time for the representatives of international voluntary agencies, who began to arrive in 1990 and early 1991, to realize the gravity of the threat of the landmines. Matt Brydon, the Somaliland representative of Doctors without Borders/Holland (MSF) returned in 1991 with an exploratory team. (MSF eventually left northern Somalia for security reasons.) Brydon recalls that at the time there were some four to five landmine casualties a day. By April 1991, Brydon had contacted the European Economic Community and the United States Agency for International Development at their regional offices in Nairobi, Kenya, presenting the urgent case for a demining operation. By the end of April, there was agreement that demining would go ahead.

Several mistakes made at the onset of the demining program in 1991 have plagued it ever since.  None of the groups planning this initial phase established mine awareness programs, such as public education on the type, location, and potential danger of mines.  These groups failed to include funding for comprehensive surveys to determine the location and number of mines, as well as the number of victims killed or injured, and the latter's access to hospital care.  While the need for an independent monitor was foreseen to gauge progress of the demining effort, none of the international agencies involved has provided funding or recruited a qualified individual for this role nor for other monitoring needs.  As one observer put it:  "Our vision of what was required was too narrow at the time.  There was no proper system of control set up, no system for setting priorities."

The European Community awarded a contract to Rimfire, a British company, which began its operations in Northern Somalia with a partial mines survey in May 1991.  Rimfire's principal functions have been training and supervision of demining personnel, defusing mines themselves, and some other intricate explosive ordnance disposal (EOD) work.  Using demining and demolition experts, usually numbering at least 14 (mostly retirees from the British armed forces), Rimfire has trained Somalis, called "Pioneers," in the basic techniques of mine detection and disposal at an old military camp on the outskirts of Hargeisa.  In its first two years of operation, Rimfire trained about 450 Somali deminers, and removed about 50,000 mines.  Most of these were in and around Hargeisa, the heavily mined airport area on the southern perimeter of the city, and other priority sites including water sources, the Hargeisa prison, and several military installations.  Two Rimfire workers had legs blown off, and two Somali employees were killed and 11 injured by mines in the same period.[77]

According to a report in May 1993, the United Nations pays for half the costs of Rimfire's operations, and the U.S., U.K., the Netherlands and the European Community share the other half.  In the same report, a Rimfire official stated that hundreds of thousands of mines remain, adding that Rimfire has identified at least 56 minefields to be cleared, each with maybe 3,000 mines.[78]

---

[77] AP wire story, untitled, by Paul Alexander, May 30, 1993.

[78] AP wire story, untitled, by Paul Alexander, May 30, 1993.

Today, in addition to Rimfire's mineclearing activities in northern Somalia, U.N. coalition troops and U.S. forces are conducting mineclearing as part of their mission in Somalia.

The United Nations has drafted a preliminary plan for demining Somalia after a political settlement and some measure of stability have been achieved. It has yet to be approved by the U.N. Special Envoy in Somalia, or by various Somali factions. According to the U.N.'s top mine expert Brigadier (Ret.) Patrick Blagden, the U.N. will have to avoid carefully having the plan appear to favor one clan over another. The plan has four elements: clear mine impediments to U.N. forces; get a demining contractor to do a survey; get a demining contractor to clear certain routes near the Ethiopian and Kenyan borders; and, create one or more mine clearance centers to train Somalis in demining.[79]

### A. Mine Awareness

There are many Somalis who have chosen to ignore the danger of mines, especially when it comes to protecting their livestock. In the course of its mission, Physicians for Human Rights witnessed one such case. On the perimeter of the Hargeisa airport, a Somali woman asked for assistance to rescue her cow, which had just had its two front legs blown off by an antipersonnel mine. The woman explained that she had already lost the rest of her animals in the vicinity of the airport. Only two weeks before, her thirteen-year-old daughter had been tending animals close by and stepped on an antipersonnel mine, losing her right leg. Despite the danger all around her, the woman brazenly walked out to the latest victim, her only surviving cow, to aid the demining team which was cautiously placing a rope around its neck. The team warned her of the danger, but to no avail. Fortunately, she was not injured. Evidently, many Somalis believe these injuries are a matter of fate and thus take enormous risks, especially when tending their livestock.

### B. Resettlement

Several hundred thousand Somali refugees are poised to return to Somaliland from border camps in Ethiopia where they have taken refuge since 1988. Hundreds of thousands returned spontaneously

---

[79]*Defense Week*, Sept. 13, 1993, p. 11.

following the defeat of Siad Barre's forces in early 1991. At first, men came alone, then women and older boys, and finally other children. This migration continues without order or direction.

Refugees and relief officials place the problem of landmines in northern Somalia high on their list of concerns. "Mines intrude on everything in Somaliland" said Gary Perkins, the UNHCR representative in Djibouti. All interviewed agreed that landmines constitute a major obstacle to the repatriation of refugees from the camps along the Ethiopian border. The UNHCR considers demining a priority for any repatriation plan.

When Somali refugees return to northern Somalia it is likely they will return to areas settled by fellow clan or subclan members. Those who raise crops and graze livestock in the greater Hargeisa, Burao, and Odwenye areas may be at greatest risk.

Regardless, an untold number will not return to a nomadic existence because, in part, of landmines. They may, by force of these circumstances, further crowd the already overburdened cities.

## IV.    Conclusion

The widespread presence of landmines in northern Somalia must be considered a humanitarian emergency, separate from, and regardless of, the other crises facing the Somali people. There is an urgent need for planning and coordination of the aid program for demining, mine awareness, and the care and rehabilitation of mine victims throughout Somalia. The United Nations should take the lead in this, in close cooperation with non-governmental organizations such as the ICRC.

Donor governments and international agencies should commit greater resources to demining operations in northern Somalia. There is no system of surveillance in place to estimate mine injuries or to keep track of where they occur. Nor have detailed maps been made of the location of mine fields. Data collection and analysis should be a part of any mine survey and eradication program.

A mines awareness program should be established in Somaliland that utilizes the schools, the mosques, and radio. Above all, children must be taught what mines look like and how to avoid them.

Donor governments and U.N. agencies should also increase assistance for upgrading acute care facilities and for rehabilitation services in Somaliland.

Finally, under no circumstances should Somali refugees in the border camps be encouraged or forcibly moved into areas where they are endangered by mines.

# 7
# MINE CLEARANCE

Given the enormity of the uncleared landmine
problem, it is obvious that there is no quick solution.
Locating uncleared landmines is a labor-intensive, slow,
dangerous, low-technology operation. Destruction of
uncleared landmines is even slower, more labor-
intensive, and extremely dangerous. It is one of the
grim ironies of landmines that they are so easy to lay,
and yet so difficult and dangerous to find and destroy.[1]

The sheer number of landmines strewn around the world is
daunting, but the situation becomes even more acute recognizing the
tremendous difficulties involved in removing those mines. More
disturbing still, the landmine situation is getting worse and is almost
certain to continue to deteriorate in the foreseeable future, absent a
global ban on production, stockpiling, trade and use.

It will take decades to clear any meaningful portion of the
approximately 100 million uncleared and unexploded landmines now
planted worldwide. Yet thousands of new landmines are being sown
every day. The human suffering caused by mines is increasing daily as
the number of mines being laid vastly exceeds the number being
removed.

As the recent U.S. State Department study on international mine
clearance points out, "It is the detection, removal and destruction of
landmines already in place that is the most critical need for populations
affected by landmines."[2] While this is true for populations already
affected by mines, it is equally clear that demining alone—even if current
efforts are increased many times over—will not be sufficient to deal with
the global landmine crisis. The ease with which mines are sown, and the
difficulty with which they are cleared, makes it altogether apparent that
mine clearance is inevitably too little, too late. Only if a ban on
production, stockpiling, trade and use of landmines is in place can the

---

[1] U.S. Department of State, *Hidden Killers: The Global Problem with Uncleared Landmines* (Washington, D.C.: U.S. Dept. of State, 1993), p. 3.

[2] DOS, *Hidden Killers*, p. 4.

international community begin to make significant headway against the killing, maiming, and socio-economic destruction caused by landmines.

The time, cost, and danger involved in demining are staggering. Those involved in mine clearing operations point out that the ratio of time to plant a mine against the time it takes to lift and disarm it is about 1:100. For modern scatterable mines delivered by aircraft or artillery, it is much worse. Some automated mine distribution systems can deliver thousands of mines in a matter of minutes. It could take weeks or perhaps months, depending on terrain, to clear mines laid in a single hour. As a rule of thumb, deminers estimate that one person can clear 20 to 50 square meters per day by hand. In Afghanistan, the United Nations expects to clear about 10 square kilometers per year.[3]

The cost ratio of planting a mine against removing it is similar to, and in some cases worse than, the time ratio. The United Nations has estimated the costs of clearance, including support and logistics costs, at somewhere between $300 and $1,000 per mine.[4] Most antipersonnel mines cost less than $25, however, and some less than $3.[5]

Large parts of the world will never be demined. Some areas mined during World War II have never been properly cleared, even after 50 years. The huge numbers of mines, the time and cost constraints of demining, and the absence of equipment capable of effective humanitarian demining on a massive scale, make the notion of an entirely demined world a utopian dream. In countries like Afghanistan and Cambodia, the mine infestations are so large that there is no hope of clearing them all. The ICRC has estimated that it could take thousands of years to clear Afghanistan.[6] In Cambodia, it is likely that many of the large border minefields will be marked but not cleared,

---

[3] Ibid., p. 28.

[4] U.N. Demining Expert Patrick Blagden gave this range at the ICRC Symposium in Montreux, April 1993. See also his comments in *Defense Week*, September 13, 1993, p. 11.

[5] See Chapter 3 for pricing information.

[6] Jody Williams, "Social Consequences of Widespread Use of Landmines," in ICRC, *Report of the Symposium on Anti-personnel Mines: Montreux*, (Geneva: ICRC, 1993) p. 6.

leaving thousands of mines in place.  Following the Falkland/Malvinas war, and unsuccessful state-sponsored attempts to clear British-laid mines, the British government made a standing offer of £1 million to anyone who could effectively clear the mines there.  There have been no takers.[7]

In areas that are cleared, it is not realistic to expect that each and every mine will be removed and destroyed.  The task is simply too huge and the level of technology insufficient.  Those engaged in humanitarian mine clearance, while aiming, in theory, for 100 percent clearance, find anything less than 99 percent clearance unacceptable.  However, as one experienced mine clearance expert put it, "Much as we might wish it otherwise, there is rarely such a thing as 100% clearance of mines.... It will not be possible in countries such as Somalia or Cambodia where there is no record of where mines have been laid nor how many, and this is the situation most often faced by humanitarian agencies."[8]  Or as noted in the State Department report, "Quite simply, demining is a business in which anything less than 100% accuracy costs lives, and 100% accuracy is difficult to achieve."[9]

Far greater resources need to be devoted to demining—both to immediate clearance and to the development of new detection and clearance equipment and technologies—by individual nations and by international organizations, public and private.  Supplier nations and mine producers bear special responsibility.

But mine clearance can never keep pace with mine infestation.  Only a successful ban on production, trade and use of landmines will allow mine clearance efforts to deal with the problems that already exist.

---

[7] DOS, *Hidden Killers*, p. 22.

[8] Alistair Craib, "Mine Detection and Demining" in ICRC, *Report of the 1993 Montreux Symposium*, pp. 150–151.

[9] DOS, *Hidden Killers*, p. 4.

## I.     What is Mine Clearance?[10]

A number of terms are used in connection with detection and removal of landmines: demining, mine clearance, area mine clearance, countermine measures, mine removal, eradication, and minefield breaching. Several of these terms are often used interchangeably. The important distinction to understand is between removal of mines for humanitarian purposes and removal of mines for military purposes. In general, "demining," "mine clearance," and "area mine clearance" are terms that are associated with humanitarian activities, while "mine countermine measures" and "breaching" are associated with military combat activities.

### A.  Humanitarian Mine Clearance

In humanitarian mine clearance, the objective is to remove each and every landmine in a minefield. United Nations demining expert Brigadier (Ret.) Patrick Blagden has stated that to be considered successful, humanitarian mine clearance requires a clearance rate of over 99 percent and preferably over 99.9 percent.[11]

Almost all humanitarian mine clearance is still done by hand, because mechanical clearance equipment is not capable of clearing such a high percentage of mines. Those involved in demining believe that the only sure way to detect a mine is by manual methods. The most common method of hand clearance is "probing" or "prodding," in which a person walks into a minefield and pokes at the ground until he encounters a mine, which is then either destroyed in place, or disarmed, removed and destroyed elsewhere. Obviously, hand clearance is extremely dangerous, very slow, and very expensive. Deminers maintain, however, that when carried out by experienced, well-trained and well-equipped operators, it

---

[10] Much of this chapter, and particularly the technical aspects of this section, draws extensively from papers on demining presented at the ICRC Symposium in Montreux in April 1993. The Arms Project and Physicians for Human Rights are particularly indebted to these authors for their expertise on this issue: Patrick Blagden, Alistair Craib, Terry Gander, Paul Jefferson, and Rae McGrath.

[11] Patrick Blagden, "Summary of United Nations Demining" in ICRC, *Report of the 1993 Montreux Symposium*, p. 118.

will usually prove to be the most efficient and reliable technique.  After having served seven months with the U.N. Protection Force in the former Yugoslavia clearing mines, Canadian Major John Thompson declared, "The most effective mine clearing resource is still a sapper armed with eyes to see, finger tips to feel the ground surface, an effective mine detector to sweep below the surface, and a prodder to feel below the surface."[12]

According to Alan Epstein of the U.S. Department of Defense's Office of the Program Manager for Mines, Countermine, and Demolitions:

> The challenges posed by [humanitarian] demining are formidable, since it is almost impossible to determine that you have removed every single mine from an area. At the present time, there is no military equipment capable of rendering this clearance reliably over an extended period of time. This means that demining will continue to be a slow, tedious process.[13]

In almost every case now encountered throughout the world, the task of demining is complicated by the fact that mines have been laid in an uncontrolled manner; the deminer has no knowledge of the exact locations or quantities of each type of mine.  Paul Jefferson, a British demining expert blinded in a mine accident, has stated that while "mine clearance should, in essence, be very simple," the obstacles are many and varied: mines are laid with malevolent intent; they are concealed and camouflaged, usually with the specific intent of defeating efforts to avoid them or find them; and, they can be laid specifically to defeat clearance methods, through combinations of different types of mines and fuzes, and booby-traps and anti-handling devices.  Moreover, topographical factors can be complicating—dense jungle, sodden or hard-baked ground, rocky

---

[12] Major John Thompson, "Demining Yugoslavia," presentation to American Defense Preparedness Association, *Symposium and Exhibition on Mines, Countermine & Demolitions* (Asheville, North Carolina, Sept. 7–9, 1993).

[13] DOS, *Hidden Killers*, p. 16.

terrain, ground with metallic fragments such as shrapnel, and other conditions all pose special difficulties.[14]

### B. Military Breaching

The military act of minefield breaching involves creating a path through a minefield, as quickly as possible, to allow troops and vehicles to pass. For breaching, any clearance rate over 80% is generally considered satisfactory, as the military accepts taking risks to achieve an objective in a timely fashion.

Breaching usually involves fairly sophisticated, higher technology equipment that clears a path either by exploding mines or pushing them aside. Minefields are generally breached explosively, with long linear charges; mechanically, by means of plows, rollers or flails; or, electronically, with magnetic signature duplication systems.[15] This equipment is discussed in greater detail below.

To date, no nation has developed equipment specifically tailored for humanitarian demining, and current military equipment is poorly suited to humanitarian clearance. As noted in the recent State Department report, "The military, for whom mine detection and removal equipment are created, do not do demining.... Unfortunately, this means that most military countermine equipment is not currently configured to be of much use for wide area [humanitarian] mine clearance."[16]

### II.    The Demining Process

The demining process can be broken down into three basic parts: location and identification of minefields; detection of individual mines; and neutralization and/or destruction of mines.

---

[14] Paul Jefferson, "An Overview of Demining, Including Mine Detection Equipment" in ICRC, *Report of the 1993 Montreux Symposium*, p. 125.

[15] DOS, *Hidden Killers*, p. 15.

[16] Ibid., p. ii.

## A.  Location of Minefields

Because of the indiscriminate fashion in which landmines are
typically used, it is often a difficult task to establish precisely where
minefields and their boundaries are located.  It almost every case, no
records will have been kept, no maps made, and no warning signs
erected.[17]   In addition to visual inspection for tell-tale signs,
information has to be gathered from locals, who may have seen mines
being laid, and from records or accounts of casualties to humans,
livestock, and equipment.

Utilizing these and other methods, survey teams draw up
generalized maps showing areas thought to be mined.  They then carry
out a more detailed survey to identify the boundaries of a minefield, and,
in some cases, the types of mines in the area.   Due to the dangers
involved, dogs are sometimes used to locate the first mines.  The outside
of the minefield is then marked with warning signs and mine clearance
teams take over.

## B.  Detection of Mines

There are four main ways to detect individual mines within a
minefield: using prodders, mine detectors, and dogs for buried mines, and
using sight for surface-laid mines.

### 1.  Prodding

The most common method of detection is prodding, also known
as probing.  It is an extremely tedious, time-consuming, and hazardous
method.  An individual pokes a prod into the ground until encountering
a mine.  A prod is usually a thin spike, about 9-12 inches long, often with
a handle; sometimes a bayonet or similar object is used.  It is pushed into
the ground at a shallow angle (about 30 degrees), so that the tip will
contact the side of a mine.

There are many dangers involved.  A mine may be buried too
deep for detection by the prod, and it is discovered only with the
deminer's next step.  A mine can be turned on its side (either on purpose

---

[17] Patrick Blagden, "Summary of United Nations Demining" in ICRC, *Report
of the 1993 Montreux Symposium,* p. 119.

or due to natural dislocation) so that the prodder hits the pressure plate rather than the side of the mine, causing it to explode. A mine can be camouflaged with flat stones around the sides of the mine. A mine can be booby-trapped with anti-handling devices, so that a slight disturbance will cause it to explode.

Obviously, the work requires careful training, constant alertness, complete dedication and slow, patient care. But experienced mine clearers maintain that, although extremely slow, prodding is the safest and most reliable way to detect all forms of buried mines, and the only way of locating 100% of mines.

## 2. Mine Detectors

Metal mine detectors are commonly used by both military and humanitarian mine clearers throughout the world. According to a recent study by the U.S. Defense Intelligence Agency, metal mine detectors are produced in at least 23 different countries.[18] Despite the widespread use of these devices, the State Department's demining report offered this rather tepid assessment of metal mine detectors: "the metallic mine detector is a reasonably effective, albeit, a rather slow method for locating buried metallic mines which have been laid for a relatively short period of time."[19]

There are two main problems with use of metal mine detectors: they detect many things they are not designed to detect, and they do not detect many things they are designed to detect. They detect not only mines, but also other types of metal, thus giving many time-consuming false signals from shrapnel, spent rounds, tin cans, and other items. Much worse, mines with low metal content are nearly impossible to locate with today's detectors. According to a report by the U.S. Defense Intelligence Agency, even though recent advances in electronics have

---

[18] U.S. Defense Intelligence Agency and U.S. Army Foreign Science and Technology Center, *Landmines Warfare — Trends & Projections*, December 1992, DST-11605-019-92, p. 4-3. This document was obtained by the Arms Project through the Freedom of Information Act. The U.S. Army is currently purchasing the AN/PSS-12 handheld metallic mine detector, made by the Austrian company Schiebel.

[19] DOS, *Hidden Killers*, p. 18.

increased both the reliability and sensitivity of metal mine detectors, "they cannot reliably locate the mines with little or no metal."[20]

Unfortunately, more and more mines are being manufactured in non-metallic materials, usually plastic. Technology has reached the point where most mines produced today have only a small amount of metal. Though often called "non-metallic" mines, most are more properly called "minimum-metal" mines, because they have some metal, usually the firing pin, a spring, or a seal. At least 18 countries, including all the world's major producers and exporters, manufacture minimum- metal mines.[21] Even the best modern mine detectors may only detect these mines under ideal conditions.

Some truly all-plastic mines are now being produced. According to U.N. demining expert Patrick Blagden, "...materials technology has now reached the stage where the use of metal is unnecessary except as a cost-savings measure. The next generation of anti-personnel mines may be completely undetectable by the present generation of electronic mine detectors."[22] In its recent report accompanying the fiscal 1994 defense authorization bill, the Senate Armed Services Committee noted that "the Defense Department has made little progress in fielding effective systems to detect and neutralize mines, especially modern anti-personnel mines. This has been a serious problem for U.S. military personnel. It is also a problem for peacekeeping operations." The Committee included $10 million for Army efforts to improve the detection and neutralization of mines, and urged the Army "to pursue technologies that can be shared in an international environment."[23]

---

[20] DIA/FSTC, p. 4-1.

[21] DIA/FSTC, p. 3-19 and the Arms Project Data Base. The countries include Argentina, Belgium, Brazil, China, Egypt, Germany, Greece, Hungary, India, Italy, the Netherlands, Pakistan, Portugal, South Africa, Spain, the United States, the former U.S.S.R., and former Yugoslavia.

[22] Patrick Blagden, "Summary of United Nations Demining" in ICRC, *Report of the 1993 Montreux Symposium*, p. 121.

[23] Senate Report 103-112, to accompany S. 1298, the National Defense Authorization Act for Fiscal Year 1994, July 27, 1993, pp. 69-70.

Various types of non-metallic mine detectors have been and continue to be developed. The DIA study notes that there are hand-held ground penetrating radar detectors which locate anomalies in the soil, but that these devices are very prone to false signals from things such as rocks and tree roots, greatly limiting their utility.[24]    The State Department report reaches the same conclusion:

> Commercially developed non-metallic mine detectors have so far proven to be impractical because of their inability to perform in dry soils and an unacceptably high false alarm rate caused by inconsistencies in the ground. This type of detector has been withdrawn from U.S. military service. However, promising research continues in this field.[25]

Deminers generally believe that the most important technological advance for humanitarian mine clearance efforts would be the development of detection equipment which would reliably locate minimum-metal mines. The Arms Project and Physicians for Human Rights believe that national governments and international organizations should devote much greater resources to this effort.

### 3. Dogs

The explosive content in mines gives off an odor which is not detectable by human beings, but can be picked up by dogs. It is difficult to make a mine non-detectable by "sniffer" dogs. Dogs are being used with success in Afghanistan, but there are many limitations in the way they operate. According to a top mine clearance specialist in Afghanistan, dogs are not infallible; they can be 95% effective if they have favorable conditions—i.e., not too windy, not too warm, and suitable soil. Even then they tire easily and can only work four to five hours per day.[26]

---

[24] DIA/FSTC, p. 4-1.

[25] DOS, *Hidden Killers*, p. 18.

[26] Kefayatullah Eblagh, "Practical Demining in Afghanistan" in ICRC, *Report of the 1993 Montreux Symposium*, p. 164.

Moreover, a dog and handler require extensive training, and a dog requires a special diet and veterinary support, although its "service" life may be short.  Finally, humanitarian clearance sometimes occurs years after mines are laid; by this time, there may be no trace odors.

### 4. Sight

Detection of even surface-laid mines can be problematic. Continuous efforts have been made to make surface mines, such as "stick" mines or Claymore-type tripwire mines, more difficult to see.  In addition, over time many surface mines become hidden in vegetation and natural overgrowth.  Deminers will often hang thin wire rods to detect tripwires.

### C.  Neutralization and Destruction

After location and detection of a mine, it must be either destroyed *in situ*, or neutralized (disarmed)—removed, and destroyed elsewhere—usually by demolition or burning.  It is safer, but more expensive, to destroy the mine by explosive without it being moved or touched.  A small explosive charge to set off the mine is placed and then initiated either electrically or with a safety fuze.

Deminers generally view neutralization, rather than *in situ* destruction, as a last resort.  While there are a variety of means of disarming a mine (for example, reinserting a safety pin; removing the detonator or striker mechanism; fitting a safety cap), it is dangerous and tricky work: some mines are fitted with booby-traps or anti-handling devices to make them explode when removed; mines linked to tripwires can be very sensitive; and, mines that get increasingly unstable with age become too dangerous to handle.  After being disarmed, mines are usually removed from the minefield area and destroyed explosively in batches in a demolition pit, or burned.  Neutralization takes skill and training, and in executing this technique, even experienced mine clearers have been killed.  Nevertheless, it is a more economical process than *in situ* destruction, and can be used when *in situ* destruction would cause unacceptable damage to the area.

## IV.    Mechanical and Other Clearance Equipment

A good deal of research and development has gone into mechanical mine clearance, in order to destroy mines more quickly and to avoid the necessity of deminers walking into minefields or making physical contact with mines at all. Unfortunately, virtually all of the research has gone into military minefield breaching, not humanitarian clearance, so that no form of clearance device currently available gives the high clearance ratio needed for humanitarian clearance.

The main mechanical equipment now used are flails, rollers, and plows. A flail is an armored vehicle fitted with a rotating drum on its front, and attached to the drum are a series of chains which are flung outwards as the drum rotates when the vehicle moves forward. Weights on the ends of chains beat the ground, hitting mines and either breaking them up or causing them to explode. However, flails do not destroy every mine in a field. In some instances, mines are driven deeper into the ground without detonating, or thrown out of the ground by the chains, landing to the side or rear of the vehicle, damaged, but not neutralized or destroyed. Mines with blast-resistant fuzes will also defeat a flail. The State Department report concludes, "Currently available flails are not really suited for area [humanitarian] clearance."[27]

Rollers, which are usually fitted to tanks or other armored vehicles, are effective in some terrain, but not on undulating or stony ground, heavily vegetated areas, or in soft soil and snow. Plow systems push tines through the ground in front of an armored vehicle, scooping up mines and pushing them off the side. Plow and roller systems are designed for military breaching; they are not reliable and have only limited applications in humanitarian clearance. They do not achieve necessary levels of clearance for re-habitation, and thus can only be used in conjunction with other methods for humanitarian clearance.[28]

In addition to the mechanical flails, rollers, and plows, the military also makes use of explosive clearance techniques for breaching under combat conditions. Explosive clearance usually involves firing a

---

[27] DOS, *Hidden Killers*, p. 20.

[28] Ibid., pp. 18-21, and DIA/FSTC, pp. 4-21 to 4-25 discuss plows, rollers and flails and their drawbacks.

# Valmara 69

This Italian-made antipersonnel bounding mine has a plastic case with a removable fuze mounted on the top. The mine is fitted with a tripwire but its fuze can also be activated by direct pressure on one or more of the five fuze prongs. To obtain a more effective fragmentation pattern, the main charge, surrounded by more than 1,000 metal splinters, is projected about half a meter into the air, by a propelling charge before detonation. The mine has a lethal radius of at least 25 meters. It is produced by Valsella Meccanotecnica SpA in Brescia, Italy and Chartered Industries of Singapore. A copy is produced by South Africa as the No. 69 Mk1. (Drawing by Pamela Blotner for the Arms Project/PHR.)

hose filled with explosives or a net of detonating cords across the minefield, so that it lies in contact with the mined ground.  The explosive charge is then detonated, destroying mines largely through overpressure. Fuel air explosives can also be used to clear minefields.[29]  In general, these methods cause too much damage to the land, are too expensive, and have insufficient reliability for humanitarian needs.  Like mechanical methods, explosives often displace mines rather than destroying them; moreover, many mines today have blast-resistant fuzes intended to defeat these explosive clearance techniques.[30]

The military has also used electronic countermeasures (e.g. magnetic signature duplication and electromagnetic devices) and high-power microwave systems (using microwave radiation to negate mines with electronic fuzes), but at the present time these methods also have insufficient reliability for humanitarian clearance.

Burning is another technique occasionally employed, and which, according to some deminers, can be useful where the mined area is covered by thick, dry, combustible vegetation, and the mines themselves are combustible and surface-laid or scattered.    Mine clearers in Afghanistan have used this method to deal with Soviet PFM-1 butterfly mines.  Perhaps more often, nonprofessional locals attempt to clear minefields by fire.  But the technique is only effective in the certain limited conditions cited.  Burning does not affect buried mines; certain surface mines are not harmed by the heating process; and, in the case of wooden stake mines, only the stake may burn up, allowing the mine to fall to the ground unharmed and dangerous.  Furthermore, the process of burning often blackens many mines, making them harder to detect.

## V.    Mine Awareness

One final element of demining that must be mentioned is mine awareness programs.  Over the years, and in many different nations, it has become apparent that an essential part of any effective demining program is providing mine awareness training to the local citizens so that they can recognize landmines and other dangerous munitions.  Mine

---

[29] DIA/FSTC, p. 4-1.

[30] DOS, *Hidden Killers*, p. 19.

awareness programs generally consist of classes and the widespread distribution of information and posters.[31]

## VI.    Who Clears Mines?

Local authorities and private contractors (both non-profit humanitarian organizations and for-profit commercial firms) are responsible for most of the actual detection and destruction of mines. Military personnel under the auspices of the United Nations and foreign national armed forces are also involved in demining in countries around the world. In many cases, the foreign mine experts train local people in mine clearing techniques—either in conjunction with or instead of removing the mines themselves.

The United Nations has become the biggest mine clearing agency in the world. Many of the world's mines are in U.N. operational areas, hampering peacekeeping and humanitarian activities. And while the U.N. has many different agencies working in mined areas, at present there is no single agency coordinating the establishment of demining programs, although the Department of Humanitarian Affairs has recently been assigned the task of coordinating humanitarian mine clearance. The U.N. also works alongside other organizations that have demining programs that benefit U.N. operations.

As a rule, the U.N. does not do the actual demining. It conducts nationwide surveys, trains local demining teams, and coordinates mine clearance activities in U.N. operational areas. Retired British Brigadier Patrick Blagden has been put in charge of coordinating U.N. mine clearance activities. He has described the aims of the U.N. demining program as providing technical assistance to all U.N. departments and agencies; setting standards for removal and a code of conduct for mine clearance companies; establishing quality assurance procedures for assessing the effectiveness of completed mine clearance; and formulating policy for U.N. mine clearance, including what kinds of programs should be set up, and who should be responsible for them.[32]   The U.N. is also in the process of establishing a database, which will include details of

---

[31] Ibid., p. 21.

[32] Patrick Blagden, "Summary of United Nations Demining" in ICRC, *Report of the 1993 Montreux Symposium*, p. 117-118.

mine infestation in each country, and the extent, methods and cost of removal efforts.

Soldiers are responsible for only a small part of the humanitarian mine clearance activities undertaken around the world. As noted earlier, humanitarian mine clearance is not a military function; armed forces, for the most part, lack the necessary expertise as they are trained in breaching techniques and not area clearance.

However, the militaries of many nations are involved in demining operations, largely but not exclusively under the auspices of various U.N. peacekeeping operations. A partial listing of nations with soldiers involved in demining in other countries now or in the recent past includes: Bangladesh in Kuwait and Cambodia; Belgium with U.N. peacekeepers; Canada with U.N. forces in the former Yugoslavia and Cyprus; France in Cambodia, Somalia, Bosnia, Kuwait, Chad, Pakistan and Lebanon; Italy in Mozambique; the U.K. in Kuwait, Cambodia, Yugoslavia and Morocco; the U.S. in Somalia; and Zimbabwe in Mozambique.[33] Moreover, Kuwait signed $700 million in demining contracts with armies or private firms from the U.S., U.K., France, Egypt, Pakistan, Turkey, and Bangladesh.

Unfortunately, local authorities often lack the capability for demining. Most developing countries, where mine infestation is greatest, simply do not have advanced mine detection equipment or experience and expertise in mine location and destruction, let alone adequate funding. Foreign funding and experience are essential for establishing priorities and procedures for demining, but these contributions need not, and in most cases cannot, continue indefinitely. It is crucial to develop an indigenous capability for mine clearance in affected countries; the time and expense factors of relying on outsiders are too great. For this reason, demining efforts should always include specialized technical training and assistance programs for local personnel, as well as mine awareness and community education components.

Mine clearance contractors can offer expert knowledge and experience. They are often staffed with military-trained explosives ordnance disposal experts, and clear mines on a contract basis for both governments and non-governmental organizations. Some of the

---

[33] DOS, *Hidden Killers*. See also, French Lt. Col. Jean Francois Gros, "De-Mining Cambodia" and Canadian Major John Thompsonr, "De-Mining Yugoslavia," presentation to the ADPA Symposium.

companies are non-profit, charitable organizations, but many others are for-profit commercial ventures.[34] Some companies that manufacture mines are also bidding for mine clearance contracts. It appears that a significant number of companies involved in the mine industry are viewing humanitarian mine clearance as a new and potentially lucrative business opportunity.[35] For example, in Mozambique more than a dozen private companies of various nationalities have competed for mine clearance contracts. Many nations with severe landmine problems cannot afford contractors, and rely on other governments, international organizations, and non-governmental organizations to provide funding.

## VII.    What does Mine Clearance Cost?

Mine clearance is not cheap. The U.N. estimates that the average cost for removing a landmine, including all support and logistics costs, is between $300 and $1,000 per mine. Thus, in a nation like Cambodia, with four to seven million landmines, seven million people and an annual per capita income of $150, to completely demine the nation would require every Cambodian to contribute every dollar of income solely to mine removal for the next five to seven years—hardly a realistic proposition.[36]

---

[34] DOS, *Hidden Killers*, p. 10. Some of the organizations involved in mine clearance include:

> Mines Advisory Group (U.K.): Afghanistan, Cambodia, Mozambique, Kurdistan, Angola, Nicaragua
> Halo Trust (U.K.): Kuwait, Cambodia, Afghanistan
> Afghan Technical Consultants: Afghanistan
> Rimfire Foundation (U.K.): Somalia
> Norwegian People's Aid: Mozambique (training)
> International Danger and Disaster Assistance Company (Belgium): El Salvador
> Disaster Aid Committee: Iraqi Kurdistan
> Gurkha Security Guards Ltd. (U.K.): Mozambique

[35] This was evident from numerous conversations with representatives of companies attending the American Defense Preparedness Association's Mines, Countermine & Demolitions Symposium, September 7-9, 1993, in Asheville, N.C.

[36] DOS, *Hidden Killers*, p. 8.

Mine clearance contractors have considerable expenses. They utilize highly trained, experienced people to do extremely dangerous work, and their fees necessarily reflect the risk. Deminers indicate that it has become increasingly difficult to find insurance for mine clearance personnel, and an annual premium of $15,000 for $400,000 coverage is average. Mechanical mine clearance equipment is also expensive—a flail, for example, costs about $350,000. Support costs for medical and casualty evacuation for injured deminers are also very high.[37]

The following are some examples of actual and estimated costs of demining operations:[38]

• The United Nations Organization for Coordinating Humanitarian Assistance to Afghanistan (UNOCHA) estimates that it can clear a priority 60 square kilometers in Afghanistan at a cost of $1 million per square kilometer, or in six years with a $10 million budget per annum.

• The U.N. has estimated that it will cost $30-40 million over a period of seven to ten years to remove an estimated two million landmines in Mozambique.

• Kuwait has signed $700 million in contracts to help remove the estimated five to seven million landmines laid during the Persian Gulf war.

• El Salvador has contracted with a private Belgian firm to remove the estimated 20,000 mines there for $4.8 million.

• The United Nations Cambodian Mines Action Center has estimated that it will require $10-12 million per year for the next five to ten years for demining activities in Cambodia.

Funding for demining comes from infested nations themselves, other governments, international organizations, and non-governmental organizations. Many nations contribute voluntarily on a bilateral basis to demining operations in various countries. For instance, the following nations have devoted money, equipment, and/or expertise to demining in Cambodia: Australia, Bangladesh, France, India, the Netherlands, Pakistan, Thailand, the U.K., the U.S., and others. Sweden, the

---

[37] Alistair Craib, "Mine Detection and Demining" in ICRC, *Report of the 1993 Montreux Symposium*, p. 151, cites these costs.

[38] These figures are culled from DOS, *Hidden Killers*.

Netherlands and Norway are providing funds for the first phase of a national demining program in Mozambique.

The U.S. State Department, including the U.S. Agency for International Development, in FY 1993 allocated more than $9 million for demining projects in Afghanistan, Mozambique, Somalia, Cambodia, and Central America. In FY 1994, the State Department hopes to more than double that allocation for United Nations demining programs and other demining projects in 18 countries. The funds will be used to help afflicted nations remove the landmines themselves. In addition, some of the money will be used to hire expert mine removal contractors to demine certain specific objectives, such as road systems.[39] In its version of the FY 1994 defense authorization bill, the U.S. Senate has added $10 million for humanitarian mine clearance activities. It is expected that these provisions will be signed into law later this year.

International organizations such as the United Nations, U.N. High Commissioner for Refugees, UNICEF, the European Community, the Organization of American States, and the Inter-American Defense Board contribute to demining operations. Non-governmental groups also contribute extensively, including the ICRC, Handicap International, and Norwegian People's Aid.

## VIII.  Mine vs. Countermine

The recent DIA study notes that "landmine technologies are constantly evolving, making landmines more deadly, more disruptive, and/or more economical."[40] As the document makes clear, and mine clearance personnel readily confirm, these new technologies also greatly complicate the task of demining—especially humanitarian mine clearance. The DIA study also makes plain that mine clearance technologies have not kept pace with advancing mine technologies, and are not likely to do so in the future. Moreover, advances in mine clearance have been almost exclusively in the realm of military minefield breaching, not humanitarian clearance. At a recent symposium, Charles Gardner from the U.S. Army Office of the Project Manager for Mines, Countermine and Demolitions, stated:

---

[39] DOS, *Hidden Killers*, pp. ii, 1.

[40] DIA/FSTC, p. 1-1.

Speaking forthrightly, I would suggest that the countermine dilemma is perhaps the greatest challenge the Army faces on today's and tomorrow's battlefield.... What we can't do very well is find mines; quickly neutralize them; and reduce their impact on our maneuver forces and soldiers.... Place yourself in the position of the U.S. soldier who is frequently exposed to randomly laid mines, mines with little to no metal content, possibly covered by direct and/or indirect fires, during hours of darkness, etc. I think you can begin to see the difficulty of producing technology which can alert soldiers and units to take evasive or other actions.... And while we look for countermine solutions, the landmine developers and producers are not sitting idle wondering what we will come up with next. Advances fuzes, new sensors, improved warheads, vertical attack, hunter mines and counter-countermeasures are the order of the day. The situation with countermine is likely to get worse before it gets better.[41]

Four technological developments of great concern to the demining community are: 1. "nondetectable" mines; 2. remotely delivered, scatterable mines; 3. anti-disturbance devices; and, 4. self-destructing and self-neutralizing mechanisms. These developments and their implications are examined at length in Chapter 2 (Development and Use of Landmines) and Chapter 10 (Future of Landmines), but deserve mention here as well, for their impact on demining operations.

Obviously, "nondetectable" mines are anathema to the demining community. While the Arms Project and Physicians for Human Rights believe that all landmine production should be terminated, as an interim measure it would be useful to require that the future production of mines be limited to those that are detectable. This could be achieved, for example, by incorporating a metal strip. In addition, a method should be found to retrofit existing mines in such a fashion.

The development of remotely delivered, scatterable mines has enabled military forces to spread a much larger quantity of mines much

---

[41] Charles Gardner, "Countermine Systems Development," presentation to the ADPA Symposium.

faster over a much wider area than ever before. What might have taken a Second World War battalion all day to emplace can now be done in minutes. Some of the remote delivery systems can dispense thousands of mines in a manner of minutes; it may take mine clearers weeks or months to remove those mines. Moreover, scatterable, remotely delivered mines cannot be reliably recorded, mapped, or marked, in the short or long run. Thus, their deployment substantially increases the danger for civilians.

According to the DIA report, scatterables also create special problems for military mine clearance:

> No longer is it practical to assume certain front-line units will be the only ones responding to the threat of landmines.... Every unit on the battlefield may be called upon to counter scatterable landmines. In fact, due to problems which may be encountered in remote delivery of mines (e.g., command and control procedures for determining where and when the landmines are to be placed, the notification of units which may need to enter those areas, and the accuracy of the emplacement systems), *friendly forces may be called upon to breach their own scatterable landmines* (emphasis added).[42]

A number of companies and governments now offer "improved" mine packages that incorporate anti-disturbance mechanisms. Some of these mines are identical in appearance to other versions which have no booby-trap capability. According to the DIA, "even well trained mine clearance teams may wrongly assume that the mine poses little difficulty in removal."[43] These mines are especially popular among Third World nations.[44]

---

[42] DIA/FSTC, p. 1-1.

[43] Ibid., pp. 3–35.

[44] Ibid. The DIA report identifies four anti-personnel, look-alike mines with antidisturbance features: a Chinese copy of the German PPM-2; the Hungarian MS-3 (a copy of the Soviet PMN); the Italian VS-50 AR (a copy of the VS-50); and, the Italian VS-MK2-E (a copy of the VS-MK2).

It is also important to note that the demining community does not believe that the development of self-destruct and self-neutralizing mines represents a significant humanitarian advance. From the deminer's point of view, these mechanisms make little practical difference. Inevitably, there is a certain failure rate for self-destruct and self-neutralizing mines; because humanitarian mine clearance aims at 100 percent clearance, deminers are compelled to clear an entire minefield just as if it contained live mines. The time and cost involved will be almost the same. Of the two mechanisms, however, deminers prefer self-destruct. Mechanisms to make a mine self-neutralizing can be tampered with to produce a booby-trap. Moreover, deminers maintain that even though self-destruct mines can explode randomly, the chance of injury is greater if people try to handle mines they believe are neutralized.

## IX.    Mine Clearance Developments

There are a variety of technologies that are being explored for detection of buried mines. Most of these are complex and expensive. Virtually all are designed to improve military mine clearance, but some could have important humanitarian clearance benefits in the future.

The DIA report notes that a variety of standoff minefield detection technologies are under development in several countries, and that research in the 1980s included thermal imaging, neutron bombardment and electromagnetic techniques. The DIA concludes that all these methods are limited by soil conditions, vegetation, mine size and composition, burial depth, and grazing angle.[45] The Swedish Defense Research Establishment for the past five years has been investigating impulse radar, multispectral reconnaissance and biosensors. The U.S. currently has three systems in development that could be useful in future demining efforts: the Airborne Stand-Off Minefield Detection System

---

[45] Ibid., p. 4-5.

(ASTAMIDS), the Vehicle Mounted Mine Detector, and the Advanced Hand-Held Mine Detector.[46]

ASTAMIDS is an airborne system that aims at providing real time locations of surface-laid or scattered minefields, using infrared sensors and artificial intelligence to analyze image data. When combined with the Global Positional System (GPS), it could provide accurate information critical to any large-scale demining effort. It cannot, however, locate individual or single mines, only minefields.[47] The Vehicle Mounted Mine Detector would increase the ability to re-open a road net closed by mines. Like ASTAMIDS, however, it cannot locate individual mines. It is hoped that the Advanced Hand-Held Mine Detector will increase the speed of manual clearance operations. Technologies are also being explored to make flails, rollers, and rakes more appropriate to humanitarian clearance, but some drawbacks will remain.

While some advanced technologies may show promise, it is likely to be years before they show tangible results in humanitarian clearance.

## X.    No Silver Bullet

Demining is thus likely to remain in its present state for the foreseeable future. Manual probing will continue to be the surest method. Colonel Richard Johnson, Program Manager of the Mines, Countermine, and Demolitions division at the Picatinny Arsenal has said that there is no "silver bullet" at the present time, or on the horizon.[48]

---

[46] DOS, *Hidden Killers*, p. 23 and Appendix D. These and other developments are also discussed in a number of presentations at the American Defense Preparedness Association Symposium in Asheville, N.C., particularly those by Charles Gardner, David Vaughn, David Heberlein, and Thomas Hafer.

[47] On August 23, 1993, Raytheon and Westinghouse were awarded contracts to continue research and development of ASTAMIDS. In about three years, one of the companies will be selected to produce the system. *Aerospace Daily*, September 3, 1993, p. 384.

[48] Interview, June 15, 1993. Charles Gardner of the Project Manager's Office in his presentation to the American Defense Preparedness Association Symposium also stated that there is "no 'silver bullet' in sight which will address the overall countermine spectrum."

As one mine clearance specialist explains:

> There seems to be an unconquerable instinct amongst
> those responsible for planning, funding and researching
> mine clearance projects to seek to develop a magic piece
> of equipment which will cure all ills.... Mine clearance
> operators...in my experience would much rather clear a
> minefield on their hands and knees, using a mine probe
> and magnetic detector, than trust to the effectiveness of
> a mechanical clearance vehicle or explosive clearance
> technique.[49]

According to the Pentagon's mine clearing expert Alan Epstein:

> There is no single device ideally suited for demining that
> will become available in the foreseeable future.
> Unfortunately, what is most apparent is that there are no
> easy solutions. Manual clearance remains the primary
> means of demining former war zones.[50]

## XI.    Conclusion

The international community must devote much greater attention
and resources to demining around the globe. The "Joint Call to Ban
Antipersonnel Landmines," among other demands, calls for establishment
of an international fund, administered by the United Nations, to promote
and finance landmine awareness, clearance, and eradication programs
worldwide, and for countries responsible for the production and
dissemination of antipersonnel mines to contribute to the international
fund.[51]

---

[49] Paul Jefferson, "An Overview of Demining, Including Mine Detection
Equipment," in ICRC, *Report of the 1993 Montreux Symposium*, p. 126.

[50] DOS, *Hidden Killers*, p. 24.

[51] "Joint Call to Ban Antipersonnel Landmines," Human Rights Watch,
Handicap International, Medico International, Mines Advisory Group, Physicians
for Human Rights, and Vietnam Veterans of American Foundation, is attached

The conclusions of the State Department report on international mine clearance is worth quoting at length; they are applicable to the governments of other countries as well:

> It is in the United States' national interest to provide demining assistance. Uncleared landmines impede the achievement of U.S. foreign policy objectives in a large number of countries.... Contributions that assist in the removal of uncleared landmines are the essential foundations for most of our foreign aid programs.... The UN Demining Expert, Brigadier Patrick Blagden RA (ret) notes that it is vital to get relief agencies to understand that demining is the fundamental precursor for any type of foreign assistance. Until the landmines are removed, money spent on other projects will not be fully effective....
>
> The UN and nongovernmental organizations cannot bear the burden of demining alone—they lack the resources and expertise. If humanity is to make an impact on the global problem with uncleared landmines it is imperative that the U.S., and the other industrialized nations, contribute technology, expertise and resources.[52]

The international community needs to spend much more money on both removal of mines and research and development of new mine detection and clearance equipment and techniques. But it is crucial that the focus be on civilian, humanitarian needs, not on military needs. The U.S. Government has acknowledged this crucial point. "In addition to working to help countries remove uncleared landmines...the US needs to emphasize the development of wide-area mine clearing techniques. The Department of Defense has already begun to take steps to address this issue."[53] The U.S. Senate has earmarked $10 million in the FY 1994

---

at Appendix 1.

[52] DOS, *Hidden Killers*, pp. 178-179.

[53] Ibid., p. ii.

defense bill for training, equipment, and other activities related to humanitarian mine clearing in civilian areas.

However, as great and urgent as the need is, if the international community focuses only on the demining effort, the landmine crisis will never sufficiently abate.  Indeed, the world will only continue to lose ground.  The fact is that mines today are being laid faster than they are being cleared, and the ratio of mines laid to mines cleared is only going to get worse in the future unless bold steps are taken.  Given the global constraints on resources available for mine clearance, and given the improbability of a technological breakthrough in demining, the worldwide landmine crisis will continue to deteriorate unless there is a ban on production, stockpiling, trade and use of landmines.

# 8
# INTERNATIONAL LAW GOVERNING LANDMINES

International law currently regulates the use of landmines, but not their production, stockpiling, transfer, or export. The Landmines Protocol, annexed to the U.N. Convention on Prohibitions or Restrictions on the Use of Certain Conventional Weapons Which May be Deemed to be Excessively Injurious and to Have Indiscriminate Effects (Weapons Convention),[1] specifically governs the use of landmines, booby-traps, and comparable delayed-action devices.[2]  In addition, the use of these

---

[1] Protocol on Prohibitions or Restrictions on the Use of Mines, Booby Traps and Other Devices (Landmines Protocol); U.N.G.A. Doc. A/Conf. 95/15 and Corr. 1-5; 19 Int'l Legal Materials 1534 (1980). In addition to the Landmines Protocol (Protocol II), two other agreements concerning Non-detectable Fragments (Protocol I) and Prohibitions or Restrictions on the Use of Incendiary Weapons (Protocol III), are attached to the Weapons Convention.  The provisions of the Weapons Convention apply to all three Protocols. The Weapons Convention and the Protocols entered into force on December 2, 1983.  Thirty-six countries are parties to the Landmines Protocol as of this writing; the United States is not among them, having signed but not ratified the treaty. See Appendix 3 for a list of states party to the Weapons Convention and the Landmines Protocol.

[2] Landmines Protocol, art. 1.  Article 2 defines these terms as follows:

"'Mine' means any munition placed under, on or near the ground or other surface area and designed to be detonated or exploded by the presence, proximity or contact of a person or vehicle, and 'remotely delivered mine' means any mine so defined delivered by artillery, rocket, mortar or similar means or dropped from an aircraft.

'Booby-trap' means any device or material which is designed, constructed or adapted to kill or injure and which functions unexpectedly when a person disturbs or approaches an apparently harmless object or performs an apparently safe act.

'Other devices' means manually-emplaced munitions and devices designed to kill, injure or damage and which are actuated by remote control or automatically after a lapse of time."

It should be noted that the term "mine" as used in the Landmines Protocol includes both antipersonnel and antitank landmines.  Here, as in other

weapons is subject to customary international humanitarian law. In fact, customary rules forbidding means of warfare that cause indiscriminate or excessive harm, particularly as codified in articles 51(4) and (5) and 35(1) and (2) of 1977 Additional Protocol I to the 1949 Geneva Conventions,[3] provide stronger protections to civilians than the Landmines Protocol itself.

The goal of the Landmines Protocol was to reduce harm to civilians from mine warfare, thus reinforcing fundamental principles of customary international law. The instrument does not, however, flatly ban the use of landmines; rather, it puts in place a thicket of limitations on how they may be used. Chief among these are provisions whose stated purpose is to prohibit both deliberate and indiscriminate use against civilians. Accordingly, under the Landmines Protocol, combatants must refrain from directing mines against civilians; attempt certain precautions to minimize collateral harm to civilians resulting from mine attacks aimed at military targets; and undertake the use of mines only in situations in which the anticipated military advantage outweighs the expected harm to civilians. In addition, the Landmines Protocol places specific restrictions on the use of remotely delivered mines and booby-traps; mandates that the location of mines be recorded and disclosed in certain circumstances; and urges that these records be used to assist demining efforts after the close of hostilities as well as to warn civilians about the location of minefields.

In the view of the Arms Project and Physicians for Human Rights, these provisions do not adequately address the unique threat that landmines pose for civilians, nor do they comport with principles of customary law. As one expert puts it, "mines are like no other type of ammunition, because they are not used for immediate effect, but are

---

chapters, the words "mine" and "landmine" will be used to refer to antipersonnel landmines, booby-traps, and other delayed-action weapons, unless otherwise specified.

[3] The Additional Protocols of June 8, 1977 to the Geneva Conventions of August 12, 1949 (Additional Protocol I Relating to the Protection of Victims of International Armed Conflicts, and Additional Protocol II Relating to the Protection of Victims of Non-international Armed Conflicts, respectively). U.N.G.A. Doc. A/32/144, Anns. I and II, Aug. 15, 1977; 16 Int'l Legal Materials 1391 (1977).

primed, concealed, and left as a hazard which remains indefinitely."[4] The Landmines Protocol fails to take into account the implications for civilian life of this delayed-action quality; it completely ignores the fact that the time lapse between the point at which a mine is planted and the point at which it explodes, virtually ensures indiscriminate effects. The Protocol's complex rules, discretionary language, and broad exceptions and qualifications to its general prohibitions further limit its utility. Moreover, because its provisions apply only to international wars, it is effectively irrelevant to the internal armed conflicts in which landmines are chiefly used.

In addition to these theoretical flaws, the Landmines Protocol fails on a practical level: even its modest restrictions have not been followed in conflicts waged since its entry into force almost ten years ago. Some combatants regularly use landmines directly against civilians. Others utilize mines without taking even minimal precautions to safeguard civilians, or in circumstances in which the likely harm to civilians outstrips anticipated military benefits. No armed force in the last decade is known to have consistently and accurately recorded the location of minefields in actual combat conditions.

This chapter proposes that the complete failure of the Landmines Protocol to control landmine use, its failure to conform to the requirements imposed by customary humanitarian law, and the extreme devastation that has resulted from mine warfare, supports a ban on the production, stockpiling, transfer, and use of landmines. Part I examines the historical development of the Landmines Protocol. Part II analyzes the Protocol's provisions in detail, and concludes that it is an utterly ineffective document both in theory and in practice, because it does not properly apply the relevant standards of customary humanitarian law, and does not serve to diminish abuses against civilians. Part III considers humanitarian rules prohibiting means of warfare that create indiscriminate or excessive harm, and demonstrates how their proper

---

[4] Lt. Col. P.R. Courtney-Green, *Ammunition for the Land Battle* (London: Brassey's UK, 1967), p. 171.

One Cambodian soldier (a farmer in civilian life) explained with respect to the enormous numbers of mines planted throughout his country:

"In the future the war will go, but the war will stay."

Asia Watch and Physicians for Human Rights, *Landmines in Cambodia: the Coward's War* (New York: Human Rights Watch, 1991), p. 38.

application requires a complete proscription on the use of landmines. This section also briefly reviews international treaties that ban the use or, alternatively, the use, production, stockpiling, transfer, and export of specific types of weapons, because they are perceived to exact unconscionable human harm, and argues that these instruments serve as valuable precedents for enacting a complete ban on landmines.

## I.    Historical Development of the Landmines Protocol

### A. Motivation for creating the Landmines Protocol

The promulgation of the Landmines Protocol stemmed from the growing perception—the same perception that led to the enactment of the 1977 Additional Protocols—that the development of modern warfare required a corresponding adaptation of the laws of war.[5] The 1977 Additional Protocols reaffirmed and refined principles of humanitarian law mandating that armed conflicts be conducted so as to inflict a minimum of suffering, and codified customary doctrine protecting civilians. Participants involved in the early discussions of the draft 1977 Protocols recommended undertaking an examination of certain conventional weapons, with a view toward crafting a set of supplementary laws to circumscribe their use.[6] The establishment of such rules was deemed critical because technological advances had led to the development of conventional weapons capable of particularly cruel effects.[7]

---

[5] Historically, the development of new weapons viewed as especially dangerous resulted in the negotiation of treaties designed to curb their use. Part III of this chapter includes a discussion of these treaties.

[6] See, e.g., Report of the Ad Hoc Committee on Conventional Weapons, 16 Official Records of the Diplomatic Conference on the Reaffirmation and Development of International Humanitarian Law Applicable in Armed Conflicts (1978), pp. 454–459, and Summary Records of the Ad Hoc Committee on Conventional Weapons, 16 Official Records of the Diplomatic Conference on the Reaffirmation and Development of International Humanitarian Law Applicable in Armed Conflicts (1978), p. 10.

[7] Ibid.

Consequently, the United Nations Diplomatic Conference on the Reaffirmation and Development of International Humanitarian Law created an ad hoc committee to consider the formulation of special restrictions on those conventional weapons, including landmines, which experts feared might be excessively injurious or indiscriminate.[8] To assist the committee in its deliberations, the International Committee of the Red Cross convened two conferences of government experts, first at Lucerne in 1974, and later at Lugano in 1976.[9] The matter was then taken up by the United Nations General Assembly, which convened two preparatory conferences in 1978 and 1979,[10] and subsequently a two-session conference in 1979 and 1980, during which the final form of the Weapons Convention, including the annexed Landmines Protocol, was

---

[8] The proceedings of the ad hoc committee are published in 16 Official Records of the Diplomatic Conference on the Reaffirmation and Development of International Humanitarian Law Applicable in Armed Conflicts (1978).

[9] The proceedings of these conferences are published respectively in ICRC, *Report on the Conference of Government Experts on the Use of Certain Weapons: Lucerne 1974* (Geneva: ICRC, 1975), and ICRC, *Report on the Conference of Government Experts on the Use of Certain Weapons: Lugano 1976* (Geneva: ICRC, 1976). For a discussion of the proceedings of the Lucerne Conference, see generally Frits Kalshoven, "Conventional Weaponry: The Law from St. Petersburg to Lucerne and Beyond" in Michael Meyers (ed.), *Armed Conflict and the New Law: Aspects of the 1977 General Protocols and the 1981 Weapons Convention*, (London: British Institute of International and Comparative Law, 1980).
In 1973 the ICRC also convened a preliminary consultation of experts to examine the use of particular weapons. Proceedings of the consultation are published in ICRC, *Weapons that may Cause Unnecessary Suffering or have Indiscriminate Effects: Report on the Work of Experts*, (Geneva: ICRC, 1973).

[10] The work of the preparatory conferences is summarized in the Report of the Preparatory Conference for the U.N. Conference on Prohibitions or Restrictions of the Use of Certain Conventional Weapons Which May be Deemed to be Excessively Injurious or to have Indiscriminate Effects,__U.N. GAOR __; U.N. Doc. A/CONF. 95/3 (May 25, 1979).

produced.[11]  Eighty-five countries participated in the final conference, including all the major military powers.[12]

## B. Drafting the Landmines Protocol:  The Conferences

### 1. General considerations

Interest in restricting the use of landmines arose for several reasons.  Technological advances had permitted the scattering of large numbers of mines over immense areas of land with great ease and rapidity, magnifying the risk of indiscriminate and unnecessary harm.[13] These technological innovations raised fears that mines would be used increasingly as offensive weapons, exposing civilians to greater danger.[14]  Moreover, concerns about the long-lasting effects of landmines on the civilian population were expressed in light of the devastation  evident in vast areas of Europe, the Middle East and North Africa that had remained  mined since World War II.

Yet there was little support for encouraging limits on the production, stockpiling, transfer, or export of mines; discussion remained

---

[11] The work of the final conferences is summarized in the Final Report of the U.N. Conference on Prohibitions or Restrictions of the Use of Certain Conventional Weapons Which may be Deemed to be Excessively Injurious or to have Indiscriminate Effects, __U.N. GAOR__; U.N. Doc. A/CONF. 95/15 (Oct. 27, 1980).

[12] See Hon. George Aldrich, Report of the United States Delegation to the United Nations Conference on Prohibitions or Restrictions of Use of Certain Conventional Weapons which may be deemed to be excessively injurious or to have indiscriminate effects—second session (1981), p. 43, for a list of participants.

[13] See Chapter 2 for a discussion of "scatterable" mines, also known as "remotely-delivered."

[14] See ibid.

centered on use. Although a few conference participants[15] contended that an agreement restricting the use of conventional weapons would be meaningless without a concomitant proscription on production, stockpiling and transfer,[16] the majority regarded such prohibitions as completely unrealistic and beyond the mandate of the conferences.[17] A consideration of this type of prohibition, in the view of most delegates, would have to be taken up separately at a disarmament conference.

## 2. Legal Criteria

Conference discussions concerning landmines, like those regarding other conventional weapons, focused on three principles of customary humanitarian law as the basis for evaluating to what extent their use should be limited. First, relying on the fundamental doctrine that parties to a conflict are not unlimited in the means by which they conduct war, participants asked whether mines cause unnecessary suffering or excessive injury relative to their military utility. Second, participants asked whether mines should be considered indiscriminate weapons. Third, they asked whether they are inherently perfidious.[18]

---

[15] Unless otherwise specified, "conference participants," "delegates," and similar terms are used generally in this chapter to refer to individuals who attended either the conferences of government experts or the diplomatic conferences on conventional weapons.

[16] Lucerne Report, p. 13; Report of the Ad Hoc Committee, p. 455.

[17] See, e.g., Lugano Report, p. 28. However, as noted in Section II of this chapter, the preamble to the Weapons Convention (to which the Landmines Protocol is annexed) expresses the wish that the treaty eventually leads to an end to the production, stockpiling and proliferation of the weapons to which it applies.

[18] Discussions concerning perfidy (perfidious acts deliberately mislead an adversary into believing that he or she will be protected under humanitarian law) focused mainly on the use of booby-traps and are not analyzed here. Provisions of the Landmines Protocol governing the use of booby-traps are discussed in Part II of this chapter.

### a.  Weighing Humanitarian and Military Considerations

The principle that the human suffering caused by a particular weapon must not exceed military necessity (sometimes referred to as the proportionality principle) is one of the oldest precepts of humanitarian law.[19]  Conference participants accordingly began their discussions by considering whether the use of landmines violated this rule.

There was, naturally, extensive disagreement about how to conceptualize the appropriate balance between humanitarian ideals and military needs.[20]  Participants agreed that "suffering" comprised such elements as mortality rate, painfulness and severity of wounds, incidence of permanent damage or disfigurement, and access to adequate treatment.  However, participants had vastly differing opinions as to the criteria by which to evaluate whether suffering was unnecessary once

---

[19] The prohibition against weapons that cause superfluous injury or unnecessary suffering is rooted in the basic humanitarian doctrine requiring a balance between military needs and humanitarian considerations.  Louise Doswald-Beck and Gerald C. Cauderay correctly note that the rule historically has been directed at preventing excessive militarily-useless harm to combatants. Louise Doswald-Beck and Gerald C. Cauderay, "The Development of New Anti-Personnel Weapons," *International Review of the Red Cross*, Nov.–Dec. 1990, p. 565.  However, at the weapons conferences, the principle was usually discussed with regard to combatants and civilians alike.  Likewise, it is codified in article 35(2) of 1977 Additional Protocol I without specific reference to combatants.  ("It is prohibited to employ weapons...of a nature to cause superfluous injury or unnecessary suffering.")  Finally, 1977 Additional Protocol I, art. 51 (5)(b) and the Landmines Protocol, art. 3 (3)(c) contain similar formulations with respect to rules against indiscriminate use.  Both articles forbid usage which "may cause incidental loss of civilian life, injury to civilians, damage to civilian objects, or a combination thereof, which would be excessive to the concrete and direct military advantage anticipated."  Therefore, because the material treated here tends not to distinguish combatants and civilians with regard to the rules against superfluous injury and unnecessary suffering, this chapter does not make the distinction, and assumes that the weighing of military and humanitarian considerations must also take into account the humanitarian impact on civilians.

[20] Frits Kalshoven notes that this discussion "provides a clear example of the type of inconclusive debate which was so characteristic of the Lucerne Conference."  Frits Kalshoven, "The Law From St. Petersburg to Lucerne" in Michael Meyers, *Armed Conflict*, p. 262.

military considerations were taken into account. It was recognized that military requirements involve complex issues and can vary widely, depending, for example, on the type of conflict involved, the economic means of the fighting forces, the degree of access to technologically sophisticated weapons, and the number of troops available to fight.

Some participants emphasized the humanitarian side of the equation, arguing that military necessity was limited to the capacity of a weapon to put an adversary out of combat, restrict enemy movement, or neutralize a military objective. Several proponents of this position asserted that in situations where two or more weapons were available with equal capacity to overcome an adversary, the less injurious must be chosen, as matter of law. Others emphasized that weapons used to destroy civilian means of subsistence could never be justified as a military necessity no matter what the circumstances. A number of delegates, emphasizing the primacy of humanitarian concerns, supported a total ban on the use of landmines. A larger number endorsed a draft convention banning specific weapons viewed as particularly egregious in their effects on civilians; remotely delivered mines, but not mines generally, were proscribed under this proposal.[21]

Delegates taking the opposite view rejected such limitations as unrealistic in wartime. They instead took an expansive view of military necessity. They considered the availability of alternative weapons, cost, destructive capability, ability to restrict enemy movement, and the effects on morale, stamina and cohesion of opposing forces. A number of delegates believed that restriction of a weapon on humanitarian grounds without carefully considering whether alternative weapons existed that would satisfy the same security function was unworkable.[22]

Significantly, many conference participants took a very traditional view of how mines are used. For example, the 1974 Report of the Conference of Government Experts stated that:

---

[21] Working paper, CDDH/IV/201 reprinted in Lugano Report, p. 198. The co-sponsors included in this proposal weapons that they believed provoked condemnation of the international community; they maintained that a mere restriction on use would distort the humanitarian objective of the conference. Ibid., p. 42.

[22] Lugano Report, p. 28.

It was widely agreed that the primary function of emplaced landmines, as well as scatterable landmines and booby-traps, was to counter enemy force mobility and to keep the enemy at tactical arm's length until such time as other weapon systems could be brought to bear on him. It was observed that landmines were primarily, although not exclusively, defensive weapons: they were used to channel enemy forces into defensible areas, to deny terrain which could not be covered by combat troops, to hinder enemy activities generally, and as close-in protective weapons for defending troops.[23]

Other examples of this perspective included the rigid classification of mine usage as either "defensive," and therefore permissible in the context of an equation balancing humanitarian and military concerns, or "offensive," thus perhaps deserving to be banned.  Association was repeatedly made between manually-emplaced mines as  defensive weapons, and remotely delivered mines as offensive.  For instance, a delegate to the 1975 Conference of Government Experts stated:

> ....the defensive use of minefields for the purpose of paralyzing enemy movements were (sic) acceptable and should not be prohibited.  On the other hand, mines scattered from aircraft over a large area presented a danger for civilians. The best solution would be to admit delayed-action weapons only as defensive weapons and to prohibit their use for offensive purposes.[24]

Several delegates also maintained that minefields were employed mainly in battlefield zones.[25]

Such views are now clearly outdated.  During the last decade, manually-emplaced mines have been regularly used as offensive weapons, often outside the context of battlefield operations, and the distinction

---

[23] Lucerne Report, p. 65.

[24] Lugano Report, p. 54.

[25] Lucerne Report, p. 65.

between offensive and defensive mine warfare frequently is too blurred to discern.

A diverse array of delegates supported the use of landmines for defensive purposes. A Canadian representative argued that because his country's armed forces are relatively small compared to its geographic size, defense of its border—presumably that with the United States—would require the extensive use of mines delivered by air.[26] The Albanian representative emphasized the need of poor nations to use mines to defend against well-armed aggressors.[27] One delegate rationalized that the defensive use of mines sometimes served humanitarian purposes. He noted that "villages protected by minefields were sometimes spared the scourge of an enemy attack on military objects in the vicinity with all the injuries and damage entailed. If a mine barrier succeeded in channelling the path of the enemy force into an uninhabited area, much was gained for the humanitarian cause."[28] Many participants also valued mines because of their relatively low cost.

The majority view was summed up clearly by a delegate who stated that mines, while particularly dangerous to civilians, nonetheless were "necessary defensive weapons."[29] Ultimately this perspective prevailed, and the drafters of the Landmines Protocol concluded that with appropriate restrictions on use in place, the necessary balance between humanitarian and military considerations could be achieved.

It is striking, however, that conference participants virtually ignored the most problematic features of mine warfare: the unique long-term risk to civilians created by the delayed-action quality of landmines; the severity of mine injuries; and the resulting massive devastation of civilian populations.

---

[26] Summary Records, p. 298. This delegate did however state that he recognized the potential risk for civilians, and "warmly welcomed" suggestions for reducing the danger. Ibid.

[27] U.N. General Assembly, 35th Session: Verbatim Record of the 37th Meeting of the First Committee, ___U.N. GAOR ___; U.N. Doc. A/C.1/35/PV.37 (Nov. 21, 1980).

[28] Summary Records, p. 407.

[29] Report of the Ad Hoc Committee, p. 512.

The records show that participants never undertook a careful exploration of how to balance the utility of mines in achieving a defined military objective with humanitarian problems that might not emerge for decades or that could last indefinitely.    There was no discussion of whether, in fact, such a calculation realistically can be made with respect to delayed-action weapons.    It would require that a field commander contemplating their use somehow assess future humanitarian risks about which he has no information—in other words, that he make a completely abstract, and, therefore, meaningless, evaluation of the human toll.[30]

While such a determination is impossibly abstract to make in a specific situation, it is clear from studies of mine use in the last decade that, in the aggregate, the military value of landmines is short-lived and quite inconsequential when compared with the ongoing wreckage they cause.  However, during discussions leading up to the enactment of the Landmines Protocol there was no serious analysis of whether, under humanitarian principles, given the long-lasting and egregious effects of landmines, it is ever possible to justify their modest military advantages.

Furthermore, the records contain no evidence that in-depth studies of the medical, social and economic effects of landmines were considered.   The fact that mines, unlike other conventional weapons, when not killing outright, usually cause permanent incapacitation resulting in traumatic or surgical amputation,[31] was not taken into account in discussions of whether their military usefulness was

---

[30] By contrast, a field commander contemplating the use of a non-delayed-action weapon can make a legitimate calculation regarding its military utility compared to humanitarian risk by carefully surveying the situation at the time he proposes to use the weapon; he can make a reasonable determination, for example, as to whether there are civilians immediately in the area who might suffer harm.  In the context of landmine use, however, such a calculation is essentially irrelevant, because it cannot deal with future dangers caused by unexploded, uncleared mines.

[31] For example, a study of Afghan mine victims admitted to a Pakistani border hospital from 1985 to shows that 73% required surgical amputation—a much higher percentage than required with victims wounded by other conventional weapons.  See J. Rautio and P. Paarolainea, "Afghan War Wounded: Experience with 200 Cases," 28 J. Trauma 523-535 (1988).  See also Courtney-Green, *Ammunition for the Land Battle*, p. 172 (noting that "whereas bullets may only incapacitate temporarily, landmines generally incapacitate permanently").

proportional to the human suffering they cause. Also ignored was the fact that minimizing the medical consequences of mine injuries requires prompt and repeated surgical care, not readily available to civilians in the developing world. The records also show that scant attention was paid to the environmental consequences of landmine use. There was little mention of the huge numbers of civilians permanently deprived of agricultural and pastoral lands due to the presence of live mines.

Although conference participants professed to strike a balance between humanitarian and military considerations, in fact their analysis was fatally incomplete. They placed unduly heavy emphasis on military need, in part because of now obsolete notions of mine warfare. On the other hand, they seriously underestimated the humanitarian costs of landmine use: the egregious nature of mine injuries, the ongoing risk that mines pose for civilians, the resulting social and economic havoc created, and the devastation caused to the natural environment. Conference participants also failed to give full consideration to the inefficacy of seeking to apply the proportionality principle to the use of a delayed-action weapon.

The Arms Project and Physicians for Human Rights believe that if the drafters of the Landmines Protocol had more closely focused on the temporal factor inherent in landmine use, they would have been forced to recognize the disutility of the proportionality principle to a commander contemplating the use of landmines in any particular instance. In addition, had they conducted a comprehensive study of the overall consequences of mine warfare, they would have had to conclude that, in the aggregate, the military value of landmines is too inconsequential to justify their long-term impact and that, therefore, humanitarian law requires that their use be banned.

Still more important, had the drafters carefully scrutinized the rules contained in 1977 Additional Protocol I, they would have recognized that the original objective of the Landmines Protocol—to codify specific rules on mines consistent with the general principles embodied in Protocol I—was not achieved.

### b. Indiscriminateness

In humanitarian law, indiscriminateness refers to the failure to distinguish between civilian and military targets. Although not fully articulated in any international legal instrument in force when negotations on the Weapons Convention began, rules requiring combatants to make such a distinction have long been part of established custom.[32]    Nonetheless, the scope of the prohibition against indiscriminateness was hotly debated at the conferences.    Some participants asserted that it included a prohibition not only on indiscriminate attacks, but also on the use of inherently indiscriminate weapons. Others argued that there was no such thing as an indiscriminate weapon, because all weapons could be used either indiscriminately or, alternatively, in a such a way as to reduce risk to civilians.    Many delegates believed that remotely delivered mines were most likely to be used indiscriminately, and that manually-emplaced landmines were "defensive" and not prone to indiscriminate use.[33]    Other delegates insisted that all landmines were inherently indiscriminate.[34]

Most participants failed to take into account the fact that landmines inevitably cause indiscriminate *effects*, because of the time lag between when they are laid and the point of detonation.    When this concern was raised at all, it was quickly dismissed through reassurances that rules requiring warnings to civilians, deactivation mechanisms, and the recording of minefields to facilitate clearance would essentially eliminate such a risk. Although several delegates pointed out that, in fact, deactivation devices often proved unreliable,[35] and that records, when

---

[32]    See, e.g., discussion in Yves Sandoz, Christophe Swinarski, and Bruno Zimmerman (eds.), ICRC Commentary on the Additional Protocols of 8 June 1977 to the Geneva Conventions of 12 August 1949 (Geneva: Martinus Nijhoff Publishers, 1987), pp. 585–589, 615.    The enactment of the 1977 Additional Protocols codified the customary proscription against indiscriminateness. See especially, 1977 Additional Protocol I, art. 51 (4) and (5).

[33]    See, e.g., Lucerne Report, p. 68.

[34]    See, e.g., ibid.

[35]    In addition to the fact that these devices can prove unreliable, mine clearance experts report that self-neutralization devices are not helpful in demining efforts, because there is no way of telling whether a mine actually has successfully self-neutralized.    Therefore, they have to be cleared anyway.    See Chapter 7 for a discussion of mine clearance. Chapter 11 discusses other reasons why self-destruct and self-neutralization mechanisms are not satisfactory solutions.

kept, were likely to be inaccurate, particularly given battlefield conditions, such considerations were given short shrift. Similarly, little mention was made of the financial costs and practical difficulties involved in mine clearance.

The drafters of the Landmines Protocol ignored the fact that where landmines are concerned, it is essential to make an analytic distinction between indiscriminate *use* and indiscriminate *effects*. Indiscriminate use signifies the failure of combatants to direct a weapon toward a specific military objective or to take precautions consistent with military necessity that might reduce harm to civilians. Landmines, of course, are frequently used in such a fashion.

By contrast, indiscriminate effects describes the problem posed by landmines *even when* combatants make a good-faith effort to distinguish between military targets and civilians. Although landmines can be directed at a military objective, and warnings given to civilians in the area, mines, because of their time-delay feature, often continue to present a danger to civilians far into the future, thus producing indiscriminate effects. Consequently, mines effectively function as indiscriminate weapons despite the fact that they may be directed towards military targets. Rules that simply regulate rather than prohibit use do not address this fundamental problem.

The Arms Project and Physicians for Human Rights believe that if the drafters of the Landmines Protocol had focused on the indiscriminate effects of landmines, rather than on the fact that landmine use can theoretically be discriminate, they would have agreed that the customary prohibition against indiscriminate means of combat requires that the use of landmines be prohibited. In particular, had the drafters properly construed the prohibitions on indiscriminate attacks set forth in 1977 Additional Protocol I, they would have concluded that a flat ban on mine use was absolutely required.[36]

### 3. Restrictions on Use vs. a Total Ban

Supporters of a total ban on landmines relied on several arguments. Some maintained that a complete ban on the use of a

---

[36] See Parts II and III of this chapter for detailed discussions of this issue.

specific type of weapon, such as landmines, could exert a moral pressure on arms producers to stop manufacture.  The example of the "dum-dum bullet," whose use was forbidden by the Third Hague Declaration of 1899, was frequently cited in this regard.  Some preferred a flat ban because it had the advantage of being precise.[37]  These advocates believed that partial restrictions would be ineffective, particularly because almost complete discretion would be given to field commanders whose determinations in the heat of battle could have devastating future consequences.  In addition, some argued, a total ban on use would be easier to implement, while prohibitions merely on certain uses would constantly be subject to strain.[38]  The breach of a complete ban would be readily evident, whereas the violation of a rule restricting use might be less obvious, and could lead to the violators arguing that they had acted within permissible limits.[39]  Some adherents of a complete proscription on use further maintained that anything short of a ban would distort the humanitarian objectives of the conference.  They persisted in asserting that landmines either were inherently indiscriminate or caused unnecessary suffering, or that they were used in ways that were indiscriminate and excessively harmful.[40]

Despite these arguments, opponents of a categorical ban on use were able to garner support for their position relatively quickly.  No one denied the practical advantage of a total proscription as likely to be most effective from a humanitarian perspective.[41]  As described above, however, a conservative application of humanitarian principles to landmine use, fostered by a widespread reliance on mines by diverse military forces, led to consensus that the harmful effects of landmine use could be sufficiently mitigated by regulations on deployment.

Such support was enhanced by the perceived need for political pragmatism and the overwhelming belief that it was unrealistic to seek

---

[37] Summary Records, p. 10.

[38] See, e.g, ibid., p. 12.

[39] Ibid., p. 10.

[40] Lugano Conference, p. 42.

[41] Ibid., p. 7; Summary Records, p. 239.

a complete proscription on mine use. As one delegate put it: "A balance had to be struck between what appeared desirable and what appeared possible," and "[w]hat was desirable was the realization of the conference's humanitarian objectives; what was possible depended on the requirements of defense and security."[42] Delegates stressed that a decision to restrict or ban the use of landmines would be made in light of security concerns, including available alternatives, and logistical and economic considerations and that, consequently, it was necessary to approach the matter with a sense of "realism."[43]

Many participants argued that a successful weapons convention required acceptance by the major powers and the main arms-producing states.[44] Anything short of that, these delegates contended, would constitute "no more than an empty moral gesture."[45] They noted, for example, that arms producing countries were largely responsible for ensuring adherence to the rules regulating weapon use contained in the Hague Agreements.[46] Delegates generally concurred that arms producers were not ready for a total ban. They pointed out that restrictions on use were more feasible given that proposals for limits, rather than a ban, came mainly from delegates whose countries were responsible for the manufacture and distribution of most conventional weapons; it was believed that this position indicated a level of regulation beyond which they were not prepared to go.

Those delegates arguing to restrict the use of landmines rather than institute a ban thus prevailed. During the last decade, however, with the marked increase in landmine use throughout the world, the fears of

---

[42] Lugano Report, p. 28.

[43] Ibid. See also Report of the Ad Hoc Committee, p. 459. The Arms Project and Physicians for Human Right's own sense of "realism," however, gained from confronting the results of the accumulation of so many millions of mines during the past ten years, urges that any measure short of a complete ban simply ignores and perpetuates the present crisis.

[44] Lugano Report, p. 40.

[45] Summary Records, pp. 15, 19.

[46] Lugano Report, p. 41.

those who supported a complete prohibition have materialized. It has become obvious that the rules adopted to diminish indiscriminate use of mines are not followed in most conflicts. It also is now strikingly clear that landmines, because of their delayed-action function, cause indiscriminate effects. Furthermore, it is evident that requiring combatants to weigh anticipated short-term military advantages with long-term humanitarian costs is futile. Finally, new studies on landmine use in diverse conflicts show that the impact of mines on civilian life is more serious and of longer duration than originally thought. The Arms Project and Physicians for Human Rights believe that a new, comprehensive examination of the full impact of landmines on civilian life inevitably must result in the enactment of a complete ban, in order to comport with existing humanitarian law.

### 4. The Special Problem of Remotely Delivered Mines

Conference participants also held special discussions regarding remotely delivered mines—particularly, their perceived offensive capabilities. The experience of the last decade shows, however, that the use of remotely delivered mines has not become as widespread as had been feared.[47] Nevertheless, the failure to ban remotely delivered mines has had terrible consequences in Afghanistan, where vast areas of land were saturated with mines delivered from the air, and in Indochina during U.S. involvement there. In addition, many concerns raised by delegates about remotely delivered mines have actually materialized in the context of the dramatic increase in the use of manually-emplaced mines. These include the increased offensive use of mines, the difficulties in discerning the borders of minefields, and the inadequacies of precautionary measures to diminish the risk of indiscriminate harm—features, that is of *all* mine use, if mines are deployed in sufficient quantities.

Whether remotely delivered mines should be categorically prohibited was the subject of one of the most heated disputes during the conferences. Although few participants seriously considered banning all mines, many more recognized the potential risks to civilians posed by

---

[47] But see Chapter 10 for a discussion of why remotely delivered mines are likely to be a prominent part of landmine deployment in the future.

mines which could be quickly dispersed over vast areas.[48]  Concerns were raised that air dispersion meant less accuracy in placement and, consequently, greater danger to civilians.  It was noted that accuracy in placement depends on the availability of sophisticated navigational and weapons guidance systems, user competence, terrain, and prevailing conditions of combat and weather; and that, therefore, a certain proportion of remotely delivered mines were inevitably lost outside targeted areas.[49]  In addition, with air dispersion, the limits of a mined area were more difficult, if not impossible, to discern, further increasing risk to civilians.  Finally, a number of delegates—particularly those from non-aligned, neutral, or developing  countries—while supporting the continued use of manually-emplaced mines because of their low cost and perceived defensive value, argued that remotely delivered mines give undue advantage to technologically advanced states, allowing them to use superior airpower against civilian populations.[50]  For some or all of these reasons, many delegates supported a complete ban on their use.[51]

Other delegates—mainly those representing the Western powers—endorsed regulation of remotely delivered mines rather than a total ban. These delegates insisted that precautions such as marking and recording of minefields, and the use of self-destruct mechanisms would eliminate or greatly reduce danger to civilians.  By the final form of the Landmines Protocol, however, the provisions dealing with these precautions had become quite weak.

Proponents of marking minefields believed that marking would provide the most complete protection for civilians.[52]  Others supported

---

[48] See, e.g., Report of the Ad Hoc Committee, p. 462.

[49] Summary Records, p. 131.

[50] See, e.g., Summary Records, pp. 16, 19.

[51] Working paper, CDDH/IV/201, stated in pertinent part, "Anti-personnel land-mines must not be laid by aircraft."  Reprinted in Lugano Report, p. 198.

[52] See, e.g., Lugano Report, p. 148.  Supporters of marking minefields noted that the procedure could take several forms:  marking the boundaries of a minefield, incorporating markers such as flares or flags into the design of each mine, or dispersing markers along with mines.

marking in theory, but pointed out that in practice the procedure would be haphazard since the perimeters of minefields, particularly those laid by remote delivery, can not be accurately defined.[53]   In the end, concerns that marking minefields would considerably reduce the military utility of mines prevailed.  The marking requirement was dropped entirely.

A number of delegates focused on mandatory self-destruct or self-neutralization features as critical to the protection of civilians—despite their rate of failure.  There was also considerable support for proposals requiring all remotely delivered mines to cease functioning  after a certain period of time.[54]   The imposition of a time limit eventually was rejected because of worries that such a rule would impede military usefulness, since the appropriate period might vary considerably in different situations.   Ultimately, the use of self-neutralizing devices remained optional, as long as combatants maintained records showing the location of their minefields.  Evidence that recording might be highly inaccurate and, in any case, of little value without mandatory demining measures was ignored. The failure of the drafters to impose an absolute requirement of self-destruct or self-neutralization mechanisms stemmed in part from concerns about their additional cost and weight, and partly from lobbying by a coalition of countries that wanted to preserve the possibility of laying mines not equipped with such devices.[55]

The dispute over whether or not to ban the use of remotely delivered mines continued even during the meeting that transmitted the final Landmines Protocol. The current, much weakened formulation,[56]

---

[53] Lugano Report, p. 54.

[54] See, e.g., Lugano Report, p. 206; Working Paper, COLU/213, reprinted in ibid., p. 189; and CDDH/IV/211 cited in Report of the Ad Hoc Committee, p. 498.

[55] See, e.g., Hon. George Aldrich, Report of the United States Delegation to the United Nations Conference on Prohibitions or Restrictions of Use of Certain Conventional Weapons Which may be Deemed to be Excessively Injurious or to Have Indiscriminate Effects--First Session (1979), p. 6.

[56] The current rules on remotely delivered mines are discussed in Part III of this chapter.

resulted from political comprises in which concessions were made to developing and non-aligned countries, mainly on such unrelated issues as language regarding mine disclosure, requirements during military occupation, and because of assurances that general rules aimed at protecting civilians from landmines also applied to the use of remotely delivered mines.[57]

Remotely delivered mines, although not used as frequently as manually-emplaced landmines, effectively illustrate the problems of manually-emplaced mines as used in contemporary armed conflict: both categories of mines have frightening offensive capabilities, cause indiscriminate harm, and are difficult to map, mark, and detect. Remotely delivered and manually-emplaced mines also share basic problems intrinsic to mine warfare: both cause egregious injuries, long-term devastation, and operate on the same delayed-action principles which render them implicitly indiscriminate weapons.

Thus, in view of the Arms Project and Physicians for Human Rights, remotely delivered mines should not be treated differently than manually-emplaced mines:    to conform to existing customary humanitarian law, the use of either type of mine must be banned.

## II.    The Landmines Protocol: Description and Analysis

### A. Applicability of the Weapons Convention

Because the Landmines Protocol is annexed to the Weapons Convention, the provisions of the Weapons Convention also govern the Protocol.

The preamble to the Weapons Convention states that it is based on three principles of customary law: that civilians should be protected from the effects of hostilities;[58] that combatants are not unlimited in

---

[57] See, e.g., the Hon. George Aldrich, Report of the United States Delegation to the Second Session of the Weapons Conference, p. 8; U.N. Disarmament Yearbook, Vol. 5:1980, pp. 305-306; Report of the Committee of the Whole, _ U.N. GAOR___; U.N. Doc. A/CONF.95/11 (1980), p. 2; 1980 Working Group Report, p.7; 1979 Conference Report, p. 20.

[58] Weapons Convention, Preamble, para. 2.

choosing the means by which they conduct war;[59] and that weapons should be prohibited that are apt to cause superfluous injury or unnecessary suffering.[60] The preamble also makes note of 1977 Additional Protocol I's prohibition against widespread, long-term and severe damage to the natural environment.[61] In addition, the preamble explicitly provides that even in cases not covered by the Weapons Convention and its Protocols, civilians always remain under the protection of the principles of customary international law, humanity, and the dictates of public conscience.[62] Particularly pertinent to the present discussion is the fact that although the Weapons Convention only governs the use of certain conventional weapons, the preamble urges that "the positive results achieved in this area may facilitate the main talks on disarmament with a view to putting an end to production, stockpiling and proliferation of such weapons."[63]

The Weapons Convention, and thus the Landmines Protocol, applies only to international armed conflicts and to a limited class of wars of national liberation.[64] Because provisions of customary law apply in all instances, however, both the prohibition against direct or indiscriminate attacks on civilians, and limits on the choice of weapons

---

[59] Ibid., Preamble, para. 3.

[60] Ibid.

[61] Ibid., Preamble, para. 4.

[62] Ibid., Preamble, para. 5. The Weapons Convention thus incorporates the so-called Martens clause, first formulated in the preamble to the Hague Convention respecting the laws and customs of war on land of 1899/1907, and enshrined in subsequent humanitarian treaties.

[63] Ibid., Preamble, para. 9.

[64] Article 1 of the Weapons Convention states that the Convention and its Protocols shall apply in situations referred to in article 2 common to the Geneva Conventions of 1949 and in paragraph 4 of article 1 of 1977 Additional Protocol I. The first situation is that of international conflict, defined as conflict between states or the occupation by one state of the territory of another. The second situation refers to armed struggle against "colonial domination, alien occupation, and racist regimes in furtherance of the right to self-determination."

and methods of combat so as not to inflict unnecessary suffering, remain in force in all armed conflicts, whether international or non-international.

In response to concerns that new types of conventional weapons would be developed which might require further international humanitarian regulation, the Weapons Convention was drafted as an open-ended treaty. Article __ provides for a review of the Convention's scope and operation as well as that of its Protocols, and permits proposals for amendments. It also allows new Protocols relating to additional categories of conventional weapons to be annexed in the future.

One of the most significant criticisms of the Weapons Convention is its failure to include enforcement provisions. It contains neither a procedure to monitor compliance, a defined venue for lodging allegations of breaches, nor a method for seeking redress or cessation of unlawful acts.[65]

### B. The Landmines Protocol

The Landmines Protocol includes the following substantive elements:

- rules to protect civilians from direct and indiscriminate mine attacks;
- recording and publication requirements for certain mines, and language encouraging international cooperation in mine removal efforts;

---

[65] Several governments made the omission of compliance procedures the subject of formal reservations. Report of the Secretary-General on the United Nations Conference on Prohibitions or Restrictions of Use of Certain Conventional Weapons Which May be Deemed to be Excessively Injurious or to have Indiscriminate Effects, U.N. Doc. A/37/199, October 5, 1982. The inclusion of such procedures was endorsed in principle by many conference participants, and representatives of several governments submitted proposals, but delegates were unable to arrive at a satisfactory agreement.

Pursuant to Article 8 of the Weapons Convention, the French government recently requested a review of the Landmines Protocol, in part because of its lack of compliance procedures.

- rules governing the deployment of non-remotely delivered mines in populated areas; and
- special regulations for remotely delivered mines and booby-traps.[66]

These are reviewed in detail below.

### 1. Restrictions on the Use of All Landmines

Article 3 of the Landmines Protocol contains general rules aimed at shielding civilians from the consequences of landmine use. These rules govern direct and indiscriminate use against civilians, and establish general precautionary measures that should be taken in waging a mine attack. Article 3 applies to the use of all mines. Unfortunately, it fails both on its face and in practice to provide meaningful protection to civilians.

### a. Prohibition of Direct Use of Mines Against Civilians

Article 3(2) of the Landmines Protocol prohibits the direct use of mines against civilians. It forbids both offensive and defensive deployment, as well as reprisals, against both the general civilian population and individual civilians. The instrument is silent as to the meaning of civilian or civilian population. However, definitions are provided in 1977 Additional Protocol I, article 50.[67]     "Civilian

---

[66] Article 8 of the Landmines Protocol also contains provisions specifically intended to protect United Nations missions and peacekeeping forces which are not discussed here. For an analysis of these rules, see Lt. Col. Burris M. Carnahan, "The Law of Land Mine Warfare: Protocol II to the United Nations Convention on Certain Conventional Weapons," 105 *Military L. Rev.* 73, 93-95 (1984).

[67] The drafters of the Land Mines Protocol turned regularly to the Geneva Conventions of 1949, and the 1977 Additional Protocols for definitions, terminology, and legal principles. They were particularly influenced by 1977 Additional Protocol I, because the Landmines Protocol was intended to supplement Protocol I's general rules regarding the conduct of war, with specific adaptations to landmine use. See historical discussion in Part I of this chapter.

population" is defined as "all persons who are civilians." A "civilian" is "anyone who is not a member of the armed forces or an organized armed group of a party to the conflict."[68] Under Protocol I, therefore, the definition of "civilian" is broad. Although the protection of civilians from attack does not extend to those who take a direct part in hostilities,[69] a clear distinction is made between direct, armed participation and general participation in the war effort.[70] Thus, for example, an individual who gives food to members of armed forces cannot legitimately become a target of mine use because of this act. Similarly, article 50(3) of Protocol I protects from attack a civilian population that has non-civilians living within it. Accordingly, a village populated by civilians cannot be subjected to mine use simply because non-civilians also happen to live there. In addition, where doubt exists as to whether a person is a civilian, article 50(1) of Protocol I requires combatants to presume that the person is a civilian.[71]

Unfortunately, although the prohibition against direct attacks on civilians is clear-cut, it is violated on a regular basis throughout the world.

---

Protocol I thus is considered *in para materia* with the Landmines Protocol.

[68] The term "armed forces" includes all organized armed forces, groups and units under a command responsible to a party to the conflict. 1977 Additional Protocol I, art. 43(1).

[69] Ibid., art. 51(3). This also was the express understanding of the Working Group on Landmines and Booby Traps. See Report of the Working Group on Landmines and Booby Traps, ____U.N. GAOR__; U.N. Doc. A/CONF./CW/7 (1980) p. 3; Report of the Conference to the General Assembly,__U.N. GAOR__; U.N. Doc. A/CONF .95/8 (1979), p. 18.

[70] ICRC, Commentary on the 1977 Protocols, p. 619.

[71] Likewise, where a question exists as to whether a particular object such as a house or school, normally dedicated to civilian purposes, also serves a military function, Additional Protocol I requires combatants to presume that it is not used for military purposes, and therefore, to refrain from attacking it.

### b.  The Prohibition Against Indiscriminate Attack

Article 3(3) purports to prohibit indiscriminate use of landmines. Indiscriminate use of weapons generally refers to the failure or inability to distinguish military targets from civilians.  Article 3(3), however, forbids only certain kinds of indiscriminate use.  It does nothing to control the basic problem of temporal indiscriminateness inherent in the use of landmines: the effects of mines that outlast their military function and place civilians at risk.  The Landmines Protocol thus fails on its own terms to provide adequate protection from this indiscriminate quality. This reflects the failure of its authors to make the analytic distinction between indiscriminate weapons *use* (which can be minimized if combatants take care to distinguish military targets from civilians), and the indiscriminate *effects* that naturally result from a mine's delayed-action operation.[72]

Article 3(3) prohibits placement of mines

(a)  which is not on or directed at a military objective; or,

(b)  which employs a method or means of delivery which cannot be directed at a specific military objective; or,

(c)  which may be expected to cause incidental loss of civilian life, injury to civilians, damage to civilian objects or a combination thereof, which would be excessive in relation to the concrete and direct military advantage anticipated.

The inadequacy of this narrow formulation is evident. Technically, mines can be directed at a legitimate military target as required by Article 3(3)(a) and (b).[73]  The problem is temporality; because of their delayed-action quality, mines essentially become indiscriminate weapons or, at least, indiscriminate in their effects.  Article 3(3) ignores this fundamental problem.

---

[72] See discussion in Part I(B)(2) of this chapter.

[73] Of course, in many conflicts the parties entirely ignore the dictates against the indiscriminate use of mines contained in Article 3(a) and (b).  Country-specific examples of indiscriminate use are discussed in Chapter 6.

In theory, Article 3(3)(c) requires that combatants seek to avoid indiscriminate use of landmines by refraining from an attack whose expected human toll would be excessive compared with a concrete anticipated military advantage. However, despite the fact that such an equation derives from a fundamental precept of customary law—that human suffering caused by warfare must not exceed military need—this formulation is insufficient to address the problem of temporal indiscriminateness central to land mine use. It does not offer guidance on how to compare the potential for long-term and essentially unknowable devastation presented by landmine use with a relatively short-term military advantage.[74]

Consider, for example, a situation where placing large quantities of mines on land traditionally used for agricultural purposes could block the movement of a column of enemy troops, thereby creating an undeniable military advantage.[75] The commander in this case does not anticipate, however, that this will cause a decisive victory. No civilian casualties are expected at the time the mines are laid, because civilians have temporarily fled the area. It is expected that this particular placement of mines will either cause the enemy to avoid the area altogether, channeling its soldiers into another location where they can be enveloped and destroyed or that some of the troops will detonate the mines and be injured or killed.

In fact, most of the mines are not exploded immediately, because once several soldiers are killed after moving across the minefield, the rest bypass it. Indeed, an important military advantage is gained because the troops, blocked by the minefield, flee to a nearby clearing, are

---

[74] In addition, the requirement of showing an anticipated "concrete and direct military advantage" is regularly ignored. Under this rule, such an advantage must be "substantial and relatively close," and "advantages which are hardly perceptible and those which would appear only in the long term should be disregarded." ICRC Commentary on the 1977 Additional Protocols, p. 684. In conflicts today, mines frequently are laid in locations where combatants speculate that at some future time, enemy troops might try to pass. This does not, in the view of the Arms Project and Physicians for Human Rights, legally satisfy the mandate that a military objective be concrete and direct.

[75] This hypothetical draws from situations in the country studies discussed in Chapter 6.

surrounded, and their formation destroyed.  After the battle, however, civilians return home.  They have been warned of the presence of mines; nevertheless, it is difficult to discern the boundaries of the minefields, and several civilians are killed by mine explosions.        Although the war ends several months later, the government cannot afford to undertake mine clearance.  International efforts are hampered by the sheer number of mines in terrain nearly impossible to clear.    Therefore, civilians remain unable to use their fields; most of the few who attempt to do so are maimed or killed.   So are their animals.   The cost of medical operations for people who succeed in reaching hospitals dwarfs average per capita income.    Unable to farm, villagers are deprived of their livelihoods, and forced to give up land used for centuries for subsistence. To survive, many of these people move to cities where they are ill-equipped to make a living; many die of malnutrition.  W a s      t h e deployment of mines in this instance justifiable within the framework of Article 3(3)(c)?  The commander's decision to launch an attack would be perfectly legitimate if his troops had been using non-delayed-action weapons; a military objective was targeted, a specific and concrete military advantage was anticipated and gained, and precautions were taken to protect civilians.  However, the temporal dimension of landmine use hopelessly complicates the calculation; it requires combatants to weigh anticipated military utility against dangers that, because of the time lag involved in mine explosions, might not emerge until far in the future.

Article 3(3)(c)'s formulation thus ignores the basic problem of indiscriminateness in landmine use: the future harm to civilians that may be caused by mines outliving their military purpose.[76]    The

---

[76] A related problem is posed by the Landmines Protocol's mandate that mines be directed at a "military objective."  Article 2(4) defines "military objective" as "any object which by its nature, location, purpose, or use makes an effective contribution to military action and whose total or partial destruction, capture or neutralization, *in the circumstances ruling at the time*, offers a definite military advantage"(emphasis added).  This definition is taken verbatim from Article 52(2) of Protocol I.  It has been noted that while Article 52(2) "constitutes a valuable guide....it will not always be easy to interpret, particularly for those who have to decide about an attack, and on the means and methods to be used."  ICRC Commentary on the 1977 Additional Protocols, p. 635.  Thus, it is acknowledged that, in general terms, following such a formulation is difficult at best.  As applied to landmines, however, it is completely unworkable because of their delayed effects.  Obligating combatants to target only those military objectives that offer

requirement that combatants weigh expected harm to civilians against anticipated military advantage fails in two respects. First, it imposes on field commanders the impossible duty of predicting future consequences of a particular use of mines.[77] Second, it ignores the essential fact of mine warfare: time delay.

Article 3(3)'s rules against indiscriminate use would have been significantly strengthened by the inclusion of several provisions contained in 1977 Additional Protocol I's prohibition against indiscriminate attacks. These rules, set forth in article 51(4), are generally recognized as expressing customary law.[78] However, as explained below, the logical result of these provisions is to ban the use of landmines altogether—a result which, given the problem of temporality, is unsurprising.

Article 51(4) of Protocol I forbids several categories of indiscriminate attacks if they "are of a nature to strike military objects and civilians or civilian objects without distinction." This language provides noncombatants with substantially more protection than the Landmines Protocol. While mines may be directed at military targets, they frequently, because of their delayed effects, strike civilians instead. Thus, they are "of a nature to strike military objects and civilians or civilian objects without distinction." Accordingly, the use of landmines is completely forbidden under this provision.

Similarly, article 51(4)(c) of Protocol I prohibits attacks "which employ a method or means of combat, the effects of which cannot be limited as required by [Protocol I]". The ICRC Commentary on the 1977 Additional Protocols notes, significantly, that "[i]t may be that mines also

---

a military advantage at the time mines are placed provides little protection to civilians after a live mine loses its military value.

[77] See discussion in part I(B)(2) (a) of this chapter.

[78] See e.g. ICRC Commentary on the 1977 Additional Protocols, pp. 598; 615–616; 619–622. The United States recognizes the rules contained in article 51(4) as customary law, although it has not ratified Additional Protocol I. See Michael J. Matheson, Deputy Legal Advisor, U.S. Dept. of State, "The United States Position on the Relation of Customary International Law to the 1977 Protocols Additional to the 1949 Geneva Conventions," 2 Am. U. J. Int'l Law and Policy 426 (Fall 1987).

come within the scope" of this provision.[79]   The Arms Project and Physicians for Human Rights believe that mines clearly do come within this prohibition because the temporal effects of landmines cannot be properly limited.

In addition, under article 51(4)(b) of Protocol I, *attacks* "which employ a method or means of combat which cannot be directed at a specific military objective" are prohibited.    Article 3(3)(b) of the Landmines Protocol, by contrast, states this rule only with respect to the *placement* of landmines; it proscribes any placement of mines "which employs a method or means of delivery which cannot be directed at a specific military objective." However, because of their delayed-action quality, it is perfectly possible to *place* mines and deliver them in a way so that they are directed at a specific military objective, and yet which still causes indiscriminate effects.

The word "attack," as used in Protocol I, has a different connotation than "placement."    The ICRC Commentary on article 51(4)(b) notes that a problem may exist; because indiscriminate attacks are forbidden, a question is raised about the point at which the use of landmines is an "attack." The commentators describe measures to protect civilians incorporated into the Landmines Protocol, but nevertheless acknowledge that, following the more stringent rule concerning prohibited attacks contained in Protocol I,

> the question may arise at what point the use of mines constitutes an attack... Is it when the mine is laid, when it is armed, when a person is endangered by it, or when it finally explodes? The participants at the meeting of the International Society of Military Law and the Law of War (Lausanne, 1982) conceded that from the legal point of view the use of mines constituted an attack in the sense of the [Protocol I] *when a person was directly endangered by such a mine* (emphasis added).[80]

The word "attack" in article 51(4)(b) of Protocol I thus focuses on the legal importance of the moment when a person is directly

---

[79] ICRC Commentary on the 1977 Additional Protocols, p. 622.

[80] Ibid.

endangered by a mine rather than the moment when it is placed and directed, as emphasized in the Landmines Protocol. The rule expressed in Article 3 (3)(b) of the Landmines Protocol is significantly weaker than that stated in article 51 (4)(b) of Protocol I; the latter rule, if "attack" is taken to be the moment of endangerment, implies a prohibition of landmine use altogether.

The drafters of the Landmine Protocol explicitly stated that the rules against indiscriminate landmine use in the Landmines Protocol were drawn from article 51 of Protocol I.[81] The obvious question is why the drafters omitted the provisions most applicable to landmines. One answer is precisely that their inclusion so evidently would prohibit, rather than restrict, landmine use. A more generous answer is that the Landmines Protocol was being drafted just as Protocol I was becoming law. It is likely that the authors of the Landmines Protocol had little opportunity to scrutinize closely the provisions of Protocol I and analyze their many implications for mine warfare. In addition, the drafters were working without the benefit of the careful interpretation and analysis provided by the ICRC Commentary on 1977 Additional Protocol I, which was not published until after the Landmines Protocol entered into force. Whatever the reason, the fact that the Landmines Protocol fails to reflect the provisions set forth in Article 51(4) of Protocol I means that the drafters failed to fulfill the original purpose of the Landmines Protocol—to supplement Protocol I's general rules on warfare.

### c. Precautionary Measures

Article 3(4) of the Landmines Protocol provides for certain precautionary measures to minimize the probability of harm to civilians, but these, again, are inadequate. Combatants are merely required to take "all feasible precautions" to protect civilians from deliberate or indiscriminate attack. "Feasible" is defined loosely as those precautions which are "practicable or practically possible taking into account all circumstances ruling at the time, including humanitarian and military considerations." This general statement is not clarified by example. Given the stated intent of Article 3 to protect civilians, these measures are remarkably vague. In fact, in a slightly different context, conference participants noted that requiring "effective" measures implied more of a

---

[81] 1980 Working Group Report at 3; 1979 Conference Report at 18.

guarantee whereas requiring only "feasible" steps without other precautions failed to place sufficient emphasis on humanitarian considerations.[82]

## 2. Recording, Publication, and Mine Clearance Provisions

In addition to general restrictions aimed at shielding civilians during an attack, the Landmines Protocol contains recording, publication, and demining provisions. These rules are extremely weak. However, even if they were significantly strengthened, they would do little to protect civilians from the problems posed by landmines.

The Protocol requires recording all "pre-planned minefields."[83] With regard to other minefields and individual mines, the parties only must "endeavour to ensure" that they are recorded.[84]    Lieutenant Colonel Burris M. Carnahan has pointed out that the term "pre-planned" was intended to refer to a degree of advance preparation beyond that covered by the word "planned."[85]    He explains that, "in a military sense," a "planned" minefield is one for which detailed efforts have been made to schedule, organize and program the minefield in advance of the actual execution of those efforts.  Since "pre-planned" means more than "planned," a "pre-planned" minefield is...one for which a detailed military plan exits considerably in advance of the proposed date of execution."[86] Carnahan then states the obvious problem which makes the recording requirement virtually useless: "Naturally, such a detailed military plan

---

[82] Report of the Preparatory Conference, Ann. II, p. 3.

[83]  Landmines Protocol, art. 7(1)(a).

[84] Ibid., art. 7(2).  In the Ad Hoc Committee meetings, this construction was criticized for being overly weak.  Report of the Ad Hoc Committee, p. 530. Recommendations for stronger language were ignored, however, because participants believed that it would be too burdensome to record other types of minefields or individual mines.  Initially, the recording requirement would have obligated combatants to record all minefields with more than twenty mines.

[85] Carnahan, *The Law of Land Mine Warfare*, p. 84.

[86]  Ibid.

could not exist for the vast majority of minefields emplaced during
wartime. In the heat of combat many minefields will be created to meet
immediate battlefield contingencies with little 'planning' or
'preplanning.'"[87] As Carnahan further points out, there is no provision
that the composition of the minefield or the pattern in which the mines
were placed be recorded. Nor is there an obligation to record the
location of individual mines within the minefield.[88]

The last decade of mine use has shown that the locations of very
few mines or minefields have been recorded. In addition, even when
combatants endeavor to keep precise and detailed maps of the mines they
lay, as the British did during the Falkland/Malvinas War, the records have
proved wildly inaccurate. The locations of landmines shift with changing
weather conditions and the passage of time. In the case of remote
delivery, many mines are placed outside the intended target area.
Finally, record-keeping is a useless exercise, even if greater accuracy were
possible, and combatants regularly kept good records, unless successful
mine clearance is undertaken in a timely fashion.

As discussed in Chapter 7, mine clearance projects worldwide are
minimal; such efforts suffer from lack of funds, accessible technology and,
more importantly, political will. Provisions in the Landmines Protocol
relating to mine removal clearly reflect this lack of will. Article 9, which
deals with demining, merely calls for international cooperation in the
removal of mines. It states in relevant part:

> After the cessation of active hostilities, the parties shall
> endeavor to reach agreement, both among themselves
> and, where appropriate with other States and with
> international organizations, on the provision of
> information and technical and material
> assistance—including in appropriate circumstances, joint

---

[87] Ibid.

[88] Ibid. The Working Group on Land Mines did write a nonbinding technical
annex with guidelines on recording. See Appendix 3. However, this annex
provides only that records should be made in such a way as to indicate the extent
of minefields, and that their location should be specified by relation to the
coordinates of a single reference point and by the estimated dimensions of the
area containing mines in relation to that single reference point.

operations—necessary to remove or otherwise render
ineffective....mines...placed in position during the conflict.

This provision has been accurately referred to as "the most
questionable variant of the rules of warfare, whose true purpose is not to
'safeguard the minimum standard of civilization' but rather to 'cover up
the inability or unwillingness to achieve this object'."[89]    The Arms
Project and Physicians for Human Rights agree.    Nothing in the
Landmines Protocol makes mine clearance mandatory or even a priority.
In addition, nothing requires that mines be built in a way that would
facilitate their removal.  Indeed, most mines today are sheathed in plastic,
making them harder to detect, further thwarting demining efforts.
Furthermore, while the Landmines Protocol merely encourages mine
clearance efforts after the end of active hostilities, a proper application
of customary law prohibiting indiscriminate attacks, particularly as
expressed in article 51 of Protocol I, would require mine removal
immediately after the military objective for which the mines were placed
ceases to exist.  This would be well before the end of an armed conflict.
"Military objective" is defined very narrowly under humanitarian law;
article 57 of Protocol I requires showing an anticipated "concrete and
direct military advantage."  Under this rule, such an advantage must be
"substantial and relatively close," and advantages which are hardly
perceptible and those which would appear only in the long-term should
be disregarded.[90]    Under this formulation demining in most cases
would be required minutes after mines are laid.  Clearly, given the time
and cost involved in mine removal, as well as wartime conditions, this
would be impossible.  Therefore, not mining at all is the only alternative
under humanitarian law.

Publication requirements contained in the Landmines Protocol
are equally ineffective.  Again, even assuming accurate records of mines,
publication of those records to allow civilians to try to avoid mined areas
is not a solution, especially where those areas include civilian homes and
fields which remain unusable until mines are removed.  In any case,

---

[89] Carnahan, "The Law of Land Mine Warfare," pp. 82-83, quoting 2 G.
Schwarzenberger, *International Law as Applied by International Courts and Tribunals*
11 (1968).

[90] ICRC Commentary on 1977 Additional Protocol I, p. 684.

thepublication requirements set forth in the Landmines Protocol are extremely weak.

Article 7 simply directs that "after the cessation of active hostilities" parties take "all necessary and appropriate measures, including the use of [mine] records, to protect civilians from the effects of....mines", and to release all information about the location of minefields to adversaries and the Secretary-General of the U.N., unless the territory of one party is still occupied by the forces of its adversary.[91] In addition, it states that "wherever possible, by mutual agreement," the parties shall provide for the release of information concerning the location of mines, "particularly in agreements governing the cessation of hostilities."[92] Requiring publication only after hostilities cease again ignores the temporal problem of landmine use.[93] It fails to take into account that because of its delayed-action feature, a mine might be directed at a military target but not detonate during military operations. At that point the mine poses a grave risk for civilians; this may well occur long *before* the cessation of hostilities, rendering the post-

---

[91] Landmines Protocol, art. 7(3)(a).

[92] Ibid., art. 7(3)(c).

[93] The phrase "cessation of hostilities" also suffers from interpretation problems; it can "begin long before a formal peace treaty enters into force," but also "refers to something more than a temporary truce or ceasefire." Carnahan, *The Law of Land Mine Warfare*, p. 87. For further discussion of this point, see ibid., pp. at 87-88.

In addition, the phrase refers to cessations which occur after the Landmines Protocol enters into force for the parties to the conflict. This is in accord with the Vienna Convention on the Law of Treaties, which provides that a treaty does not bind a party in relation to any act or fact which occurred before entry into force. Thus, for example, if North Korea and South Korea both become parties to the Landmines Protocol, no new obligation to disclose mines as a result of the 1953 cessation of hostilities between the two countries would arise. Ibid., p. 88.

conflict provision irrelevant.[94] Considering how many serious conflicts have persisted a decade or more, the problem is significant.

Moreover, the provision directing parties to undertake "necessary and appropriate measures" to shield civilians from the effects of mines is not sufficiently mandatory, and fails to give specific guidance. Finally, language calling for release of information about the location of mines "wherever possible, by mutual agreement" is too precatory to be of any real use.

### 3. Additional Restrictions on Certain Types of Landmines

In addition to the general rules reviewed in the preceding section which are applicable to the use of all landmines, the Landmines Protocol includes additional restrictions on particular kinds of mines.

### a. Restrictions on Non-Remotely Delivered Mines in Populated Areas

Article 4 of the Landmines Protocol contains rules that apply to non-remotely delivered mines used in populated areas. The provisions are confusing because they actually appear in certain respects to undercut the Protocol's mandate to avoid attacks on civilians. Article 4(2) prohibits the use of the defined weapons in "any city, town, village or other area containing a similar concentration of civilians" where there is no active or imminent ground combat. However, this apparent ban on landmine use in peaceable civilian concentrations is vitiated by two major exceptions. First, such use is permitted either if mines are placed in the "close vicinity of a military objective belonging to or under the control of" the enemy, or, second, if measures are taken "to protect civilians from their effects."[95] Specific measures are not enumerated. Instead, Article

---

[94] In addition, the language of the Landmines Protocol appears to make an exception where active hostilities have ceased, but the forces of one party occupy the territory of the adverse party; in such cases, disclosure of the location of mines to the adverse party and the U.N. is not strictly mandatory, although undertaking" all necessary and appropriate measures...to protect civilians" is. Art. 7(3)(a).

[95] Landmines Protocol, art. 4(2)(a) and 4(2)(b), respectively.

4 gives only a short list of examples: the posting of warning signs or sentries, the issue of warnings, and the provision of fences.[96] None of these are mandatory.

This either/or formulation lawfully permits, for example, mines to be placed near an enemy weapons silo (a legitimate military objective) located in the middle of a heavily populated city that has never been under military attack, without warning civilians living across the street.[97]

Given that the attacking party is subject to Article 3's protections for civilians—such as weighing expected harm to civilians against the specific military advantage anticipated—Article 4's affirmative sanctioning of attacks on military objectives in otherwise peaceful civilian areas without warning is confusing at best. It appears to undercut seriously the Landmines Protocol's attempts to limit injury and death to civilians and damage to civilian property generally. Article 4 exemplifies the startling lax protections contained in the Landmines Protocol. It does not constitute an acceptable standard under customary international law.

---

[96] At the Preparatory Conference, it was proposed by some delegates that the Landmines Protocol require "effective" measures. Others recommended or that "all feasible" measures be required. The former Soviet Union opposed the first formulation out of concern that it might be considered a guarantee that civilians not be harmed. The Western powers opposed the "all feasible" alternative as not placing enough emphasis on humanitarian factors, permitting commanders to justify taking no protective measures because they were not feasible. The present formulation is a compromise, which requires that some measures be implemented to safeguard civilians, but does not ensure the effectiveness of the measures. Carnahan, *The Law of Land Mine Warfare*, p. 73.

[97] The peculiar drafting also would seem to allow the mining of a non-military objective as long as precautions are taken pursuant to Landmines Protocol, art. 4(2)(b). This makes no sense in light of Article 3's mandate that only military objectives be targeted.

# PFM-1

The Soviet-made PFM-1 is a small air-delivered plastic antipersonnel mine. When large numbers of these green, wing-shaped mines were dropped in Afghanistan, Afghan tribesmen named it the "Green Parrot." It is also called the "Butterfly" mine. The PFM-1 is also made of white or sand-colored low-metallic signature plastic and is usually sown by Mi-8 Hip or similar helicopters. The mine drifts to the ground where it becomes activated. From then on, any distortion of the plastic body will cause the mine to detonate. This distortion may be produced by stepping on or kicking the mine or by the accumulation of light pressures such as those produced by handling. Afghan children, mistaking the mine for a toy, have been killed or maimed. (Drawing by Pamela Blotner for the Arms Project/PHR.)

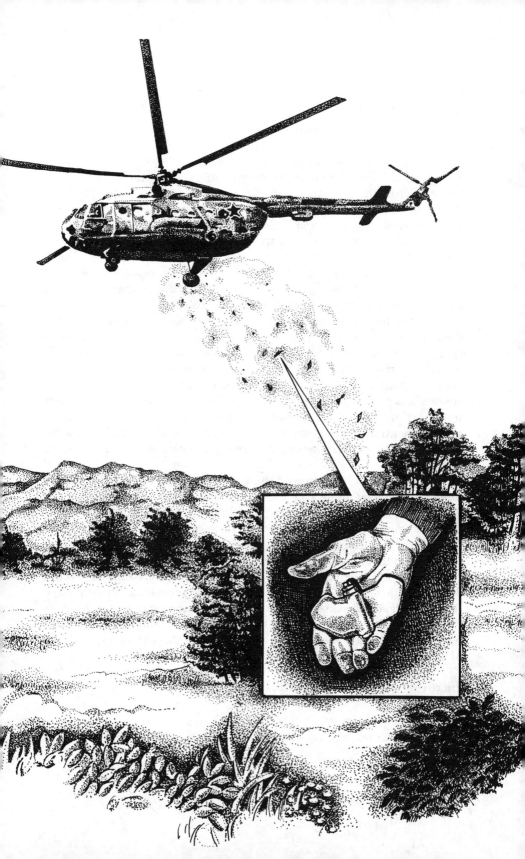

## b. Remotely Delivered Mines[98]

As discussed in Part I of this chapter, very serious consideration was given to banning remotely delivered mines altogether, even as late as the meeting that transmitted the final draft of the Landmines Protocol. Two concerns fueled the attempt to completely proscribe their use: first, that they cause a greater risk of harm to civilians and, second, that they give unfair advantage to countries with greater access to advanced military technology.    The present provisions governing the use of remotely delivered mines are the result of political compromise, some of which had little to do with remotely delivered mines themselves, but instead with other parts of the Landmines Protocol.

The deployment of remotely delivered mines is always subject to the general restrictions placed on landmine use discussed earlier.  Rules specifically governing remotely delivered mines are three-fold.  There is a threshold requirement that they can be used only within an area which is itself a military objective or which contains military objectives.  If this condition is met, combatants must take one of the following steps: they must record the location of mines *or* they must equip them with "an effective neutralizing mechanism."  Finally, the use of remotely delivered mines requires "effective advance warning" to civilians if "circumstances permit."

The initial limitation of the use of remotely delivered mines to military objectives reinforces the Landmines Protocol's prohibition on using mines either directly against the civilian population or in a manner whereby mines cannot be directed at a specific military objective. Although this formulation attempts to shield civilians from harm, it suffers from the same shortcomings discussed earlier with regard to those rules.  It fails to take into account that remotely delivered mines, even if directed at a military object, can become indiscriminate in two ways: first, as with all mines, with respect to time, if they survive their military function and, second, by missing their mark due to the large quantities of mines dispersed across vast areas of land, and the virtual impossibility of accurate targeting during remote delivery.

The precautions set forth in the Landmines Protocol do not deal effectively with these problems.   First, despite evidence presented at

---

[98] The rules on remotely-delivered mines are contained in Article 5 of the Landmines Protocol.

experts meetings that the lack of sophisticated navigational systems frequently led to inaccurate delivery, the Landmines Protocol does not require specialized equipment for delivery. Second, it omits a minefield marking requirement, despite repeated recommendations that one be imposed.[99] The current formulation, allowing either marking of mine locations *or* the use of an effective neutralizing mechanism is remarkably weak. Although these methods are flawed—and rarely followed—the inclusion of rules mandating that both be used at least might have provided modestly increased protection.

Morover, as explained previously, the Landmines Protocol's recording requirements are limited because they are mandatory only with respect to pre-planned minefields, and because there is no obligation to record the composition of the minefield or the location of individual mines within the field. In addition, because remotely delivered mines are often quickly laid during fluid battlefield conditions, and dropped far into enemy territory, it can prove difficult, if not impossible, to record the location of remotely delivered mines.[100]

The alternative to recording—equipping remotely delivered mines with self-destruct or self-neutralization mechanisms—has its own problems. First, like the recording requirement, the mandate to use such mechanisms frequently is ignored. The result is that remotely delivered mines often are placed without either precaution being taken. Second, self-destruct and self-neutralizations mechanisms do not always function properly, a concern expressed by some conference participants, but never resolved. Third, there is no time period designated within which the devices must deactivate or destroy the mines. The unfortunate result is that the "specific and concrete military objective" required by the Landmines Protocol as necessary for a landmine attack might cease to be

---

[99] It is important to note, however, that marking minefields is of only limited utility. Current technology does not permit the marking of the precise perimeters of mined areas.

[100] Carnahan, *The Law of Landmine Warfare*, p. 89.

important after one day, but a mine equipped with such a device might not deactivate for months or years.[101]

The warning requirement, is also weak, especially when compared to the grave, often long-term dangers caused by remotely delivered mines.  In practice, very few mine deliveries have been preceded or followed by warnings of any kind.

The Landmines Protocol requires only that "[e]ffective advance warning shall be given of any delivery or dropping of remotely delivered mines which may affect the civilian population, unless circumstances do not permit."[102]  Although this language is identical to that set forth in 1977 Additional Protocol I's general warning requirement,[103] the latter instrument also requires that other precautions be taken to safeguard civilian interests.

In addition, the Landmines Protocol does not require warnings to civilians *after* remotely delivered mines are laid.  This omission is troubling, since a warning often will be perfectly possible after mines are delivered, even though security considerations (the safety of the aircraft, for example) might have justified not issuing a prior warning.[104] Carnahan believes that subsequent warnings would still be required under Landmines Protocol Article 3(4) which states that "all feasible precautions shall be taken to protect civilians from the effects of mines."[105] However, given the admittedly heightened risks to civilians from remotely delivered mines, this should have been spelled out.  The failure to include an explicit requirement to issue subsequent warnings seems to

---

[101] It is also important to note that the neutralizing option contained in the Landmines Protocol allows either turn-off or self-destruct devices. Mine clearance experts have voiced serious reservations about the utility of the turn-off mechanisms, because the existing technology does not indicate whether the mine actually is turned off or remains live. Therefore, those mines have to be cleared as though they were live anyway.

[102] Landmines Protocol, art. 5(2).

[103] 1977 Additional Protocol I, art. 57.

[104] Carnahan, *The Law of Land Mine Warfare*, p. 80.

[105] Ibid.

confirm that the drafters of the Landmines Protocol did not focus on the unique temporal dimension that makes mines so dangerous to civilians. With other weapons, once an attack is over, there generally is no need to provide a warning; the damage is done.    In the case of landmines, however, subsequent warnings are critical.

### c. Booby-traps

Boobytraps are defined as "any device or material which is designed, constructed or adapted to kill or injure and which functions unexpectedly when a person disturbs or approaches an apparently harmless object or performs an apparently safe act."[106]    Particular concern was raised at both the experts' and diplomatic conferences that booby-traps are inherently perfidious.[107]    Consequently, there was a fair amount of support for a total ban.    However, many delegates maintained that because booby-traps could be rigged up with scarce resources, they were militarily essential. The result was a compromise which led to the banning of certain kinds of booby-traps considered to be particularly perfidious.

Permissible classes of booby-traps are subject to Article 3's prohibitions on direct deployment against civilians and indiscriminate use, as well as rules pertaining to recording and disclosure, and use in areas of civilian concentrations.  Two categories of booby-traps are proscribed. First are booby-traps in the "form of an apparently harmless, portable object which is specifically designed and constructed to contain explosive material and to detonate when it is disturbed or approached."[108] Second are those in any way attached to or associated with the following: internationally recognized protective emblems such as the Red Cross or Red Crescent; the wounded or the dead; medical facilities and equipment; children's toys or other portable objects or products designed for the well-being of children; food and drink; civilian kitchen utensils; objects of a

---

[106] Landmines Protocol, art. 2(2).

[107] "Perfidious" refers to acts which intentionally mislead an adversary into believing that he will be protected under humanitarian principles. See, e.g., Protocol I, art. 37.

[108] Landmines Protocol, art. 6(1)(a).

clearly religious nature; historic monuments; works of art which are part of the cultural or spiritual heritage of people; and animals or their carcasses.[109]

The first category forbids "prefabricated" booby-traps which could be mass-produced.[110] This prohibition effectively means the proscription of remotely delivered booby-traps. The second category derives from prohibitions contained in the Geneva Conventions of 1949 and the 1977 Additional Protocols, and from discussions at the various conferences about what constituted "perfidious" uses of booby-traps. The specific enumeration of forbidden objects is refreshing in a document containing so much general and precatory language. However, one possible draw-back is that combatants might come to see the list as all-inclusive, despite Article 6(1)'s statement that the rules regarding booby-traps are without prejudice to general humanitarian principles relating to perfidy and treachery.

The Landmines Protocol also explicitly forbids the use of any booby-trap designed to cause superfluous injury or unnecessary suffering. Of course, under customary international law, the use of any weapon apt to lead to such results is prohibited. The specific inclusion of such language with respect to booby-traps is meant to provide some protection against particularly heinous types—principally non-portable, non-explosive booby-traps—not expressly banned by the designated categories.

Although the rules governing the use of booby-traps fall short of a total ban, they are stronger than the rest of the regulations contained in the Landmines Protocol. The language used is more clear-cut; the basic rules are not subject to the kinds of exceptions, qualifications, and discretionary formulations that characterize the other provisions. In addition, unlike other regulations, those relating to booby-traps make specific reference to rules of customary international law which provide broader protections than the Landmines Protocol.

### C. Summary

The purpose of the Landmines Protocol was to adapt general humanitarian principles, particularly those expressed in 1977 Additional

---

[109] Ibid., art. 6(1)(b).

[110] 1979 Conference Report, p. 20.

Protocol I, to the peculiar vagaries of mine warfare. It has failed to achieve this goal, either in theory or in fact.

The Landmines Protocol does not effectively address the most serious aspect of indiscriminateness posed by mine warfare: a mine that does not explode during military operations, and is not removed, becomes indiscriminate, creating a long-term threat to civilians. Article 3's limited prohibition on indiscriminate use—focused on whether a mine is directed at a military objective rather than the effects caused by its time-delayed quality—does not take this temporality problem into account.

Despite the failure of the Landmines Protocol, both on its face and in practice, the Arms Project and Physicians for Human Rights support convening a comprehensive review conference to reconsider the treaty. Under Article 8 of the Weapons Convention, such a conference would permit the contracting parties to review the scope and operation of the Landmines Protocol and urge changes. This would allow for a full discussion and debate of the issues raised in this book. In particular, it would provide an opportunity to bring the Landmines Protocol in line with customary law, especially with the relevant provisions contained in 1977 Additional Protocol I.

Of course, it is likely that bringing the Landmines Protocol into conformity with Protocol I would be tantamount to banning use.[111] The application of rules prohibiting indiscriminate attacks set forth in articles 51(4) and 51(5)(b) of Protocol I requires a ban on the use of landmines. Likewise, an in-depth examination of the range of medical, social, and economic consequences of landmines would support a ban under articles 35(1) and (2) of Protocol I, which together provide that the right of the parties to a conflict to choose and employ weapons must be limited when those weapons are of a nature to cause superfluous injury or unnecessary suffering. It is clear that nothing short of a wholesale ban on the use of landmines within the framework of humanitarian law, and on production, stockpiling, and transfer of mines within the framework

---

[111] One approach, within the framework of the Landmines Protocol, would be to insert a simple proviso into Article 3 providing that any use of antipersonnel mines is always indiscriminate and hence always prohibited. Since the Landmines Protocol also deals, for example, with antitank mines, it does not render the rest of the treaty wholly superfluous.

of disarmament law, can effectively curb the intractable problems caused by a weapon that is not only frequently subject to indiscriminate use, but also because of its delayed-action quality, is virtually always indiscriminate in effect.

### III.     How International Law Supports a Ban on Landmines

#### A. Prohibiting the Use of Landmines Under Customary Law

In analyzing the failures of the Landmines Protocol, Part II of this Chapter explains how prohibitions against indiscriminate means of combat in Article 51(4) of 1977 Additional Protocol I provide stronger protections to civilians from the indiscriminate effects of landmines than does the Landmines Protocol itself.  Article 35 of Additional Protocol I, which forbids the use of weapons that cause unnecessary suffering or superfluous injury, also supports a ban on the use of mines. These provisions are rooted in three fundamental principles of customary humanitarian law:

1.  parties to a conflict are not unlimited in choosing the means by which they wage war;
2.  military needs must yield to humanitarian considerations when weapons cause unnecessary suffering; and
3.  combatants must endeavor to protect civilians from the effects of hostilities and, therefore, are required to employ means of combat that can distinguish between civilian and military objectives.[112]

---

[112] These principles are generally recognized as customary law.  In addition to being codified in the Protocol I art. 35(1) and (2), and art. 51(1)–(5), they were expressly stated in U.N. General Assembly Resolution 2444, "Respect for Human Rights in Armed Conflicts," which was adopted by unanimous vote on January 13, 1969.  The first two also formed the basis for early humanitarian treaties, these treaties are discussed in Part III(B) of this chapter.

The U.S. government expressly recognizes the three principles as declaratory of existing customary international law.  For example, the U.S. Air Force's *Pamphlet on the Conduct of Armed Conflict and Air Operations* 110-31 recognizes "...a specific prohibition against unnecessary suffering and a

These principles, refined and codified in Protocol I, were considered in detail by the participants in the conferences that led to the drafting of the Landmines Protocol.[113] However, as described in Part I of this chapter, the delegates placed undue emphasis on the military utility of landmines, gave short-shrift to humanitarian concerns and ignored, in particular, the indiscriminate effects on civilians implicit in the use of mines. As a result, while liberally citing established principles of humanitarian law, the authors of the Landmines Protocol failed to give them proper effect. In failing properly to apply humanitarian law, the Landmines Protocol also fails to achieve its purpose as originally articulated at the conferences on the Reaffirmation and Development of Humanitarian Law: to apply the general customary rules codified in Protocol I to the specifics of mine warfare.[114]

---

requirement of proportionality," and "confirms the basic immunity of the civilian population and civilians from being objects of attack during armed conflict." Similar rules are contained in the other U.S. armed services manuals.

See also Remarks of Michael J. Matheson, Deputy Legal Advisor, United States Dept. of State, "The United States Position on the Relation of Customary International Law to the 1977 Protocols Additional to the 1949 Geneva Conventions," in The Sixth Annual American Red Cross—Washington College of Law Conference on International Law, *American U.J. Int'l Law and Policy* (Fall 1987), p. 419, 424–426. Matheson notes specifically that the U.S. supports the principle contained in Article 35(1) and (2) of Protocol I that means of warfare are not unlimited, and that parties to a conflict must refrain from using weapons "of a nature to cause superfluous injury or unnecessary suffering," Ibid., p. 424. He further explains that the U.S. supports the provisions in articles 51 and 52 of Protocol I that aim to protect civilians and civilian objects from deliberate and indiscriminate attacks.

[113] Indeed, these principles are explicitly recognized in the preamble to the Weapons Convention as the basis for the rules contained in the annexed Protocols, including the Landmines Protocol.

[114] See Report of the Ad Hoc Committee, p. 454, Summary Records of the Ad Hoc Committee, p. 10; and discussion in Part IA of this chapter.

Fine-tuning the Landmines Protocol will not ameliorate the defining features of mine warfare:

1.  the severity of mine injuries and long-term devastation caused to civilians; and
2.  the operation of mines on delayed-action principles, which significantly magnify risks to civilians.

The first of these features justifies a prohibition on mine use under customary rules which forbid means of warfare that cause unnecessary suffering.[115]  These rules are codified in articles 35(1) and (2) of Additional Protocol I.  While the principle is subject to diverse interpretations, the basic tenet holds that violence which exceeds the minimum militarily necessary is unlawful.[116]  Earlier chapters document the extent to which damage caused by landmines exceeds military gains.  In light of these facts, a re-evaluation of landmine use under humanitarian principles recognizing that means of warfare are limited at the point they cause unnecessary suffering, must lead to a complete prohibition against mine warfare.

The second salient feature of landmine use—the indiscriminate effects caused by its delayed-action function—justifies a ban on use landmines under humanitarian principles forbidding means of warfare that have indiscriminate effects.  As explained earlier in this chapter, rules against indiscriminateness contained in the Landmines Protocol address only indiscriminate use and not indiscriminate effects.  Nevertheless, as detailed Part II (B), customary principles, particularly as codified in article 51(4) of Additional Protocol I, explicitly forbid means of warfare that have indiscriminate effects.  Briefly, Article 51(4) forbids as indiscriminate, attacks "of a nature to strike military objects and civilians or civilian objects without distinction,"[117] or which "employ a method

---

[115] See, e.g., codification of this principle in 1977 Additional Protocol I, art. 35(1) and (2).

[116] See, e.g., ICRC Commentary on the 1977 Additional Protocols, p. 396.

[117] 1977 Additional Protocol I, art. 51(4).

or means of combat, the effects of which cannot be limited..."[118]  In addition, article 51(4)(b) forbids attacks "which employ a method or means of combat which cannot be directed at a specific military objective."  The meaning of "attack" in this provision, specifically with respect to landmines, has been interpreted by the International Society of Military Law and the Law of War as being the point at which a person is directly endangered by a mine, thus   implying a prohibition on landmine use altogether.[119]

Thus, both the general customary principle prohibiting means of combat that cannot distinguish between civilian and military objectives, and the specific rules codified in article 51(4) of Additional Protocol I require a proscription on landmine use.  A ban would also be consistent with the ICRC's recommendation that under international humanitarian law

> belligerents should refrain from using weapons...which on account of their imprecision or their effects harm civilian populations and combatants without distinction...[and] whose consequences escape from the control of those employing them, in space or time.[120]

It is the inherent nature of mine warfare that makes it simply impossible to regulate the use of landmines in a manner consistent with customary law.  Landmines cause particularly gruesome injuries and ongoing devastation to civilians, and their delayed-action function essentially renders them indiscriminate weapons.  Customary laws

---

[118] 1977 Additional Protocol I, art. 51(4)(c).  See also ICRC Commentary on the 1977 Additional Protocols, p. 621.

[119] See discussion in Part II of this chapter, and ICRC Commentary on the 1977 Additional Protocols, p. 622.

[120] ICRC, *Report on the Reaffirmation and Development of the Laws and Customs Applicable in Armed Conflicts*, submitted to the Twenty-first International Conference of the Red Cross (Istanbul, 1969) quoted in Aubert, Maurice, "The International Committee of the Red Cross and the problem of excessively injurious or indiscriminate weapons," *International Review of the Red Cross* (November–December 1990), pp. 479-480.

prohibiting means of warfare that cause indiscriminate and excessive injury therefore require a complete prohibition on landmine use. Simply tinkering with rules on use cannot bring the Landmines Protocol into conformity with customary law.

### B. Protection of the Environment

Principles regarding the protection of the environment also support a ban on the use of mines. While such rules likely are not yet customary law, the preamble to the Weapons Convention itself takes note of the prohibition against "widespread, long-term and severe damage to the natural environment".[121] The preamble also states that civilians always remain under the principles of humanity and the dictates of public conscience.[122] Given the growing concern throughout the world about the destruction of the natural environment, as well as the codification of measures to safeguard the environment in international treaties, the protection of the environment could be construed as constituting a principle of humanity and a dictate of public conscience.

Landmine use is problematic with respect to the environment under at least two rules codified in Protocol I: article 35(3)'s proscription against means of warfare which "are intended or may be expected to cause widespread, long-term and severe damage to the natural environment," and article 55(1)'s prohibition against means of warfare that "are intended or may be expected to cause damage to the natural environment and thereby to prejudice the health or survival of the population."[123]

---

[121] Weapons Convention, Preamble, para. 4. It is worthwhile to note that the Landmines Protocol contains no language giving direct effect to this provision.

[122] Ibid, para. 5.

[123] Article 54(2) of Protocol I also may be applicable in some cases. It states in pertinent part: "It is prohibited to attack, destroy, remove or render useless objects indispensable to the survival of the civilian population, such as foodstuffs, agricultural areas for the production of foodstuffs, crops, livestock, drinking water installations and supplies and irrigation works, for the specific purpose of denying them for their sustenance value to the civilian population...." Thus, destroying fields of crops to prevent the enemy using it for cover is permissible,

Article 35(3) of Protocol I was drafted with three purposes: to protect the natural environment from means of warfare deliberately directed against it; to protect the environment from collateral, but long-lasting damage from war; and to safeguard the civilian population from the effects of a ravaged environment.[124] The scope of the prohibition still requires refinement[125], but it is clear that the provision applies to the use of landmines. The ICRC Commentary on article 35(3) makes this explicit. The commentators explain that

> Landmines and booby-traps have in some cases been scattered in astronomical quantities in certain theatres of war. Once the war is over, these devices can only be eliminated with considerable risk by patient efforts which must continue for many years. Meanwhile, they form a serious and constant threat to the population....[I]n reality all delayed-action devices or those which have not exploded, for whatever reason, have a similar effect on the environment, with ominous consequences.[126]

---

but destroying them to prevent the enemy from consuming the crops is forbidden." ICRC Commentary on the 1977 Additional Protocols, p. 655. The ICRC summarizes the gist of Article 54(2): "....the meaning is clear: the objects indicated must be respected in order to guarantee the survival of the population, unless....military necessity requires that they be attacked, destroyed, removed or rendered useless." Ibid., p. 656.

[124] See generally ibid., pp. 410-420.

[125] For example, there has been much debate about the meaning of "long-term" damage. It is now generally agreed that within the terms of Protocol I, the words "long-term" should be interpreted as a matter of decades. Ibid., p. 416. The meaning of the terms "widespread" and "severe" are less clear, but imply a degree of damage that is quite serious and not easily remedied. See generally ibid., pp. 410-420.

[126] Ibid., p. 411. See also U.N. General Assembly Resolution 3571, "Problem of Remnants of War," adopted December 5, 1980. The Resolution acknowledges that "the presence of material remnants of war, particularly mines, on the territories of certain developing countries seriously impedes their development efforts and entails loss of life and property."

Thus, there is consensus at least that landmine use may be expected to cause environmental damage that is severe, long-lasting, and widespread.  Accordingly, under article 35(3) of Protocol I, the complete prohibition on use of landmines is justified.

Article 55(1)'s prohibition against means of warfare that may be expected to damage the environment, thereby prejudicing the health or survival of the population, also supports a prohibition on mine warfare. In regions where subsistence is based on agriculture or pastoralism, the presence of the mines can prevent inhabitants from working the land, depriving them of their livelihoods, and seriously threatening their health and the ongoing survival of the population as a whole.

### C.  Legal Precedents For Banning Categories of Weapons

A complete ban on the use of landmines as a weapon would not be unprecedented in international law.  International agreements have banned other categories of weapons and means of warfare considered to pose intolerable human harm.  A ban on landmines would be part of an established legal tradition.

### 1. The St. Petersburg Declaration[127]

The St. Petersburg Declaration of 1868 is the first major modern international agreement prohibiting the use of specific weapons in war. Drafted by an international military commission convened in response to the invention of a bullet designed to explode on contact with a soft surface and shatter, the Declaration bans the use in war of projectiles weighing less than 400 grams which are either explosive or inflammable.  It does so on humanitarian grounds, noting that there are "technical limits at which the necessities of war ought to yield to the requirements of humanity," and that the employment of arms which uselessly aggravate human suffering is contrary to the "laws of humanity." Recognizing the effect that the development of modern technology could have on armaments, the drafters specifically acknowledge the possibility

---

[127] The Declaration Renouncing the Use, in Time of War, of Explosive Projectiles under 400 Grammes Weight, December 11, 1868, reprinted in ICRC, *International Law Concerning the Conduct of Hostilities*, (Geneva 1989), p. 165.

of drawing up new agreements "in order to maintain the principles which they have established."

The St. Petersburg Declaration is viewed as expressing, with respect to a specific weapon, the customary principle prohibiting means of warfare causing unnecessary suffering, and requiring conciliation of the necessities of war with the laws of humanity. It led to the adoption of other international agreements forbidding particular means of warfare on such grounds.

## 2. The Hague Agreements

Premised on the customary principle codified in the St. Petersburg Declaration, several declarations renouncing the use of specific weapons were concluded at the First Hague Peace Conference of 1899 and the Second Hague Peace Conference of 1907. The rule is also incorporated in article 23 of the Regulations annexed to 1899 Hague Convention II and 1907 Hague Convention IV.

The Second Hague Declaration prohibits the use of projectiles whose only object is to diffuse asphyxiating gases.[128] It derives from the customary rule against using weapons that cause unnecessary suffering, and specifically from custom prohibiting the use of poison. It laid the foundation for subsequent, more comprehensive treaties prohibiting gas warfare.

The Third Hague Declaration outlaws the use of expanding bullets, best known as "dum-dum" bullets.[129]  Despite several objections that such bullets did not expand in a way that created wounds of exceptional cruelty, the treaty was adopted, again on the basis of the rule prohibiting unnecessary suffering.

---

[128] The Declaration concerning asphyxiating gases, The Hague, July 29, 1899, reprinted in A. Roberts and R. Guelff, eds., *Documents on the Laws of War*, (New York: Oxford U. Press, 1982), pp. 36-37.

[129] The Declaration concerning expanding bullets, the Hague, July 29, 1899 reprinted in ICRC, *International Law Concerning the Conduct of Hostilities*, p. 167.

Article 23 of the Hague Regulations[130] forbids the use of poison and poison arms, the treacherous killing or wounding of enemy civilians and combatants, and the use of arms, projectiles, or material of a nature to cause superfluous injury.[131]

### 3. The 1925 Geneva Protocol for the Prohibition of the Use in War of Asphyxiating, Poisonous or other Gases, and of Bacteriological Methods of Warfare[132]

Like earlier agreements prohibiting specific means of war, the 1925 Geneva Protocol banning the use of asphyxiating gases and bacteriological means of warfare derived from general principles of customary law prohibiting poison and materials that cause unnecessary suffering. Although not explicitly stated in the text, the 1925 Geneva Protocol, in banning chemical and biological warfare, goes a step further than previous agreements prohibiting certain weapons, by proscribing means of warfare that not only cause unnecessary suffering but which are inherently indiscriminate; chemical and biological weapons are incapable of distinguishing military targets from civilians. The fact that it has been the subject of relatively few breaches (mainly by states not party to the 1925 Geneva Protocol) may be attributed, in part, to the fact that it constitutes a flat ban on use.[133]

---

[130] Regulations respecting the laws and customs of war on land annexed to the Convention respecting the laws and customs of war on land, the Hague, October 18, 1907, reprinted in ibid.

[131] The First Hague Declaration, which forbids the discharge of projectiles and explosives from balloons, obviously failed in achieving its underlying objectives. However, the failure of the First Declaration , particularly in light of the relative success of other treaties banning specific categories of weapons or means of combat, should not be seen as mitigating against new efforts to ban particular weapons because of their human costs.

[132] The 1925 Geneva Protocol for the Prohibition of the Use in War of Asphyxiating, Poisonous or other Gases, of Bacteriological Methods of Warfare, June 17, 1925, reprinted in *International Law Concerning the Conduct of Hostilities*, p. 174.

[133] See, e.g., Summary Records, p. 10.

## 4. The 1972 Biological Weapons Convention[134]

The 1972 Biological Weapons Convention is the first international agreement banning not just the use, but the production, stockpiling, and transfer of a whole category of weapons.[135] It was negotiated as a disarmament treaty in an effort to mitigate "the horrors of war," and because of the conviction that the use of biological and toxin weapons "would be repugnant to the conscience of mankind and that no effort should be spared to minimize this risk."[136] The 1972 Biological Weapons Convention forbids the parties "in any circumstances to develop, produce, stockpile or otherwise acquire or retain" biological agents that have no justification for peaceful purposes, and weapons, equipment or means of delivery designed to use such agents or toxins for hostile purposes or in armed conflict.[137] In addition, each party to the Convention must undertake to destroy or divert to peaceful purposes all agents, toxins, weapons, equipment and means of delivery specified above.[138] The parties to the Convention also are bound not to transfer "to any recipient whatsoever, directly or indirectly, and not in any way to assist, encourage, or induce any State" or other entity, "to manufacture or acquire" any of the proscribed items.[139] While the 1972 Biological Weapons Convention has been criticized for failing to

---

[134] Convention on the Prohibition of the Development, Production and Stockpiling of Bacteriological (Biological) and Toxin Weapons and on their Destruction, April 10, 1972 (entered into force on March 26, 1975) reprinted in E. Geissler, ed., *Biological and Toxin Weapons Today*, (New York: Oxford U. Press, 1986), p. 135.

[135] Its development was predicated on the fear that the 1925 Protocol might not be adequate to deal with chemical and microbiological methods of warfare that had since emerged. Ibid., p. 138.

[136] Ibid., Preamble.

[137] Ibid., art. 1.

[138] Ibid., art. 2.

[139] Ibid., art. 4.

include a regular verification mechanism, it does provide for parties to lodge allegations of breaches by other parties with the U.N. Security Council, which may investigate the charges.[140] It also obligates parties to consult and cooperate to resolve problems relating to implementation or application.[141]

### 5. Application to Landmines

Signatories to the St. Petersburg Declaration recognized more than one hundred years ago the need to adapt the laws of war to the circumstances engendered by the invention of increasingly sophisticated weapons. Since then, the principle that military utility must give way to humanitarian considerations when warfare causes unnecessary suffering, has served as the basis for treaties banning particular types of weapons. In addition, as discussed earlier, the principles forbidding indiscriminate warfare have led to codification of rules banning means and methods of combat that cause indiscriminate effects. Furthermore, within the framework of disarmament law, the production and transfer of biological and toxin weapons was banned, in an effort to reduce the grave risks they present.

The proposal to ban land mines is thus not a break with humanitarian or disarmament law; instead, it should be viewed in the tradition of developing new treaties prohibiting specific weapons and means of war because of their uselessly harsh effects. Landmine use is so common that perhaps, for those unfamiliar with its effects, it may not initially evoke the horrific visions of chemical or biological warfare. However, the largely indiscriminate effects of landmine use, the grotesque injuries mines cause, and their terrible potential for long-term and widespread devastation, urge that landmines be banned just as those agents have been banned. The legal step to ban production, stockpiling, transfer, and use is a step forward, but it is not so large as it might first seem, since it is wholly within the tradition of existing principles of humanitarian and disarmament law.

---

[140] Ibid., art. 6.

[141] Ibid., art. 5.

## IV.    Conclusion

This chapter has analyzed at length the history and text of the Landmines Protocol, shown how it fails both on its face and in practice, and explained why international law already supports a ban on landmines. The drafters of the Landmines Protocol intended to apply customary principles to the use of landmines; indeed, their mandate was to develop specific rules for mine use grounded in the customary rules embodied in 1977 Additional Protocol I. This mandate was not fulfilled, primarily for two reasons.

First, the drafters gave undue weight to military concerns and short- shrift to the devastating medical, social, economic, and environmental consequences of landmine use. The Landmines Protocol therefore does not give proper effect to the customary principle now codified in articles 35(1) and (2) of Additional Protocol I, forbidding the use of weapons which cause unnecessary suffering or superfluous injury. Second, the drafters ignored the fundamental temporal problem of landmine use; because mines operate on time delay, the likelihood of indiscriminate effects is virtually ensured. Consequently, the Landmines Protocol fails to apply correctly customary laws, now set forth in article 51(4) and (5) of Additional Protocol I, which prohibit indiscriminate attacks.

The result is an utterly ineffective document which fails to comport with customary law, and which does not and, indeed, on its own terms, cannot, significantly diminish abuses against civilians.

The Arms Project and Physicians for Human Rights believe that the proper application of customary law, particularly as codified in articles 51(4) and (5) and 35(1) and (2) of Additional Protocol I, already requires a ban on the use of landmines. Furthermore, the basis in disarmament law for a ban on indiscriminate weapons that produce unconscionable harm provides a strong foundation for prohibiting the production, stockpiling, and transfer of landmines. The Landmines Protocol should be amended to bring it into conformity with the rest of customary law.

In addition to the legal reasons for a ban on landmines, there are very pragmatic ones as well. It is evident from the record of landmine use throughout the world during the last decade that the rules in the Landmines Protocol have not been respected. As the drafters of the Landmines Protocol themselves realized, and as the Arms Project and

Physicians for Human Rights believe, a total ban is much easier to enforce—for practical and political reasons—than a set of complex and unworkable regulations.

# 9
# INITIATIVES TO CONTROL LANDMINES

Other than routine licensing requirements, few countries have domestic laws restricting the use, production, stockpiling, transfer, or export of landmines. However, mounting evidence of the devastation caused by widespread use of mines in conflicts throughout the world has prompted several countries to consider unilateral measures to prohibit their transfer and sale, and to limit their use. A number of governments also have expressed interest in revising the international Landmines Protocol to make its regulation of landmine use much stronger, and in eventually banning mines altogether.[1] Humanitarian agencies are actively engaged in educating governments about the effects of landmines in an effort to persuade them to adopt strong domestic landmine restrictions, and to promote an international ban on production, stockpiling, transfer and sale of mines. This chapter briefly reviews current initiatives to control landmines at national and international levels.

## I.    United States

The United States has enacted the leading domestic legislation, the Landmine Moratorium Act, which imposes a one year ban on the sale, export, and transfer abroad of landmines.[2] It specifically forbids the sale or financing of a sale, as well as the transfer of landmines, and prohibits

---

[1] Chapter 8 contains a detailed analysis of the limited regulations on mine use contained in the Landmines Protocol.

[2] National Defense Authorization Act for Fiscal Year 1993, Pub. L. No. 102-484, sec. 1365 (the Landmine Moratorium Act or Leahy-Evans Amendment), reproduced as Appendix 7. The implementing regulations appear at *Federal Register*, Vol. 57, p. 228, Nov. 25, 1992, reproduced at Appendix 7.

The legislation was introduced in the U.S. Senate by Senator Patrick Leahy (D-VT) in July 1992. Parallel legislation was introduced in the House of Representatives by Congressman Lane Evans (D-IL). It was passed as an amendment to the defense authorization bill for fiscal year 1993. A second amendment, introduced by Senator Edward Kennedy, requiring a study of international mine clearance efforts in situations involving the repatriation and resettlement of refugees and displaced persons also was included in the defense authorization bill. Ibid., sec. 1364, also reproduced as Appendix 7.

their licensing for export. Signed into law on October 23, 1992, the Landmine Moratorium Act, also known as the Leahy-Evans Amendment, is the first such legislation in the world, as far as the Arms Project and Physicians for Human Rights are aware.

The Landmine Moratorium Act is based on Congressional findings that landmines "have been used indiscriminately in dramatically increasing numbers" and that "noncombatant civilians, including tens of thousands of children have been the primary victims."[3]  In addition to imposing a year-long ban on the sale, export, and transfer abroad of landmines, the amendment calls on the President to submit to the Senate for advice and consent to ratification the Weapons Convention, which through its annexed Landmines Protocol, includes restrictions on landmine use.[4]

The legislation also states the policy of the United States to seek verifiable international agreements prohibiting the sale, transfer, or export of landmines, and further limiting their use, production, possession, and deployment.

Senator Patrick Leahy, who authored the legislation, recently wrote in an article published in *Arms Control Today* that he hopes the Landmine Moratorium Act will influence other governments to adopt similar laws and support an international agreement banning landmines.[5]  However, until a complete international ban is achieved, Senator Leahy envisions several possible interim steps.  He suggests that the Clinton Administration work to obtain agreements from supplier countries to transfer landmines only to countries that have ratified the Landmines Protocol, or to reach a bilateral understanding with potential suppliers to abide by its terms.[6]

---

[3] Pub. L. No. 102-484, sec. 1365 (a)(1).

[4] The Weapons Convention, and particularly the Landmines Protocol, are discussed at length in Chapter 8.

[5] Senator Patrick Leahy, "Landmine Moratorium: A Strategy for Stronger International Limits," *Arms Control Today*, Jan.-Feb. 1993, p. 11, reproduced as Appendix 4.

[6] Ibid., p. 13.

In addition, he calls for an international conference to review the Landmines Protocol, with an eye toward strengthening its regulations. Leahy proposes several immediate modifications of the Landmines Protocol.[7] First, he emphasizes the importance of procedures to monitor compliance, such as establishing an international registry under U.N. auspices of national stockpiles of numbers and types of mines, a list of facilities where mines are manufactured, and notification of sales or transfers.[8] He also suggests a compliance mechanism similar to that contained in 1977 Additional Protocol I to the Geneva Conventions of 1949 which authorizes complaints to be made to a fact-finding body empowered to conduct investigations.[9] Second, Leahy endorses the ICRC's recommendation that the Landmines Protocol be extended to apply to internal as well as international conflicts. Finally, he supports limiting the kinds of mines that may be produced and used, and the manner in which they are deployed.[10]

In July 1993, Senator Leahy and Representative Evans introduced legislation that extends the export moratorium for three years.[11] In introducing the Landmine Moratorium Extension Act of 1993, Senator Leahy stated:

> The landmine moratorium has two purposes. It shows that the United States intends to be a leader in stopping the spread of these insidious weapons. It will also

---

[7] Ibid.

[8] Ibid.

[9] Ibid., p. 14.

[10] Ibid.

[11] The Landmine Moratorium Extension Act of 1993 was introduced on July 22, 1993 in the Senate as S. 1276 and in the House as H.R. 2706. S. 1276 is reproduced as Appendix 8.

strengthen the position of the United States to negotiate stronger limits on the sale, manufacture, and use of landmines by setting an example for other nations.[12]

On September 14, 1993, the Senate passed by a vote of 100-0 a modified version of the bill as an amendment to the Fiscal Year 1994 Defense Authorization bill (S. 1298).[13] Another amendment, sponsored by Senator Leahy and Senator Edward Kennedy and passed by voice vote, authorizes the expenditure of $10 million for humanitarian (as opposed to military) mine clearing. According to Senator Leahy, "The purpose of this amendment is specifically to get U.S. military personnel involved in training, technical assistance, and provision of equipment, and other activities in support of landmine clearing in a humanitarian context."[14] It is expected that the House of Representatives will also agree to the amendments and that the President will sign them into law before the end of the year.

There have been encouraging signs that the Clinton Administration is quite concerned about the global landmine crisis, and is preparing to take meaningful steps to help alleviate the situation. When Secretary of State Warren Christopher appeared before the Senate Appropriations Committee in March 1993, he told Senator Leahy:

> I agree with your views on the need to take action on landmines. In February the State Department established an interagency Demining Coordination

---

[12] *Congressional Record*, July 22, 1993, p. S9291, reproduced as Appendix 8.

[13] The original bill, which had 59 co-sponsors in the Senate, stated that it shall be the policy of the United States to seek verifiable international agreements not only prohibiting sales and further limiting manufacture, possession, and use, but also "eventually, terminating the manufacture, possession and use of anti-personnel landmines." S. 1276, section 3(a). The amendment dropped the latter phrase, at the urging of the Chairman of the Armed Services Committee, Senator Sam Nunn. See *Congressional Record*, September 10, 1993, pp. S11376-77, S11391-95, and S11452-3 for the amendment text and debate, and the *Congressional Record*, September 14, 1993, p. S11616 for the vote.

[14] *Congressional Record*, September 10, 1993, p. S11395.

Group that is working with the Department of Defense to develop a comprehensive U.S. strategy to address the problem of global demining. However, we recognize that if we are to make an impact on the enormous worldwide problem with uncleared mines, we must couple our efforts to remove and destroy existing landmines with appropriate prohibitions or restrictions on their future sale and use.... We support measures to control landmines and will support efforts to impose such prohibitions and restrictions.[15]

In July 1993, the State Department issued a major report on international demining, which begins with the premise, "Uncleared landmines pose a significant challenge to the achievement of key U.S. foreign policy objectives."[16] The report concludes that "it appears that the U.S. Government can make its greatest contribution towards solving the global problem with uncleared landmines by providing assistance in four general areas: Education, Technical Expertise, Equipment and Technology, and diplomatic efforts to restrict the sale and use of landmines."[17]

## II.    France

A petition with more than 22,000 signatures was submitted by representatives of Handicap International to French President Francois Mitterand on February 10, 1993 in Phnom Penh, Cambodia, asking the French government to declare a moratorium on the sale, export and transfer of landmines. The next day, President Mitterand stated that France already voluntarily abstains from exporting antipersonnel landmines, and called upon other states to proclaim a moratorium on

---

[15] Transcript from hearing before Senate Appropriations Subcommittee on Foreign Operations, March 30, 1993.

[16] U.S. Department of State, *Hidden Killers: The Global Problem with Uncleared Landmines*, July 1993, p. i. Parts of this 185-page report are reproduced as Appendix 5.

[17] DOS, *Hidden Killers*, p. 180.

such exports. In July 1993, French Foreign Minister Alain Juppe informed Handicap International in writing that France "confirmed, last February, the moratorium on exports of anti-personnel landmines that it in fact has respected since 1985, and has called upon the international community to follow in this path."[18]

In a very important development, the French government has asked the Secretary-General of the U.N. to convene an international conference to review the Weapons Convention and its annexed Landmines Protocol. It is expected that the review conference will take place in late 1994 or early 1995.

### III.    United Kingdom

In the United Kingdom, an early day motion entitled "Moratorium on the Export of Landmines," based on the Leahy-Evans amendment, was introduced in Parliament on March 11, 1993. Noting that landmines are indiscriminate weapons, and congratulating Senator Leahy and Congressman Evans on their initiative, the motion calls for an immediate and indefinite moratorium on the export of landmines from the United Kingdom. It also asks for British ratification of the Weapons Convention, and requests the government to seek to negotiate an international agreement or modification of the Weapons Convention to prohibit the sale, transfer or export of landmines. In addition, the motion demands that resources be made available for mine clearance.

### IV.    Belgium

The Belgian government reportedly has announced that it has stopped all production of antipersonnel landmines, and will not permit the transit of such mines within its territory. Belgium is also moving to ratify the Landmines Protocol.[19]

---

[18] Letter dated July 26, 1993 from Foreign Minister Alain Juppe to Philippe Chabasse, Director of Handicap International.

[19] The Belgian actions were cited by Senator Leahy in the *Congressional Record*, Sept. 10, 1993, p. S11392.

## V.     Australia

A petition entitled "Landmines in Cambodia" was recently presented to the Australian House of Representatives early in 1992.[20] Submitted on behalf of 1,400 Australian citizens, the petition requests the Australian House to call for a U.N. review of the Weapons Convention, and ask U.N. member states for a total ban on the manufacture and use of landmines. It also urges the Australian government to ensure that priority be given to mine clearance in aid packages to Cambodia.

## VI.    Europe

The European Parliament passed a resolution, introduced on December 14, 1992, which demands that all member states "as an emergency measure" declare a five year moratorium on the export of mines and on the training to place them. The resolution also calls on member states to ratify the Weapons Convention and make it applicable to internal conflicts. It further asks member states that are also members of the Security Council to treat mine clearance as a matter of great urgency.[21]

On October 8, 1993, the 12 European Community member states, plus Austria, Finland, Norway, and Sweden, introduced a draft resolution in the United Nations General Assembly deploring the adverse consequences of landmines and urging the United Nations, other international bodies, and individual states to do more to resolve the problem of landmines as a "matter of urgency." The resolution asks the Secretary-General to submit a comprehensive report on the problems caused by the increasing presence of mines, and on further measures the United Nations can take to help with mine clearance. It specifically asks the Secretary-General to consider the establishment of a voluntary trust fund to finance mine clearance and training programs.[22]

---

[20] "Landmines in Cambodia", Feb. 27, 1992, *Weekly House Hansard*, p. 301.

[21] The resolution is reproduced as Appendix 13.

[22] Draft Resolution before the General Assembly, 48th Session, Agenda Item 155, re "Assistance in Mine Clearance," A/48/L.5, October 8, 1993, reproduced as Appendix 11.

# M18A1

The American-made M18A1 "Claymore" is a directional, fixed fragmentation mine that is usually used for defense or ambush purposes. The mine is normally fired from a distance by an M57 firing device, but can also be activated by a pull wire or a tripwire. When detonated, a fan-shaped sheaf pattern of 700 steel balls is projected in a 60 degree arc covering a casualty area of 50 meters. The M18A1 is produced in the Thiokol/U.S. Army facility in Louisiana and elsewhere in the U.S. Several countries, such as Chile and South Korea, also produce the mine. Similar mines are produced by the former Soviet Union, South Africa, Pakistan, and other countries. (Drawing by Pamela Blotner for the Arms Project/PHR.)

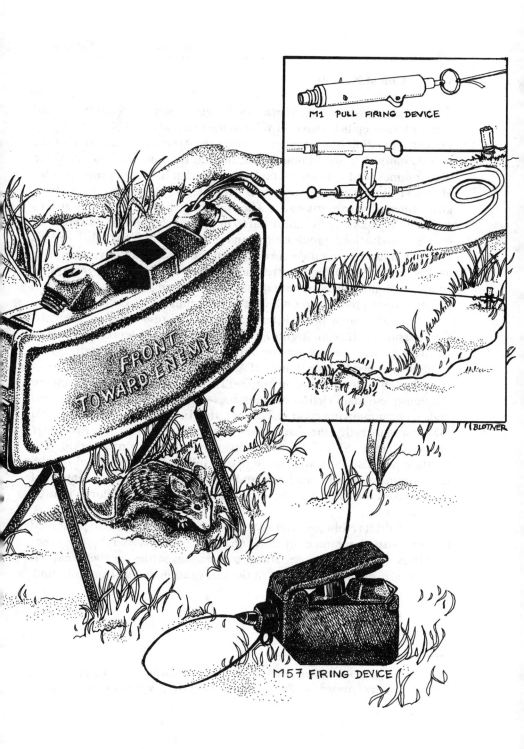

FRONT TOWARD ENEMY

M1 PULL FIRING DEVICE

M57 FIRING DEVICE

BLOTNER

## VII.    United Nations

In addition to these initiatives, various countries and humanitarian agencies have introduced measures at the U.N. encouraging further regulation of landmines. During the March 1993 meeting of the U.N. Commission on Human Rights, the International Federation Terre des Hommes read a statement on landmines that had been prepared with Handicap International, and was signed by seventeen other non-governmental organizations.[23] The statement urged member states to ratify the Weapons Convention and to implement a five year moratorium on the production, proliferation and use of mines.  It also invited member states to undertake a revision of the Weapons Convention with a view toward applying its provisions to internal conflicts, instituting compliance and sanction mechanisms, and studying the possibility of an eventual total prohibition on antipersonnel mines.

At the same time, France submitted a resolution to the U.N. Commission on Human Rights focusing on the consequences of war, and particularly the use of antipersonnel landmines, on children.  This resolution, called "Consequences of Armed Conflicts on Children's Lives," was adopted without a vote on March 11, 1993.  It notes that children are frequently the main victims of landmines—often long after conflicts have ended, encourages international cooperation in mine removal efforts, and asks states to ratify the Landmines Protocol as well as the two other Protocols annexed to the Weapons Convention.  In addition, the resolution calls on states to support fully the prevention of the indiscriminate use of landmines, and, as required by the Convention of the Rights of the Child, to take all possible steps to assist children injured by mines.

A draft resolution on the Weapons Convention was also presented to the First Committee by Sweden, and co-sponsored by 18 other countries.  The draft urges states to become parties to the Weapons Convention, encourages review of the Convention and its Protocols, and

---

[23]    See also Resolution 1993/83 of the Commission on Human Rights, "Consequences of Armed Conflicts on Children's Lives," reproduced as Appendix 14.

asks the Secretary-General to inform periodically the General Assembly regarding adherence. The resolution was adopted without vote by the Committee on November 12, 1992 for recommendation to the General Assembly.

In August 1993, UNICEF Geneva informed the Vietnam Veterans of America Foundation that "UNICEF Geneva after consultation with our colleagues in New York Headquarters has decided to give priority attention to the issue of landmines and its negative impact on [the] world's children. We plan to inform the European public opinion and to advocate for the ban of landmines."[24]

## VIII.    United Nations Conference to Review the Landmines Protocol

The French government recently requested the Secretary-General of the U.N. to convene an international conference to review the Weapons Convention and its annexed Landmines Protocol. As a result, a review conference is to be scheduled in 1994 or 1995.

Pursuant to Article 8 of the Weapons Convention, such a conference permits the contracting parties to review the scope and operation of the Weapons Convention and any of its Protocols, and make changes. The Arms Project and Physicians for Human Rights support convening a conference on the Landmines Protocol.

However, the conference must have a broad-based agenda and not be limited to minor revisions. To be meaningful, it must include an in-depth consideration of the serious long-term medical, social, economic, and environmental effects of mine warfare. It must also take into account that the delayed-action quality of landmines implicitly means that they produce indiscriminate effects—which constitutes a violation of customary international law, particularly as expressed in 1977 Additional Protocol I.[25] A comprehensive review conference would allow a full analysis of the facts and the relevant law, and in the opinion of the Arms Project and Physicians for Human Rights, would lead to widespread support for a complete ban on landmines.

---

[24] Letter dated August 16, 1993 from Bilge Ogun-Bassani, Deputy Director of the Geneva Office of UNICEF to Stuart Maslen of the Vietnam Veterans of America Foundation.

[25] Chapter 8 includes a detailed analysis of these points.

## IX.    Non-Governmental Organizations

In addition to the measures described above, non-governmental organizations are undertaking efforts in other countries to educate governments and the public about landmines, and, in many cases, to press governments to consider a ban on landmine use, manufacture and proliferation. Such campaigns are currently underway in a number of countries—notably in Germany, Sweden, New Zealand, Denmark, the Netherlands, Switzerland, Slovakia and Spain.

An ad hoc group coordinating the activities of non-governmental organizations on landmines consists of the Vietnam Veterans of America Foundation (U.S.), Handicap International (France), Human Rights Watch (U.S.), Medico International (Germany), Mines Advisory Group (U.K.), and Physicians for Human Rights (U.S.).

Other non-governmental organizations involved include Adelaide Diocesan Justice and Peace Commission (Australia), Amok (Netherlands), Arms Transfers Working Group (U.S.), British Refugee Council, Buko (Germany), Cambodia Trust (U.K.), Campaign Against the Arms Trade (U.K.), CARDRI (U.K.), Community Aid Abroad (Australia), the European Network Against the Arms Trade, Greenpeace International, Gulf Information Project (U.K.), the Human Rights Council of Australia, Inc., International Federation Terre des Hommes, International Peace Bureau (Switzerland), International Physicians for the Prevention of Nuclear War (Australia, Canada, Germany, U.S., and U.K. branches), Jaipur Limb Campaign (U.K.), Lawyers for Social Responsibility (Canada), Mercy Refugee Service (Australia), Monitese (Italy), National Peace Council (U.K.), Oxfam America, Oxfam U.K., Pax Christi Netherlands, Save the Children U.K., Swedish Peace and Arbitration Society, Swedish Red Cross, United Nations Association of New Zealand, Women's Commission for Refugee Women and Children of the International Rescue Committee (U.S.), and World Vision International (Australia, New Zealand, Switzerland, and U.K. branches).

In addition, in September 1992, the Lutheran World Federation voted to promote international efforts that would lead to the banning of production and use of landmines and other inhumane weapons.[26]

The ICRC has played a crucial role in raising international

---

[26] Minutes of the Meeting of the Lutheran World Federation Council, Madras, India, September 13-23, 1992, "Statement on the Banning of Landmines."

awareness of the global landmines problem and in encouraging the international community to take steps to begin to remedy it. The ICRC-sponsored Symposium on Antipersonnel Landmines held in Montreux, Switzerland, April 21-23, 1993, was an important gathering of landmine experts aimed at sharing information and developing strategies to cope with the landmine problem.

Several national Red Cross chapters are actively involved in the landmines issue. Perhaps most notably, the Swedish Red Cross announced on June 14, 1993 that it has launched a campaign against the international arms trade, starting with Swedish exports of antipersonnel landmines. The American Red Cross has issued a statement "condemning the pervasive horror in our world due to wanton and indiscriminate use of antipersonnel mines," and declaring that the "human suffering caused by the senseless and inhumane use of landmines should not be tolerated by the international community."[27]

The International Federation of Red Cross/Red Crescent Societies commissioned a study to identify options for actions related to the issue of landmines. A consideration of these options has been scheduled for the October 1993 Federation meeting in the United Kingdom.

## X. Conclusion

As discussed in the previous chapter, one of the principal reasons that the drafters of the Landmines Protocol rejected the idea of a total ban on the use of landmines was because of their perception that the major military powers would never support such a measure. Times have changed. The United States now is taking a leadership role in efforts to institute a complete proscription. The governments of France, Great Britain, and other countries are actively considering the possibility. An international ban on landmine production, transfer and use is much more politically feasible now than it was a decade ago. However, until a total ban is established, it is crucial that individual governments adopt unilateral measures to control the flow, use, and effects of landmines.

---

[27] See Appendix 6.

# 10
# THE FUTURE OF LANDMINES

The stark reality is that many more mines are deployed every day than are removed. Unless a worldwide ban on production, stockpiling, transfer, and use is instituted, it can be expected on the whole that the landmines situation will continue to worsen, possibly at a rate exceeding that of the past several decades, and even if some future developments serve to ease the human suffering and socio-economic dislocation caused by landmines.

The dark future of the landmines situation has various causes: renewed hostilities in existing landmine-afflicted nations; the likelihood of increased ethnic and religious conflict around the world; changes in strategies for using landmines; increasing involvement of more nations in landmine production and trade; and technological development in landmines.[1]

As noted by a leading U.S. Army landmines expert, landmines are the "poor man's" weapon of choice, and "are likely to remain the weapon of choice when the 'little guy' is looking to control movements of his own people or the threat of intervention by the U.S."[2] At the same time, increased use of landmines in the future is also likely on account of evolving technologies and strategies for employing landmines.

This chapter examines the issues of military strategies and requirements for landmines, technological developments in landmine design, and potential future measures aimed at controlling the production, trade, and use of landmines. In so doing, this chapter addresses frontally three key questions for policymakers and governments: first, are mines militarily *essential* and not just militarily useful? Second, why is a ban on all landmines necessary, rather than simply a ban on landmines that do not self-destruct or self-neutralize? Third, what from the standpoint of arms control and disarmament, and not just humanitarian law, are the policy options for controlling future landmine proliferation?

---

[1] These factors are discussed in detail in Chapter 1.

[2] Charles Gardner, Office of the Project Manager for Mines, Countermine and Demolitions, U.S. Army, presentation to the American Defense Preparedness Association's Mines, Countermine and Demolitions Symposium, September 7-9, 1993, Asheville, NC, p. 10.

## I. Future Military Requirements

This book has argued at length that landmines ought to be banned, and indeed already *are* banned, under principles of humanitarian law. Yet notwithstanding that landmines ought to be outlawed solely on the basis of their indiscriminate qualities, and without regard for their military utility, it would be fruitless to deny that the political ability to secure a ban on landmines depends, in large part, on perceptions of the military utility of the weapon. Perceptions of the military usefulness of landmines, rather than their militarily incidental, albeit horrific, effects on civilians, are likely to be the main criteria by which many governments will decide to keep or eliminate the weapon. Indeed, for too many governments it is likely to be the military's own determination of the utility of a weapon, without adequate civilian political input, that ultimately decides.[3] For this reason it is necessary to address directly the question of whether, apart from humanitarian or legal considerations, landmines are not just useful but indispensable to certain essential military missions.

This criterion of indispensability, rather than incidental utility, is, however, consistent with the general principle of the laws of war that a means of warfare, such as landmines, must be not only militarily useful (i.e., contribute to the ends of victory) but further that its contribution must outweigh the non-military damage it causes (the principle of proportionality). Although this book has argued that the principle of distinction (viz., that indiscriminate methods of attack are disallowed in war) ought to ban landmines altogether, setting aside that principle solely for purposes of discussing the actual military usefulness of landmines does not mean that landmines should be evaluated solely on the basis of their incidental usefulness. Rather, the level of non-military damage they cause is so great that even as a matter of proportionality, and without regard for the prohibition against indiscriminate attacks, they would have to be *indispensable* to remain legally defensible. Thus, indispensability is the threshold level of military utility against which this chapter judges landmines.

---

[3] The importance of this point is developed by William Arkin in his paper presented to the NGO Conference on Antipersonnel Landmines held in London, May 24, 1993, p. 1.

Framed as a question of indispensability, the military value of landmines to the armed forces of the world is an open question.  Many professional military people maintain that landmines serve many useful functions, as part of the basic purpose of "killing, destroying, or otherwise incapacitating enemy personnel and/or equipment."[4]  Military functions most often cited are route and area denial, protection of bases and installations—particularly protection of antitank mine fields—diversion of enemy forces, ambush, and demoralization of enemy forces.  Formal U.S. tactical doctrine emphasizes their role as a time denial, rather than area denial, weapon, used to slow the advance of armor through antitank minefields by requiring enemy commanders to choose between casualties and loss of materiel, on the one hand, and time-consuming mine breaching methods, on the other.

Conventional militaries also view mines as an inexpensive force multiplier.  For example, Lieutenant Colonel Hamish Rollo of the British Ministry of Defence, speaking at the ICRC conference on landmines in Montreux in April 1993, stated that landmines enhance the effectiveness of a considerable number of land and air weapons systems.  He claimed that the "cost effectiveness" of those systems may be increased "by up to a factor of 3" when deployed with  mines.[5]

However, it is not at all clear that landmines are an *essential* weapon for modern, professional militaries.  In an interview with the Arms Project, for example, Colonel Richard Johnson, then-Project Manager of the U.S. Army's Mines, Countermine and Demolitions division, stated that there was no longer a requirement for traditional, hand-emplaced mines like the Claymore, since U.S. military doctrine now rejects the notion of a static war of attrition.  He further stated that scatterable antipersonnel mines had but one key function: protection of antitank minefields.[6]

The Congressional Research Service supported this assessment in its recent landmines paper: "Anti-personnel landmines are a minor system

---

[4] "U.S. Mine Warfare Policy," as cited in Congressional Research Service, Memorandum to Sen. Patrick Leahy, Jan. 13, 1993, p. 6.

[5]  Lt. Col. N. Hamish Rollo, "The Military Use of Anti-Personnel Mines," Report Presented at the ICRC Symposium, April 1993, p. 2.

[6]  Interview at Picatinny Arsenal, June 15, 1993.

in U.S. doctrine, primarily used to protect the more important anti-tank minefields.... Conventional mines are very labor intensive to emplace, and have serious side effects such as potential fratricide and innocent civilian casualties. For those reasons, the United States now prefers mechanically scatterable mines that self-destruct...."[7]

Yet even with respect to scatterables, the U.S. military to date apparently has not conducted a rigorous evaluation of either their military utility or indispensability, let alone such an evaluation of mines generally. Colonel Johnson indicated that he was unaware of any recent analytical study of the effectiveness of antipersonnel landmines in protecting antitank minefields; he could recall only a U.S. Army study conducted sometime in the early 1970s.[8] Scatterable mines, whether self-destructing or not, pose special humanitarian problems, apart from the problems of landmines generally.

One of the bases on which military officers have questioned the military utility of landmines is the danger they may create to friendly military forces. In private conversations with active duty and retired military personnel, the Arms Project found an ambivalence toward landmines for this reason; while there was a conviction that if your enemy had landmines, you should have them, too, there was also often recognition that the dangers to military personnel may equal or exceed the military benefits. In Vietnam, for example, U.S. forces often found themselves moving through areas they had previously mined. Deborah

---

[7] Congressional Research Service, Memorandum to Senator Patrick J. Leahy, January 13, 1993, p. 6.

[8] Interview at Picatinny Arsenal, June 15, 1993. In response to a follow-up letter from the Arms Project, Col. Johnson wrote that "this information [regarding the effectiveness of A/P mines] was developed many years ago, and difficult to locate. AP mines depend on the psychological factor of fear to inhibit the manual clearance of AT mines." Letter to Stephen Goose, the Arms Project, dated July 12, 1993. The Arms Project has thus far been unable to locate a copy of that study.

# Type 72

This Chinese-made, pressure-operated mine has been extensively used in Cambodia. There are three versions of this mine: Type 72, Type 72B, and Type 72C (sometimes designated as Type 72, 72A, and 72B). All three mines are externally identical with a green plastic casing and minimal metal parts. This makes detection difficult especially in areas where metal fragments are present. The 34-gram explosive charge is small but is sufficient to produce severe injuries. The 72B and 72C are designed to ensure detonation when the device is handled or disturbed in any way, making it extremely unstable. The basic version of the Type 72 operates by pressure alone. Type 72B and 72C use electronic circuitry and operate either as pressure mines or anti-disturbance mines, ensuring detonation when the device is handled or disturbed in any way. Type 72C is similar to 72B with the addition of a self-destruct function in the electronics package. A similar mine is manufactured in South Africa. This is one of the most commonly found mines in the world. (Drawing by Pamela Blotner for the Arms Project/PHR.)

Shapley, in her biography of former Secretary of Defense Robert McNamara, notes that the Pentagon facilitated a study, based on a database of actions in the ground war, which uncovered the alarming fact that, "although the army kept asking for more mines, one fifth to one third of all U.S. deaths were caused by these devices, while they killed relatively few enemy in exchange."[9]

Some believe this lesson remains true today. At a recent symposium, a U.S. Army mine warfare expert gave his opinion of the threat landmines pose to U.S. forces:

> Speaking forthrightly, I would suggest that the Countermine dilemma is perhaps the greatest challenge the Army faces on today's and tomorrow's battlefield. We can make tanks which are better armored and gunned than the other guy's; we can make missiles which bring down other missiles...but what we can't do very well is find mines, quickly neutralize them, and reduce their impact on our maneuver forces and soldiers.... Mines are clearly the inexpensive weapon of choice for less powerful armies, particularly those which have to come up against a formidable and well-trained force such as that of the United States.... Place yourself in the position of the U.S. soldier who is frequently exposed to randomly laid mines, mines with little to no metal content, possibly covered by direct and/or indirect fire, during hours of darkness, etc. I think you can begin to see the difficulty of producing technology which can alert soldiers and units to take evasive or other actions.[10]

---

[9] Deborah Shapley, *Promise and Power: The Life and Times of Robert McNamara*, (Boston: Little Brown & Co., 1993), p. 414. Shapley notes that factual information of this sort was published in *Southeast Asia Report*, a classified journal. The Arms Project is seeking to have this information released publicly.

[10] Charles Gardner, U.S. Army Office of the Project Manager for Mines, Countermine and Demolitions, presentation to the ADPA symposium, September 7-9, 1993, Asheville, NC, pp. 1-2.

At the same symposium, and further echoing the lessons of Vietnam, former Marine Corps Commandant General Alfred Gray, Jr., made even more striking comments, which call into question the effectiveness of mines and emphasizes the dangers they pose to U.S. forces:

> We kill more Americans with our mines than we do anybody else. We never killed many enemy with mines... What the hell is the use of sowing all this [airborne scatterable mines] if you're going to move through it next week or next month?... I know of no situation in the Korean War, nor in the five years I served in Southeast Asia, nor in Panama, nor in Desert Shield-Desert Storm where our use of mine warfare truly channelized the enemy and brought them into a destructive pattern.... In the broader sense, I'm not aware of any operational advantage from broad deployment of mines.... I'm not downgrading the need for the best [technology] in mine warfare, all I'm saying is we have many examples of our young warriors trapped by their own minefields or by the [old] French minefields [in Southeast Asia]—we had examples even in Desert Storm.[11]

In the case of the United States, it may be that a global ban on mines, in which neither the U.S. nor its potential adversaries employ mines, would prove to be a net benefit for U.S. forces. It does seem clear that landmines today are probably of greater use to U.S. adversaries than they are to U.S. forces, as the deaths of U.S. servicemen in Somalia by landmines suggests. The emphasis in current U.S. military doctrine on maneuver warfare has lessened the importance of mine warfare to U.S. forces, as has the shift in emphasis from fighting a major conventional war in Europe to fighting lesser conflicts principally in the developing world.

It appears that to date, neither the U.S. military nor any other country's armed forces has explored whether other systems and technologies are now available, or could be developed, to fulfill the military missions of landmines but which pose less danger to civilians and

---

[11] Speech to the ADPA Symposium, September 9, 1993.

cause less long-term damage. Thus the question of whether landmines are an indispensable, rather than merely useful, weapon remains unanswered. Indeed, there are at least some grounds for doubt even in the minds of some military officers themselves.

Even if there are voices that question the traditional wisdom of mine use, the predominant trend of military thought tends to favor, if anything, expanding rather than contracting missions for landmines in the future. British Lieutenant Colonel Rollo's presentation at the ICRC Montreux symposium is particularly illuminating. According to Lieutenant Colonel Rollo, "Historically, [mine] use has mainly been considered in the context of defensive operations, however the increasing availability of low cost technologies could result in wider use... New delivery systems have significantly reduced laying times and can provide a far more flexible response to the realities of the battlefield."[12] Referring to the defensive role and the delaying-nuisance role of mines, Lieutenant Colonel Rollo stated that "the opportunity to extend both roles is presented as new weapons and concepts of operations evolve." He listed such potential future uses: guarding so-called "autonomous" weapons (such as antitank mines); using landmines to compensate for a decreasing number of troops available to protect vital points and areas; attacking rear area targets (for example, logistics dumps, routes, fording sites, and engineer construction sites) with new rocket and air delivery systems; and denying landing areas and exit routes to helicopters.[13]

Finally, Lieutenant Colonel Rollo detailed the characteristics armies will seek in future landmine designs: greater flexibility of use; greater speed in laying; reduction in logistics, manpower, and training needed for deploying systems; ability to lay mines over larger areas and wider frontages than before; and adaptability for remote laying by aircraft, rocket, or artillery shell.[14]

Much of this wish list of future "requirements" is, of course, a prescription for future humanitarian disasters. New, aggressive roles for

---

[12] Rollo, p. 2.

[13] Ibid, pp. 7-8.

[14] Ibid, p. 12.

landmines—striking deeper and covering more territory more quickly through remote delivery—become available through advanced technology, and they do not bode well for the future.

## II.    Future Technological Developments

New technologies tend to make landmines more attractive to militaries, and they also tend to make mines more attractive to manufacturers, because of the potential for higher profits from more expensive, value-added systems. But new technologies are not likely to reduce significantly the landmine threat to civilians in the developing world, despite the claims of some enthusiasts. Technological developments will not make the world safe for landmines.

New, so-called smart mines are not being developed in order to make them more humane. For all their sophisticated electronic components, microchips, software, and advanced sensors, smart mines will not differentiate between a civilian and a soldier. Moreover, some maintain that the greater the degree of electronic sophistication, the greater the likelihood of malfunction. In any case, smart mines will be susceptible to jamming, electronic countermeasures and sensor spoofing.

Several technological trends are likely to compound the destruction and human suffering wrought by landmines. The recent DIA report notes that the "massive infusion of technology in the 1970s and 1980s has drastically altered landmine holdings the world over," most notably with the proliferation of remotely deliverable scatterable mines, and hard-to-detect plastic mines.[15] The trends toward scatterable mines and plastic mines are most disconcerting from a humanitarian perspective. Another disturbing development is the proliferation of submunitions which function as landmines.

### A. Detectability

The world's stockpile of mines increasingly consists of mines constructed almost entirely of plastic. At least 18 countries, including all of the world's major producers and exporters of mines, manufacture "minimum-metal" mines, which contain only a very small amount of

---

[15] DIA/FSTC, p. xvii.

metal (often the firing pin or a spring or seal).[16]    United Nations demining expert Brigadier (Ret.) Patrick Blagden has stated, "Materials technology has now reached the stage where the use of metal is unnecessary except as a cost-savings measure.  The next generation of antipersonnel mines may be completely undetectable by the present generation of electronic mine detectors."[17]    Indeed, truly all-plastic mines are apparently being produced by a number of nations, including Italy, China, and Yugoslavia.[18]

Even minimum-metal mines often can be detected only by the best equipment under very favorable conditions.   While obviously anathema to mine clearers, these mines offer some advantages to producers and armies; they are lighter weight and more durable.  Some users may believe nondetectability to be a desirable feature, since it might conceivably inflict greater damage on the enemy, and slow the enemy down to a greater degree.  However, the Arms Project and Physicians for Human Rights have never encountered a professional military person who believed that there is a military requirement for a nondetectable mine.

Thus, while the Arms Project and Physicians for Human Rights believe that all landmine production should be terminated, they favor a requirement that all mines produced in the interim should be detectable. This could be achieved by adding a metal ring to plastic mines, or by a number of other ways.  Existing mines should also be retrofitted in some fashion to make them detectable, perhaps by simply applying strips of metal tape. National governments and international organizations should

---

[16] DIA/FSTC, p. 3-19 and the Arms Project data base.  The countries include Argentina, Belgium, Brazil, China, Egypt, Germany, Greece, Hungary, India, Italy, the Netherlands, Pakistan, Portugal, South Africa, Spain, the United States, the former U.S.S.R., and the former Yugoslavia.

[17] Paper presented at the ICRC Symposium, p. 6.

[18] China and Italy were cited in an interview with representatives of the U.S. Army Countermine Systems Directorate, April 23, 1993; Yugoslavia was cited by John Taffe, of Explosive Ordnance Disposal World Services, who encountered all-plastic Yugoslav mines in Kuwait. Taffe maintains that there are now more than two dozen different types of all-plastic mines. Interview with Stephen Goose, the Arms Project, September 30, 1993.

devote much greater resources to developing detection equipment to reliably locate minimum-metal mines.

The limited significance of such an interim measure is underscored by the fact that many demining experts believe that making all mines detectable, without other restrictions on use, would not greatly help mine clearance, since probing, not metal detection, is the main method used to find mines.[19] Metal detection is useful to mine clearers principally to establish the existence of a minefield and its approximate boundaries, rather than definitively establishing the location of individual mines. It is unlikely that making all mines detectable would have a significant impact on the devastation and suffering associated with landmines.

### B. Scatterable Mines

Virtually all future technological developments will focus on scatterable mine systems. Details on the development and technical aspects of scatterable mines are contained in Chapters 2 and 3. In essence, however, scatterable systems allow many more mines to be spread much faster over much wider areas than ever before. Some automatic mine distribution systems can deliver thousands of mines in a matter of minutes. While scatterables are not yet an important factor in the global deployment of landmines outside of Iraq, Kuwait, Indochina, and Afghanistan, they are clearly the wave of the future for those who can afford them.

From a humanitarian perspective, scatterable systems are a disaster. Scattering mines converts mines from a defensive, tactical weapon into an offensive, theater-wide weapon. Afghanistan, for example, became the world's most extensively mined country in a relatively short period of time because of scatterable technologies and new strategies for their use.

Scatterable, remotely delivered mines cannot be reliably recorded, mapped, or marked, in the short or long run. The degree to which scatterables are indiscriminate is clear from the fact that they endanger not only civilians, but also the very military forces which lay them. The recent DIA study notes: "In fact, due to problems which may be

---

[19] This point was made by several mine clearance experts at the ICRC Symposium in Montreux, Switzerland, April 21-23, 1993.

encountered in remote delivery of mines (e.g. command and control procedures for determining where and when the landmines are to be placed, the notification of units which may need to enter those areas, and the accuracy of emplacement systems), friendly forces may be called upon to breach their own scatterable landmines."[20]

Moreover, scatterable mines are increasingly designed to elude detection and overcome deactivation. While these are understandable objectives from a military perspective, they obviously greatly complicate the task of mine clearance.

The Landmines Protocol prohibits remotely delivered mines unless they can be accurately recorded (a virtual impossibility), or contain "an effective neutralizing mechanism."[21] While all U.S. scatterable mines now being produced or under development contain a self-destruct mechanism, most scatterable mines produced elsewhere have neither a self-destruct nor self-neutralizing feature.

### C. Self-Destructing and Self-Neutralizing Mines

Many people who are sensitive to the problem of landmines believe that the best solution is simply to require that all mines contain a mechanism to render the mine inert. The two basic options are self-destructing and self-neutralizing mechanisms. A self-destructing mine is designed to simply explode after a pre-determined period of time, just as if a person had detonated it. A self-neutralizing mine, by contrast, does not explode, but becomes inert because its batteries expire, or by some other mechanical, chemical, or electronic means.

Both military personnel and those engaged in mine clearance express strong preferences for self-destructing as opposed to self-neutralizing mines. Understandably, neither soldiers nor deminers have confidence that mines that are supposedly neutralized are in fact neutralized. It is difficult to persuade anyone to walk into a minefield where mines are still visible. Civilians will not know for certain when a mine is no longer active, and if they cannot be sure it is safe, they will

---

[20] DIA/FSTC, p. 1-1. This was a common problem in Vietnam; see Chapter 2.

[21] See Chapter 8 for a discussion of the Landmines Protocol's provisions concerning remote delivery.

not return to occupy the land. Not only will civilians be denied use of the land, but deminers will also have to clear entire fields just as if each mine were live. It involves virtually the same amount of time and cost. Another problem with self-neutralizing mines is that the explosive charge remains in the ground, and over time can become more dangerous as it chemically degrades and becomes unstable. It can also be dug up and reused or resold. In addition, mechanisms to make a mine self-neutralizing, and mechanisms to indicate if a mine is neutralized, could be complex and costly, and could be tampered with to produce a booby-trap. Deminers maintain that even though self-destructing mines could explode randomly, the chance of injury is greater if people try to handle mines they believe are neutralized.

Self-destructing mines, while perhaps preferable to self-neutralizing mines, are not a panacea for the landmines crisis. Self-destruct mines obviously endanger civilians merely by the fact that the civilians have no idea when the mines will explode. Minefields could be deliberately set to randomly self-destruct. Like every other type of mine, self-destruct mines can and will be used in an indiscriminate fashion. The Landmines Protocol does not establish a time limit for self-destruct mechanisms; and whether they blow up in a matter of years, months, weeks, or days, the mines can be used in an indiscriminate fashion posing dangers to civilian non-combatants. Most mines of this type currently being produced are scatterable mines, which are indiscriminate by nature. The failure rate of the self-destruct mechanism is also of grave concern, especially for scatterable mines that are sown thousands at a time,[22] given that humanitarian mine clearance requires 99.9% accuracy.

Most importantly, however, self-destructing mines are more difficult to manufacture and more expensive to purchase, and are therefore not attractive to poorer armies. This is what makes the prospect of a requirement that mines be self-destructing or self-neutralizing attractive to arms producers, who see the opportunity to convert the unsophisticated, low-margin, pure commodity landmine into a value-added product. But it is unlikely that less developed nations, few

---

[22] At the ICRC Symposium in Montreux in April 1993, mine experts cited a likely 10% failure rate. The Project Manager of the U.S. Army Mines, Countermine and Demolitions division told the Arms Project, however, that U.S. self-destructing mines have a hazardous dud rate of between 1 in 10,000 and 1 in 100,000 (Interview, June 15, 1993).

of whom make self-destructing mines, would agree to a ban on the mines they manufacture, and can afford both to buy *and to sell*, while permitting technologically more advanced nations to continue producing and selling the latest mines in their arsenals. It may be, as some developing world diplomats and military officers have indicated privately to the Arms Project, that the real problem of self-destructing and self-neutralizing mines is unfortunately as much a desire by developing world mine exporters to preserve their sales markets as it is pressure from developing world purchasers who want to buy mines. But in either case, permitting only self-destructing mines would create an intractable political problem: poorer armies in developing countries and insurgency an undue technological advantage to wealthier nations and simply ignore such a rule. Developing countries, unable to cost-effectively introduce the new, advanced technologies, and enjoying a competitive advantage principally in labor costs, would reject a ban that would undercut their export markets. The likely result would be an irresolvable North-South conflict and no movement whatsoever toward control of landmines of any type.

If there is to be a successful ban on landmines, it is necessary to have one single standard for all nations of the world, both from a moral and a practical standpoint. Landmines should be treated in the same way as chemical and biological weapons—those who use them are outlaws, and should be stigmatized as such. Moreover, a total ban on landmines would be easier to monitor and enforce than one with broad exemptions. A mine with a self-destructing mechanism is preferable to a mine without. A requirement that all mines have self-destruct mechanisms would likely save lives, while nonetheless having only a marginal impact on the global crisis, in part because of uncleared mines and in part because the mere existence of self-destructing mines on the market is not likely to change the patterns of developing world mine users. There is no such thing as a "good" mine.

### D. Submunitions

Technological developments and tactical strategies have made it increasingly difficult to determine precisely what constitutes an antipersonnel mine. Particularly disturbing in this regard is the proliferation of submunitions.[23]  "Submunitions," commonly referred to as bomblets, cluster bombs, and grenades, are delivered by aircraft, surface artillery, and rockets.  In some instances, these submunitions are purposely used as an antipersonnel weapon; in other instances, they are intended as an anti-armor weapon which incidently kills and maims people.  Of greatest concern, however, is that when these submunitions fail to explode on initial contact with the ground (or after a preset time), they in essence become landmines.  The "dud rate"—the percent of submunitions that do not explode as intended—is high.  Manufacturers claim two to five percent, but many observers believe 10-20 percent more accurate based on experience in Iraq.  Even at a conservative five percent, more than one million submunitions remained live following the Persian Gulf war.

     An air attack, or an artillery or rocket barrage, typically disperses thousands of submunitions within a small space, roughly 100 x 50 meters. Submunitions are produced by many nations, in huge numbers, and they are inexpensive.  The U.S. is estimated to have manufactured an astounding 750 million submunitions for artillery and rockets alone.  A 155 millimeter artillery shell with 72 grenades costs $400.  The CBU-87 air-delivered cluster bomb with 202 bomblets costs about $15,000.  One analyst has estimated that some 30 million submunitions were expended during the Persian Gulf war, and that 30% of the total number of weapons dropped by aircraft in the Gulf War were cluster bombs.[24]

     In considering measures to limit, restrict, or ban landmines, every effort should be made to include those submunitions which are functionally equivalent to mines.

### III.     Future Options for Controlling Landmines

     While a total ban on production, stockpiling, trade, and use of landmines is the only measure that will ultimately permit the international community to come to grips with the landmines crisis, there are a number of interim steps, short of a total ban, that should be considered, in addition to the "technical fixes" addressed above such as

---

[23] This section is largely drawn from the paper by William Arkin presented to the NGO Conference on Antipersonnel Landmines in London, May 24, 1993.

[24]  Arkin, p. 5.

requirements for detectability and self-destruct mechanisms.[25]

The extension of current export bans by the United States and France, and the adoption of similar moratoria by other nations, is an important step.  An export moratorium is valuable as an interim measure that sets a standard for state behavior, focuses world attention on the use of mines, and provides momentum toward more far-reaching limitations.

A related possibility is the establishment of a multilateral voluntary regime along the lines of the Australia Group (which limits exports on dual-use chemicals) and the Missile Technology Control Regime.  Such a regime would regionalize and/or internationalize the control of export of mines.

All states could take steps to strengthen national controls over illegal or quasi-legal exports of landmines, particularly by enhancing the role of customs authorities.

There is clearly a need for the development and exchange of information at the international level on production, stockpiles and exports of mines.[26]  Particularly important is the addition of landmines to the U.N. Register of Conventional Arms.

Governments should ratify the Landmines Protocol, and then actively participate in the U.N. review conference with the objective of enacting a total ban.

These steps are useful only as a prelude to a multilateral agreement to ban development, manufacture, stockpiling, transfer, and use of landmines.  In and of themselves, none of these interim steps—nor even a widespread ban on export of landmines—will significantly impact on the humanitarian disaster brought about by landmines.

---

[25]  Much of the following discussion is drawn from the Report of Working Group 6, "Possible Arms Control Measures relating to the Commerce in Mines and their Stockage," at the ICRC Symposium in Montreux, April 21-23, 1993. See also the discussion of interim measures in Chapter 11, Conclusion.

[26]  See Chapter 4 on transparency.  In addition to those technical fixes, the use, trade, and production in any instance of anti-handling and anti-disturbance devices in connection with antipersonnel mines should be prohibited, as an interim measure.  Anti-handling and anti-disturbance devices, when used in connection with mines, are prima facie evidence that the force laying the mines does not intend to remove them.  Once activated, they are typically uncontrollable even by the force laying them.

From an arms control perspective, there are many issues to be considered in a multilateral agreement to ban mines, including:

• technical definitions of what constitutes an antipersonnel mine, production facility, dual-use componentry, and mine delivery systems. In this regard, special attention needs to be devoted to the blurring of the line between antitank and antipersonnel mines, and the need to include submunitions and other ordnance that can function as landmines.
• a routine verification regime, which would include declarations and inspections.
• a special challenge inspection regime.
• destruction of stockpiles in an extremely limited time period and on-site verification of destruction.
• sanctions provisions in the case of non-compliance.
• strict national legislation and enforcement to support the terms of the multilateral agreement.
•allowance for certain permitted purposes, such as research for the improvement of demining equipment, mine countermeasures, and for protection of troops.[27]

Obviously, adherence as wide as possible to such an agreement is vital. Undoubtedly, clandestine commerce would continue, and rogue states and sub-national actors would continue to produce, trade and use mines. The difficulties in dealing with continued use, production and trade by states that are not parties to the agreement would be serious. But the advantages of a comprehensive ban are many and obvious.

---

[27] These various arms control measures are discussed in Congressional Research Service report to Sen. Leahy, March 11, 1993, Appendix E and F.

# 11
# CONCLUSION

The need is urgent to secure a worldwide ban on the production, stockpiling, transfer, and use of antipersonnel landmines.

A total ban is supported by international humanitarian laws prohibiting the use of weapons which cause indiscriminate and excessive injury, and by disarmament principles forbidding the production, stockpiling, and transfer of weapons which exact unconscionable human harm. The facts presented in this book support a ban within this legal framework. Preceding chapters have documented the proliferation of landmines in recent decades; the escalation of deliberate mine use against non-combatants as well as indiscriminate attacks resulting in serious collateral harm to civilians; the insidious nature of mine injuries; the long-term social and economic consequences of mine warfare; and the even deadlier uses of mines predicted for the future. The book has also described the multitude of problems inherent in undertaking mine eradication—lack of funds and political will, technological developments that make it virtually impossible to detect the location of mines, inadequate mapping, the danger and slowness of demining procedures, and the heavy economic burden of clearance.

Even if mine deployment ceased today forever, many countries would still be engaged in attempting to clear mines, and many thousands of civilians would still be killed and maimed, for decades to come. Without stringent controls, the number of landmines produced and deployed around the world will continue to increase, very likely at a rate faster than experienced in the past. The result is a deadly accumulation that gradually creates a potential for mass destruction.

There are reasons to believe that the global landmines situation is going to deteriorate further in the future, and perhaps quite rapidly: renewed hostilities in nations such as Angola that already have serious landmine problems; the likelihood of increased ethnic and religious conflict around the world; changes in strategies for using landmines; increasing involvement of more nations in landmine production and trade; and technological developments that can make mines even deadlier.

## I.    The Legal Necessity of a Ban

While some military experts have expressed doubts about the absolute military importance of landmines, particularly for modern, professional conventional armies,[1] there is no doubt at all about their steep costs to non-combatants, communities, and entire countries. Even accepting that landmines have military value, under humanitarian law it is necessary to weigh military benefits against human suffering caused. This calculation must take into account the grotesque injuries caused by mines, their inability to distinguish civilians from combatants, and the long-term economic and social costs of unusable fields, uninhabitable villages, medical treatment and rehabilitation, mine clearance, and rebuilding.

It is the opinion of the Arms Project and Physicians for Human Rights that, given the overall humanitarian costs of landmines, the military role they play in contemporary warfare[2] is too limited to justify their use. However, even if the calculation tipped in favor of landmines because of their military usefulness, they would still have to be banned because of their indiscriminate qualities.[3] Under customary international law, and as codified in article 51(4) of 1977 Additional

---

[1] See discussions in Chapters 2 and 10.

[2] The last decade has seen a dramatic shift in the use of mines from primarily defensive and tactical battlefield weapons to offensive, strategic weapons used to consolidate control over vast areas of land. Concomitant with this transformation, mines now are used increasingly against civilians, to spread terror, destroy agriculture and food supplies, and destabilize civilian populations in an effort to weaken military opponents. Such uses undoubtedly have military value, but are not legitimate under humanitarian law. See discussion in Chapter 2.

[3] As emphasized throughout this book, unless unexploded mines are removed or deactivated immediately after the end of the specific military operation during which they were laid (a task virtually impossible during war), mines, because of their delayed-action operation, will produce indiscriminate effects—essentially becoming indiscriminate weapons unable to differentiate civilian and military targets.

Protocol I, weapons which are by their nature indiscriminate or cause uncontrollable indiscriminate effects are forbidden no matter what their military utility.

## II.    Political Feasibility of a Total Ban

Although delegates to the conferences culminating in enactment of the Landmines Protocol acknowledged that a flat ban on landmines would be more effective and easier to enforce than a series of complicated rules, they concurred that such a measure was not politically acceptable.  In particular, delegates believed that a flat ban would fail because it would not be supported by the major military powers.

Today, a decade later, the situation is substantially different. Mounting evidence of the extreme devastation caused by massive use of mines world-wide has prompted several countries, including major military powers, to consider measures to forbid their transfer and sale, and to restrict their use.  The United States has imposed a unilateral ban on mine transfer, and there is support in the U.S. government for extending such a ban to prohibit the use of mines; members of Congress and the administration are now taking a world leadership role in efforts to institute an international export proscription.  France has announced that it has ended all sale of mines.  Belgium reportedly has stopped production of antipersonnel landmines, and has forbidden the transit of such mines within its borders.  A motion has been introduced in the British Parliament calling for British ratification of the Landmines Protocol and negotiation of an international agreement or modification of the Protocol to prohibit the sale, transfer and export of landmines.  In Australia, a petition supporting a ban on the manufacture and transfer of landmines has been submitted to the House of Representatives.  Finally, the French government, among others, has requested that a conference be convened by the United Nations to review the efficacy of the Landmines Protocol.

A reevaluation of the human costs of landmine use also makes a total ban more politically feasible.  Participants in conferences leading up to the Landmines Protocol did not consider the full impact of mine warfare.  Consequently, imposing restrictions on use rather than a ban was deemed sufficient. Studies conducted during the last decade documenting the egregious medical, social, and economic effects of landmines are, however, causing governments to recognize that the immediate as well as long-term toll on civilian society cannot justify their use.

The Landmines Protocol was intended to apply the general humanitarian rules contained in 1977 Additional Protocol I to the specifics of mine warfare. However, the Landmines Protocol was being written just as Additional Protocol I was becoming law. Now, with more than ten years of analysis of and commentary on Protocol I, as well as accumulating evidence of the devastating effects of landmine use, it has become clear that the Landmines Protocol does not give full effect to the requirements of Protocol I—nor, indeed, to basic precepts of customary humanitarian law forbidding indiscriminate weapons and those that cause indiscriminate effects, as well as weapons that exact humanitarian costs that exceed military necessity. Under these principles, particularly as they are embodied in Protocol I, landmines must be banned.

Finally, the failure of the Landmines Protocol, both on its face and in practice, to diminish abuse of civilians is starting to create a consensus that the only effective response is complete proscription. Indeed, in the decade since the Landmines Protocol entered into force, mine use has proliferated and attacks on civilians have multiplied manyfold.

For a ban to be truly politically feasible, however, it is necessary to have a single standard applied equally to all fighting forces. In particular, it is unrealistic to expect that less developed nations will agree to a ban on manually-emplaced mines that do not contain de-activation devices, but accept that wealthier countries can continue to manufacture, sell, and use scatterable mines incorporating such mechanisms.

## III.    Pragmatic Feasibility of a Total Ban

A total ban on landmines has pragmatic advantages over a web of rules merely restricting use. A total ban is easier to monitor and enforce than complex restrictions on use, as even drafters of the Landmines Protocol recognized. Moreover, from a practical enforcement perspective, a total ban makes it possible to stigmatize landmines as a weapon. This is not possible, however, if some uses are considered acceptable and some are not; there would be an endless and inconclusive debate as to the military judgment made in landmine use. By contrast, if the weapon is banned altogether, then any use of it can be stigmatized.

The same principle applies to the supply and export of

landmines.  If some export is legal, then there will always be an inconclusive debate as to whether exports in a given situation are legal. Only if all export is illegal is it possible to stigmatize violations—in the international media, in diplomatic relations, and in other venues.

It has been suggested that seeking a total ban on production, stockpiling, transfer, and use is a hopelessly quixotic exercise, because it is not politically feasible and therefore not a realistic goal.  However, the Arms Project and Physicians for Human Rights see it quite the other way around.  Any legal measure short of a ban is an invitation to abuse and precludes the possibility of using the pragmatic tools of the human rights and humanitarian movement—denunciation and stigmatization—because there will always be an argument as to whether a particular export or use of landmines was in fact legal.   Only a total ban eliminates that argument.  In addition, even the fact that not all suppliers are likely to leave the market does not render a ban pointless, because a reduction in supply may raise the political and economic costs of landmines and induce changes in combatant behavior.

A realistic assessment of the landmines crisis world-wide makes the pragmatic argument for a ban even stronger.  Experience has shown, in the decade the Landmines Protocol has been in force, that parties who fight wars will, if they have access to relatively cheap and unlimited landmines, virtually always abuse them.  Only a total ban is a realistic goal because landmines, if available, are an irresistible weapon.

## IV.    Interim Measures Short of a Total Ban

The Arms Project and Physicians for Human Rights understand that international abolition of the production, stockpiling, transfer, and use of landmines will not happen overnight.  There are still several important interim measures that governments should take to diminish the harm caused by landmines and build toward a total ban:

- adopt unilateral legislation to control landmine production and export, renounce their use in armed conflict, and press for a total international ban;
- ratify the Landmines Protocol and actively participate in the United Nations review conference to the end of enacting a total ban;

- ensure that the review conference undertake a full examination of the Landmines Protocol, and not permit an agenda based on mere fine-tuning of its provisions;
- provide more funds for humanitarian mine clearance, establish better training for mine clearers and better coordination of mine clearance efforts, fund programs to develop new mine clearance technologies, and fund rehabilitation and medical programs to deal with landmine victims worldwide;
- press avenues of disarmament law to draft conventions and protocols to establish regimes of compliance and verification covering production, stockpiling, and export, including but not limited to extending the United Nations Register of Conventional Arms;
- require domestic mine producers to manufacture and sell only mines that are readily detectable in order to facilitate clearance efforts, and permit their own armies to use only such mines.

## V.     A Call to Action

The deadly accumulation of landmines world-wide is now too great to be ignored.    Landmines are, when all their effects are considered, the equivalent of a weapon of mass destruction in slow motion.  They are a weapon aimed particularly at the developing world. The Arms Project and Physicians for Human Rights do not take lightly the breadth of the call that they, along with an increasing number of non-governmental organizations, make to governments of the world to enact and enforce a total ban on landmines.  But neither do the Arms Project and Physicians for Human Rights regard the call for a total ban as mere idealism.  It is, rather, the pragmatic and realistic response to a weapon that, if available, will be abused, but which can no longer be tolerated.

# APPENDICES

# APPENDICES

# APPENDIX 1

## HANDICAP INTERNATIONAL, HUMAN RIGHTS WATCH, MEDICO INTERNATIONAL, MINES ADVISORY GROUP, PHYSICIANS FOR HUMAN RIGHTS

### and

## VIETNAM VETERANS OF AMERICA FOUNDATION

### have come together to issue

## A JOINT CALL TO BAN ANTIPERSONNEL LANDMINES

Whereas antipersonnel mines that detonate on contact are indiscriminate weapons that remain hidden and lethal long after the end of a conflict; and

Whereas antipersonnel mines have killed or mutilated tens of thousands of civilians and rendered large tracts of agricultural and pastoral land unusable, preventing the subsistence and economic development of rural populations; and

Whereas the 1981 United Nations Protocol on Prohibitions or Restrictions on the Use of Mines, Booby Traps and Other Devices has failed to prevent the indiscriminate use of antipersonnel mines;

HANDICAP INTERNATIONAL, HUMAN RIGHTS WATCH, MEDICO INTERNATIONAL, MINES ADVISORY GROUP, PHYSICIANS FOR HUMAN RIGHTS, and the VIETNAM VETERANS OF AMERICA FOUNDATION call for:

\* An international ban on the use, production, stockpiling, and sale, transfer or export of antipersonnel mines; and

*   The establishment of an international fund, administered by the United Nations, to promote and finance landmine awareness, clearance and eradication programs worldwide; and

*   Countries responsible for the production and dissemination of antipersonnel mines to contribute to the international fund.

# APPENDIX 2

## The Six Non-Governmental Organizations

## Convening the Campaign to Ban

## Antipersonnel Landmines

Handicap International
13 Place de Rungis
75013 Paris
France
Attn:   Philippe Chabasse
        Tim Carstairs

Human Rights Watch
The Arms Project
485 Fifth Avenue, 3rd Floor
New York, New York  10017
USA
Attn:   Kenneth Anderson
        Stephen D. Goose

Medico International
Obermainanlage 7
D-6000 Frankfurt/Main 1
Germany
Attn:   Angelika Beer

Mines Advisory Group
54a Main Street
Cockermouth
Cumbria  CA13 9LU
Great Britain
Attn:   Rae McGrath

Physicians for Human Rights
100 Boylston Street, 7th Floor
Boston MA 02116
USA
Attn:   Eric Stover
        Susannah Sirkin

Vietnam Veterans of America Foundation
2001 S Street, N.W., Ste. 740
Washington, D.C.  20009
USA
Attn:   Jody Williams
        Bobby Muller

# APPENDIX 3

## Convention on Prohibitions or Restrictions on the Use of Certain Conventional Weapons Which May be Deemed to be Excessively Injurious or to Have Indiscriminate Effects

*The High Contracting Parties,*

*Recalling* that every State has the duty, in conformity with the Charter of the United Nations, to refrain in its international relations from the threat or use of force against the sovereignty, territorial integrity or political independence of any State, or in any other manner inconsistent with the purposes of the United Nations,

*Further recalling* the general principle of the protection of the civilian population against the effects of hostilities,

*Basing themselves on the principle of* international law that the right of the parties to an armed conflict to choose methods or means of warfare is not unlimited, and on the principle that prohibits the employment in armed conflicts of weapons, projectiles and material and methods of warfare of a nature to cause superfluous injury or unnecessary suffering,

*Also recalling* that it is prohibited to employ methods or means of warfare which are intended, or may be expected, to cause widespread, long-term and severe damage to the natural environment,

*Confirming their determination* that in cases not covered by this Convention and its annexed Protocols or by other international agreements, the civilian population and the combatants shall at all times remain under the protection and authority of the principles of international law derived from established custom, from the principles of humanity and from the dictates of public conscience,

*Desiring* to contribute to international detente, the ending of the arms race and the building of confidence among States, and hence to the realization of the aspiration of all peoples to live in peace,

*Recognizing* the importance of pursuing every effort which may contribute to progress towards general and complete disarmament under strict and effective international control,

*Reaffirming* the need to continue the codification and progressive development of the rules of international law applicable in armed conflict,

365

*Wishing* to prohibit or restrict further the use of certain conventional weapons and believing that the positive results achieved in this area may facilitate the main talks on disarmament with a view to putting an end to the production, stockpiling and proliferation of such weapons,

*Emphasizing* the desirability that all States become parties to this Convention and its annexed Protocols, especially the military significant States,

*Bearing in mind* that the General Assembly of the United Nations and the United Nations Disarmament Commission may decide to examine the question of a possible broadening of the scope of the prohibitions and restrictions contained in this Convention and its annexed Protocols,

*Further bearing in mind* that the Committee on Disarmament may decide to consider the question of adopting further measures to prohibit or restrict the use of certain conventional weapons,

*Have agreed as follows:*

### Article 1 — *Scope of application*

This Convention and its annexed Protocols shall apply in the situations referred to in Article 2 common to the Geneva Conventions of 12 August 1949 for the Protection of War Victims, including any situation described in paragraph 4 of Article 1 of Additional Protocol I to these Conventions.

### Article 2 — *Relations with other international agreements*

Nothing in this Convention or its annexed Protocols shall be interpreted as detracting from other obligations imposed upon the High Contracting Parties by international humanitarian law applicable in armed conflict.

### Article 3 — *Signature*

This Convention shall be open for signature by all States at United Nations Headquarters in New York for a period of twelve months from 10 April 1981.

### Article 4 — *Ratification, acceptance, approval or accession*

1. This Convention is subject to ratification, acceptance or approval by the Signatories. Any State which has not signed this Convention may accede to it.

2. The instruments of ratification, acceptance, approval or accession shall be deposited with the Depositary.

3. Expressions of consent to be bound by any of the Protocols annexed to this Convention shall be optional for each State, provided that

at the time of the deposit of its instrument of ratification, acceptance or approval of this Convention or of accession thereto, that State shall notify the Depositary of its consent to be bound by any two or more of these Protocols.

4. At any time after the deposit of its instrument of ratification, acceptance or approval of this Convention or of accession thereto, a State may notify the Depositary of its consent to be bound by any annexed Protocol by which it is not already bound.

5. Any Protocol by which a High Contracting Party is bound shall for that Party form an integral part of this Convention.

### Article 5 — Entry into force

1. This Convention shall enter into force six months after the date of deposit of the twentieth instrument of ratification, acceptance, approval or accession.

2. For any State which deposits its instrument of ratification, acceptance, approval or accession after the date of the deposit of the twentieth instrument of ratification, acceptance, approval or accession, this Convention shall enter into force six months after the date on which that State has deposited its instrument of ratification, acceptance, approval or accession.

3. Each of the Protocols annexed to this Convention shall enter into force six months after the date by which twenty States have notified their consent to be bound by it in accordance with paragraph 3 or 4 of Article 4 of this Convention.

4. For any State which notifies its consent to be bound by a Protocol annexed to this Convention after the date by which twenty States have notified their consent to be bound by it, the Protocol shall enter into force six months after the date on which that State has notified its consent so to be bound.

### Article 6 — Dissemination

The High Contracting Parties undertake, in time of peace as in time of armed conflict, to disseminate this Convention and those of its annexed Protocols by which they are bound as widely as possible in their respective countries and, in particular, to include the study thereof in their programmes of military instruction, so that those instruments may become known to their armed forces.

### Article 7 — Treaty relations upon entry into force of this Convention

1. When one of the parties to a conflict is not bound by an annexed Protocol, the parties bound by this Convention and that annexed Protocol shall remain bound by them in their mutual relations.

2. Any High Contracting Party shall be bound by this Convention and any Protocol annexed thereto which is in force for it, in any situation contemplated by Article 1, in relation to any State which is not a party to this Convention or bound by the relevant annexed Protocol, if the latter accepts and applies this Convention or the relevant Protocol, and so notifies the Depositary.

3. The Depositary shall immediately inform the High Contracting Parties concerned of any notification received under paragraph 2 of this Article.

4. This Convention, and the annexed Protocols by which a High Contracting Party is bound, shall apply with respect to an armed conflict against the High Contracting Party of the type referred to in Article 1, paragraph 4, of Additional Protocol I to the Geneva Conventions of 12 August 1949 for the Protection of War Victims:

  (a) where the High Contracting Party is also a party to Additional Protocol I and an authority referred to in Article 96, paragraph 3, of that Protocol has undertaken to apply the Geneva Conventions and Additional Protocol I in accordance with Article 96, paragraph 3, of the said Protocol, and undertakes to apply this Convention and the relevant annexed Protocols in relation to that conflict; or

  (b) where the High Contracting Party is not a part to Additional Protocol I and an authority of the type referred to in subparagraph (a) above accepts and applies the obligations of the Geneva Conventions and of this Convention and the relevant annexed Protocols in relation to that conflict. Such an acceptance and application shall have in relation to that conflict the following effects:

    (i) the Geneva Conventions and this Convention and its relevant annexed Protocols are brought into force for the parties to the conflict with immediate effect;

    (ii) the said authority assumes the same rights and obligations as those which have been assumed by a High Contracting Party to the Geneva Conventions, this Convention and its relevant annexed Protocols; and

    (iii) The Geneva Conventions, this Convention and its relevant annexed Protocols are equally binding upon all parties to the conflict.

The High Contracting Party and the authority may also agree to accept and apply the obligations of Additional Protocol I to the Geneva Conventions on a reciprocal basis.

*Article 8 — Review and amendments*
1. (a) At any time after the entry into force of this Convention any High Contracting Party may propose amendments to this Convention or any annexed Protocol by which it is bound. Any proposal for an amendment shall be communicated to the Depositary, who shall notify it to all the High Contracting Parties and shall seek their views on whether a conference should be convened to consider the proposal. If a majority, that shall not be less than eighteen of the High Contracting Parties so agree, he shall promptly convene a conference to which all High Contracting Parties shall be invited. States not parties to this Convention shall be invited to the conference as observers.
   (b) Such a conference may agree upon amendments which shall be adopted and shall enter into force in the same manner as this Convention and the annexed Protocols, provided that amendments to this Convention may be adopted only by the High Contracting Parties and that amendments to a specific annexed Protocol may be adopted only by the High Contracting Parties which are bound by that Protocol.
2. (a) At any time after the entry into force of this Convention any High Contracting Party may propose additional protocols relating to other categories of conventional weapons not covered by the existing annexed Protocols. Any such proposal for an additional protocol shall be communicated to the Depositary, who shall notify it to all the High Contracting Parties in accordance with subparagraph 1 (a) of this Article. If a majority, that shall not be less than eighteen of the High Contracting Parties so agree, the Depositary shall promptly convene a conference to which all States shall be invited.
   (b) Such a conference may agree, with the full participation of all States represented at the conference, upon additional protocols which shall be adopted in the same manner as this Convention, shall be annexed thereto and shall enter into force as provided in paragraphs 3 and 4 of Article 5 of this Convention.

3. (a) If, after a period of ten years following the entry into force of this Convention, no conference has been convened in accordance with subparagraph 1 (a) or 2 (a) of this Article, any High Contracting Party may request the Depositary to convene a conference to which all High Contracting Parties shall be invited to review the scope and operation of this Convention and the Protocols annexed thereto and to consider any proposal for amendments of this Convention or of the existing Protocols. States not parties to this Convention shall be invited as observers to the conference. The conference may agree upon amendments which shall be adopted and enter into force in accordance with subparagraph 1 (b) above.

(b) At such conference consideration may also be given to any proposal for additional protocols relating to other categories of conventional weapons not covered by the existing annexed Protocols. All States represented at the conference may participate fully in such consideration. Any additional protocols shall be adopted in the same manner as this Convention, shall be annexed thereto and shall enter into force as provided in paragraphs 3 and 4 of Article 5 of this Convention.

(c) Such a conference may consider whether provision should be made for the convening of a further conference at the request of any High Contracting Party if, after a similar period to that referred to in subparagraph 3 (a) of this Article, no conference has been convened in accordance with subparagraph 1 (a) or 2 (a) of this Article.

*Article 9 — Denunciation*

1. Any High Contracting Party may denounce this Convention or any of its annexed Protocols by so notifying the Depositary.

2. Any such denunciation shall only take effect one year after receipt by the Depositary of the notification of denunciation. If, however, on the expiry of that year the denouncing High Contracting Party is engaged in one of the situations referred to in Article 1, the Party shall continue to be bound by the obligations of this Convention and of the relevant annexed Protocols until the end of the armed conflict or occupation and, in any case, until the termination of operations connected with the final release, repatriation or re-establishment of the persons protected by the rules of international law applicable in armed conflict, and in the case of any annexed Protocol containing provisions concerning situations in which peace-keeping, observation or similar functions are performed by

United Nations forces or missions in the area concerned, until the termination of those functions.

3. Any denunciation of this Convention shall be considered as also applying to all annexed Protocols by which the denouncing High Contracting Party is bound.

4. Any denunciation shall have effect only in respect of the denouncing High Contracting Party.

5. Any denunciation shall not affect the obligations already incurred, by reason of an armed conflict, under this Convention and its annexed Protocols by such denouncing High Contracting Party in respect of any act committed before this denunciation becomes effective.

*Article* 10 — *Depositary*
1. The Secretary-General of the United Nations shall be the Depositary of this Convention and of its annexed Protocols.

2. In addition to his usual functions, the Depositary shall inform all States of:
- (*a*) signatures affixed to this Convention under Article 3;
- (*b*) deposits of instruments of ratification, acceptance or approval of or accession to this Convention deposited under Article 4;
- (*c*) notifications of consent to be bound by annexed Protocols under Article 4;
- (*d*) the dates of entry into force of this Convention and of each of its annexed Protocols under Article 5; and
- (*e*) notifications of denunciation received under Article 9, and their effective date.

*Article* 11 — *Authentic texts*
The original of this Convention with the annexed Protocols, of which the Arabic, Chinese, English, French, Russian and Spanish texts are equally authentic, shall be deposited with the Depositary, who shall transmit certified true copies thereof to all States.

\* \* \*

# Protocol on Non-Detectable Fragments (Protocol I)

It is prohibited to use any weapon the primary effect of which is to injure by fragments which in the human body escape detection by X-rays.

* * *

# Protocol on Prohibitions or Restrictions on the Use of Mines, Booby Traps and Other Devices (Protocol II)

*Article 1 — Material scope of application*

This Protocol relates to the use on land of the mines, booby-traps and other devices defined herein, including mines laid to interdict beaches, waterway crossings or river crossings, but does not apply to the use of anti-ship mines at sea or in inland waterways.

*Article 2 — Definitions*

For the purpose of this Protocol:

1. 'Mine' means any munition placed under, on or near the ground or other surface area and designed to be detonated or exploded by the presence, proximity or contact of a person or vehicle, and 'remotely delivered mine' means any mine so defined delivered by artillery, rocket, mortar or similar means or dropped from an aircraft.

2. 'Booby-trap' means any device or material which is designed, constructed or adapted to kill or injure and which functions unexpectedly when a person disturbs or approaches an apparently harmless object or performs an apparently safe act.

3. 'Other devices' means manually-emplaced munitions and devices designed to kill, injure or damage and which are actuated by remote control or automatically after a lapse of time.

4. 'Military objective' means, so far as objects are concerned, any object which by its nature, location, purpose or use makes an effective contribution to military action and whose total or partial destruction, capture or neutralization, in the circumstances ruling at the time, offers a definite military advantage.

5. 'Civilian objects' are all objects which are not military objectives as defined as defined in paragraph 4.

6. 'Recording' means a physical, administrative and technical operation designed to obtain, for the purpose of registration in the official records, all available information facilitating the location of minefields, mines and booby-traps.

*Article 3 — General restrictions of the use of mines, booby-traps and other devices*

1. This Article applies to:

   (a)  mines;

(*b*)　booby-traps; and

(*c*)　other devices.

2. It is prohibited in all circumstances to direct weapons to which this Article applies, either in offence, defence or by way of reprisals, against the civilian population as such or against individual civilians.

3. The indiscriminate use of weapons to which this Article applies is prohibited. Indiscriminate use is any placement of such weapons:

(*a*)　which is not on, or directed at, a military objective; or

(*b*)　which employs a method or means of delivery which cannot be directed at a specific military objective; or

(*c*)　which may be expected to cause incidental loss of civilian life, injury to civilians, damage to civilian objects, or a combination thereof, which would be excessive in relation to the concrete and direct military advantage anticipated.

4. All feasible precautions shall be taken to protect civilians from the effects of weapons to which this Article applies. Feasible precautions are those precautions which are practicable or practically possible taking into account all circumstances ruling at the time, including humanitarian and military considerations.

*Article 4 — Restrictions on the use of mines other than remotely delivered mines, booby-traps and other devices in populated areas*

1. This Article applies to:

(*a*)　mines other than remotely delivered mines;

(*b*)　booby-traps; and

(*c*)　other devices.

2. It is prohibited to use weapons to which this Article applies in any city, town, village or other area containing a similar concentration of civilians in which combat between ground forces is not taking place or does not appear to be imminent, unless either:

(*a*)　they are placed on or in the close vicinity of a military objective belonging to or under the control of an adverse party; or

(*b*)　measures are taken to protect civilians from their effects, for example, the posting of warning signs, the posting of sentries, the issue of warnings or the provision of fences.

*Article 5 — Restrictions on the use of remotely delivered mines*

1. The use of remotely delivered mines is prohibited unless such mines are only used within an area which is itself a military objective or which contains military objectives, and unless:

(a) their location can be accurately recorded in accordance with Article 7(1)(a); or

(b) an effective neutralizing mechanism is used on each such mine, that is to say, a self-actuating mechanism which is designed to render a mine harmless or cause it to destroy itself when it is anticipated that the mine will no longer serve the military purpose for which it was placed in position, or a remotely-controlled mechanism which is designed to render harmless or destroy a mine when the mine no longer serves the military purpose for which it was placed in position.

2. Effective advance warning shall be given of any delivery or dropping of remotely delivered mines which may affect the civilian populations, unless circumstances do not permit.

*Article 6 — Prohibition on the use of certain booby-traps*

1. Without prejudice to the rules of international law applicable in armed conflict relating to treachery and perfidy, it is prohibited in all circumstances to use:

(a) any booby-trap in the form of an apparently harmless portable object which is specifically designed and constructed to contain explosive material and to detonate when it is disturbed or approached, or

(b) booby-traps which are in any way attached to or associated with:

    (i)     internationally recognized protective emblems, signs or signals;

    (ii)    sick, wounded or dead persons;

    (iii)   burial or cremation sites or graves;

    (iv)   medical facilities, medical equipment, medical supplies or medical transportation;

    (v)    children's toys or other portable objects or products specially designed for the feeding, health, hygiene, clothing or education of children;

    (vi)   food or drink;

    (vii)   kitchen utensils or appliances except in military establishments, military locations or military supply depots;

    (viii)  objects clearly of a religious nature

    (ix)   historic monuments, works of art or places of worship which constitute the cultural or spiritual heritage of peoples;

    (x)    animals or their carcasses.

2. It is prohibited in all circumstances to use any booby-trap which is designed to cause superfluous injury or unnecessary suffering.

*Article 7 — Recording and publication of the location of minefields, mines and booby-traps*
1. The parties to a conflict shall record the location of:
   (*a*)  all pre-planned minefields laid by them; and
   (*b*)  all areas in which they have made large-scale and pre-planned use of booby-traps.
2. The parties hall endeavour to ensure the recording of the location of all other minefields, mines and booby-traps which they have laid or placed in position.
3. All such records shall be retained by the parties who shall:
   (*a*)  immediately after the cessation of active hostilities:
   (i)  take all necessary and appropriate measures, including the use of such records, to protect civilians from the effects of minefields, mines and booby-traps; and either
   (ii)  in cases where the forces of neither party are in the territory of the adverse party, make available to each other and to the Secretary-General of the United Nations all information in their possession concerning the location of minefields, mines and booby-traps in the territory of the adverse party; or
   (iii)  once complete withdrawal of the forces of the parties from the territory of the adverse party has taken place, make available to the adverse party and to the Secretary-General of the United Nations all information in their possession concerning the location of minefields, mines and booby-traps in the territory of the adverse party;
   (*b*)  when a United Nations force or mission performs functions in any area, make available to the authority mentioned in Article 8 such information as is required by that Article;
   (*c*)  whenever possible, by mutual agreement, provide for the release of information concerning the location of minefields, mines and booby-traps, particularly in agreements governing the cessation of hostilities.

*Article 8 — Protection of United Nations forces and missions from the effects of minefields, mines and booby-traps*

375

1. When a United Nations force or mission performs functions of peacekeeping, observation or similar functions in any area, each party to the conflict shall, if requested by the head of the United Nations force or mission in that area, as far as it is able:

    (*a*)   remove or render harmless all mines or booby-traps in that area;

    (*b*)   take such measures as may be necessary to protect the force or mission from the effects of minefields, mines and booby-traps while carrying out its duties; and

    (*c*)   make available to the head of the United Nations force or mission in that area, all information in the party's possession concerning the location of minefields, mines and booby-traps in that area.

2. When a United Nations fact-finding mission performs functions in any area, any party to the conflict concerned shall provide protection to that mission except where, because of the size of such mission, it cannot adequately provide such protection. In that case it shall make available to the head of the mission the information in its possession concerning the location of minefields, mines and booby-traps in that area.

*Article 9 — International co-operation in the removal of minefields, mines and booby-traps*

After the cessation of active hostilities, the parties shall endeavour to reach agreement, both among themselves and, where appropriate, with other States and with international organizations, on the provision of information and technical and material assistance — including, in appropriate circumstances, joint operations — necessary to remove or otherwise render ineffective minefields, mines and booby-traps placed in position during the conflict.

* * *

# TECHNICAL ANNEX TO THE PROTOCOL ON PROHIBITIONS OR RESTRICTIONS ON THE USE OF MINES, BOOBY-TRAPS AND OTHER DEVICES (PROTOCOL II)

## Guidelines on recording

Whenever an obligation for the recording of the location of minefields, mines and booby-traps arises under the Protocol, the following guidelines shall be taken into account.

1. With regard to pre-planned minefields and large-scale and pre-planned use of booby-traps:

   (a) maps, diagrams or other records should be made in such a way as to indicate the extent of the minefield or booby-trapped area; and

   (b) the location of the minefield or booby-trapped area should be specified by relation to the co-ordinates of a single reference point and by the estimated dimensions of the area containing mines and booby-traps in relation to that single reference point.

2. With regard to other minefields, mines and booby-traps laid or placed in position:

   In so far as possible, the relevant information specified in paragraph 1 above should be recorded so as to enable the areas containing minefields, mines and booby-traps to be identified.

2. CONVENTION ON PROHIBITIONS OR RESTRICTIONS ON THE USE OF CERTAIN CONVENTIONAL WEAPONS WHICH MAY BE DEEMED TO BE EXCESSIVELY INJURIOUS OR TO HAVE INDISCRIMINATE EFFECTS (AND PROTOCOLS)

*Concluded at Geneva on 10 October 1980*

ENTRY INTO FORCE: 2 December 1983, in accordance with article 5, paragraphs 1 and 3.
REGISTRATION: 2 December 1983, No. 22495.
TEXT: United Nations, *Treaty Series*, vol. 1342, p. 137; depositary notifications C.N.356.1981. TREATIES-7 of 14 January 1982 (procès-verbal of rectification of the Chinese authentic text) and C.N.320.1982. TREATIES-11 of 21 January 1983 (procès-verbal of rectification of the Final Act).
STATUS: Signatories: 52. Parties: 35.

| Participant | Signature | Ratification, acceptance (A), approval (AA), accession (a), succession (d) | Acceptance pursuant to article 4, paragraphs 3 and 4[1] Protocols I | II | III |
|---|---|---|---|---|---|
| Afghanistan | 10 Apr 1981 | | | | |
| Argentina | 2 Dec 1981 | | | | |
| Australia | 8 Apr 1982 | 29 Sep 1983 | x | x | x |
| Austria | 10 Apr 1981 | 14 Mar 1983 | x | x | x |
| Belarus | 10 Apr 1981 | 23 Jun 1982 | x | x | x |
| Belgium | 10 Apr 1981 | | | | |
| Benin | | 27 Mar 1989 *a* | x | | x |
| Bulgaria | 10 Apr 1981 | 15 Oct 1982 | x | x | x |
| Canada | 10 Apr 1981 | | | | |
| China | 14 Sep 1981 | 7 Apr 1982 | x | x | x |
| Cuba | 10 Apr 1981 | 2 Mar 1987 | x | x | x |
| Cyprus | | 12 Dec 1988 *a* | x | x | x |
| Czechoslovakia | 10 Apr 1981 | 31 Aug 1982 | x | x | x |
| Denmark | 10 Apr 1981 | 7 Jul 1982 | x | x | x |
| Ecuador | 9 Sep 1981 | 4 May 1982 | x | x | x |
| Egypt | 10 Apr 1981 | | | | |
| Finland | 10 Apr 1981 | 8 May 1982 | x | x | x |
| France | 10 Apr 1981 | 4 Mar 1988 | x | x | |
| Germany[2] | 10 Apr 1981 | 25 Nov 1992 | x | x | x |
| Greece | 10 Apr 1981 | 28 Jan 1992 | x | x | x |
| Guatemala | | 21 Jul 1983 *a* | x | x | x |
| Hungary | 10 Apr 1981 | 14 Jun 1982 | x | x | x |
| Iceland | 10 Apr 1981 | | | | |
| India | 15 May 1981 | 1 Mar 1984 | x | x | x |
| Ireland | 10 Apr 1981 | | | | |
| Italy | 10 Apr 1981 | | | | |
| Japan | 22 Sep 1981 | 9 Jun 1982 A | x | x | x |
| Lao People's Democratic Republic[3] | [ 2 Nov 1982] | 3 Jan 1983 *a* | x | x | x |
| Liechtenstein | 11 Feb 1982 | 16 Aug 1989 | x | x | x |
| Luxembourg | 10 Apr 1981 | | | | |
| Mexico | 10 Apr 1981 | 11 Feb 1982 | x | x | x |
| Mongolia | 10 Apr 1981 | 8 Jun 1982 | x | x | x |
| Morocco | 10 Apr 1981 | | | | |
| Netherlands[4] | 10 Apr 1981 | 18 Jun 1987 A | x | x | x |
| New Zealand | 10 Apr 1981 | | | | |
| Nicaragua | 20 May 1981 | | | | |
| Niger | | 10 Nov 1992 *a* | x | x | x |
| Nigeria | 26 Jan 1982 | | | | |

| Participant | Signature | Ratification, acceptance (A), approval (AA), accession (a), succession (d) | Acceptance pursuant to article 4, paragraphs 3 and 4[1] Protocols | | |
|---|---|---|---|---|---|
| | | | I | II | III |
| Norway .......................... | 10 Apr 1981 | 7 Jun 1983 | x | x | x |
| Pakistan ........................ | 26 Jan 1982 | 1 Apr 1985 | x | x | x |
| Philippines ...................... | 15 May 1981 | | | | |
| Poland ......................... | 10 Apr 1981 | 2 Jun 1983 | x | x | x |
| Portugal ........................ | 10 Apr 1981 | | | | |
| Romania ........................ | 8 Apr 1982 | | | | |
| Russian Federation ................ | 10 Apr 1981 | 10 Jun 1982 | x | x | x |
| Sierra Leone ..................... | 1 May 1981 | | | | |
| Slovenia ........................ | | 6 Jul 1992 d | x | x | x |
| Spain .......................... | 10 Apr 1981 | | | | |
| Sudan .......................... | 10 Apr 1981 | | | | |
| Sweden ......................... | 10 Apr 1981 | 7 Jul 1982 | x | x | x |
| Switzerland ..................... | 18 Jun 1981 | 20 Aug 1982 | x | x | x |
| Togo ........................... | 15 Sep 1981 | | | | |
| Tunisia ......................... | | 15 May 1987 a | x | x | x |
| Turkey ......................... | 26 Mar 1982 | | | | |
| Ukraine ......................... | 10 Apr 1981 | 23 Jun 1982 | x | x | x |
| United Kingdom of Great Britain and Northern Ireland ........... | 10 Apr 1981 | | | | |
| United States of America ........... | 8 Apr 1982 | | | | |
| Viet Nam ....................... | 10 Apr 1981 | | | | |
| Yugoslavia ...................... | 5 May 1981 | 24 May 1983 | x | x | x |

---

## XXVI.2  CONVENTION ON PROHIBITIONS OR RESTRICTIONS ON THE USE OF CERTAIN CONVENTIONAL WEAPONS WHICH MAY BE DEEMED TO BE EXCESSIVELY INJURIOUS OR TO HAVE INDISCRIMINATE EFFECTS (AND PROTOCOLS)

### Concluded at Geneva on 10 October 1980

---

### Actions effected between 1 January and _____ 1993 *

| | Participant/Authority | Action | Date |
|---|---|---|---|
| 1. | Latvia | Accession | 4 January 1993 1/ |
| 2. | Czech Republic | Succession | 22 February 1993 2/ |
| 3. | Slovakia | Succession | 28 May 1993 |
| 4. | Bosnia and Herzegovina | Succession | 1 September 1993 |

1/ Latvia also acceded to Protocols I, II and III.
2/ The Czech Republic also succeded to Protocols I, II and III.

* Subject to the deposit of outstanding instruments.

# APPENDIX 4

## LANDMINE MORATORIUM: A STRATEGY FOR STRONGER INTERNATIONAL LIMITS

*Senator Patrick Leahy*

*Senator Patrick Leahy (D-VT), chairman of the Foreign Operations subcommittee, has been a member of the Senate since 1975. He is the author of legislation establishing the current U.S. landmine moratorium and has visited El Salvador, Honduras, Uganda and other countries where he has met with landmine victims.*

*This article is reprinted with the kind permission of Arms Control Today, from the January-February 1993 issue.*

With international attention focused on agreements for dramatic cuts in nuclear weapons, bans on nuclear tests and the manufacture or possession of chemical weapons, and new prohibitions on conventional arms sales and distribution, this may not seem the time to be pushing for new laws to restrict the export and use of landmines.

But in fact, urgent action must be taken because landmines, especially anti-personnel landmines, pose a real and present danger to civilian populations in dozens of countries. Hundreds of thousands—perhaps millions—of people, many of them children, have already lost their lives, their legs or arms or their eyesight from stepping on landmines. Some mines are relics of past wars, others are being strewn in today's conflicts; all turn peaceful fields, jungle paths and main travel routes into potential death traps for innocent civilians long after the conflicts end and the causes of war are forgotten.

Landmines are cheap, easy to get, easy to carry, highly effective and can make whole areas inaccessible. Thus, whatever their source and wherever they are used, landmines have advantages for insurgents and poor countries as well as technologically advanced countries.

It may be decades before Afghanistan rids itself of the estimated 10 million landmines left there from the Soviet occupation and the ensuing civil war. And in Cambodia, at least 20,000 people have lost limbs and hundreds of people each month are reportedly still being maimed or killed by landmines. It takes a week for a team of 20 trained people to clear mines from a piece of Cambodian jungle the size of two football fields, at great personal risk. According to an American prosthetist I spoke to, "Cambodia is being de-mined an arm and a leg at a time." At the present rate, it will be hundreds of years before the Cambodian people will be safe from these weapons.

One characteristic that makes landmines particularly insidious is that they can remain lethal long after the fighting ends. People are still being killed in Laos and Vietnam by mines strewn by American and Vietnamese forces from both sides more than 20 years ago.

Old mines are also killing and maiming people, mainly civilians, in Somalia, Angola, Mozambique and many other countries in Central America, Asia and the Middle East. It is time for the United States to lead the way in stopping the deadly trade in these weapons, and to strengthen current international limits on their use. Ultimately, our goal should be to ban landmines outright, as we have done with biological weapons.

**A One-Year Moratorium**

Four years ago I started the "War Victims Fund" in the U.S. foreign aid program to send American doctors and prosthetists to help landmine victims. In addition, in the Fiscal Year (FY) 1993 foreign aid bill we earmarked military aid funds for de-mining efforts. While these programs aid the victims and reduce the threat, they have not stopped the killing and maiming by landmines.

That is why, joined by 35 co-sponsors I introduced the Landmine Moratorium Act in July 1992. Congressman Lane Evan (D-IL) introduced identical legislation in the House, and, in conference, it was included in the FY93 defense authorization bill signed into law by President Bush on October 23, 1992.

This legislation imposes a one-year U.S. moratorium on the sale, export or transfer abroad of anti-personnel landmines. It declares the "Sense of the Congress" that the president should actively seek verifiable international agreements or a modification of the existing international landmine protocol to prohibit the sale, transfer or export of anti-personnel landmines. The ultimate goal is to achieve change in international law along the line of the current, unilateral one-year U.S. moratorium. The moratorium legislation also states that it is the policy of the United States to seek verifiable international agreements to further limit the use, production, possession and deployment of anti-personnel landmines.

The United States is one of about 37 countries that export anti-personnel landmines. However, our exports are quantitatively insignificant. In the past 10 years, the departments of State and Defense have licensed sales and exports of anti-personnel landmines valued at less than $1.9 million. Clearly, these minuscule sales are neither necessary for our national security nor significant in terms of U.S. jobs. However our failure to show leadership in limiting or...this deadly trade has a terrible significance for the victims and for their families.

**International Landmine Protocol**

The new moratorium imposes the first limitations on these weapons in U.S. law, but there is a precedent in international law. Eleven years ago the United States joined 52 other countries in signing the 1981 landmine protocol, formally known as the "Second Protocol to the 1981 United Nations Convention on Prohibitions or Restrictions on the Use of Certain Conventional Weapons Which May be Deemed To Be Excessively Injurious or To Have Indiscriminate Effects."

The landmine protocol seeks to regulate the use of "mines" (any munition placed under, on or near the ground or other surface area and designed to be detonated or exploded by the presence, proximity or contact of a person), "booby-traps" (devices designed to kill or injure when a person disturbs or approaches an apparently harmless object or performs an apparently safe act), and certain other devices actuated by remote control or automatically after a lapse of time and designed to kill, injure or damage.

The protocol prohibits the direct use of mines against civilians, and their indiscriminate use, such as by a method of delivery that cannot be directed at a specific military objective or that may be expected to kill or injure civilians. It prohibits the use of mines in densely populated areas unless certain measures are taken to warn civilians. It also prohibits the remote delivery (for example, by aircraft) of mines unless their location can be accurately recorded or they contain a neutralizing mechanism designed to render them harmless when they no longer serve a military purpose. The protocol also contains a commitment by the contracting parties to record the location of minefields and, after the cessation of hostilities, take measures to protect civilians from mines and inform the United Nations of their location.

**Protocol Ratification Stalled**

When the United States signed the landmine protocol April 8, 1982, the Reagan administration expressed its strong support by including this statement as a footnote attached to the document:

> "The United States Government
> welcomes the adoption of this Con-
> vention, and hopes that all States will
> give the most serious consideration to
> ratification or accession. We believe
> that the Convention represents a
> positive step forward in efforts to
> minimize injury or damage to the civilian
> population in time of armed conflict.
> Our signature of the Convention reflects
> general willingness of the United States
> to adopt practical and reasonable
> provisions concerning the conduct of
> military operations, for the purpose of
> protecting noncombatants."

The landmine protocol focused attention on the international threat to civilians from landmines and contains many potentially important limitations on their use. But so far the protocol has had little practical effect. Since 1983, when the protocol entered into force, the use of landmines has multiplied, resulting in the crippling and deaths of many more thousands of non-combatants.

The carnage continues to spread because few countries have shown an interest in limiting conventional weapons, and underdeveloped countries have been particularly resistant to limits on weapons they can afford. If the protocol is to become an effective barrier to indiscriminate use of anti-personnel landmines, a major effort to gain wider adherence to it must be launched. This will take U.S. leadership.

Unfortunately, the United States is in the embarrassing position of having signed, but not yet ratified, the 1981 U.N. convention and its three accompanying protocols governing the use of non-detectable fragments, landmines, and incendiary weapons. Although the United States encouraged other countries to ratify the convention—and enough did so for it to enter into force on December 2, 1983—neither the Reagan nor Bush administrations submitted it to the Senate for ratification. To this day, the convention and its three protocols—including the widely supported landmine protocol—languish in "ratification limbo." The fact that only 32 countries have ratified the convention is almost certainly due, in part, to the failure of the United States to ratify it and to then pressure others to do likewise.

The failure of the Reagan and Bush administrations to seek ratification of the convention or any of its three protocols was due partly to a dispute with Congress over ratification of two earlier, unrelated international agreements: protocols to the 1949 Geneva Conventions on the laws of war, both of which the United States signed in 1977. The Reagan administration supported ratification of the more limited Protocol II of the 1949 conventions (which extend some of the laws of war protections to a wider range of conflicts), but the Senate Foreign Relations Committee has not acted, waiting for the administration to also submit the more comprehensive Protocol I of the 1949 conventions (which broadens the laws of war protections). This logjam was partly responsible for the Reagan and Bush administrations' refusal to submit for ratification the 1981 convention and its protocols—including the landmine protocol.

While there has also been disagreement within the executive branch over other parts of the 1981 convention containing the landmine protocol, particularly the protocol on incendiary weapons, there appears to be virtually no opposition within the Defense or State departments to ratification of the landmine protocol itself. But because of the 1981 convention's link to other internationally accepted protocols to the 1949 Geneva Conventions on the laws of war, the United States—by failing to ratify the landmine protocol—is losing the leadership role it would have in seeking further limits on the use of landmines against civilian populations.

## An Early Task for Clinton

The Clinton administration should immediately review *all* the laws of war agreements on which the Reagan and Bush administrations failed to act, with a view to sending them to the Senate for prompt ratification. If there are aspects of these agreements that require reservations by the United States on national security grounds, that should also be recommended by the new administration and considered by the Senate. But whatever happens on these other agreements, the Clinton administration should seek rapid ratification of the landmine protocol. We can afford no further delay.

By imposing a unilateral moratorium on the sale, export or transfer of anti-personnel landmines, my amendment to the FY93 defense authorization bill sets an example for other countries to do likewise. The next step is for President Clinton to use the influence that accrues from setting an example with this policy of unilateral restraint to negotiate a binding international ban on the sale, export and transfer of anti-personnel mines.

This will not be easy. At least 35 countries manufacture landmines and any sale or transfer restrictions might cause more countries to develop at least a rudimentary production capability. Moreover, monitoring the transfer of a weapon that can fit in a shoebox is far more difficult than monitoring missile shipments. On the positive side, landmines are cheap, and restraints on exports would be less vulnerable to the enormous economic incentives to export that pose daunting obstacles for other arms sales restraints. Nor are landmines the major tool of foreign policy that other arms sales have become.

If an international ban on exports proves elusive, it should be possible to obtain agreement among supplier countries, perhaps as part of negotiations already underway for restraint in conventional arms sales, to limit transfers of anti-personnel landmines to countries that have ratified the landmine protocol, or give a bilateral undertaking to potential suppliers to abide by its terms. This could provide leverage, ensuring that more countries adhere to the limitations specified in the protocol as a condition to continued access to landmines.

## The United States Can Lead

While the ultimate goal should be an international agreement outlawing these inhumane weapons, it is very unlikely that an outright ban will occur soon. In the meantime, the U.S. export moratorium can move us toward global export restraints, and U.S. ratification of the landmine protocol can give new momentum to a global campaign to limit the use of landmines. It would also set the stage for addressing the protocol's three principal weaknesses: the lack of compliance and verification procedures; overly modest limitations on the use of anti-personnel landmines; and the current international apathy and lack of interest, as manifest by the small number of countries that have ratified the protocol so far.

The first of these weaknesses, the lack of compliance procedures, was raised by the United States when it signed the convention. At the time, the Reagan administration also included the following as an official statement attached to the document:

> "[W]e want to emphasize that formal adherence by States to agreements restricting the use of weapons in armed conflict would be of little purpose if the parties were not firmly committed to taking every appropriate step to ensure compliance with those restrictions after their entry into force. It would be the firm intention of the United States and, we trust, all other parties to utilize the procedures and remedies provided by this Convention, and by the general laws of war, to see to it that all parties to the Convention meet their obligations under it. *The United States strongly supported proposals by other countries during the Conference to include special procedures for dealing with compliance matters, and reserves the right to propose at a later date additional procedures and remedies, should this prove necessary, to deal with such problems.*" (Emphasis added.)

For the protocol to have any significant impact in curtailing the worldwide carnage, there must be stronger incentives to comply with its limitations during conflict. In December, the required 10 years will have elapsed since the protocol entered into force, and any country that is a party to it may then petition for review. With support from the former Soviet states, a consensus for effective compliance and verification procedures may be within reach.

Because the United States has not ratified the protocol, it cannot call for a review conference. France has indicated that is plans to press for one, however, and as a signatory the United States could actively participate. A review conference will open the door to modifications of the protocol to establish an effective basis for monitoring compliance—such as an international registry under U.N. auspices—of national stockpiles of numbers and types of landmines, a list of facilities where anti-personnel landmines are manufactured and notification of sales or transfers of anti-personnel landmines.

**Lessons From Other Agreements**

One of the most successful arms limitation compliance mechanisms has been the concept of a Standing Consultative Commission (SCC) established under the Strategic Arms Limitations Talks (SALT I) agreements, and being continued under another name in the Strategic Arms Reduction treaties (START I and II). As a forum for addressing questions of interpretation of treaty provisions as well as resolving compliance issues, the SCC could offer a model for managing a compliance regime under the landmine protocol.

Another practical compliance measure could be to apply the voluntary "fact-finding" mechanism already in existence under Article 90 of the 1977 Protocol I to the 1949 Geneva Conventions. Under this regime, upon complaint to the fact-finding body, parties to the agreement would agree to permit this international group of experts to seek information that would allow other states to determine whether the landmine protocol is being observed. When the Clinton administration carries out its review of the 1977 protocols, it should agree to participate in this international fact-finding mechanism, as many of our allies have already done. However, applying the Geneva Conventions' fact-finding regime could require amendment to the landmine protocol, as would some of the other measures I have suggested.

Some arms control experts consider this risky because it might weaken, rather than strengthen, the current limitations. Others contend that it should be possible to find acceptable ways to make the Article 90 mechanism apply to the landmine protocol, without amending the protocol itself. That is an approach worth considering. However if additional useful—and feasible—limitations on the use of anti-personnel landmines can be identified, I believe reopening the landmine protocol to amendment is a risk worth taking if it is to become more than a symbolic measure.

A major weakness of the landmine protocol is that it applies only to international conflicts. The majority of today's conflicts are internal, or a mixture of internal and international. The International Committee of the Red Cross has rightly suggested that the protocol be modified to apply to internal conflicts as well. But the difficulty and controversy of implementing such a step should not be underestimated. Many developing countries, while prepared to see the laws of war (such as the landmine protocol) apply to international conflicts, are opposed to their application to civil wars or insurgencies. Nevertheless, if the landmine protocol is to be an effective protection of civilians against indiscriminate use of anti-personnel landmines, we are going to have to press for an extension of the protocol to internal conflicts as well.

The landmine protocol's specific limitations should also be strengthened. For example, the protocol permits the use of remotely delivered mines, such as those scattered by aircraft, even if they have no means of being deactivated, as long as the user maintains records of where the mines are located. This is unacceptable.

The United States should therefore propose modifications that sharply limit the kinds of landmines that may be manufactured and used, and the manner in which they are deployed. For example, only landmines that deactivate without detonating after a finite period of time should be permitted. Deployment of landmines by projectile or aircraft should be prohibited; it is simply not possible to ensure that they will be deployed in a way that guarantees they will not endanger civilians. While these steps fall short of a total ban on the use of landmines, they could, if coupled with an effective compliance mechanism, significantly reduce the number of civilian casualties.

As indicated earlier, getting these changes will not be easy, but the first step is for the United States to ratify the landmine protocol. We should then work to ensure that the ideas just outlined (many of them incorporated in our own one-year unilateral export moratorium law and its accompanying policy statement) gain the kind of support and consensus needed to change dramatically the way landmines are viewed—and used—around the world.

Landmines obviously are not weapons of mass destruction as are nuclear and chemical weapons, but they have resulted in far more casualties because they are used so widely and indiscriminately. The end of the Cold War has rekindled interest in seeing the United Nations finally become the forum for resolving conflicts and global problems envisioned by its founders. With the 10th anniversary of the landmine protocol at hand and the recent inauguration of a global campaign against landmines by non-governmental organizations, the United States has an opportunity to show real leadership on an important arms control issue with no risk to national security, and to do something concrete to begin to stop the slaughter of innocent people.

## APPENDIX 5

Excerpts from:

# HIDDEN KILLERS

## The Global Problem
## with Uncleared Landmines

*A Report on International Demining
prepared by the*

## United States Department of State
## Political-Military Affairs Bureau
## Office of International Security Operations

IN IMPLEMENTATION OF SECTION 1364 OF THE
NATIONAL DEFENSE AUTHORIZATION ACT FOR
FISCAL YEAR 1993

# TABLE OF CONTENTS

# EXECUTIVE SUMMARY

The State Department estimates that there are more than 85 million uncleared landmines scattered in 62 countries around the world, and more are being laid each day. Roughly 150 people around the world are killed or injured by landmines each week. Most of these are civilians.

Uncleared landmines pose a significant challenge to the achievement of key U.S. foreign policy objectives. They inhibit the repatriation of refugees, hinder economic reconstruction and development, and provide a continuing element of chaos in countries striving for political stability.

The traditional use of mines is as obstacles to movement, laid in mapped minefields by organized military units. To be effective barriers to movement, such minefields must be covered by defending fire. Uncovered minefields are quickly breached by standard military breaching techniques and equipment. However, the last two decades has seen an increasing use of landmines in non-traditional ways. Increasingly, guerilla and terrorist groups are using landmines to achieve political and economic, rather than military, objectives.

Landmines laid by insurgent forces are commonly used to disrupt the political and economic infrastructure of the state, and to place strains upon the social fabric of the society as a whole. In response, mines are often laid by government forces to protect or defend key economic infrastructure. Mines are commonly placed by both sides on roads and railways, around bridges, along power lines, and around water plants and irrigation systems. Such mines isolate the national infrastructure in many countries making it difficult to maintain or improve roads, bridges, sanitation facilities, power supplies, and agricultural productivity. This in turn creates economic dislocation that often exacerbates local problems and makes countries ever more dependent upon foreign aid.

The economic impact of these uncleared landmines is significant. Even a few uncleared landmines laid in arable land essentially make that land unproductive for agricultural use until civilians are confident that the mines have been cleared both from the land and from water delivery systems. The disruption of the transportation system produced by even a few mines results in local scarcities of products, lessened exports and balances of the hard currency they bring, inflation, and sometimes famine. Economic infrastructure such as bridges, roads, and powerlines, are denied regular

i

maintenance and consequently breakdown. Finally, the local healthcare system in most countries is inadequate to provide the high level of care required by mine victims. For example, there are currently more than 20,000 amputees in Angola who were victims of landmines. The surgical facilities and the medicines required to treat mine victims on this scale simply do not exist in many countries.

It is one of the characteristics of mines that while they are extremely easy to lay, they are also extremely difficult to detect and destroy. The technology does not yet exist that would allow the standoff detection and/or destruction of all of the mines in a minefield. The military, for whom mine detection and removal equipment are created, do not do demining. The military mission is to clear a lane through, or breach, a minefield. The military typically blows a lane through a minefield, followed by plows and rakes that move most of the remaining mines to the side, so that troops and equipment can move speedily through the obstacle. Unfortunately, this means that most military countermine equipment is not currently configured to be of much use for wide area mine clearance. Landmines are detected and removed by personnel equipped with hand-held mine detectors and non-metallic prods. Many of the lesser developed countries in which landmines were laid do not have even this level of training or equipment with which to remove them.

The U.S. State Department has moved forward to address this issue. In FY93 the U.S. State Department, including USAID, allocated more than $9 million for demining projects in Afghanistan, Mozambique, Somalia, Cambodia, and Central America. In FY94 the State Department hopes to more than double that allocation. These funds will be used to fund training and equipment purchases that will allow afflicted nations to remove the landmines themselves. In addition, some funds will be used to hire expert demining contractors to demine certain specific objectives, such as road systems. For the near future, the focus of State Department allocations will be to provide countries with the ability and equipment to remove landmines themselves.

In addition to working to help countries remove uncleared landmines by training them in manual mineclearing techniques and providing hand held detection equipment, the U.S. needs to emphasize the development of wide-area mine clearing techniques. The DOD has already begun to take steps to address this issue, and while demining will remain a low-tech procedure for the near future, long term development may eventually bring a high tech solution to this global problem.

# INTRODUCTION

From Afghanistan to Nicaragua, from Angola to Cambodia, the world is littered with uncleared landmines. Landmines may be the most toxic and widespread pollution facing mankind. In a time of high-tech, target-specific weaponry, landmines are perhaps the weapons most consistently dangerous to noncombatants. They kill soldiers and civilians alike, without preference. Bombs can be aimed at military targets, bullets fired by soldiers at other soldiers, artillery directed by forward observers; but, while landmines can be employed for legitimate military purposes, they are by nature hidden underground and kill or wound whoever triggers them. They do not differentiate between tanks and relief trucks, soldiers or children, and can remain deadly for decades.

Inexpensive and easy to lay, mines have become the weapon of choice in many developing countries. Some Antipersonnel (AP) mines can be bought for less than $3 per mine, and some Antitank mines are available for less than $75 each. They are readily available on the international market to any party with cash. In addition, for years landmine warfare was an integral part of the tactical doctrine taught by Soviet advisors to their Third World clients. This doctrine emphasized the use of massive minefields to protect strategic areas and to form barriers designed to channel enemy forces into fields of fire. During the height of its influence, the Soviet Union and its allies provided tens of millions of landmines to client states around the world. Unfortunately, once the Soviet advisors left, the disciplined military use of mines that they taught, including the mapping of active minefields, disappeared. Instead, large stockpiles of effective mines were left in the hands of forces with neither the skill nor the inclination to lay and map their minefields in a disciplined manner. Mines are now routinely used as weapons of terror; and in countries such as Angola, Cambodia, and Mozambique, where knowledge of the location of old minefields has been lost, mines have become indiscriminate menaces to everyone, soldier and civilian alike.

The deadly residue of decades of civil strife and regional conflict, landmines kill or wound more than 150 people per week worldwide - most of them unarmed civilians. Children fall easy prey to landmines because they often wander unaware through areas marked by their elders, or because childish curiosity causes them to turn brightly colored mines into play things. Farmers are victimized because survival often requires that they plant or harvest crops in fields were mines have been laid. Women are maimed or killed by landmines as they fetch water from communal wells, or work in the fields. Landmines inhibit the repatriation of refugees, impede the reconstruction of rural economies, isolate impoverished and often starving populations, and provide a continuing element of chaos in countries striving for stability.

Our best estimate is that there are roughly 85-90 million uncleared landmines in the world today. This estimate is based on survey data contained in this report, as well as data gathered from host governments and various non-governmental organizations (NGOs). However, it is important to note that this data is inexact. It is impossible to give an exact estimate of the number of uncleared landmines laid around the world. By their nature mines are extremely difficult to locate. They are specifically made to lie hidden underground, undetected. Most nations do not themselves know the locations or numbers of landmines laid on their soil. Therefore, the numbers within this report should be viewed as the best, most reliable, estimates that could be gathered.

Given the enormity of the uncleared landmine problem, it is obvious that there is no quick solution. Locating uncleared landmines is a labor-intensive, slow, dangerous, low-technology operation. Destruction of uncleared landmines is even slower, more labor intensive, and extremely dangerous. It is one of the grim ironies of landmines that they are so easy to lay, and yet so difficult and dangerous to find and destroy.

Mines inhibit the return of refugees dislocated by war or civil unrest. In Afghanistan, land mines are a major impediment to the repatriation of the remaining 2 million refugees in Pakistan and the 1.5 million in Iran. For those who have already begun their journey home, the greatest danger from landmines occurs not on their trip, but rather as they attempt to resettle and resume productive lives. They are not used to living with mines, and do not have the local knowledge which would allow them to avoid dangerous areas. As a consequence, the ICRC reports a significant increase in mine injuries since the rate of repatriation surged in the summer of 1992.

The impact of uncleared landmines on a developing economy is tremendous. During civil strife or regional conflict it is common to lay mines around key economic installations such as electric plants and powerlines, water treatment plants, key road nets, major market centers, warehouses and harbor installations, and government buildings. These are the key installations required to support a rebuilding economy. When the economic infrastructure has been isolated by landmines, it can not sustain economic development. As a consequence, economic reconstruction is delayed until the roads, the electric power system, and the water system, etc. can be cleared of landmines.

3

In Sudan, Somalia, Ethiopia, and Mozambique landmines have
isolated regions and populations stricken by drought,
exacerbating the famine.  In such areas farmers can no longer
plant their fields for fear of being killed by landmines.
Landmines also prevent aid from reaching stricken populations.
Mined river banks, water plants, and irrigation systems prevent
farmers from delivering water to drought stricken crops.  In
regions of Southern Sudan, landmines are reported to have
created nearly impenetrable barriers to movement, effectively
trapping thousands of people in an enormous, impoverished,
drought-stricken prison.  Unless these minefields can be
breached, some relief organizations believe that Southern Sudan
could face mass starvation on a huge scale .

On the positive side, it is not immediately necessary to
remove every one of the roughly 85 million landmines currently
in place around the world.  Those landmines laid in remote
areas, away from population centers, that do not pose a direct
threat to local inhabitants, can be cordoned off.  In such
areas mine awareness campaigns are essential to educate the
local populace.  Perhaps as many as 30% of the mines in the
world fall into this category.  However, it has to be
recognized that this is only a temporary solution.  For
example, as population pressures have mounted in Egypt, the
Egyptian government has begun to search for ways to clear and
develop land sewn with World War II landmines.  These mines,
having been marked off and left untouched for 40 years are
proving extremely difficult to detect and clear.

Cutting off the supply of additional landmines can help
contain the size of the global landmine problem.  However, it
is the detection, removal, and destruction of landmines already
in place that is the most critical need for populations
affected by landmines.  Unfortunately, while landmines are
inexpensive, and easy to lay, they are generally difficult to
detect and extremely dangerous to remove or destroy.  Few
countries possess sophisticated mine detection equipment, and
even the most sophisticated mine detection equipment still
requires mine detection personnel to enter the minefield.
Contrary to popular belief, there is not yet a reliable
standoff mine detection system.  In general, the most reliable
piece of mine detection equipment is the non-metallic probe,
which in many parts of the world is a wooden stick.  Mine
detection personnel use these to probe the ground in front of
them, locating mines by touch.  Needless to say, this is an
extremely dangerous undertaking.

The removal and destruction of landmines poses additional
problems.  It is almost impossible for even the most
experienced ordnance disposal teams to be sure that they have
removed every landmine from an area - and every landmine left
in the ground is a potential killer.  Even a 99% success rate
in a minefield with 1000 mines leaves ten mines uncleared.
Quite simply, demining is a business in which anything less
than 100% accuracy costs lives, and 100% accuracy is difficult
to achieve.

# CONCLUSION

BY

DAVID GOWDEY
OFFICE OF INTERNATIONAL SECURITY OPERATIONS
BUREAU OF POLITICAL - MILITARY AFFAIRS
U.S. DEPARTMENT OF STATE

It is in the United States' national interest to provide demining assistance. Uncleared landmines impede the achievement of U.S. foreign policy objectives in a large number of countries. Uncleared landmines prevent the repatriation of refugees, inhibit the reconstruction of war damaged economies, and provide a continuing element of chaos in countries striving for political stability. Many of these countries - such as Kuwait, Afghanistan, El Salvador, Honduras, and Lebanon - are vital to U.S. political, strategic, and economic interests.

Contributions that assist in the removal of uncleared landmines are the essential foundations for most of our foreign aid programs. It is useless to donate farm equipment and agricultural assistance to countries in which farmers can not plant crops because their fields are sewn with landmines. By the same count, it is illogical to contribute money for the repair and rebuilding of national infrastructure if those roads and bridges are isolated by landmines. The U.N. Demining Expert, Brigadier Patrick Blagden RA (Ret.), notes that it is vital to get relief agencies to understand that demining is the fundamental precursor for any type of foreign assistance. Until the landmines are removed, money spent on other projects will not be fully effective.

In an era of shrinking budgets and scarce resources it is inevitable that questions will be raised as to whether the United States should be involved in demining. The U.S. bears little blame for the global problem with uncleared landmines, having been a selective exporter of limited numbers of landmines. Less than 15% of the landmines in countries with uncleared landmine problems originated in the U.S. By any definition, the U.S. has limited responsibility for the global uncleared landmine problem, and so, some would say, has relatively little obligation to assist in the expensive and dangerous job of removing and destroying these landmines.

Such arguments ignore the fact that since the U.S. is one of the few countries with the technology, expertise, and equipment to provide demining assistance, there is a strong humanitarian imperative to do so. The U.N. and nongovernmental organizations cannot bear the burden of demining alone - they lack the resources and expertise. If humanity is to make an impact on the global problem with uncleared landmines it is imperative that the U.S., and the other industrialized nations, contribute technology, expertise, and resources. What is certain is that, should the U.S. as a nation decide not to provide demining assistance to countries in need, many innocent people will die needlessly in years to come from landmine explosions.

In the past, the U.S. approach to demining was disjointed and relatively inefficient. Resources were allocated by a variety of agencies and bureaus on a case by case basis, and only the scarcity of resources prevented excessive duplication of effort. In the twelve months since June of 1992, the U.S. State Department, including USAID, allocated approximately $9 million for demining assistance in Afghanistan, Central America, Mozambique, Cambodia, and Somalia. The Department of Defense also conducted limited demining operations in Somalia in support of Operation Restore Hope.

In February of 1993, the Department of State established the interagency Demining Coordination Group (DCG), consisting of representatives from various regional and functional bureaus within the State Department, the Department of Defense, and the Joint Chiefs of Staff. The objective of this group is to develop a comprehensive global strategy for the allocation of U.S. Government demining resources. Such a strategy will allow the U.S. government to pool demining resources from various departments and agencies, prioritize and focus our demining assistance, and avoid duplication of effort and unnecessary expenditures. The DCG has been able to draw upon the expert knowledge of personnel from the U.S. Army's Foreign Science and Technology Center at Charlottesville, Virginia; the Office of the Program Manager for Mines, Countermine, and Demolitions program, and the U.S. Army Countermine Research, Development and Engineering Center at Fort Belvoir, Virginia. In addition, the group has worked very closely with Mr. Patrick Blagden, the U.N. Demining Expert, and has drawn freely on his expert knowledge.

In considering the question of what type of assistance the U.S. government can provide to countries afflicted by uncleared landmines, the Demining Coordination Group carefully examined U.S. countermine resources. Certain parameters soon became clear. The first of these is that U.S. military personnel will not physically remove landmines. There is a general agreement that the global problem with uncleared landmines is a humanitarian problem that does not affect U.S. interests closely enough to justify risking the lives of American Soldiers and Marines in foreign minefields. The adverse publicity that would result from significant

American casualties clearing foreign mines from foreign
minefields would adversely impact all U.S. demining
assistance. The second parameter that became clear is that the
U.S. has tremendous training and technological assets that
could be brought to bear on the demining problem, but that
these assets are currently focused elsewhere. It will be
necessary to refocus their attention on the demining issue.
Finally, it became clear that U.S. assistance will have to be
conducted with limited resources.

Given these parameters, it appears that the U.S. Government
can make its greatest contribution towards solving the global
problem with uncleared landmines by providing assistance in
four general areas: Education, Technical Expertise, Equipment
and Technology, and diplomatic efforts to restrict the sale and
use of landmines. Contractors, while extremely knowledgeable
and efficient, are expensive. Given limited resources, the
U.S. Government will likely fund contractors to conduct
specific demining operations, or to work in areas where there
is no central authority. However, the focus of our efforts
will probably be in the following four categories.

## EDUCATION

From March 8 to April 8, 1993 the U.S. Army conducted its
first demining training course for foreign instructors at the
School of the Americas at Fort Benning, Georgia. This program
trained 15 instructors from various Latin American countries in
the skills they will need to supervise on the ground the OAS
demining program in Nicaragua. Reviews of this program by
outside experts, Army personnel, Interamerican Defense Board
officials, and the students themselves were outstanding.
Results in the field have justified these assessments. The
students are competent to handle most situations they might
encounter in clearing landmines in Nicaragua, and they know
that if there is a situation that is beyond the scope of their
knowledge, U.S. military experts are available to assist them.
This IADB program, under OAS auspices, was largely funded by
U.S. contributions.

This training program has provided an excellent model for
the type of educational demining assistance the U.S. can
provide. The Army has preserved all of the course materials
for this training program, and, after translating the materials
into appropriate languages, are prepared to teach students from
all around the world. The costs of this type of training are
low, less than $4,000 per student, and the results are
impressive.

In addition to training courses run in the U.S., the U.S. Special Forces Command has conducted successful demining training courses under UN auspices in the field in Afghanistan. Lessons learned from this course have been incorporated in course materials, and the U.S. Special Forces command now believes that it has an excellent training course that it can present in the field to local populations. The linguistic and teaching skills of the Special Forces personnel make them extremely flexible in tailoring their course of instruction to meet local conditions. In chaotic political situations, where a central government is not strong enough to sustain a national demining effort, Special Forces training programs can be used to begin demining efforts on a regional, provincial, or village level.

## TECHNICAL EXPERTISE

The U.S. Department of Defense has one of the greatest collection of experts in the field of mines, mine detection, mine removal, mine destruction, and countermine technology in the world. The human resources available at places like the U.S. Army's Foreign Science Technology Center in Charlottesville, Virginia; the U.S. Army Belvoir Research, Development and Engineering Center at Fort Belvoir, Virginia; the Office of the Program Manager for Mines, Countermines, and Demolitions at Picatinny Arsenal, N.J., and the Department of Defense EOD experts at the Naval facility at Indian Head, Maryland, are impressive.

These experts are capable of providing technical advice on any facet of demining, from equipment to render-safe procedures. Unfortunately, their talents are being underutilized in terms of demining. A cumbersome declassification system often prevents them from providing even the most innocent information to other governments or organizations on a timely basis. This information is quite often of life saving importance, and the tortuous efforts it has taken to get critical information within regulations to friendly demining personnel has been a source of constant frustration to all concerned.

One of the most important contributions these personnel could make is the assembly of a comprehensive landmine data base that includes known technical information about all mines in the world. Such a data base has been assembled, but it is classified. An unclassified version should be created that could be given to foreign demining personnel or the U.N.

Understandably, questions have been raised about the liability of the U.S. Government should such information be improperly used. However, the critical importance of this type of data base being made publicly available should provide sufficient incentive to work out some form of legal release system. Fear of lawsuits should not delay the release of such important humanitarian information, for more people are killed as a result of the lack of such information than will ever be killed as a result of its publication.

In addition to the data base, it is important that an official communication channel be established in the demining community. There needs to be a channel through which foreign and U.N. personnel can request technical information from the U.S. government and receive a speedy answer. The Demining Coordination Group is working on establishing such a channel.

## TECHNOLOGY AND EQUIPMENT

As noted in Chapter 3, current U.S. countermine technology is not generally designed for wide-area mine clearance (demining). Since the military generally requires only that its countermine technology enable troops to quickly brief minefield obstacles, military procurement specifications for countermine equipment are tailored toward minefield breaching. Much of this same technology, especially detection equipment and mechanical mine removal equipment (flails, plows, and rakes) has demining as well as breaching applications. With some modifications, the technology could prove effective in the demining role. The DCG and DOD are working to identify ongoing research programs with demining applications that can be transferred to foreign governments. However, because demining is not a military mission, and there is not a military requirement for demining equipment, there are few resources to fund the development of true demining equipment and technology.

As a consequence, the U.S. has generally been limited to giving in-minefield detection equipment, and equipment with which to conduct manual mine clearing operations, to countries that it is assisting with mine clearing efforts. While the significance of such assistance should not be underestimated, there is undoubtedly a place for mechanical equipment that can rapidly and efficiently clear roads, and for stand-off detection equipment. Mine neutralizing technology would also be of inestimable value in solving global demining problems. Perhaps ironically, the development of such technology, technology that permits the stand-off detection of minefields, detection of nonmetallic mines, and new clearance techniques would be high payoff programs that would give the U.S. Armed Forces much greater countermine capabilities.

Given resource limitations, the modification of existing technology and the development of new technologies can only be done by the Department of Defense working in conjunction with other agencies such as the Department of Energy. Such a shift in the emphasis of DOD research will only come about as a result of a policy decision by the U.S. government. Until that time, the U.S. government will be limited in the types of resources and equipment it can contribute to the global demining effort.

## DIPLOMATIC EFFORTS

While each of the above categories of assistance is targeted towards the removal or destruction of mines already emplaced, U.S. diplomatic efforts will be targeted more toward the prevention of the emplacement of new mines. As bad as the global problem with uncleared landmines currently is, the problem is daily growing worse. New landmines are being laid on a daily basis in countries like Bosnia Herzegovina, Sudan and Angola. As we remove and destroy existing landmines in one country, others are being laid continents away. Clearly we can not hope to solve the global landmine problem without achieving some limitations on their sale and use.

Recently, there has been a great deal of international attention focused on the idea of an international landmine ban. The ICRC conference held in April of this year in Montreaux, and the London NGO conference in May addressed this topic. In fact, the U.S. has led the way on this issue with its unilateral one year moratorium on the export of landmines for FY 1993. France has announced a similar moratorium, and the EC is looking at enacting a ban on the export of landmines. France has also called for a review conference of the Landmine Protocol of the 1980 Conventional Weapons Convention with the idea of placing stricter international restrictions on the use of landmines.

Unfortunately, the chance of such measures making a significant impact on the numbers and use of landmines around the world is slight. As was shown in Somalia, nations are able to evade national and international restrictions with regards to the procurement of weapons quite easily. European weapons systems that legally should never have been sold or exported to Somalia were found in large numbers in the country by UNITAF forces. In addition, fighting parties in most of the world routinely ignore current international regulations concerning the mapping of minefields and the prohibition on their use against civilian populations. It is unlikely that further restrictions on use will increase their level of compliance.

However, if legal restrictions on the sale and export of landmines are coupled with measures to make all landmines produced in the world more easily detectable and self neutralizing, we might be able to eventually solve this problem. There are roughly 42 mine manufacturing countries in the world today. Such countries could ensure that a sufficient amount of metal were installed in all plastic mines to make them easily detectable by current technology. By the same token, electronic fusing systems powered by limited life batteries are a very simple and inexpensive way to ensure

that landmines do not remain lethal for years after their
employment. More expensive self destructing fuses, such as
those carried by U.S. mines, would be better still. If such an
agreement among mine producing countries could be coupled with
ongoing international efforts to ban the export and restrict
the use of landmines, the effect on the landmine problem would
be extraordinary.

The State Department has begun to review US Government
policy toward this issue. As the U.S. is already in compliance
with most of the measures we are advocating concerning the
manufacture of landmines. the impact on U.S. defense efforts
would be minimal. However, policy decisions will have to be
taken that will allow the State Department to achieve the best
possible agreements in this area consistent with U.S. security
requirements.

CONCLUSION:

It is obvious that the U.S. has a great deal to contribute
towards the global demining effort. U.S. technical expertise
can assist UN and other efforts around the world. U.S.
equipment and technology, if appropriately modified, and new
technology developed, could play a key role in global demining
efforts, as well as providing export earnings for U.S.
companies. Education of local demining personnel is a mission
for which the U.S. government is prepared already. Education,
combined with demining equipment and technical support can give
countries the ability to rid themselves of their landmine
problem.

Given the limited resources available for demining programs
at the present time, it is difficult to provide meaningful
assistance. The Demining Coordination Group is attempting to
locate excess DOD mine detection equipment, medical support
equipment, protective equipment, and general supplies that can
be donated to countries requiring demining assistance. By
coupling this assistance with appropriate training, we can give
many countries with no ability to conduct demining operations
at least a rudimentary capability.

Finally, by focusing our assistance on giving countries the
ability to deal with their internal demining problems, we are
achieving a significant psychological objective as well. The
populations of these countries are the ones that suffer the
most from uncleared landmines. It is they who can most
accurately determine which minefields should be cleared first,
and how demining resources should be allocated. They are the
ones with the most incentive to get the landmines cleared as
soon as possible. All successful demining efforts to date were
completed by countries in the aftermath of World War II.
Countries such as Belgium, the Netherlands, Russia, Germany,
and China dealt themselves with the millions of mines left

littering their soil. They did so in a more effective and efficient manner than any outside power could achieve, and in so doing they gave themselves experience and knowledge of demining operations that they continue to possess today. Not only is it not necessary to have U.S. forces removing minefields in a foreign country, it is undesirable. It is the empowerment of the more than 62 countries with landmine problems to deal with this problem themselves that is, and should be, the goal of U.S. demining policy.

# COUNTRIES WHICH HAVE REPORTED LANDMINE INCIDENTS*

## (GROUPED BY REGION)

### PREPARED BY PM/ISO: DAVID M. GOWDEY

COUNTRY | SEVERITY OF THE PROBLEM (1=Most Severe)

## AFRICA

| COUNTRY | SEVERITY |
|---|---|
| ANGOLA | 1 |
| BOTSWANA | 3 |
| CHAD | 2 |
| DJIBOUTI | 1 |
| EGYPT | 3 |
| ETHIOPIA | 1 |
| LIBERIA | 2 |
| LIBYA | 3 |
| MALAWI | 1 |
| MAURITANIA | 2 |
| MOROCCO | 2 |
| MOZAMBIQUE | 1 |
| NAMIBIA | 3 |
| RWANDA | 2 |
| SOMALIA | 1 |
| SOUTH AFRICA | 3 |
| SUDAN | 1 |
| ZIMBABWE | 2 |

## LATIN AMERICA

| COUNTRY | SEVERITY |
|---|---|
| CHILE | 3 |
| COLOMBIA | 3 |
| COSTA RICA | 3 |
| CUBA | 3 |
| EL SALVADOR | 1 |
| GUATEMALA | 2 |
| HONDURAS | 2 |
| NICARAGUA | 1 |

## EAST ASIA/PACIFIC

| COUNTRY | SEVERITY | |
|---|---|---|
| BURMA | 2 | |
| CAMBODIA | 1 | |
| CHINA | 2 | |
| INDONESIA | 3 | (Sea Mines) |
| LAOS | 2 | |
| MALAYSIA | 3 | |
| NEW CALEDONIA | 3 | |
| THAILAND | 3 | |
| VIETNAM | 1 | |

| COUNTRY | SEVERITY OF THE PROBLEM (1=Most Severe) |
|---|---|
| **EUROPE** | |
| ARMENIA | 2 |
| AZERBAIJAN | 2 |
| BELGIUM | 3 |
| BOSNIA/HERZEGOVINA | 1 |
| BULGARIA | 3 |
| CROATIA | 1 |
| CYPRUS | 3 |
| ESTONIA | 3 |
| GEORGIA | 2 |
| GERMANY | 3 |
| THE NETHERLANDS | 3 |
| LATVIA | 3 |
| LITHUANIA | 3 |
| POLAND | 3 |
| RUSSIA | 3 |
| SERBIA | 3 |
| TADJIKSTAN | 2 |
| TURKEY | 3 |
| | |
| **NEAR EAST** | |
| IRAQ | 1 |
| IRAN | 2 |
| ISRAEL | 2 |
| KUWAIT | 1 |
| LEBANON | 2 |
| OMAN | 3 |
| SYRIA | 2 |
| YEMEN | 2 |
| | |
| **SOUTH ASIA** | |
| AFGHANISTAN | 1 |
| INDIA | 3 |
| PAKISTAN | 3 |
| SRI LANKA | 2 |

NOTE: Countries which have had landmine incidents may not have reported a problem with uncleared landmines. Such incidents may have been isolated.

# APPENDIX 6

FOR IMMEDIATE RELEASE
[April 21, 1993]

CONTACT: ANN STINGLE
202-639-3395
(H) 703-323-9232

## STATEMENT BY ELIZABETH DOLE ON THE USE OF ANTIPERSONNEL MINES

Elizabeth Dole, president of the American Red Cross issued the following statement today in support of the International Red Cross symposium on the use of antipersonnel mines:

*The American Red Cross joins with the International Committee of Red Cross in condemning the pervasive horror in our world due to wanton and indiscriminate use of antipersonnel mines. The scale of human suffering caused by the senseless and inhumane use of landmines should not be tolerated by the international community. Each month, 800 people are killed and 450 people are injured by land mines. Little children are killed or maimed, long after the fighting, by landmines that are scattered like deadly toys where they live and play. The use of these weapons of terror is prohibited by international humanitarian law and immediate compliance must be demanded by all men and women of conscience.*

# RED CROSS CALLS FOR END TO INDISCRIMINATE USE OF LANDMINES

Washington, April 21--The American Red Cross today joined its international counterparts in appealing for an end to the carnage caused by the indiscriminate use of anti-personnel mines. The Red Cross cites U.N. Figures saying there are more than 100 million landmines scattered throughout the world, most undetectable until it is too late.

At a press conference held in Geneva today at the opening of a symposium on mines, the International Committee of the Red Cross and the Federation of Red Cross and Red Crescent Societies pointed out that landmines are increasingly used to spread terror among civilians and to keep them away from sources of food. The presence of large numbers of unrecorded and undetectable landmines makes vast tracts of land inaccessible, prevents refugees and displaced persons from returning home and hinders humanitarian work.

Elizabeth Dole, president of the American Red Cross, said "Each month, 800 people are killed and 450 people are injured by landmines. Little children are killed or maimed, long after the fighting is over, by landmines that are scattered like deadly toys where they live and play."

Participants in the symposium this week are representatives of arms manufacturers, humanitarian organizations, government officials, mine clearance specialists, military officers, doctors and lawyers.

The use of mines is covered by general rules of international humanitarian law governing the use of all weapons:

- Parties to a conflict must always distinguish between civilians and combatants. Civilians may not be directly attacked and indiscriminate attacks and the use of indiscriminate weapons are prohibited.
- It is prohibited to use weapons which cause unnecessary suffering. The use of weapons whose damaging effects are disproportionate to their military purpose are prohibited.

The American Red Cross has several projects to help those who have been victimized by mines and other weapons. One is the American Red Cross Prosthesis Program, funded by USAID. It provides technical assistance, equipment and materials to programs aimed at assisting disabled victims of war to live their lives more fully. Sites for the project include Mozambique, Angola and Cambodia. The American Red Cross also has a bi-lateral prothesis project for war victims at Kom Pong Speu, Cambodia.

**SEC. 1364. REPORT ON INTERNATIONAL MINE CLEARING EFFORTS IN REFUGEE SITUATIONS.**

(a) FINDINGS.—The Congress finds that—

(1) an estimated 10-20 million mines are scattered across Cambodia, Afghanistan, Somalia, Angola, and other countries which have experienced conflict; and

(2) refugee repatriation and other humanitarian programs are being seriously hampered by the widespread use of anti-personnel mines in regional conflicts and civil wars.

(b) REPORT.—(1) The President shall provide a report on international mine clearing efforts in situations involving the repatriation and resettlement of refugees and displaced persons.

(2) The report shall include the following:

(A) An assessment of mine clearing needs in countries to which refugees and displaced persons are now returning, or are likely to return within the near future, including Cambodia, Angola, Afghanistan, Somalia and Mozambique, and an assessment of current international efforts to meet the mine clearing needs in the countries covered by the report.

(B) An analysis of the specific types of mines in the individual countries assessed and the availability of technology and assets within the international community for their removal.

(C) An assessment of what additional technologies and assets would be required to complete, expedite or reduce the costs of mine clearing efforts.

(D) An evaluation of the availability of technologies and assets within the United States Government which, if called upon, could be employed to augment or complete mine clearing efforts in the countries covered by the report.

(E) An evaluation of the desirability, feasibility and potential cost of United States assistance on either a unilateral or multilateral basis in such mine clearing operations.

(3) The report shall be submitted to the Congress not later than 180 days after the date of the enactment of this Act.

**SEC. 1365. LANDMINE EXPORT MORATORIUM.**                    22 USC 2778
                                                             note.

(a) FINDINGS.—The Congress makes the following findings:

(1) Anti-personnel landmines, which are specifically designed to maim and kill people, have been used indiscriminately in dramatically increasing numbers, primarily in insurgencies in poor developing countries. Noncombatant civilians, including tens of thousands of children, have been the primary victims.

(2) Unlike other military weapons, landmines often remain implanted and undiscovered after conflict has ended, causing untold suffering to civilian populations. In Afghanistan, Cambodia, Laos, Vietnam, and Angola, tens of millions of unexploded landmines have rendered whole areas uninhabitable. In Afghanistan, an estimated hundreds of thousands of people have been maimed and killed by landmines during the 14-year civil war. In Cambodia, more than 20,000 civilians have lost limbs and another 60 are being maimed each month from landmines.

(3) Over 35 countries are known to manufacture landmines, including the United States. However, the United States is not a major exporter of landmines. During the past ten years the Department of State has approved ten licenses for the

commercial export of anti-personnel landmines valued at $980,000, and during the past five years the Department of Defense has approved the sale of 13,156 anti-personnel landmines valued at $841,145.

(4) The United States signed, but has not ratified, the 1981 Convention on Prohibitions or Restrictions on the Use of Certain Conventional Weapons Which May Be Deemed To Be Excessively Injurious or To Have Indiscriminate Effects. The Convention prohibits the indiscriminate use of landmines.

(5) When it signed the Convention, the United States stated: "We believe that the Convention represents a positive step forward in efforts to minimize injury or damage to the civilian population in time of armed conflict. Our signature of the Convention reflects the general willingness of the United States to adopt practical and reasonable provisions concerning the conduct of military operations, for the purpose of protecting noncombatants.".

(6) The President should submit the Convention to the Senate for its advice and consent to ratification, and the President should actively negotiate under United Nations auspices or other auspices an international agreement, or a modification of the Convention, to prohibit the sale, transfer or export of anti-personnel landmines. Such an agreement or modification would be an appropriate response to the end of the Cold War and the promotion of arms control agreements to reduce the indiscriminate killing and maiming of civilians.

(7) The United States should set an example for other countries in such negotiations, by implementing a one-year moratorium on the sale, transfer or export of anti-personnel landmines.

(b) STATEMENT OF POLICY.—(1) It shall be the policy of the United States to seek verifiable international agreements prohibiting the sale, transfer, or export, and further limiting the use, production, possession, and deployment of anti-personnel landmines.

(2) It is the sense of the Congress that the President should actively seek to negotiate under United Nations auspices or other auspices an international agreement, or a modification of the Convention, to prohibit the sale, transfer, or export of anti-personnel landmines.

(c) MORATORIUM ON TRANSFERS OF ANTI-PERSONNEL LANDMINES ABROAD.—For a period of one year beginning on the date of the enactment of this Act—

(1) no sale may be made or financed, no transfer may be made, and no license for export may be issued, under the Arms Export Control Act, with respect to any anti-personnel landmine; and

(2) no assistance may be provided under the Foreign Assistance Act of 1961, with respect to the provision of any anti-personnel landmine.

(e) DEFINITION.—For purposes of this section, the term "anti-personnel landmine" means—

(1) any munition placed under, on, or near the ground or other surface area, or delivered by artillery, rocket, mortar, or similar means or dropped from an aircraft and which is designed to be detonated or exploded by the presence, proximity, or contact of a person;

(2) any device or material which is designed, constructed, or adapted to kill or injure and which functions unexpectedly when a person disturbs or approaches an apparently harmless object or performs an apparently safe act;

(3) any manually-emplaced munition or device designed to kill, injure, or damage and which is actuated by remote control or automatically after a lapse of time.

## Bureau of Politico-Military Affairs

[Public Notice 1727]

## Suspension of Transfers of Anti-Personnel Mines

**AGENCY:** U.S. Department of State.

**ACTION:** Notice.

**SUMMARY:** Notice is hereby given that all licenses, approvals, sales or transfers of landmines specifically designed for anti-personnel use, regardless of method of delivery, are suspended until further notice. Additionally, all existing authorizations for the sale, export, or transfer of such defense articles are revoked until further notice. This action has been taken pursuant to sections 2. 38 and 42 of the Arms Export Control Act, and section 1365 of the National Defense Authorization Act for Fiscal Year 1993.

**EFFECTIVE DATE:** November 25, 1992.

**FOR FURTHER INFORMATION CONTACT:** Terry Davis, Compliance Analysis Division, Office of Defense Trade Controls, Bureau of Politico-Military Affairs, U.S. Department of State. Phone: (703–875–6650).

**SUPPLEMENTARY INFORMATION:** On October 23, the President signed into law the National Defense Authorization Act for Fiscal Year 1993 (Pub. L. 102–484). Section 1365 of that Act contains a statutory moratorium on transfers of anti-personnel landmines to foreign nations. Therefore, effective immediately, it is the policy of the U.S. Government to deny all applications for licenses and other approvals, including letters of offer and acceptance (LOAs). to export or otherwise transfer landmines specifically designed for anti-personnel use to foreign persons or foreign nations. In addition, U.S. manufacturers and exporters and any other affected parties are hereby notified that the Department of State has revoked or suspended all previously issued licenses, approvals, and LOAs authorizing the export, sale, or other transfer of landmines specifically designed for anti-personnel use.

The licenses and approvals that have been revoked or suspended include any manufacturing licenses, technical assistance agreements, technical data, and commercial military exports of any kind involving landmines specifically designed for anti-personnel use. This action also precludes the use in connection with such landmines of any exemptions from licensing or other approval requirements included in the International Traffic in Arms Regulations (ITAR) (22 CFR Parts 120–130).

This action has been taken pursuant to sections 2, 38, and 42 of the Arms Export Control Act (22 U.S.C. 2752, 2778, and 2791), § 126.7 of the ITAR, and section 1365 of the National Defense Authorization Act for FY 1993.

Dated: November 18, 1992.

Pamela L. Frazier,

*Acting Deputy Assistant Secretary, Bureau of Politico-Military Affairs, U.S. Department of State.*

[FR Doc. 92-28460 Filed 11-24-92; 8:45 am]

BILLING CODE 4710-25-M

# APPENDIX 8

STATEMENTS ON INTRODUCED
BILLS AND JOINT RESOLUTIONS

By Mr. LEAHY (for himself, Mr. MITCHELL, Mr. DOLE, Mr. INOUYE, Mr. PELL, Mr. KERREY, Mr. KERRY, Mr. MOYNIHAN, Mr. DeCONCINI, Mr. D'AMATO, Mr. SPECTER, Mr. DODD, Mr. JEFFORDS, Mr. WOFFORD, Mr. SIMON, Mr. LAUTENBERG, Mr. EXON, Mr. KENNEDY, Ms. MIKULSKI, Mr. RIEGLE, Mr. ROCKEFELLER, Mr. BUMPERS, Mr. BRYAN, Mr. HARKIN, Mrs. FEINSTEIN, Mrs. MURRAY, Mr. METZENBAUM, Mr. DASCHLE, Mr. BRADLEY, Mr. GRAHAM, Mr. FORD, Mr. FEINGOLD, Mrs. BOXER, and Mr. LEVIN):

S. 1276. A bill to extend for 3 years the moratorium on the sale, transfer or export of anti-personnel landmines abroad, and for other purposes; to the Committee on Foreign Relations.

LANDMINE MORATORIUM EXTENSION ACT OF 1993

Mr. LEAHY. Mr. President, the United States signed the convention to outlaw the manufacture, possession, and use of chemical weapons. We know what chemical weapons do. They do not distinguish between combatants and innocent victims.

I remember how outraged everyone was in this country when Saddam Hussein used chemical weapons against the Kurds. But I wonder how many people realize that all of the deaths from chemical, biological, even nuclear weapons are only a fraction of the number of people who have been killed or maimed by landmines.

What do chemical and biological weapons have in common with landmines? They do not discriminate. A landmine will blow the leg or the arm off of whoever steps on it. It does not make any difference whether it is a combatant, a civilian, older person, or a child.

Antipersonnel landmines, which are designed specifically to maim and kill people, have been used in dramatically increasing numbers around the world. Unlike other weapons, landmines often remain undiscovered for weeks, months, or years. Sometimes even after a conflict has ended, and people no longer remember what they were fighting about, active landmines are still there.

We have seen the horrifying photographs, photographs like this one of a child with his leg blown off. This child was not a combatant. This child just happened to be in an area where landmines were used, not just as weapons of war but as weapons of terror. And the terror, of course, was imposed not against the combatants but upon this young child who stepped on a landmine and had his leg blown off at the knee, and his arm blown off to the elbow.

Mr. President, I could show hundreds of photographs like this. We have seen what landmines did in Afghanistan where the Russians scattered millions of mines from the air. Hundreds of thousands of people—most of them civilians—have lost limbs, and huge areas of that country today are uninhabitable and will remain that way for decades.

In Cambodia, refugees are finally going home only to be killed or crippled by the millions of landmines that lie hidden in the jungle there. I spoke to one American who runs a program to make artificial legs. He told me "The mines in Cambodia are being cleared one leg, one arm, one life at a time."

The same thing is happening in Mozambique, where this boy lives. He lost both legs above the knee, in a country where he will probably have to earn a living at physical labor. He will walk on these artificial legs for the rest of his life.

Another victim of a landmine, an American, wrote about what happened to him in Vietnam. Let me read what he said:

I was thrown violently through the air. When I threw my arms out in front of me, I saw in shocked amazement that my left arm was gone from above the elbow. A white splintered bone jutted out of a bloody stump of tangled and torn flesh. The flesh on my right arm had been blasted away from the elbow to the hand, and I could see both bones glistening white against bloody pulp.

The horror, the sheer horror, of that statement. But hundreds of thousands of people could say the same thing.

As many as 100 million landmines have been strewn in at least 62 countries. The State Department estimates there are more than 10 million in Afghanistan, 9 million in Angola, 4 million in Cambodia, 3 million in Iraqi Kurdistan, and 2 million each in Somalia, Mozambique, and the former Yugoslavia.

Think of the horror of living day to day in a country where at any moment you could lose a leg, or your life, or your child's life, because of these hidden weapons. Where any open field, or patch of trees, or roadside ditch is a potential death trap. That is a way of life for tens of millions of people around the world.

Today, advanced technologies are used to manufacture landmines that can be scattered by aircraft or artillery tubes, at a rate of more than 1,000 per hour. These mines are by their nature nondiscriminatory, because no one can be sure where they fall.

Four years ago, I started a special fund in the foreign aid program to send American doctors and prosthetists to aid landmine victims abroad. That program has enabled thousands of people crippled by landmines to walk again. But each year the number of landmine victims continues to grow.

I started that program, Mr. President, because I went to a field hospital in Honduras, where I met a young boy who had lost his leg from a landmine. When I asked him which side in the war had put it there, he did not know. What difference did it make? Both sides used landmines. But he was crippled for life, and he was living in the hospital because he had no place else to go. I started the War Victims Fund for people like that Honduran boy.

But I also felt something had to be done to stop this senseless slaughter. I sponsored last year legislation to impose a 1-year moratorium on the sale, transfer, and export abroad of antipersonnel landmines from the United States. The amendment became part of the defense authorization act, and it was signed into law by President Bush on October 23, 1992.

Today, I am introducing legislation to extend the landmine moratorium for 3 years.

I send to the desk and ask for the appropriate referral of my landmine legislation.

The PRESIDING OFFICER. The bill will be received and appropriately referred.

Mr. LEAHY. Mr. President, this legislation is sponsored by myself, Senators MITCHELL, DOLE, INOUYE, PELL, KERREY, KERRY, MOYNIHAN, DECONCINI, D'AMATO, SPECTER, DODD, JEFFORDS; the distinguished Presiding Officer, Mr. WOFFORD; Senators SIMON, LAUTENBERG, EXON, KENNEDY, MIKULSKI, RIEGLE, ROCKEFELLER, BUMPERS, BRYAN, HARKIN, FEINSTEIN, MURRAY, METZENBAUM, DASCHLE, BRADLEY, GRAHAM, FEINGOLD, and FORD.

Mr. President, as is noted by both the Democratic and Republican leaders of the Senate, this is not a partisan issue. It is an issue of humanity.

The landmine moratorium has two purposes. It shows that the United States intends to be a leader in stopping the spread of these insidious weapons. It will also strengthen the position of the United States to negotiate stronger international limits on the sale, manufacture, and use of landmines by setting an example for other nations.

Since last October when the U.S. moratorium took effect, the response has surpassed our expectations.

The President of France announced that France no longer sells or exports antipersonnel landmines, and has called on other European nations to do the same. France has formally requested the United Nations to hold a conference to review the 1980 landmine protocol.

The European Parliament has issued a resolution calling on its members to impose a 5-year moratorium on sales and exports of antipersonnel landmines.

Members of the British Parliament have introduced a resolution calling for an indefinite British moratorium on exports, and for an international ban on exports.

Secretary of State Warren Christopher, testifying before Congress, expressed support for limits on the sale and use of landmines.

The International Committee of the Red Cross sponsored a conference on landmines, attended by representatives of governments including the United States, and nongovernmental organizations.

The American Committee on Red Cross issued a public statement condemning the horror caused by the indiscriminate use of landmines.

The Swedish Red Cross launched a campaign to stop Swedish exports of antipersonnel landmines.

Mr. President, people everywhere want to stop the killing and maiming of civilians by landmines. Our moratorium has showed that it is possible.

At least 300 types of antipersonnel landmines have been manufactured by about 44 countries, including the United States. However, the United States is not a major exporter of landmines. During the past 10 years, the administration has approved only 10 licenses for the commercial export of antipersonnel landmines with a total value of $980,000, and the sale under the Foreign Military Sales Program of only 102,129 antipersonnel landmines.

Obviously, these sales are neither significant in terms of American jobs nor necessary for U.S. security. But they have terrible significance for the victims who are crippled for life, and for their families.

The landmine moratorium does not affect U.S. manufacture, or use of landmines by U.S. forces. Nor does it affect exports of antitank mines. But I would have introduced the moratorium even if it did, because we have to do more than just talk about this problem. The moratorium has given momentum to a global campaign to put limits on antipersonnel landmines, or to ban them altogether.

And it has put pressure on other countries that are exporting millions of landmines, even to our enemies. Thousands of sophisticated Italian mines with antidetection and antineutralization devices were discovered in Iraqi arsenals after the gulf war.

Ten years ago the United States joined 52 other countries in signing the landmine protocol, the only international agreement that seeks to regulate the use of mines to reduce their indiscriminate effect on civilians.

The protocol called world attention to the scourge of landmines, but it needs to be significantly strengthened. While the United States was actively involved in negotiating the protocol and is a signatory, neither the Reagan or Bush administrations forwarded it to the Senate for ratification. Apparently, the problems the previous administrations had were not with the landmine protocol itself, but with other protocols on the laws of war. The United States needs to ratify the landmine protocol so that it can play a leadership role in negotiating stronger limits.

The legislation I am introducing today states that it is the sense of the Congress that the President should submit the 1980 Convention on Conventional Weapons to the Senate for ratification, and I am pleased that the administration is reviewing the convention with that in mind.

It also calls on the administration to participate in a U.N. conference to review the landmine protocol, and actively seek to negotiate an international prohibition on the sale, transfer or export of antipersonnel landmines, and further limits on their manufacture, possession and use.

With France and other European countries pressing for a review of the protocol late next year, there is no time to lose. The administration needs to become actively involved in planning for the conference to ensure that the agenda covers the full range of issues.

Mr. President, in the Foreign Operations Subcommittee this year, Secretary of State Christopher testified about the "enormous number of deaths from landmines" and the need for "prohibitions or restrictions on their sale and use." I believe the administration will support this legislation, and will be a leader in the U.N. review conference.

Mr. President, I have spoken about this subject many times. I appreciate the support of my colleagues in helping me get the money for the War Victim's Fund. It was first used in Mozambique, and because of our great Ambassador, Melissa Wells, we have used it in many other countries.

I have visited the hospitals, along with my wife who is a registered nurse. We have seen the tremendous good that has been done with the War Victims Fund with little money but with dedicated American volunteers. They have trained local people to carry on the work of repairing the horrible damage and relieving some of the suffering caused by landmines.

Mr. President, I think you would agree with me—and I think most of the American people would agree—that it would be wonderful if there were no need to do it in the first place. Maybe we can make that day come.

Mr. President, I ask unanimous consent that the text of the bill and a factsheet on it be printed in the RECORD.

There being no objection, the material was ordered to be printed in the RECORD, as follows:

### S. 1276

Be it enacted by the Senate and the House of Representatives of the United States of America in Congress assembled,

SECTION 1. SHORT TITLE.

This Act may be cited as the "Landmine Moratorium Extension Act of 1993."

SEC. 2. FINDINGS.

The Congress makes the following findings:

(1) Anti-personnel landmines, which are designed to maim and kill people, have been used indiscriminately in dramatically increasing numbers around the world. Hundreds of thousands of noncombatant civilians, including children, have been the primary victims. Unlike other military weapons, landmines often remain implanted and undiscovered after conflict has ended, causing massive suffering to civilian populations.

(2) Tens of millions of landmines have been strewn in at least 62 countries, often making whole areas uninhabitable. The State Department estimates there are more than 10 million landmines in Afghanistan, 9 million in Angola, 4 million in Cambodia, 3 million in Iraqi Kurdistan, and 2 million each in Somalia, Mozambique, and the former Yugoslavia. Hundreds of thousands of landmines

were used in conflicts in Central America in the 1980s.

(3) Advanced technologies are being used to manufacture sophisticated mines which can be scattered remotely at a rate of 1000 per hour. These mines, which are being produced by many industrialized countries, were discovered in Iraqi arsenals after the Persian Gulf War.

(4) At least 300 types of anti-personnel landmines have been manufactured by at least 44 countries, including the United States. However, the United States is not a major exporter of landmines. During the past ten years the Administration has approved ten licenses for the commercial export of anti-personnel landmines with a total value of $980,000, and the sale under the Foreign Military Sales program of 109,129 anti-personnel landmines.

(5) The United States signed, but has not ratified, the 1980 Convention on Prohibitions or Restrictions on the Use of Certain Conventional Weapons Which May Be Deemed To Be Excessively Injurious or To Have Indiscriminate Effects. Protocol II of the Convention, otherwise known as the Landmine Protocol, prohibits the indiscriminate use of landmines.

(6) When it signed the 1980 Convention, the United States stated: "We believe that the Convention represents a positive step forward in efforts to minimize injury or damage to the civilian population in time of armed conflict. Our signature of the Convention reflects the general willingness of the United States to adopt practical and reasonable provisions concerning the conduct of military operations, for the purpose of protecting noncombatants.".

(7) The United States also indicated that it had supported procedures to enforce compliance, which were omitted from the Convention's final draft. The United States stated: "The United States strongly supported proposals by other countries during the Conference to include special procedures for dealing with compliance matters, and reserves the right to propose at a later date additional procedures and remedies, should this prove necessary, to deal with such problems.".

(8) The lack of compliance procedures and other weaknesses have significantly undermined the effectiveness of the Landmine Protocol. Since it entered into force on December 2, 1983, the number of civilians maimed and killed by anti-personnel landmines has multiplied.

(9) Since the moratorium on United States sales, transfers and exports of anti-personnel landmines was signed into law on October 23, 1992, the European Parliament has issued a resolution calling for a five year moratorium on sales, transfers and exports of anti-personnel landmines, and the Government of France has announced that it has ceased all sales, transfers and exports of anti-personnel landmines.

(10) On December 2, 1993, ten years will have elapsed since the 1980 Convention entered into force, triggering the right of any party to request a United Nations conference to review the Convention. Amendments to the Landmine Protocol may be considered at that time. The Government of France has made a formal request to the United Nations Secretary General for a review conference. With necessary preparations and consultations among governments, a review conference is not expected to be convened before late 1994 or early 1995.

(11) The United States should continue to set an example for other countries in such negotiations by extending the moratorium on sales, transfers and exports of anti-personnel landmines for an additional three years. A moratorium of this duration would extend the current prohibition on the sale, transfer and export of anti-personnel landmines a sufficient time to take into account the results of a United Nations review conference.

SEC. 3. POLICY.

(a) It shall be the policy of the United States to seek verifiable international agreements prohibiting the sale, transfer or export, further limiting the manufacture, possession and use, and eventually, terminating the manufacture, possession and use of anti-personnel landmines.

(b) It is the sense of the Congress that the President should submit the 1980 Convention on Certain Conventional Weapons to the Senate for ratification. Furthermore, the Administration should participate in a United Nations conference to review the Landmine Protocol, and actively seek to negotiate under United Nations auspices a modification of the Landmine Protocol, or another international agreement, to prohibit the sale, transfer or export of anti-personnel landmines, and to further limit their manufacture, possession and use.

SEC. 4. MORATORIUM ON TRANSFER OF ANTI-PERSONNEL LANDMINES ABROAD.

For a period of three years beginning on the date of enactment of this Act—

(1) no sale may be made or financed, no transfer may be made, and no license for export may be issued, under the Arms Export Control Act, with respect to any anti-personnel landmine; and

(2) no assistance may be provided under the Foreign Assistance Act of 1961, with respect to the provision of any anti-personnel landmine.

SEC. 5. DEFINITION.

For purposes of this section, the term "anti-personnel landmine" means—

(1) any munition placed under, on, or near the ground or other surface area, or delivered by artillery, rocket, mortar, or similar means or dropped from an aircraft and which is designed to be detonated or exploded by the presence, proximity, or contact of a person;

(2) any device or material which is designed, constructed, or adapted to kill or injure and which functions unexpectedly when a person disturbs or approaches an apparently harmless object or performs an apparently safe act;

(3) any manually-emplaced munition or device designed to kill, injure, or damage and which is actuated by remote control or automatically after a lapse of time.

LANDMINE MORATORIUM EXTENSION ACT—
FACT SHEET

The Leahy bill extends the current moratorium on the export of anti-personnel landmines from the United States. The moratorium, which became law in October 1992, stems from a provision offered last year by Senator Leahy and 35 Senate cosponsors.

The moratorium does not affect U.S. manufacture, stockpiles or use of anti-personnel landmines, or exports of anti-tank landmines. The moratorium expires on October 1, 1993.

The Landmine Moratorium extension Act now being offered by Senator Leahy and others would extend the moratorium an additional three years—a sufficient time to take into account the results of a United Nations conference on limitations on anti-personnel landmines, expected to begin in late 1994 or early 1995.

The United States signed, but has not ratified, the 1980 Landmine Protocol. The Leahy bill urges the President to submit the 1980 Landmine Protocol to the Senate for ratification, and to seek to negotiate an international ban on exports and further limits on the manufacture, possession and use of anti-personnel landmines.

What impact will the moratorium have on U.S. exports and jobs?

Exports of anti-personnel landmines from the United States have been insignificant. In the past decade, only 10 licenses have been approved for the commercial export of anti-personnel landmines valued at a total of $980,000. Only 109,129 anti-personnel landmines have been sold under the Foreign Military Sales Program during the past 10 years.

Several U.S. companies manufacture landmines or components for U.S. use. However, with the decrease in the U.S. defense budget, some manufacturers are seeking export markets for anti-personnel landmines. One manufacturer speculates that the potential foreign market for U.S. anti-personnel landmines could be $500 million over the next several years.

The number of American workers engaged in producing anti-personnel landmines for export is extremely small. Estimates of the number of potential U.S. jobs that could be affected by the moratorium have ranged from 30 in late 1992, to 1000 in April 1993, to 2000 in June 1993.

Why not include an exception in the moratorium for "self-destructing" or "self-neutralizing" mines?

Self-destructing and self-neutralizing anti-personnel landmines are the only types of anti-personnel landmines made in the United States that are offered for export. An exception for these types of mines would nullify the moratorium.

Such mines are scattered remotely by aircraft, artillery tubes, or other launching devices. They are therefore by nature indiscriminate and pose a danger to noncombatants. In addition, there is no way for civilians to know when self-destruct mines will explode, or if self-neutralizing mines are active. Thousands of Italian mines with anti-neutralizing devices were found in Iraqi arsenals after the Gulf War.

Estimates of the failure rate of self-destruct mines range from 2-10 percent. Thus, for every 10,000 mines delivered, 200-1000 may be defective. For self-neutralizing mines, the explosive charge remains intact and can be reactivated.

The purpose of the moratorium is to enable the U.S. to exercise leadership in negotiating stronger international limits on anti-personnel landmines by setting an example for other countries. It is unlikely that less developed countries that do not produce self-destruct or self-neutralizing mines would agree to limits on mines they produce while permitting the advanced countries to continue exporting more sophisticated mines.

Any exceptions for the manufacture, export or use of specific kinds of mines should be agreed to in an international negotiation on the Landmine Protocol.

Have any other nations taken steps to limit exports of anti-personnel landmines as a result of the U.S. example?

The French Government announced that it has ceased all sales and exports of anti-personnel landmines.

The European parliament issued a resolution calling on its members to adopt a five-year moratorium.

Members of the British Parliament introduced a resolution calling for an indefinite moratorium on exports from the United Kingdom, for the U.K. to ratify the Landmine Protocol and negotiate an international ban on exports.

The Swedish Red Cross launched a campaign for a moratorium in Sweden.

LANDMINE AMENDMENT

Mr. LEAHY. Mr. President, many of us have seen photographs like this. It is a horrible photograph. It is not one that any of us like looking at. A photograph of a young boy, one leg badly burned, damaged, crippled, the other leg torn off, one arm torn off.

I do not show this picture simply to upset my colleagues. It is a picture of just one of hundreds and hundreds of thousands of landmine victims worldwide; innocent children, legs and arms blown off by landmines.

I show the picture, though, because it has to touch the morality of every man and women in this Chamber. It does not make any difference whether we are conservative, liberal, moderate, Democrat or Republican, we have to understand how terrible these things are.

I recall the first time I met one of these children in a field hospital in the jungles of Honduras, a little boy who lost his leg and lived in that hospital because he had no other place to go. He was from a peasant family, and could no longer work.

I asked him how it happened. He said it was a landmine on a jungle trail. I ask him if it was put there by the Contras or the Sandinistas? He did not know. But one thing he did know, was that his life was horribly changed.

Bombs and artillery can target military targets and soldiers can aim, at other combatants. But, like chemical weapons, landmines do not discriminate. A landmine will blow the arm or leg off anybody who steps on it, civilian or military. Usually it is a civilian.

Landmines are used more and more as weapons of terror against civilian populations.

The Senator from New Jersey has kindly yielded to me for a few moments. I will return later and offer up my landmine amendment. Fifty-nine Members of this body have already cosponsored it. Both leaders, the Republican leader and the Democratic leader, have. Again, Senators who range across the political spectrum.

But today it is estimated that at least 85 million landmines are scattered in 62 countries, and they kill or maim hundreds of innocent people every month.

In Cambodia alone there are four million landmines, and those mines are being cleared, as they say, an arm and a leg at a time. Much of the arable land in that country may never be safe for farming because the people cannot even walk in the fields without dying.

Kuwait has already spent $700 million to get rid of some of the seven million Iraqi landmines, many of which were sold to Iraq by NATO countries. Afghanistan, Lebanon, El Salvador, Mozambique, Armenia, even the Falkland Islands—these are some of the countries strewn with landmines, some dating back to World War II. My amendment extends the moratorium on exports of landmines an additional 3 years. By doing so we can pressure other countries to stop exporting them, and finally to give the same onus to landmines that we give to chemical and biological weapons. Then we can say once and for all that people of any morality, of any respect for humanity, will not use landmines.

For me, this is a moral issue. And the most powerful nation on Earth, the only superpower, can set the example.

Mr. President, I thank my good friend from New Jersey for his courtesy.

Mr. KENNEDY. Will the Senator yield very, very briefly?

Mr. LEAHY. The Senator from New Jersey has the floor.

Mr. KENNEDY. I just need 1 minute.

Mr. LAUTENBERG. I am happy to yield, without losing my right to the floor.

The PRESIDING OFFICER. Without objection, the Senator from Massachusetts is recognized.

Mr. KENNEDY. Mr. President, I join in commending the Senator from Vermont for this proposal. I am also grateful to the chairman of the Armed Services Committee and the ranking minority member for also being willing to accept a corollary amendment that will permit an authorization of up to $10 million to permit surplus Army equipment that could be helpful and useful in clearing up these mines, permit some technical help and assistance, when appropriate and available, to be utilized in the country.

I have heard, as chairman of the Refugee Committee, if you talk to any of the nongovernmental agencies or any of the international agencies, the No. 1 concern that they have is how to clear up these landmines.

We have some very considerable capability to do it. I commend the Senator from Vermont, who has been a great leader in this area.

And I am grateful to the chairman of the committee for being willing to accept a very modest amendment which would permit up to $10 million in the O&M account to be utilized in ways that can further advance this humanitarian cause.

I have heard the chairman of the Armed Services Committee in our markups and in our considerations speak very eloquently about this problem, as well. I really think that this is something that will be very modest but very useful, particularly for the children in many of these war-torn lands.

I thank the Senator.

Mr. NUNN. Will the Senator yield for 30 seconds?

Mr. LAUTENBERG. I am happy to yield.

Mr. NUNN. Mr. President, I commend the Senator from Vermont. I will recommend to the Senate that we accept this amendment, as well as the amendment of the Senator from Massachusetts.

This is a tragedy that occurs every day. It is beyond human imagination the number of innocent women and children and people having nothing to do whatsoever with battles that are going on around the world that are victims of this.

I am not sure that this amendment will alleviate much of it because there are so many mines out there now, but at least it puts us on record in strong support of this kind of conduct.

I remember very well visiting with our American military people in Cambodia. Most people do not realize we had American people in Cambodia. They were assigned as observers; unarmed observers, of course. They told of the horrors they witnessed. As they walked from one village to another as observers, they had to follow oxen down the trail because there were so many mines in the area. They have one story after another about the horrors of dealing with this and the number of atrocities they have seen.

So, at the appropriate time, I would certainly recommend the acceptance of both of these amendments.

Mr. LAUTENBERG addressed the Chair.

The PRESIDING OFFICER. The Senator from New Jersey.

Mr. LAUTENBERG. First, Mr. President, I commend the Senator from Vermont for his proposed amendment. I think it is appropriate that, as much as possible, we remove the ability to destroy, maim, and kill people who had no involvement with the conflict at the time, and that we should do whatever we can to protect those lives.

I ask unanimous consent that I be included as a cosponsor of the amendment.

The PRESIDING OFFICER. Without objection, it is so ordered.

LEAHY (AND OTHERS)
AMENDMENT NO. 821

Mr. LEAHY (for himself, Mr. MITCHELL, Mr. PELL, Mr. INOUYE, Mr. MOYNIHAN, Mr. DeCONCINI, Mr. KERREY, Mr. KERRY, Mr. DODD, Ms. MIKULSKI, Mr. WOFFORD, Mr. SIMON, Mr. KENNEDY, Mr. BRYAN, Mr. LAUTENBERG, Mr. RIEGLE, Mr. EXON, Mr. ROCKEFELLER, Mr. BUMPERS, Mrs. FEINSTEIN, Mrs. MURRAY, Mr. FORD, Mr. HARKIN, Mr. METZENBAUM, Mr. DASCHLE, Mr. BRADLEY, Mr. GRAHAM, Mr. DORGAN, Mrs. BOXER, Mr. LEVIN, Mr. FEINGOLD, Mr. SARBANES, Mr. AKAKA, Mr. REID, Mr. KOHL, Mr. WELLSTONE, Mr. MATHEWS, Mr. PRYOR, Mr. SASSER, Mr. ROBB, Mr. BINGAMAN, Mr. CAMPBELL, Mr. GLENN, Mr. BYRD, Ms. MOSELEY-BRAUN, Mr. DOLE, Mr. JEFFORDS, Mr. D'AMATO, Mr. SPECTER, Mr. HATFIELD, Mr. DURENBERGER, Mr. McCAIN, Mr. DOMENICI, Mr. MURKOWSKI, Mr. CHAFEE, Mrs. KASSEBAUM, Mr. LUGAR, Mr. SIMPSON, Mr. BURNS, Mr. GRASSLEY) proposed an amendment to the bill S. 1298, supra, as follows:

At the appropriate place insert the following:

SEC. . LANDMINE MORATORIUM EXTENSION ACT.

(a) This section shall be titled the "Landmine Moratorium Extension Act of 1993".

(b) FINDINGS.—The Congress makes the following findings:

(1) Anti-personnel landmines, which are designed to maim and kill people, have been used indiscriminately in dramatically increasing numbers around the world. Hundreds of thousands of noncombatant civilians, including children, have been the primary victims. Unlike other military weapons, landmines often remain implanted and undiscovered after conflict has ended, causing massive suffering to civilian populations.

(2) Tens of millions of landmines have been strewn in at least 62 countries, often making whole areas uninhabitable. The State Department estimates there are more than 10 million landmines in Afghanistan, 9 million in Angola, 4 million in Cambodia, 3 million in Iraqi Kurdistan, and 2 million each in Somalia, Mozambique, and the former Yugoslavia. Hundreds of thousands of landmines were used in conflicts in Central America in the 1980s.

(3) Advanced technologies are being used to manufacture sophisticated mines which can be scattered remotely at a rate of 1000 per hour. These mines, which are being produced by many industrialized countries, were found in Iraqi arsenals after the Persian Gulf War.

(4) At least 300 types of anti-personnel landmines have been manufactured by at least 44 countries, including the United States. However, the United States is not a major exporter of landmines. During the past ten years the Administration has approved ten licenses for the commercial export of anti-personnel landmines with a total value of $980,000, and the sale under the Foreign Military Sales program of 108,852 anti-personnel landmines.

(5) The United States signed, but has not ratified, the 1980 Convention on Prohibitions or Restrictions on the Use of Certain Conventional Weapons Which May Be Deemed To Be Excessively Injurious or To Have Indiscriminate Effects. Protocol II of the Convention, otherwise known as the Landmine Protocol, prohibits the indiscriminate use of landmines.

(6) When it signed the 1980 Convention, the United States stated: "We believe that the Convention represents a positive step forward in efforts to minimize injury or damage to the civilian population in time of armed conflict. Our signature of the Convention reflects the general willingness of the United States to adopt practical and reasonable provisions concerning the conduct of military operations, for the purpose of protecting noncombatants.".

(7) The United States also indicated that it had supported procedures to enforce compliance, which were omitted from the Convention's final draft. The United States stated: "The United States strongly supported proposals by other countries during the Conference to include special procedures for dealing with compliance matters, and reserves the right to propose at a later date additional procedures and remedies, should this prove necessary, to deal with such problems.".

(8) The lack of compliance procedures and other weaknesses have significantly undermined the effectiveness of the Landmine Protocol. Since it entered into force on December 2, 1983, the number of civilians maimed and killed by anti-personnel landmines has multiplied.

(9) Since the moratorium on United States sales, transfers and exports of anti-personnel landmines was signed into law on October 23, 1992, the European Parliament has issued a resolution calling for a five year moratorium on sales, transfers and exports of anti-personnel landmines, and the Government of France has announced that it has ceased all sales, transfers and exports of anti-personnel landmines.

(10) On December 2, 1993, ten years will have elapsed since the 1980 Convention entered into force, triggering the right of any party to request a United Nations conference to review the Convention. Amendments to the Landmine Protocol may be considered at that time. A formal request has been made to the United Nations Secretary General for a review conference. With necessary preparations and consultations among governments, a review conference is not expected to be convened before late 1994 or early 1995.

(11) The United States should continue to set an example for other countries in such negotiations by extending the moratorium on sales, transfers and exports of anti-personnel landmines for an additional three years. A moratorium of this duration would extend the current prohibition on the sale, transfer and export of anti-personnel landmines a sufficient time to take into account the results of a United Nations review conference.

(c) STATEMENT OF POLICY.—

(1) It shall be the policy of the United States to seek verifiable international agreements prohibiting the sale, transfer or export, and further limiting the manufacture, possession and use of anti-personnel landmines.

(2) It is the sense of the Congress that the President should submit the 1980 Convention on Certain Conventional Weapons to the Senate for ratification. Furthermore, the Administration should participate in a United Nations conference to review the Landmine Protocol, and actively seek to negotiate under United Nations auspices a modification of the Landmine Protocol, or another international agreement, to prohibit the sale, transfer or export of anti-personnel landmines, and to further limit their manufacture, possession and use.

(d) MORATORIUM ON TRANSFERS OF ANTI-PERSONNEL LANDMINES ABROAD.—For a period of three years beginning on the date of enactment of this Act—

(1) no sale may be made or financed, no transfer may be made, and no license for export may be issued, under the Arms Export Control Act, with respect to any anti-personnel landmine; and

(2) no assistance may be provided under the Foreign Assistance Act of 1961, with respect to the provision of any anti-personnel landmine.

(e) DEFINITION.—For purposes of this section, the term "anti-personnel landmine" means—

(1) any munition placed under, on, or near the ground or other surface area, or delivered by artillery, rocket, mortar, or similar means or dropped from an aircraft and which is designed to be detonated or exploded by the presence, proximity, or contact of a person;

(2) any device or material which is designed, constructed, or adapted to kill or injure and which functions unexpectedly when a person disturbs or approaches an apparently harmless object or performs an apparently safe act;

(3) any manually-emplaced munition or device designed to kill, injure, or damage and which is actuated by remote control or automatically after a lapse of time.

---

## KENNEDY (AND LEAHY) AMENDMENT NO. 822

Mr. LEAHY (for Mr. KENNEDY, for himself and Mr. LEAHY) proposed an amendment to the bill S. 1298, supra, as follows:

On page 81, between lines 7 and 8, insert the following:

SEC. 207. FUNDS FOR CLEARING LANDMINES.

Of the funds authorized to be appropriated in section 301, not more than $10,000,000 is authorized for activities to support the clearing of landmines for humanitarian purposes (as determined by the Secretary of Defense), including the clearing of landmines in areas in which refugee repatriation programs are on-going.

AMENDMENT NO. 821

Mr. LEAHY. Mr. President, I send an amendment to the desk and ask for its immediate consideration.

The PRESIDING OFFICER. The clerk will report.

The bill clerk read as follows:

The Senator from Vermont [Mr. LEAHY], for himself, Mr. MITCHELL, Mr. PELL, Mr. INOUYE, Mr. MOYNIHAN, Mr. DECONCINI, Mr. KERREY, Mr. KERRY, Mr. DODD, Ms. MIKULSKI, Mr. WOFFORD, Mr. SIMON, Mr. KENNEDY, Mr. BRYAN, Mr. LAUTENBERG, Mr. RIEGLE, Mr. EXON, Mr. ROCKEFELLER, Mr. BUMPERS, Mrs. FEINSTEIN, Mrs. MURRAY, Mr. FORD, Mr. HARKIN, Mr. METZENBAUM, Mr. DASCHLE, Mr. BRADLEY, Mr. GRAHAM, Mr. DORGAN, Mrs. BOXER, Mr. LEVIN, Mr. FEINGOLD, Mr. SARBANES, Mr. AKAKA, Mr. REID, Mr. KOHL, Mr. WELLSTONE, Mr. MATHEWS, Mr. PRYOR, Mr. SASSER, Mr. ROBB, Mr. BINGAMAN, Mr. CAMPBELL, Mr. GLENN, Mr. BYRD, Ms. MOSELEY-BRAUN, Mr. DOLE, Mr. JEFFORDS, Mr. D'AMATO, Mr. SPECTER, Mr. HATFIELD, Mr. DURENBERGER, Mr. McCAIN, Mr. DOMENICI, Mr. MURKOWSKI, Mr. CHAFEE, Mrs. KASSEBAUM, Mr. LUGAR, Mr. SIMPSON, Mr. BURNS, and Mr. GRASSLEY, proposes an amendment numbered 821.

Mr. LEAHY. Mr. President, I ask unanimous consent that reading of the amendment be dispensed with.

The PRESIDING OFFICER. Without objection, it is so ordered.

The amendment is as follows:

At the appropriate place insert the following:

SEC. LANDMINE MORATORIUM EXTENSION ACT.

(a) This section shall be titled the "Landmine Moratorium Extension Act of 1993".

(b) FINDINGS.—The Congress makes the following findings:

(1) Anti-personnel landmines, which are designed to maim and kill people, have been used indiscriminately in dramatically increasing numbers around the world. Hundreds of thousands of noncombatant civilians, including children, have been the primary victims. Unlike other military weapons, landmines often remain implanted and undiscovered after conflict has ended, causing massive suffering to civilian populations.

(2) Tens of millions of landmines have been strewn in at least 62 countries, often making whole areas uninhabitable. The State Department estimates there are more than 10 million landmines in Afghanistan, 9 million in Angola, 4 million in Cambodia, 3 million in Iraqi Kurdistan, and 2 million each in Somalia, Mozambique, and the former Yugoslavia. Hundreds of thousands of land mines were used in conflicts in Central American in the 1980s.

(3) Advanced technologies are being used to manufacture sophisticated mines which can be scattered remotely at a rate of 1000 per hour. These mines, which are being produced by many industrialized countries, were found in Iraqi arsenals after the Persian Gulf War.

(4) At least 300 types of anti-personnel landmines have been manufactured by at least 44 countries, including the United States. However, the United States is not a major exporter of landmines. During the past ten years the Administration has approved ten licenses for the commercial export of anti-personnel landmines with a total value of $980,000, and the sale under the Foreign Military Sales program of 108,852 anti-personnel landmines with a total value of $980,000, and the sale under the Foreign Military Sales program of 108,852 anti-personnel landmines.

(5) The United States signed, but has not ratified, the 1980 Convention on Prohibitions or Restrictions on the Use of Certain Conventional Weapons Which May Be Deemed To Be Excessively Injurious or to have Indiscriminate Effects. Protocol II of the Convention, otherwise known as the Landmine Protocol, prohibits the indiscriminate use of landmines.

(6) When it signed the 1980 Convention, the United States stated: "We believe that the Convention represents a positive step forward in efforts to minimize injury or damage to the civilian population in time of armed conflict. Our signature of the Convention reflects the general willingness of the United States to adopt practical and reasonable provisions concerning the conduct of military operations, for the purpose of protecting noncombatants.".

(7) The United States also indicated that it had supported procedures to enforce compliance, which were omitted from the Convention's final draft. The United States stated: "The United States strongly supported proposals by other countries during the Conference to include special procedures for dealing with compliance matters, and reserves the right to propose at a later date additional procedures and remedies, should this prove necessary, to deal with such problems.".

(8) The lack of compliance procedures and other weaknesses have significantly undermined the effectiveness of the Landmine Protocol. Since it entered into force on December 2, 1983, the number of civilians maimed and killed by anti-personnel landmines has multiplied.

(9) Since the moratorium on United States sales, transfers and exports of anti-personnel landmines was signed into law on October 23, 1992, the European Parliament has issued a resolution calling for a five year moratorium on sales, transfers and exports of anti-personnel landmines, and the Government of France has announced that it has ceased all sales, transfers and exports of anti-personnel landmines.

(10) On December 2, 1993, ten years will have elapsed since the 1980 Convention entered into force, triggering the right of any party to request a United Nations conference to review the Convention. Amendments to the Landmine Protocol may be considered at that time. A formal request has been made to the United Nations Secretary General for a review conference. With necessary preparations and consultations among governments, a review conference is not expected to be convened before late 1994 or early 1995.

(11) The United States should continue to set an example for other countries in such negotiations by extending the moratorium on sales, transfers and exports of anti-personnel landmines for an additional three years. A moratorium of this duration would extend the current prohibition on the sale, transfer and export of anti-personnel landmines a sufficient time to take into account the results of a United Nations review conference.

(c) STATEMENT OF POLICY.—

(1) It shall be the policy of the United States to seek verifiable international agreements prohibiting the sale, transfer or export, and further limiting the manufacture, possession and use of anti-personnel landmines.

(2) It is the sense of the Congress that the President should submit the 1980 Convention on Certain Conventional Weapons to the Senate for ratification. Furthermore, the Administration should participate in a United Nations conference to review the Landmine Protocol, and actively seek to negotiate under United Nations auspices a modification of the Landmine Protocol, or another international agreement, to prohibit the sale, transfer or export of anti-personnel landmines, and to further limit their manufacture, possession and use.

(d) MORATORIUM ON TRANSFERS OF ANTIPERSONNEL LANDMINES ABROAD.—For a period of three years beginning on the date of enactment of this act—

(1) no sale may be made or financed, no transfer may be made, and no license for export may be issued, under the Arms Export Control Act, with respect to any anti-personnel landmine; and

(2) no assistance may be provided under the Foreign Assistance Act of 1961, with respect to the provision of any anti-personnel landmine.

(e) DEFINITION.—For purposes of this section, the term "anti-personnel landmine" means—

(1) any munition placed under, on, or near the ground or other surface area, or delivered by artillery, rocket, mortar, or similar means or dropped from an aircraft and which is designed to be detonated or exploded by the presence, proximity, or contact of a person;

(2) any device or material which is designed, constructed, or adapted to kill or injure and which functions unexpectedly when a person disturbs or approaches an apparently harmless object or performs an apparently safe act;

(3) any manually-emplaced munition or device designed to kill, injure, or damage and which is actuated by remote control or automatically after a lapse of time.

Mr. LEAHY. Mr. President, on July 22 when I introduced the Landmine Moratorium Extension Act, I spoke at length about the urgent need to stop the slaughter of innocent people by landmines.

My amendment today is simple. It extends the current U.S. moratorium on the sale, transfer, and export of antipersonnel landmines for an additional 3 years. The moratorium was passed last year but it will expire this October unless we extend it.

With one minor change, my amendment is the same as the legislation I introduced in July, which has 59 cosponsors, including the majority and minority leaders of the U.S. Senate.

In addition to myself and Senators MITCHELL and DOLE, the cosponsors are Senators INOUYE, BYRD, MOYNIHAN, ROBB, SASSER, JEFFORDS, MCCAIN, DECONCINI, GLENN, KERRY, KERREY, LUGAR, KASSEBAUM, DODD, PELL, SPECTER, HATFIELD, DURENBERGER, D'AMATO, MIKULSKI, WOFFORD, MURKOWSKI, CHAFEE, SIMON, EXON, DOMENICI, LAUTENBERG, KENNEDY, ROCKEFELLER, BRYAN, BUMPERS, FEINSTEIN, MURRAY, HARKIN, METZENBAUM, BRADLEY, DASCHLE, FORD, GRAHAM, DORGAN, FEINGOLD, LEVIN, RIEGLE, BOXER, SARBANES, AKAKA, REID, KOHL, WELLSTONE, MATHEWS, PRYOR, CAMPBELL, SIMPSON, MOSELEY-BRAUN, BINGAMAN, BURNS, and GRASSLEY.

I mention their names because I defy anybody to find an ideological root in this. You have Senators across the political spectrum, from all parts of the country. They join together because this is not a political or economic issue as much as it is a statement of moral leadership on the part of the United States.

When we passed the moratorium last year, there was not a great deal of notice, initially. Certainly no notice, as I recall, in the press in Washington or anywhere else. But like so many other seeds that take root, the effect was great.

Let me tell you what has happened since we passed it, I think largely because of the moral leadership of the United States.

The French Government has announced that it ceased all exports of antipersonnel landmines. In fact, it went further and urged all other European countries to do the same.

The European Parliament issued a resolution calling upon its members to support a 5-year landmine moratorium.

Belgium has stopped all production of the antipersonnel landmines, and has said it will not permit the transit of landmines within its territory. It is also moving to ratify the Landmine Protocol.

Members of the British Parliament introduced a resolution for an indefinite moratorium.

The French, Swedish, and Dutch Governments have asked the United Nations to schedule a conference to review the 1980 Landmine Protocol.

UNICEF has called for a worldwide ban on production and trade in landmines.

The Secretary of State, Warren Christopher, testified in the Foreign Operations Subcommittee in support of restrictions or prohibitions on the export and use of landmines, and the State Department has said it supports an extension of the moratorium and has called on other countries to adopt similar laws.

Mr. President, everyone has seen the horrifying pictures, like this one, of innocent children with their legs and arms blown off from landmines. These are not combatants.

Bombs and artillery can be aimed at military targets, and bullets fired by soldiers at other combatants. But, like chemical weapons, landmines do not discriminate. A landmine will blow the arm or leg off whoever steps on it, and usually it is a civilian.

According to a recent State Department report titled "Hidden Killers," the first report of its kind produced by the U.S. Government on the global problem of landmines, at least 85 million landmines are scattered in 62 countries.

The magnitude of the death and destruction caused by these insidious weapons is absolutely incredible. Landmines kill or maim hundreds of people every month, most of them innocent noncombatants, many of them children, who just happen to walk in the wrong place.

Cambodia, where there are over 4 million landmines, is being cleared of mines an arm, a leg, and a life at a time. Large areas of that country will never be rid of these timeless death traps.

Kuwait has already spent over $700 million to get rid of some of the 7 million Iraqi landmines, many of which the NATO countries exported to Iraq.

Afghanistan, Lebanon, El Salvador, Mozambique, Somalia, Cyprus, Bosnia, Armenia. Even the Falkland Islands. These are a few of the countries strewn with millions and millions of landmines, some of them dating from the Second World War and still capable of blowing off an arm or a leg.

The United States is not a major exporter of landmines, but I would offer this amendment even if it were. We simply must show leadership. Landmines are increasingly being used as weapons of terror, and once they are sold there is no way of knowing where they end up, or how they are used.

High-technology landmines are capable of being scattered from the air by the thousands. Some are made to self-destruct after a period of weeks or months, but they also endanger civilians and can end up in the wrong hands.

Let me read what Gen. Patrick Blagden, head of the U.N. demining program says about self-destruct mines.

Blagden's deminers found 181 unexploded "self-destruct" mines in southern Iran, 2 years after they were sown. I am quoting him:

If they so successfully self-destruct, how come I've got one?

I don't know how many were sown, so I don't know the proportion that did self-destruct. But it certainly wasn't 99 percent. If somebody is going to prove to me that there is a 99 percent chance of self-destruction, then I am going to say, "OK, fine." But until that time, no way.

This amendment sets an example for other countries that are major landmine exporters, but it does not affect the manufacture of landmines by U.S. companies for use by U.S. forces.

Obviously, by itself, this amendment will not get rid of this horrendous problem. But it does call on the President to seek to negotiate an international agreement to prohibit the export of antipersonnel landmines and further limit their manufacture, possession, and use.

If other countries follow our example, as they are beginning to, and controls on exports are coupled with measures to limit the kinds of landmines that are manufactured and used, that would go a long way toward banning these weapons altogether.

I make no bones about it. I believe that should be our goal. Like chemical weapons, there is simply no way these weapons can be designed so they distinguish between combatants and civilians. They are inherently indiscriminatory, and they are inherently inhumane. They should be outlawed.

We are a long way from seeing that day. But in the meantime, by this amendment, we can continue the momentum we have begun.

Let me emphasize two other points. There is an international treaty that deals with landmines, but the United States has not ratified it. The administration needs to send the Landmine Protocol to the Senate for ratification without further delay.

And next year, or in early 1995, the United Nations will sponsor a conference to review the Landmine Protocol, for the purposes of strengthening it. A dialogue has already begun to define the agenda for that conference. The administration should assert an active, creative role in those discussions. The agenda should be broad enough in scope to encompass a wide range of ideas for correcting the flaws and weaknesses in the treaty.

Mr. President, I appreciate the support of all the cosponsors of this legislation.

It gives me a great deal of pride in the U.S. Senate that this amendment will be adopted on Tuesday, and I applaud those Senators of both parties.

We discuss many weighty issues on this floor. Next week we will have the signing of the first steps toward real peace in the Middle East. Perhaps like last year, what we do on landmines will be missed by the newspapers, but it is an idea taking root around the world. Here in the U.S. Senate we lit the spark, we lit the fire.

Mr. President, I ask for the yeas and nays on this amendment.

The PRESIDING OFFICER. Is there a sufficient second?

There is a sufficient second.

The yeas and nays were ordered.

Mr. LEAHY. I thank the Chair. Mr. President, I understand that rollcall will now occur on Tuesday; is that correct?

The PRESIDING OFFICER. That is correct.

Mr. LEAHY. I ask unanimous consent that when we begin the rollcalls after 2:15, according to the distinguished majority leader's original request, this be the first of the rollcalls to occur.

The PRESIDING OFFICER. Without objection, it is so ordered.

Mr. LEAHY. Mr. President, I know the Senator from Arkansas is here to speak. We have a second amendment. I am simply going to put it into the RECORD because it is going to be accepted. It is offered on behalf of myself and Mr. KENNEDY. But I had wanted the managers of the bill on the floor to do that.

Mr. PRYOR addressed the Chair.

Mr. LEAHY. I yield to the Senator from Arkansas.

Mr. BROWN addressed the Chair.

The PRESIDING OFFICER. Has the Senator yielded for a question?

Mr. LEAHY. Mr. President, I yield to the Senator from Arkansas for——

The PRESIDING OFFICER. The Senator has a right to yield to the Senator for a question. The Senator from Colorado is seeking recognition.

Mr. LEAHY. Mr. President, I am reluctant for a moment to give up the floor. I am only going to hold it for about a minute. I just was hoping that——

Mr. PRYOR. I was going to make a suggestion as to how to get us out of our dilemma.

Mr. LEAHY. I ask unanimous consent to yield for that purpose without losing my right to the floor.

The PRESIDING OFFICER. Without objection, it is so ordered.

Mr. PRYOR. I am wondering, I certainly do not want to take over from the Senator from Colorado, because I think he may want to go next with an amendment. I am not in the business of yielding time. I wonder if we might temporarily lay the Senator's amendment aside for a moment to allow the Senator from Colorado to go forward with his statement and then perhaps return to the amendment of the Senator from Vermont.

Mr. LEAHY. I am perfectly willing to do that. I think I can do it in about 20 seconds, now that the distinguished chairman is here.

The PRESIDING OFFICER. The Senator from Vermont has the floor.

Mr. LEAHY. I have completed my discussion of my amendment. We have ordered the yeas and nays. The vote will be on Tuesday. I ask if I might simply insert a statement on behalf of Senator KENNEDY, a statement on behalf of myself, and an amendment on behalf of Senator KENNEDY and myself and ask for its acceptance on the subject of authorizing funds for clearing landmines.

Mr. NUNN. Is this the second amendment we discussed that has been cleared that basically provides surplus funds for the purpose of clearing landmines?

Mr. LEAHY. That is right.

Mr. NUNN. I recommend acceptance.

Mr. THURMOND. Mr. President, I share the concerns expressed by the senior Senator from Vermont, Senator LEAHY, and the senior Senator from Massachusetts, Senator KENNEDY regarding the tragic accidental deaths and injuries suffered by innocent civilians as a result of antipersonnel landmines left on former battlefields around the world.

Unfortunately, the weapons of war are intended to maim and kill. Antipersonnel landmines are particularly bad because they may remain in battle areas long after the battles are over causing injury and death to innocent civilians.

I support Senator KENNEDY's amendment to utilize resources of the Department of Defense to assist in the removal of these mines and for research to develop better ways to detect and neutralize residual antipersonnel landmines.

I appreciate the cooperative manner in which Senator LEAHY's staff has worked with members of my staff. I understand that Senator LEAHY has agreed to maintain the wording of the current law with respect to the policy of the United States regarding the manufacture, possession, and use of antipersonnel landmines.

Last year the Senator from Vermont agreed that the moratorium on sale, transfer, or export of antipersonnel landmines should be for only 1 year. This year, he proposes that the moratorium should be extended for 3 more years. Unfortunately, because of this proposed moratorium, the U.S. manufacturers will continue to be prohibited from exporting antipersonnel landmines with self-destruct features.

Antipersonnel landmines manufactured by the United States have self-destruct or self-neutralizing features rendering them harmless after reasonable periods of time. Obviously, these mines do not pose the threat to innocent civilians that less sophisticated mines do.

As a result, countries seeking to buy such mines from the U.S. firms will be forced to buy elsewhere and may buy the more dangerous mines without self-destruct features, thereby making the situation Senator LEAHY has described, and which we all abhor, even worse.

In fact, the protocol of the 1980 convention cited throughout Senator LEAHY's amendment does not preclude the use of antipersonnel mines with self-destruct or self-neutralizing features. But Senator LEAHY's amendment prohibits the sale or export of such mines.

Mr. President, I am also concerned that the United States will be prohibited from transferring antipersonnel landmines to allies and coalition parties even when hostilities are imminent or have begun.

I hope that the Senator from Vermont does not intend to propose limitations on the future use of mines by our own forces. Our military forces should not be required to go into battle with unilaterally imposed restrictions which greatly increase their risks. Our forces may arrive in areas of combat outnumbered, requiring the use of economy of force measures where the employment of both antitank and antipersonnel mines are essential to deny the enemy key terrain and critical avenues of approach.

Mr. President, all of us share the concern expressed by Senator LEAHY's amendment. However, I believe that the moratorium proposed in this amendment may have a symbolic effect but will do little to alleviate the situation.

Mr. President, I yield the floor.

AMENDMENT NO. 822

(Purpose: To authorize the use of funds by the Department of Defense for the clearing of landmines for humanitarian purposes)

Mr. LEAHY. Mr. President, I send the amendment to the desk and ask for its immediate consideration.

The PRESIDING OFFICER. Under the request of the Senator from Arkansas, the amendment that has been discussed here the past hour or so by the Senator from Vermont is laid aside.

The clerk will report.

The bill clerk read as follows:

The Senator from Vermont [Mr. LEAHY], for Mr. KENNEDY, for himself and Mr. LEAHY, proposes an amendment number 822.

Mr. LEAHY. Mr. President, I ask unanimous consent that the reading of the amendment be dispensed with.

The PRESIDING OFFICER. Without objection, it is so ordered.

The amendment is as follows:

On page 81, between lines 7 and 8, insert the following:

SEC. 307. FUNDS FOR CLEARING LANDMINES.

Of the funds authorized to be appropriated in section 301, not more than $10,000,000 is authorized for activities to support the clearing of landmines for humanitarian purposes (as determined by the Secretary of Defense), including the clearing of landmines in areas in which refugee repatriation programs are on-going.

Mr. NUNN. Could the Senator from Vermont bring me up to date on what the status of his first amendment is?

Mr. LEAHY. I want to make sure I understand. Mr. President, am I correct in that we debated my first amendment and it is before the Senate? I have asked for the yeas and nays and, under the earlier unanimous-consent request, a vote will now occur as the first of whatever series of votes we have following the caucuses on Tuesday.

Mr. NUNN. I thank the Senator.

The PRESIDING OFFICER. The statement of the Senator from Vermont is correct.

Mr. LEAHY. I further understand Senator KENNEDY's amendment, cosponsored by me, is now before the Senate?

The PRESIDING OFFICER. Amendment No. 822 is now before the Senate.

Mr. LEAHY. I will accept a voice vote on that.

Mr. KENNEDY. Mr. President, this amendment continues an effort begun by last year's defense bill to address a serious worldwide humanitarian problem—the tens of millions of uncleared, unexploded land mines that plague large numbers of Third World nations around the globe. My amendment would provide $10 million to the Defense Department to support current and planned efforts to remove these mines.

This problem has been carefully studied. Last year, I sponsored a provision in the fiscal year 1993 Defense Authorization Act that required a report from the President on the status of international mine-clearing efforts in situations involving the repatriation and resettlement of refugees. That report,

"Hidden Killers: The Global Problem With Uncleared Land Mines," was issued this past July. It paints a devastating picture of uncleared mines as a scourge of war-torn nations trying to rebuild themselves after the conflict ends.

According to the report, more than 85 million landmines scattered around the world kill 150 people each week, maim countless more, and pose a devastating obstacle to efforts to repatriate refugees and resettle lands in areas that were formerly war zones.

If mines are not cleared from these areas of habitable land, refugees cannot return to these areas and rebuild their lives and their societies. Farmers cannot plant crops in fields littered with mines. Injuries from mine explosions overwhelm health care facilities. The cost of demining is a heavy burden to struggling economies. To demine up to 7 million landmines spread across Cambodia, that nation's entire GDP for 5 years would have to be devoted to nothing else but clearing these mines.

The "Hidden Killers" report outlines practical steps that the United States can take to address this enormous problem. The solution involves training foreign military personnel and civilians to conduct demining operations, and providing them with the equipment and technical assistance to carry · out the job themselves. U.S. know-how and equipment can help these nations to help themselves.

In particular, the report focuses on the interagency Demining Consultative Group. This group, consisting of representatives of the Office of the Secretary of Defense, the Joint Chiefs of Staff, regional bureaus of the State Department, and selected demining experts of the Defense Department, brings together experts on the technical and policy problems of demining to formulate a national strategy for addressing the global problem.

The specific recommendations contained in the report emphasize three main areas: education and training, technical assistance, and equipment and technology.

The report points to two training methods that have proved effective to date. The first consists of bringing foreign personnel to the United States for training as demining instructors. In the spring of 1993, the U.S. Army conducted its first demining training course for foreign mine clearing instructors. The course was a success, and the report recommends continuing this form of training, which costs less than $4,000 per trainee.

The second method consists of sending Special Operations Forces overseas to conduct training on mine clearing in the nations that need it. The Special Operations Command has already conducted a successful demining training course under U.N. auspices in Afghanistan. The command has used this experience to develop a demining training course that it can tailor to local conditions around the world.

With respect to technical assistance, the Defense Department has outstanding experts on mine detection and removal located at several key centers around the Nation. They have compiled a comprehensive database on mines and demining. This database should be put in declassified form and made available to foreign demining personnel and to the U.N.

The Demining Coordination Group is currently looking at ways to establish an official communications channel between the United States and other nations. This system can make technical assistance available on a regular basis.

Finally, we can provide equipment to foreign personnel trained by our forces to clear mines. Much of this material consists of excess stocks maintained by our Armed Forces, and will require no additional procurement. We should also pursue new technologies for wide-area mine clearing.

The committee bill provides $10 million in research and development for advanced counter-mine warfare capability, and I hope that the needs of civilian mine clearing will be considered in that program as well.

This amendment provides $10 million to the Defense Department to implement these recommendations. This sum is an investment that will help remove a main obstacle to the reconstruction of war-torn nations, and I urge the Senate to approve it.

Mr. LEAHY. Mr. President, I rise to offer an amendment on behalf of Senator KENNEDY and myself to authorize up to $10 million for activities to support clearing landmines. When the Defense appropriations bill comes to the floor I intend to offer an amendment to make these funds available.

I want to applaud Senator KENNEDY for sponsoring this amendment, which I understand has been accepted by both sides.

Five years ago I started a fund in the foreign aid program to get medical aid to landmine victims. Last year I sponsored a moratorium on the export of antipersonnel landmines from the United States. This amendment is the third leg of this effort to stop the slaughter of innocent people by landmines.

There are 100 million landmines scattered around the world in over 62 countries. Think of what that means for the people of those countries, who live in constant fear that they, or their children, will inadvertently step on one of these explosives and lose a leg, or an arm, or their life.

In Cambodia, over 4 million mines have turned huge areas of that country into death traps for returning refugees. The same is true of Afghanistan, Nicaragua, Mozambique, Somalia, Bosnia. The list goes on.

The Defense Department has a long history of involvement in mine clearing, but from a military perspective. Its focus has been in countermine warfare, not getting rid of mines in humanitarian situations, to enable civilians to return to their land after a conflict.

The purpose of this amendment is specifically to get U.S. military personnel involved in training, technical assistance, and provision of equipment, and other activities in support of landmine clearing efforts in a humanitarian context.

We are not contemplating that these Americans will get involved in actual mine clearing. That is for the people of those countries. but our people have the expertise and the resources to assist countries that are trying to deal with their own landmine problems.

I look forward to discussions with the administration on the specifics of implementing this program.

Mr. President, long after the conflict has ended and people have forgotten why they were fighting, millions of landmines continue to kill and maim innocent people. The human and economic costs of these weapons is incalculable. This amendment is another step towards stopping this senseless slaughter.

VOTE ON AMENDMENT NO. 821

The PRESIDING OFFICER. The question is on adoption of the Leahy amendment No. 821. On this question, the yeas and nays have been ordered, and the clerk will call the roll.

The assistant legislative clerk called the roll.

The PRESIDING OFFICER. Are there any other Senators in the Chamber desiring to vote?

The result was announced—yeas 100, nays 0, as follows:

[Rollcall Vote No. 258 Leg.]

YEAS—100

| | | |
|---|---|---|
| Akaka | Feingold | McConnell |
| Baucus | Feinstein | Metzenbaum |
| Bennett | Ford | Mikulski |
| Biden | Glenn | Mitchell |
| Bingaman | Gorton | Moseley-Braun |
| Bond | Graham | Moynihan |
| Boren | Gramm | Murkowski |
| Boxer | Grassley | Murray |
| Bradley | Gregg | Nickles |
| Breaux | Harkin | Nunn |
| Brown | Hatch | Packwood |
| Bryan | Hatfield | Pell |
| Bumpers | Heflin | Pressler |
| Burns | Helms | Pryor |
| Byrd | Hollings | Reid |
| Campbell | Hutchison | Riegle |
| Chafee | Inouye | Robb |
| Coats | Jeffords | Rockefeller |
| Cochran | Johnston | Roth |
| Cohen | Kassebaum | Sarbanes |
| Conrad | Kempthorne | Sasser |
| Coverdell | Kennedy | Shelby |
| Craig | Kerrey | Simon |
| D'Amato | Kerry | Simpson |
| Danforth | Kohl | Smith |
| Daschle | Lautenberg | Specter |
| DeConcini | Leahy | Stevens |
| Dodd | Levin | Thurmond |
| Dole | Lieberman | Wallop |
| Domenici | Lott | Warner |
| Dorgan | Lugar | Wellstone |
| Durenberger | Mack | Wofford |
| Exon | Mathews | |
| Faircloth | McCain | |

NAYS—0

So the amendment (No. 821) was agreed to.

Mr. LEAHY. Mr. President, I move to reconsider the vote.

Mr. GLENN. I move to lay that motion on the table.

The motion to lay on the table was agreed to.

The PRESIDING OFFICER. The Chair reminds the body the remaining votes will be 10 minutes each.

VOTE ON AMENDMENT NO. 840

The PRESIDING OFFICER. The question is on agreeing to the Grassley amendment.

Mr. GLENN. Madam President, I move to table the Grassley amendment, and I ask for the yeas and nays.

The PRESIDING OFFICER. Is there a sufficient second?

There is a sufficient second.

The yeas and nays were ordered.

The PRESIDING OFFICER. The question is on agreeing to the motion of the Senator from Ohio.

The clerk will call the roll.

# Injuries from land mines

## *Doctors should work for a ban on these indiscriminate weapons*

For the past 25 years land mines have ravaged rural communities in some of the poorest countries of the world. This manmade epidemic went largely unreported until early 1988, when relief workers drew attention to the thousands of limbless victims of mines in Afghanistan and Cambodia. Now, antipersonnel mines are injuring large numbers of civilians each year in Burma, Mozambique, Ethiopia, Somalia, Iraq, Nicaragua, and Angola.

The first use of antipersonnel mines dates back to the second world war, when German and allied troops used them to prevent enemy soldiers from removing larger antitank mines. In the late 1960s the United States introduced a new class of antipersonnel mine, scattered from the air and known as remotely delivered mines or "scatterbabies," to stop the flow of men and material from North to South Vietnam through Laos.[1] When stepped on, the device, weighing only 20 g, could tear off a foot. Even today these mines continue to take a toll of lives and limbs among Laotian farmers.

Further technological advances made antipersonnel mines much easier to hide than to find. Modern mines are often all but undetectable by the usual metal detection gear. Some antipersonnel mines are about the size of a tobacco tin, so a soldier can easily strew scores of them during a single patrol.

What makes land mines so abhorrent is the indiscriminate destruction they cause. Unlike bombs or artillery shells, which are designed to explode when they approach or hit their target, mines lie dormant until a person, a vehicle, or an animal triggers their detonating mechanism. Mines do not distinguish between the footfall of a soldier and that of a child. Mines recognise no ceasefire, and long after the fighting has stopped they can maim or kill the children or grandchildren of the soldiers who laid them.

Those civilians most likely to encounter antipersonnel mines are the rural poor who live far from proper medical facilities.[2] Peasants foraging for wood and food or tilling their fields are particularly at risk. Children herding livestock are vulnerable as they often traverse wide tracts of land in search of fresh pastures.

Even when civilians injured by mines reach medical facilities they often fail to receive proper care because blood and medical supplies are unavailable. Victims of mine blasts are also more likely to require amputation[3][4] and remain in hospital longer than those wounded by other munitions.[5] In many cases amputation is required because those helping the victims fail to loosen tourniquets on the wounded limbs at regular intervals.

Land mines, as indicated by Coupland and Korver (p 1509),[6] have ruinous effects on the human body. They drive dirt, bacteria, clothing, and metal and plastic fragments into the tissue, causing secondary infections. The shock wave from an exploding mine can destroy blood vessels well up the leg, forcing surgeons to amputate much higher than the site of the primary wound.[7] Field surgeons report that plastic fragments from the casing of some mines become embedded in tissue or bone.[8] Because these fragments are difficult to detect by x ray examination they must be located by eye and extracted. When such fragments are overlooked they can lead to serious infections, including osteomyelitis.

In many developing countries mine amputees leave hospital without artificial limbs and return to their villages with little hope for the future. There are few, if any, rehabilitation centres, and in agrarian societies, where muscle power means survival, amputees are often viewed by their families and communities as unproductive and simply another mouth to feed.

Given a situation so grave what can the international medical community do to prevent the use of land mines? Casualties can be reduced by clearing and destroying mines already placed and by imposing an international ban on their future use. A campaign for a ban has recently been started by two organisations based in the United States, Physicians for Human Rights and Human Rights Watch. The medical profession could lend its weight to this lobby by studying and publicising the effects of mines on rural communities throughout the world. Individual doctors and medical agencies, such as the International Committee of the Red Cross, Médecins Sans Frontières, and Médecins du Monde, can help future mine clearing efforts by keeping records on injuries caused by mines, including the date and place where they occurred.

The task of ending the use of land mines will not be easy. Government and private arms manufacturers, particularly in Europe, have invested heavily in their production to meet the demand from government and rebel armies worldwide. Governments and industry, however, are not immune to international opinion and pressure. Medical professionals can help document the physical and mental suffering exacted from civilians by land mines. They can also ensure that this information becomes public knowledge in countries that pay for their use.

RAE McGRATH

Director,
Mines Advisory Group

ERIC STOVER

Physicians for Human Rights,
100 Boylston Street,
Boston, Massachusetts 02116,
USA
(Correspondence to Mr Stover)

1 Martin ES, Hiebert M. Explosive remnants of the second Indo China war in Vietnam and Laos. In Westing AH, ed. *Explosive remnants of war: mitigating the environmental effects*. London: Taylo and Francis, 1985:39-49.
2 Fasol R, Irvine S, Zilla P. Vascular injuries caused by anti-personnel mines. *J Cardiovasc Sur (Torino)* 1989;30:467-72.
3 Rautio J, Paavolainen P. Afghan war wounded: experience with 200 cases. *J Trauma* 1988;28:523-5
4 Johnson DE, Panijayanond P, Lumjiak S, Crum JW, Boonkrapu P. Epidemiology of comba casualties in Thailand. *J Trauma* 1981;21:486-8.
5 Johnson DE, Crum JW, Lumjiak S. Medical consequences of the various weapons systems used i: Thailand. *Milit Med* 1981;146:632-4.
6 Coupland RM, Korver A. Injuries from antipersonnel mines: the experience of the International Committee of the Red Cross. *BMJ* 1991;303:1509-12.
7 Traverso LW, Fleming A, Johnson DE, Wongrukmitr B. Combat casualties in northern Thailand emphasis on land mine and levels of amputation. *Milit Med* 1981;146:682-5.
8 Asia Watch and Physicians for Human Rights. *Land mines in Cambodia: the coward's war*. New York Asia Watch and Physicians for Human Rights, 1991.

# APPENDIX 10

*Reprinted from the* **BRITISH MEDICAL JOURNAL,**

*14th December 1991, Vol. 303, Pages 1509-1512*

# Injuries from antipersonnel mines: the experience of the International Committee of the Red Cross

Robin M Coupland, Adriaan Korver

**Abstract**

*Objective*—To describe and quantify patterns of injury from antipersonnel mines in terms of distribution of injury, drain on surgical resources, and residual disability.

*Design*—Retrospective analysis.

*Setting*—Two hospitals for patients injured in war.

*Subjects*—757 patients with injuries from antipersonnel mines.

*Main outcome measures*—Distribution and number of injuries; number of blood transfusions; number of operations; disability.

*Results*—Pattern 1 injury results from standing on a buried mine. These patients usually sustain traumatic amputation of the foot or leg; they use most surgical time and blood and invariably require surgical amputation of one or both lower limbs. Pattern 2 injury is a more random collection of penetrating injuries caused by multiple fragments from a mine triggered near the victim. The lower limb is injured but there is less chance of traumatic amputation or subsequent surgical amputation. Injuries to the head, neck, chest, or abdomen are common. Pattern 3 injury results from handling a mine: the victim sustains severe upper limb injuries with associated face injuries. Eye injuries are common in all groups.

*Conclusions*—Patients who survive standing on a buried mine have greatest disability. Non-combatants are at risk from these weapons; in developing countries their social and economic prospects after recovery from amputation are poor.

## Introduction

The International Committee of the Red Cross (ICRC) deploys surgical teams for treating victims of war in 13 hospitals in Asia and Africa; these are served by first aid posts near the conflict areas. The teams are recruited from national Red Cross societies for three or six months of service.

Mine warfare is commonly used in developing countries, and antipersonnel mines may injure both combatants and non-combatants during and after a conflict. Surprisingly little attention has been paid to this subject in the medical literature; the medical implications of injury patterns and their severity have not been described.

This study was undertaken after the observation that victims of antipersonnel mines present with recognisable patterns of injury. Each pattern carries its own implication for the surgeon, the blood transfusion service, and patients' long term disability.

Three recognisable patterns of injury are seen in ICRC hospitals. In pattern 1 injury the victims trigger a buried mine by standing on the device. They usually have traumatic amputation of part of the lower limb[1-3] with less severe injuries elsewhere; earth and the remains of the foot are blown upwards. Such mines may consist of explosive only or include fragments of metal or plastic. Many are specifically designed to incapacitate by traumatic amputation of all or part of the foot (fig 1). Pattern 2 injury results from a fragment mine being triggered. The pattern of wounding is more random, consisting of multiple fragment wounds (fig 2). Such mines may resemble a grenade and be triggered by a tripwire or they may be ejected from the ground to explode at waist height. The person who triggers the ejected mine rarely survives,[4] but fragment mines are likely to injure others in the vicinity. In pattern 3 injury a mine explodes while being handled. Anyone digging up or defusing mines, laying mines (which is usually denied), or, in the case of children, playing with mines risks injury to the hands and face (fig 3).

This article is intended to promote understanding of the management and plight of victims of antipersonnel mines. The principles of neutrality and impartiality by which the ICRC works preclude identifying the location of the hospitals in this study.

## Method

The hospital records of all patients admitted with the diagnosis of mine injury were reviewed for a calendar year in two different ICRC hospitals (hospitals A and B). The following information was recorded: hospital number; age; sex; time between injury and admission; the distribution of injuries (head, neck, chest, abdomen, genitals, limbs) and whether there was traumatic amputation of limbs; whether the patient died; whether the patient underwent surgical amputation; whether there was another disability and if so of what nature; the total number of times the patient went to the operating theatre; the number of units of blood received by the patient.

Each patient was allotted an injury pattern number according to the clinical record. "Stood on a mine," "injured by mine fragments," and "was handling a mine" are typical descriptions of injury patterns and correspond to patients with patterns 1, 2, and 3 respectively. Injury patterns could also be allocated according to the distribution of injuries as marked on the homunculus on the admission card and the operating notes. When there was insufficient information in the records to give a pattern number or the pattern was ambiguous the form was marked with "N" (no pattern); these records were analysed alongside those of other patterns.

Patients who discharged themselves from hospital against medical advice were excluded from the study.

For the purposes of this study non-combatants were defined as women, boys less than 16 years old, and men over 50 years old.

## Results

The records of 757 patients were reviewed, 276 from hospital A and 481 from hospital B. Table I shows the time between injury and admission to the two hospitals; table II shows the proportion of patients with each injury pattern admitted to the hospitals. Most patients were admitted 6-24 hours after injury, and most patients had pattern 2 injuries.

TABLE I—*Time between wounding and admission to hospital*

| No of hours | No of patients in hospital A* | No of patients in hospital B |
|---|---|---|
| <6 | 47 | 34 |
| 6-24 | 130 | 309 |
| 24-72 | 36 | 87 |
| >72 | 39 | 51 |

*24 Records did not contain this information.

TABLE II—*Number (percentage) of patients with different injury patterns*

| | Hospital A (n=276) | Hospital B (n=481) |
|---|---|---|
| Pattern 1 (traumatic amputation of part of lower limb, less severe injuries elsewhere) | 66 (24) | 135 (28) |
| Pattern 2 (multiple fragment wounds) | 133 (48) | 236 (49) |
| Pattern 3 (injury to hands and face) | 17 (6) | 24 (5) |
| Insufficient information or ambiguous pattern | 60 (22) | 86 (18) |

Table III shows the non-combatant population injured by mines. Twelve of the 30 non-combatants were admitted to hospital A in one 24 hour period; this incident was related to smuggling. Of the pattern 3 patients, one in hospital A was a child; seven in hospital B were children.

TABLE III—*Number (percentage) of non-combatants admitted to the hospitals with a diagnosis of mine injury*

| | Hospital A (n=276) | Hospital B (n=481) |
|---|---|---|
| Women | 20 (7) | 12 (2) |
| Men >50 years | 10 (4) | 77 (16) |
| Children (aged <16) | 7 (3) | 55 (11) |

PATTERN OF INJURY

Six patients (0·8%) died in hospital: two patients with pattern 1 injury, three patients with pattern 2, and one patient with an ambiguous pattern. The number of injuries sustained in different parts of the body is shown in table IV according to injury pattern. Table V shows the demand that patients with different injury patterns make on surgical time and the transfusion service: patients with pattern 1 injuries require more operations, and more such patients require blood transfusions, than patients with other injury patterns. The implications for permanent disability carried by each pattern of injury as indicated by the number and level of amputations and other disabilities are shown in table VI.

For the patients with each pattern the proportion of limbs injured (not including those traumatically amputated) that eventually required amputation is given by the formula:

(total number of amputations −number of traumatic

TABLE IV — *Total number of regional injuries, limb injuries, and limb traumatic amputations sustained by all 757 patients. Patients may have more than one injury*

| | Injury pattern 1 (n=201) | Injury pattern 2 (n=369) | Injury pattern 3 (n=41) | Insufficient information or ambiguous pattern (n=149) |
|---|---|---|---|---|
| Central injuries (head, neck, chest, abdomen) | 38 | 290 | 26 | 61 |
| Upper limb: | | | | |
|   Injuries | 98 | 219 | 20 | 57 |
|   Traumatic amputation | 5 | 5 | 33 | 12 |
| Lower limb: | | | | |
|   Injuries | 156 | 398 | 12 | 134 |
|   Traumatic amputation | 186 | 4 | 1 | 12 |
| Genital injuries | 27 | 14 | 2 | 6 |

TABLE V — *Use of surgical and transfusion resources by patients injured by mines*

| | Injury pattern 1 | Injury pattern 2 | Injury pattern 3 | Insufficient information or ambiguous pattern |
|---|---|---|---|---|
| Mean No of operations/patient | 4·6 | 2·5 | 3·0 | 2·4 |
| No (%) patients given blood transfusion | 151 (74) | 51 (14) | 5 (12) | 23 (15) |
| Mean No of blood units/patient | 4·1 | 3·8 | 3·0 | 2·1 |

TABLE VI — *Residual disability according to injury pattern*

| | Injury pattern 1 (n=201) | Injury pattern 2 (n=369) | Injury pattern 3 (n=41) | Insufficient information or ambiguous pattern (n=149) |
|---|---|---|---|---|
| Upper limbs amputated | 12 | 14 | 39 | 19 |
|   Hand | | | 25 | |
|   Forearm | | | 13 | |
|   Arm | | | 1 | |
| Lower limbs amputated | 210 | 22 | 1 | 19 |
|   Foot | 7 | 3 | | |
|   Below knee amputation | 149 | 13 | | |
|   Above knee amputation | 54 | 6 | | |
| Other disability | 8 | 34 | 10 | 12 |

amputations)÷number of limb injuries. By this formula, 15% (210−186÷156) of the injured lower limbs of patients with pattern 1 injuries were eventually amputated; in patients with pattern 2 injuries 5% (22−4÷398) of injured lower limbs were amputated; in patients with pattern 3 injuries 30% (39−33÷20) of injured upper limbs were amputated.

A total of 64 patients had other injuries: 59 had eye injuries with variable loss of vision; in patients with pattern 1 injuries one nerve palsy was recorded; in patients with pattern 2 injuries two nerve palsies and one urethral stricture were recorded and one patient was rendered deaf and blind.

## Discussion

The study presented here relates to victims of antipersonnel mines admitted to ICRC hospitals. The long and difficult evacuation to these hospitals (most wounded arrived six hours or more after injury) means that those most seriously injured are not seen. This is verified by the low hospital mortality. The less seriously injured may not come to the hospital, making do with local treatment. It is known that the ICRC hospitals see only a small proportion of the injured from the conflicts in their regions. Information available in both locations is that there are many varieties of mines. The similar proportion of pattern 1 to pattern 2 injuries in each hospital would support this.

Civilians in both conflicts are at risk from these weapons, especially those with access to hospital B. It is particularly distressing that here, also, children seem to be susceptible, lending support to rumours that they may be used to walk ahead of combatants in areas where there is a risk of mines; other children may be tempted to pick up mines that have been dropped by air. It is possible that wounded non-combatants, especially women, are not as readily brought to first aid posts as wounded combatants.

### IMPLICATIONS OF INJURY PATTERNS

The study confirms the observation that the patterns of mine injuries and their severity are related to the demand on surgical resources and the blood bank, and it provides a yardstick for any other medical staff who manage or are planning to manage patients injured by mines. It affirms predictable disability from each pattern.

With a pattern 1 injury, in addition to receiving traumatic amputation of one foot or leg, the victim, if he or she survives, has a high chance of contralateral lower limb injury and arm injury and a lower chance of genital and central injuries. The observation that pattern 1 injuries are the most severe is confirmed by their being the greatest drain on surgical and transfusion resources. In pattern 1 there are more amputations, and lower limbs injured but not amputated by the weapon have a higher chance of subsequent surgical amputation, with the result that the patient is usually a bilateral amputee. The larger number of visits to the operating theatre made by these patients reflects difficulty in closing the amputations and in salvaging the other leg. This should be noted by surgeons unfamiliar with these injuries. The difficulties of making the decision to amputate and the operations needed for correct amputation or limb salvage are persistently underestimated. A related observation in ICRC hospitals is that, of all patients, those with limb injuries from mines use most blood.

In pattern 2 there is widespread injury from fragments, with a predilection for the lower limbs. The injury is less severe than in pattern 1, as indicated by the smaller proportion of injured lower limbs requiring amputation. It is interesting that the higher proportion of central injuries associated with pattern 2 does not apparently increase the hospital mortality or blood use.

The injury distribution in pattern 3 is entirely in keeping with the history of handling a mine; not surprisingly, most patients require amputation of part or all the hand. Eye injuries were sustained in nearly a quarter of the patients (10 of 41).

Patients designated "N" had a low number of operations and low blood consumption; this indicates that one reason for the poor documentation may be less severe injury. The number of upper and lower limb amputations compared with those in patients with patterns 1, 2, and 3 injuries indicates that pattern N contains a mixture of other patterns.

In pattern 1 and 3 injuries there is close contact between the limb and the device when it explodes. Possible explanations for the difference in surgical demand between the two patterns are that amputation or salvage of the upper limb is technically easier; the mines that are handled may be smaller; a mine triggered by a foot is buried and so the blast, directed upwards, contains earth and grass; and the leg is more prone to an extreme compartment syndrome, which may be overlooked.[3]

It is known that severity of injury is only one factor determining the level of amputation. Others are the delay in presentation, the judgment and capability of the surgeon, and the type of footwear worn by the victim.[5] In ICRC hospitals the surgeons are encouraged to make every effort to maintain a tibial stump of acceptable length because this may be the factor that determines whether the patient can eventually work and therefore support his or her family.

In the hospitals involved in this study the only specialty emergency that is routinely referred to other agencies is penetrating eye injury. About 8% of patients have eye injury; there is no information about the number with permanently impaired vision. Our experience is that eye injury is sustained from fragments, mud, or sand thrown up by the explosion. Many victims lose one eye and have a variable degree of injury to the other; a minority are totally blinded.

The incidence of other disabilities in these patients is certainly higher than indicated here. Numerous nerve palsies are not documented, probably because they represent only one aspect of the successful salvage of a severely injured limb.

There is little information about the number of patients who discharged themselves from hospital. We are sure that this is quite a small number. The commonest reason for leaving hospital against medical advice is the cultural or religious unacceptability of amputation; some patients prefer to die. Had these patients remained in hospital there would have been a slightly higher number of eventual amputations.

This study focuses on the surgical aspects of antipersonnel mine injuries; one must bear in mind that the prospects for amputees in developing countries may be divorce, unemployment, or crime. The effect on the society of several thousand amputees may be considerable. The ICRC runs rehabilitation centres in many countries and worldwide produces 9000 prostheses a year, most of which are for victims of antipersonnel mines.

We thank Mr Heinz Weiler, Ms Ariane Curdy, and Ms Irene Deslarzes for their invaluable help with the database of this study.

1 Jones EL, Peters AF, Gasior RM. Early management of battle casualties in Vietnam. *Arch Surg* 1968;97:1-15.
2 Cheng XM, Lin YQ, Guo RF, Lian WK, Wang DT. Analysis of wound ballistics in 2414 cases of battle casualties. *J Trauma* 1990;6(suppl):169-72.
3 Coupland RM. Amputation for antipersonnel mine injuries of the leg: preservation of the tibial stump using a medial gastrocnemius myoplasty. *Ann R Coll Surg Engl* 1989;71:405-8.
4 Adams DB, Schwab CW. Twenty one year experience with land mine injuries. *J Trauma* 1988;28(suppl):S159-62.
5 Traverso LW, Fleming A, Johnson DE, Wongrukmitr B. Combat casualties in northern Thailand: emphasis on land mine injuries and levels of amputation. *Milit Med* 1981;146:682-5.

*(Accepted 26 September 1991)*

# APPENDIX 11

[United Nations
General Assembly]

[A/48/L.5
8 October 1993]

[Forty-eighth session
Agenda item 155]

## ASSISTANCE IN MINE CLEARANCE

Austria, Belgium, Denmark, Finland, France, Germany, Greece, Ireland, Italy, Luxembourg, Netherlands, Norway, Portugal, Spain, Sweden and the United Kingdom of Great Britain and Northern Ireland:
Draft Resolution

The General Assembly,

Gravely alarmed by the increasing presence of mines and other unexploded devices as a result of armed conflicts,

Dismayed by the high number of victims of mines, especially among civilian populations, and taking note in this context of resolution 1993/83 of the Commission on Human Rights of 10 March 1993,[1] on the effects of armed conflicts on children's lives,

Gravely concerned by the serious humanitarian, social, economic and ecological disruption which can be caused by the failure to remove mines and other unexploded devices,

Bearing in mind the serious threat which mines and other unexploded devices constitute to the safety, the health and the lives of personnel participating in humanitarian, peace-keeping and rehabilitation operations,

---

[1] See Official Records of the Economic and Social Council, 1993, Supplement No. 3 (E/1993/23), chap. II, sect. A.   442

Aware that mines constitute an obstacle to reconstruction and economic development as well as to the restoration of normal social conditions,

Considering that, in addition to the responsibilities incumbent upon States, there is scope for the United Nations to strengthen its contribution to the solution of problems relating to mine clearance,

Noting with interest, in this regard, the recommendations made by the Secretary-General in paragraph 58 of his report of 17 June 1992 entitled "An Agenda for Peace",[2] as well as in his report of 15 June 1993,[3]

Recalling its resolution 47/120 B of 20 September 1993 on the "Agenda for Peace",

Taking note also of the statement made by the President of the Security Council on 26 February 1993,[4]

Recalling its resolution 47/56 of 9 December 1992 on the Convention on Prohibitions or Restrictions on the Use of Certain Conventional Weapons Which May Be Deemed to Be Excessively Injurious or to Have Indiscriminate Effects, and in particular on the Protocol on Prohibitions or Restrictions on the Use of Mines, Booby Traps and Other Devices (Protocol II),[5]

Noting with interest, in this regard, the convening, by the Secretary-General of the United Nations, of a Conference to review and amend the above-mentioned Convention and in particular its Protocol II,

Noting with satisfaction the inclusion in the mandate of several peace-keeping operations of provisions relating to mine clearance,

---

[2] A/47/277-s/24111.

[3] A/47/965-s/25944.

[4] s/25344.

[5] See The United Nations Disarmament Yearbook, vol. 5: 1980 (United Nations publication, Sales No. E.81.IX.4), appendix VII.

Commending the activities already undertaken by the United Nations system, the International Committee of the Red Cross and non-governmental organizations to address the solution of problems relating to the presence of mines,

Welcoming the establishment, within the Secretariat, of a coordinated mine-clearance programme,

1.     Deplores the adverse consequences which can be caused by the failure to remove mines and other unexploded devices remaining in place after armed conflicts, and considers it a matter of urgency that a solution to these problems be found;

2.     Stresses the importance of coordination by the United Nations of activities, including those by regional organizations, related to mine clearance, in particular those activities relating to information and training with a view to improving the effectiveness of activities in the field;

3.     Invites all relevant programmes and bodies, multilateral or national, to include, in a coordinated manner, activities related to mine clearance in their humanitarian, social and economic assistance activities;

4.     Requests the Secretary-General to submit to it, before its forty-ninth session, a comprehensive report on the problems caused by the increasing presence of mines and other unexploded devices resulting from armed conflicts and on the manner in which the United Nations contribution to the solution of problems relating to mine clearance could be strengthened;

5.     Also requests the Secretary-General to include in his report consideration of the financial aspects of activities related to mine clearance and, in this context, of the advisability of establishing a voluntary trust fund to finance, in particular, information and training programmes relating to mine clearance and to facilitate the launching of mine-clearance operations;

6.     Urges all Member States to extend full assistance and cooperation to the Secretary-General in this respect and to provide him with any information and data which could be useful in drawing up the above-mentioned report;

7. <u>Decides</u> to include, in the provisional agenda of its forty-ninth session, the item entitled "Assistance in mine clearance."

## APPENDIX 12

### HOUSE OF COMMONS
#### LONDON SW1A 0AA

11 December 1992

*Q. Michael Heseltine,*

Please find enclosed a fax I have received from the Vietnam
Veterans of America Foundation regarding their campaign for an
international ban on the trade in landmines which, as you will
be aware, have been the cause of enormous suffering in
countries like Cambodia and Afghanistan and which will continue
to inflict heavy casualties for many years to come.

I understand that the US Congress has recently passed a bill
calling for a one year moratorium on the trade in US anti-
personnel mines.  The bill, sponsored by Senator Patrick Leahy
and Congressman Lane Evans, became law on 23 October.  The
object of the moratorium is to create conditions in which
international action can be taken against the trade in such
weapons.

I will be grateful to know:

1. What types of anti-personnel weapons of the sort covered by
Senator Leahy's bill are produced in this country ?

2. To which countries such weapons have been exported in the
last five years ?

3. If HMG is willing to contemplate legislation along the lines
enacted by the US Congress ?

4. What part HMG is willing to play in initiating an
international ban on the trade in these weapons ?

5. What contribution HMG is making to the clearance of mines in
Cambodia and Afghanistan and to assisting those organisations
who are attempting to cope with the victims of accidents caused
by mines ?

contd.

**HOUSE OF COMMONS**
LONDON SW1A 0AA

Because I appreciate that these are questions for a number of
departments, I am addressing similar letters to the Secretary
of State for Defence and the Minister for Overseas Development.

Chris Mullin MP


Rt Hon Michael Heseltine MP
President of the Board of Trade
Department of Trade and Industry
Ashdown House
123 Victoria Street
London SW1H OET


cc: Vietnam Veterans of America Foundation
    Senator Patrick Leahy
    Congressman Lane Evans

    Defence correspondents of:
    The Guardian
    The Independent
    The Times
    The Financial Times
    The Daily Telegraph

    The Editor, Jane's Weekly

22 January 1993

Chris Mullin MP
House of Commons
London
SW1A 0AA

Foreign &
Commonwealth
Office

London SW1A 2AH

*From The Minister of State*

*Dear Chris*

Thank you for your letter of 11 December to Lynda Chalker
enclosing one from the Vietnam Veterans of America
Foundation about an international ban on the trade in
anti-personnel mines. I am replying as minister responsible
for defence sales at the FCO. I am also replying on behalf
of Michael Heseltine and Malcolm Rifkind to whom you
addressed similar letters.

To take your questions in order: the only type of weapons
produced in the UK which are covered by Senator Leahy's bill
are air-delivered area denial and area attack mines. They
form part of a bomb and are designed to impede the repair of
damage caused to military installations. We do not comment
in detail on those countries to which Britain exports arms;
nor do we disclose information on specific export licence
applications.

We are not contemplating separate legislation to cover the
export of anti-personnel mines similar to that recently
adopted by the US Congress. We believe that our current
stringent controls on the export of defence equipment, which
include controls on all mines, are sufficient to stop the
sale of these weapons to countries which may use them in an
irresponsible manner.

We further believe that attention should be focused on the
observance of the large body of law which implicitly or
explicitly relates to the use of mines rather than the
introduction of new regulations or an international ban on
their trade. We are a signatory to the 1981 Convention on
Prohibitions or Restrictions on the Use of Certain
Conventional Weapons Which May Be Deemed to be Excessively
Injurious or to Have Indiscriminate Effects. Protocols I
and II of the convention introduced strict rules concerning
the use of mines. We are not at present a party to the
Convention but are now considering ratification.

In June 1992 the ODA approved a grant of £173,736 to the
Halo Trust in support of the Cambodia Mine Clearance
Project.  The Halo Trust is actively engaged in demining in
rural Cambodia, focussing on areas of importance to the
community such as areas to which internally displaced people
are expected to return.  The ODA expects shortly to approve
a small grant in support of BBC radio broadcasts on mine
awareness, which will be disseminated via UNTAC radio in
Cambodia.  In addition, £160,000 has been given this year to
the Cambodia Trust for prosthetics training in cooperation
with the ICRC and Harding International.

As part of our response to UN appeals for humanitarian
assistance to Afghanistan in 1992 the ODA has contributed
£0.5m this financial year towards mine clearance programmes
of the UN Office of the Coordinator for Afghanistan (UNOCA).
The ODA expects to continue financial contributions to UNOCA
in support of their demining programmes.  We have provided
£1m this financial year to the ICRC which among other things
has supported a major hospital in Kabul and clinics
elsewhere in the country.  War injuries, including those
caused by mines, have been a major preoccupation of these
medical facilities.  The Halo Trust has also received
£163,000 for its demining of Afghanistan.

I am sending a copy of my reply to Malcolm Rifkind and
Michael Heseltine.

Douglas Hogg

# APPENDIX 13

Strasbourg, 14th December 1992

[The European Parliament]
MOTION FOR A RESOLUTION
pursuant to Rule 64 of the Rules of Procedure
by Mme. Veil, Mrs. Larive and Mme. Andre on behalf of the LDR Group
on the havoc caused by mines

<u>The European Parliament,</u>

A. Conscious of the havoc wrought in Afghanistan, Angola, Cambodia,
   Iraqi Kurdistan, Mozambique, Laos and Somalia in some parts of
   Central America and increasingly in Bosnia-Herzegovina, by the
   planting of mines which are designed to mutilate rather than to kill
   and of whom the most numerous victims are civilians, including
   thousands of children;

B. Aware that, according to non-governmental organisations which are
   struggling with this evil, the number of such mines in Afghanistan
   total 10-12 million and that at the present rate of clearance it will
   take 1000 years to dispose of all the mines;

C. Aware that in Cambodia there are already 36,000 people who have
   lost limbs as a result of these mines;

D. Shocked by the role played by Member States in the production and
   sale of the mines;

E. Disturbed that the work of clearing these mines is held up by the
   failure of Member States and other members of the UN to provide
   the minimum finances required;

1. Calls on all Member States which have not yet ratified the UN
   Convention on Prohibitions or Restrictions on the Use of Certain
   Conventional Weapons Which May be Deemed to be Excessively
   Injurious or to Have Indiscriminate Effects to do so;

2.  Urges on the Ministers meeting in political cooperation the need to extend this Convention to internal conflicts;

3.  Demands that all Member States as an emergency measure, agree to a five year moratorium on their sale of, transfer or export of anti-personnel mines and the military skills to plant them;

4.  Insists on the need to ensure that the specialist military units and NGOs working on clearing mines be provided with the necessary resources to continue and, as more trained people become available, to expand their work;

5.  Calls on Member States, which are Members of the Security Council, to raise the question of how to ensure that the removal of the mines is treated as matter of the greatest urgency;

6.  Stresses that the presence, in vast quantities, of these mines makes economic recovery, especially in predominantly agricultural or pastoral societies impossible;

7.  Instructs its President to transmit this resolution to the Commission, the Council, the Ministers meeting in EPC, the Members of the Security Council and Secretary-General of the UN.

# APPENDIX 14

**UNITED
NATIONS**

## Economic and Social Council

Distr.
LIMITED

E/CN.4/1993/L.11/Add.8
11 March 1993

Original: ENGLISH

COMMISSION ON HUMAN RIGHTS
Forty-ninth session
Agenda item 30

DRAFT REPORT OF THE COMMISSION

Rapporteur: Mr. Zdzislaw KEDZIA (Poland)

CONTENTS*

---

    * E/CN.4/1993/L.10 and addenda will contain the chapters of the report relating to the organization of the session and the various items on the agenda. Resolutions and decisions adopted by the Commission, as well as draft resolutions and decisions for action by, and other matters of concern to, the Economic and Social Council will be contained in documents E/CN.4/1993/L.11 and addenda.

GE.93-12148 (E)

**1993/83.  Consequences of armed conflicts on children's lives**

The Commission on Human Rights,

Welcoming the promptness with which a large number of States have ratified the Convention on the Rights of the Child, which is evidence of unprecedented mobilization by the international community,

Noting in particular the fundamental importance of every child's inherent right to life, as recognized in article 6 of the Convention,

Reaffirming that this right is to be applied especially in times of armed conflict, when children's lives and physical integrity are particularly threatened,

Noting with interest that the Committee on the Rights of the Child, at its second session, decided to hold its first general discussion on the situation of children in armed conflicts (see CRC/C/10), thereby acknowledging the fundamental importance of this issue for the promotion and protection of children's rights and the role of the Convention in this regard,

Noting with consternation the very large number of innocent civilians who continue to be the victims of all forms of armed conflicts now taking place in the world,

Deploring the continued practice of enlisting children in the armed forces,

Deeply concerned at the alarming figures for deaths and serious injuries entailing life-long disability among children in areas of conflict,

Alarmed at the information that some particularly injurious weapons, especially anti-personnel mines, continue to strike long after conflicts have ended,

Noting with distress that children are often among the main victims of such weapons, and especially of anti-personnel mines,

Fully aware in this respect of the importance of operations for the effective detection, clearance and destruction of unremoved mines, operations that cannot be conducted without resources or special skills, and anxious to promote international cooperation in this field,

Noting the commitments entered into by States in fields pertaining to humanitarian law, and particularly the Geneva Conventions of 12 August 1949 and their Additional Protocols,

Recalling that, on that basis both of international humanitarian law and of the provisions of the Convention on the Rights of the Child, States must take all possible measures to ensure special protection and suitable care and the physical and psychological recovery, as well as social reintegration, of children affected by an armed conflict,

Also recalling in this regard the specific commitments entered into by States that have ratified the 1980 Convention on Prohibitions or Restrictions on the Use of Certain Conventional Weapons Which May Be Deemed to Be Excessively Injurious or to Have Indiscriminate Effects, and particularly Protocol II, on Prohibitions or Restrictions on the Use of Mines, Booby Traps and Other Devices, and calling on States to consider ratifying these instruments,

1.    Expresses its deep concern and indignation at the serious consequences of armed conflicts on children, directly or indirectly involved, who are often among the main victims of the indiscriminate use of anti-personnel mines;

2.    Expresses its gratitude to the Committee on the Rights of the Child for its views, at its second session, on the issue of children in armed conflicts, in particular on the need to strengthen preventive measures and to implement effective protection for children, and notes the recommendations made by the Committee at its third session on means to improve the protection of children against adverse consequences of armed conflicts (see CRC/C/16), including the recommendation made to the General Assembly to undertake a study in the light of article 45 (c) of the Convention;

3.    Expresses its gratitude to the International Committee of the Red Cross for its efforts to foster awareness of the issue of anti-personnel mines;

4.    Encourages efforts to promote international cooperation to assist in the detection and clearance of unremoved mines;

5.    Requests all States to render full support to prevention of the indiscriminate use of anti-personnel mines and to protection and assistance for the victims;

6.    Invites the relevant organizations in the United Nations system as well as other intergovernmental organizations to intensify their efforts to ensure that all possible assistance is given to child victims of anti-personnel mines, who are often disabled for life, with a view to their physical and psychological recovery and social reintegration, and also to support to this end the activities of non-governmental organizations in the field.

67th meeting
10 March 1993
[Adopted without a vote. See chap. XXIV.]

# APPENDIX 15


# COMITÉ INTERNATIONAL DE LA CROIX-ROUGE


## UNITED NATIONS

## GENERAL ASSEMBLY (47th Session 1992)


## FIRST COMMITTEE


Convention on Prohibitions or Restrictions on the Use of Certain Conventional Weapons which May Be Deemed to Be Excessively Injurious or to Have Indiscriminate Effects


## STATEMENT BY THE

## INTERNATIONAL COMMITTEE OF THE RED CROSS (ICRC)

## TUESDAY, OCTOBER 27TH 1992

1.  The Mandate of the ICRC and the 1980 Convention

International humanitarian law prohibits the use of means or methods of warfare that are indiscriminate or cause excessive injury, and the ICRC has the mandate to work for the faithful application of this law and to prepare suitable developments. The ICRC has taken a number of initiatives in the past to develop treaty rules that implement the basic rules of international humanitarian law as well as steps to encourage a better application of them. One of these initiatives was the appeal made by the ICRC to governments and to the League of Nations to take action to prohibit the use of chemical weapons and this contributed to the adoption of the 1925 Geneva Protocol. We are therefore very pleased that States have decided to more vigourously pursue the goal of the total non-use of these weapons by also prohibiting their manufacture and stockpiling. It is certainly a great achievement that the treaty that has been so carefully negotiated for this purpose is now near adoption.

Another important initiative of the ICRC was the Conference of Government Experts that it convened in order to study the possibility of a treaty regulation of certain weapons that could be considered to be excessively injurious or having indiscriminate effects. These experts met in Switzerland in 1974 and 1976 and the results of their work was used as a basis for the United Nations Conference that adopted this Weapons Convention in 1980. Given the important role that the ICRC played in the initial preparation of this Convention, as well as the mandate of the ICRC in general, we take a particular interest in the extent to which this Convention is being adhered to and its provisions applied in practice.

2.  Protocol II to the 1980 Convention on Mines Booby-Traps and Other Devices

Probably the most pertinent of the Convention's Protocols, in the light of the situation we are faced with today, is the second one regulating the use of mines, booby-traps and other devices. Given the greater awareness that exists today on the immense problems created by the use of landmines, in particular anti-personnel landmines, it is worth recalling that this Protocol provides some important basic restrictions on their use. First of all it reaffirms the

456

basic rules of international humanitarian law by outlawing the indiscriminate use of mines. Thus it provides that they may only be directed at military objectives and that all feasible precautions are to be taken to protect civilians. There are specific further restrictions on the use of remotely-delivered mines which may not be used unless their location is accurately recorded or they are fitted with an effective neutralising mechanism. The treaty also requires that parties record all pre-planned minefields and endeavour to ensure the recording of all others. There is also a provision requiring parties to try to take the necessary measures to clear minefields or otherwise render them harmless after the end of hostilities.

Unfortunately, as we know only too well, the actual use of mines tends to reflect anything but conformity with these rules. We have seen such a massive indiscriminate use of mines that there are now millions of mines strewn in countries that have been involved in armed conflict. These mines, and those who have been responsible for their use, have blindly killed or injured countless innocent victims and they continue to do so after the conflicts are over. Huge expanses of land are now uncultivatable, preventing people from returning to their homes. The full extent of this scourge has become apparent in countries where mine-clearance teams are presently facing an unbelievably slow and dangerous task. The experience of these teams shows that it takes many years to clear only very small areas, and casualties among mine-clearance teams is frighteningly high.

We need to ask ourselves why such a situation has arisen in order to work out the steps that absolutely need to be taken to prevent its worsening. Apart from the obviously indiscriminate use of these mines, the easy availability and relative cheapness of these weapons has clearly enabled such an incredibly widespread use. The fact that the vast majority of these mines are not fitted with neutralising or self-destruct mechanisms means that they continue to be dangerous long after the military purpose for which they were laid has expired. Finally, mine-clearing has become so incredibly difficult because mines are increasingly manufactured so as to be undetectable. Unless urgent and effective action is taken to deal with this situation, it will only worsen because yet more of these devices will be laid in the same fashion in future conflicts.

3.    Strengthening the 1980 Convention

At present only 32 States are party to the 1980 Convention, a very disappointing rate of participation. Yet the present catastrophe caused by indiscriminate mines' use proves just how relevant and important this treaty's provisions are. States must now as a matter of urgency indicate their concern by ratifying the treaty themselves and by actively encouraging its universal ratification. They must also, of course, take the necessary steps to see to it that its provisions are taught to the armed forces so that the rules are effectively carried out.

Thought should also be given to an appropriate strengthening of this Convention which could be undertaken during a revision conference which is provided for in the Convention. Thus measures for implementation of its provisions, including perhaps verification, could be usefully considered.

The Convention also foresees the possible adoption of additional Protocols so that new weapons' developments and use are in conformity with the basic principles of international humanitarian law and with the humanitarian needs of society. The ICRC continues to inform itself on such developments. In this connection we may mention here that the ICRC will be publishing in one volume the four reports of the meetings of experts that were held on blinding laser weapons and that this publication will be available in English, French and Spanish at the beginning of 1993.

Finally, serious thought should be given to the applicability of the rules found in the 1980 Convention to non-international armed conflicts. At present, the Convention only applied to international armed conflicts, but the majority of today's conflicts are internal or a mixture of internal and international. Many of them last for very long periods creating the kind of severe problems that we see in relation to mines' use. Surely the need to avoid this extent of human suffering transcends the theoretical distinction between international and internal conflicts and we need to recognise the value of restraining indiscriminate and excessively cruel weapons' use in all types of conflicts.

In this respect, the wishes of the ICRC and those working in disarmament are the same, namely, to take practical measures which are aimed at solving the real problems that we are faced with. We sincerely hope that every effort will be made to find the most effective solutions and to implement them.

DDM/JUR 92/LDB/jp
19.10.1992

# APPENDIX 16

JIMMY CARTER

August 28, 1992

To Jody Williams

Thank you for sending me the material on the campaign to ban the use, production and trade in landmines. I am pleased to endorse your efforts and am impressed with the good plans that are in place.

Please extend my best wishes to all who are giving of their time and talents for such a significant cause.

Sincerely,

Jimmy Carter

Mr. Jody Williams
Coordinator
Landmines Campaign
Vietnam Veterans of America Foundation
2001 "S" Street, N.W.
Suite 740
Washington, D.C.  20009

# APPENDIX 17

# Antipersonnel Landmine Types and Producers

## Argentina

### Argentina Ministry of Defense
Direccion Generale de Fabriacaciones Militaires

| Weapon | Material | Characteristics |
|--------|----------|-----------------|
| FMK-1 | Plastic | Blast |
| MAPG | Metal | Blast, press or pull |
| MAPPG | Metal | Bounding |

## Austria

### Armaturen-Gesellschaft GmbH

| Weapon | Material | Characteristics |
|--------|----------|-----------------|
| ARGES M89 | | Clay, dir, frag |
| ARGES M80 | | Clay, dir, frag |
| ARGES M80A1 | | Clay, dir, frag |
| SpM75 | | Bound, frag, trip |

### Dynamit-Nobel Wien

| Weapon | Material | Characteristics |
|--------|----------|-----------------|
| DNW HM 1000 | Plastic | Dir, frag |

### Hirtenberger AG

| Weapon | Material | Characteristics |
|--------|----------|-----------------|
| APM-1 | | Clay, dir, frag |
| APM-2 | | Clay, dir, frag |
| APM-3 | | Frag |

### Sudsteirische Metall-Industrie GmbH

| Weapon | Material | Characteristics |
|--------|----------|-----------------|
| SMI 17/4C | | Dir, frag |
| APM 19 | | Clay, dir, frag |
| APM 29 | | Clay, dir, frag |
| AVM 100 | | Clay, dir, frag |
| AVM 195 | | Clay dir frag |
| 21/11C | | Clay, dir, frag |
| 21/3C | | Clay, dir, frag |
| 20/1C | | Clay, dir, frag |

## Belgium

### Giat Industries
#### Poudres Reunie de Belgue (PRB SA)

| Weapon | Material | Characteristics |
|--------|----------|-----------------|
| NR 257 | Metal | Press |
| NR 409 | Plastic | Press |
| NR 413 | Metal | Trip, frag |
| NR 430 | | Bound, frag, press or pull |
| NR 442 | | Bound, frag, press or pull |
| PRB BAC | Plastic | Blast, frag |
| PRB M35 | | Blast, press |
| U/1 | | Blast, press |

## Brazil

### Britanite Industrias Quimicas Ltda.

| Weapon | Material | Characteristics |
|--------|----------|-----------------|
| T-AB-1 | Plastic | Press |

### Quimica Tupan SA

| Weapon | Material | Characteristics |
|--------|----------|-----------------|
| AP NM AE T1 | Non-metal | |

## Bulgaria

### Kintex (marketing agency)

| Weapon | Material | Characteristics |
|--------|----------|-----------------|
| PSM-1 | Metal | Bound, frag |
| PSM-10b | Metal | |
| PM-79 | Metal | Press |

## Canada

### SNC Industrial Technologies Inc.

| Weapon | Material | Characteristics |
|--------|----------|-----------------|
| C3A1  (Elsie) | Plastic | Press,  blast |

## Chile

### FAMAE Fabricas y Maestranzas del Ejercito

| Weapon | Material | Characteristics |
|---|---|---|
| MAPP 78-F2 | Plastic | Press, Blast |
| MAPT 78-F2 | Plastic | Trip, Blast |
| M18 | | Dir, frag |

### Metalnor SA

| Weapon | Material | Characteristics |
|---|---|---|
| AP | Metal | Blast, frag |
| AP II | | Bound, blast, frag; press or trip |
| M18 | | Clay, Dir, Frag |

## China

### China North Industries Corporation

| Weapon | Material | Characteristics |
|---|---|---|
| Type 69 | | Frag, bound, press or trip |
| Portable | | Bound, Frag |
| Type 72 | Plastic | Blast, press |
| Directional steel frag. | Metal | Blast or frag, trip |
| Type 72B | Plastic | Blast, press, anti-handle |
| Type 72C | Plastic | Blast, press |

### Chinese State Arsenals

| Weapon | Material | Characteristics |
|---|---|---|
| POMZ-2 | Metal | Frag, stake |
| PPM-2 | | Frag |
| PMN | Plastic | Press |
| PMD-6 | Wood | Blast; press or trip |
| Type 66 | | Dir, frag |
| Type 59 | Metal | Frag, stake |

## Cyprus

### Not known

| Weapon | Material | Characteristics |
|---|---|---|
| BPD SB-33 | | |

## Czechoslovakia (ex)

### Czechoslovak State Factories

| Weapon | Material | Characteristics |
|---|---|---|
| PP-Mi-Ba | Plastic | |
| PP-Mi-D | Wood | Blast |
| PP-Mi-Sb | Metal & Concrete | Stake, frag, press |
| PP-Mi-Sk | Metal & Concrete | Stake, frag, pull |
| PP-Mi-Sr | Metal | Bound, frag, pull or press. |
| PP-MI-ST-46 | Metal | Frag, pull |

## Denmark

### Not known

| Weapon | Material | Characteristics |
|---|---|---|
| AIPD 51 | | |
| M 47-1 | Wood or bakelite | Blast |
| M14 | Plastic | Press, blast |
| M16 | Metal | Press or trip, bound, frag |

## Egypt

### Ministry of War Production
#### Heliopolis Company for Chemical Industries

| Weapon | Material | Characteristics |
|---|---|---|
| T/78 | Plastic | Blast |

#### Kaha Company for Chemical Industries

| Weapon | Material | Characteristics |
|---|---|---|
| A/P jumping | | Bound, frag, jump |

#### Maasara Company for Engineering Industries

| Weapon | Material | Characteristics |
|---|---|---|
| A/P plastic | Plastic | |
| A/P fragmentation | | Clay, dir, frag |
| A/P jumping | | Jump, trip |

## El Salvador

### Not known

| Weapon | Material | Characteristics |
|---|---|---|
| Claymore-type | Wood | Clay, dir, frag |

# France

## Not known

| Weapon | Material | Characteristics |
|---|---|---|
| A/P Fragm. plate | | Dir, frag |
| M 1948 SCHU | | Blast |
| M-1956 | Plastic | Press, Blast |
| MiAPMB 51/55 | Metal | Bound, frag |
| DV-56 | Plastic | Blast, press |
| A/P directed frag | Metal | Dir, frag |
| Belouga Bomblet | Metal | |

## Societe d'Armement et d'Etudes Alsetex

| Weapon | Material | Characteristics |
|---|---|---|
| MAPED F1 | Metal | Clay dir frag; com, trip or electr. |
| Mark 61 | | Press, stake, Frag |
| Mark 63 | | Press, frag, stake, anti-lift |
| M 59 (Mi APDV 59) | Plastic | |
| M 1951/55 | Metal | Frag, bound |
| M 1951 | Plastic | Blast |
| M 51 | Metal | Bound, frag |

# Germany (ex-F.R.G.)

## DIEHL
### Ordnance Division

| Weapon | Material | Characteristics |
|---|---|---|
| DM11 | "Non-metal" | Circular, press, blast |
| DM31 | Metal | Bound, blast |
| MUSA | Metal | Frag |
| MUSPA | Metal | Frag, self-dest |

## Daimler-Benz
### Messerschmitt-Bolkow-Blohm (MBB)

| Weapon | Material | Characteristics |
|---|---|---|
| MUSA | Metal | Frag |
| MUSPA | Metal | Frag, self-dest |

## Dynamit Nobel AG
### Defense Technology Division

| Weapon | Material | Characteristics |
|---|---|---|
| AP2 | Metal | Frag, scat |

## Germany (ex-F.R.G.)

### Rheinmetal GmbH

| Weapon | Material | Characteristics |
|--------|----------|-----------------|
| MUSA | Metal | Frag |
| MUSPA | Metal | Frag, self-dest |

## Germany (ex-G.D.R.)

### Former East German state factories

| Weapon | Material | Characteristics |
|--------|----------|-----------------|
| PPM-2 | | Press, electr., blast |
| PMP 71/2 | | Blast, frag |
| SM-70 | Metal | Dir, frag, electr |
| POMS-2 | Metal | Frag, stake |
| POMS-2M | Metal | Frag, stake |

## Germany (not given)

### Not known

| Weapon | Material | Characteristics |
|--------|----------|-----------------|
| DM-39 | Metal or plastic | Press, blast, delay, anti-lift |
| K-2 | Metal | Bound, frag, press or trip |
| Remote bounding | | bound, comm |
| S-Mine 35 | Metal | bound, frag |
| SD-2 | Metal | blast, frag |
| Truppmina 11 | Metal | bound, frag |
| W-1 | | Blast |
| PM-60 | Plastic | Blast; press or pull |

## Greece

### ELVIEMEK SA

| Weapon | Material | Characteristics |
|--------|----------|-----------------|
| EM 20 | Plastic | |

### Hellenic Arms Industry SA

| Weapon | Material | Characteristics |
|--------|----------|-----------------|
| M16A2 | | |

## Hungary

### Hungarian State Factories

| Weapon | Material | Characteristics |
|---|---|---|
| Gyata-64 | Some metal | Blast, frag |
| M62 | Plastic | Press, blast |
| M49 | Wood | Press, blast, trip, anti-lift |
| MS-3 | Plastic | Press, anti-dist. |
| A/P Bounding | | Bound, frag, trip |
| RAMP | Metal | Blast |
| CVP-1 dual purpose | Metal | Press, blast |

## India

### Ordnance Factory Board

| Weapon | Material | Characteristics |
|---|---|---|
| M 14 | Plastic | Press, blast |
| M16A1 | Metal | Bound, frag |

## Iran

### Not known

| Weapon | Material | Characteristics |
|---|---|---|
| Claymore M18A1 | | Clay, dir, frag |

## Iraq

### Not known

| Weapon | Material | Characteristics |
|---|---|---|
| VS-69 | | Bound, jump, frag |
| P-25 | Plastic | Trip |
| P-40 | Plastic | Bound, frag, jump |
| PMN-1 | | |
| ICM | | Frag |

## Israel

### Explosive Industries Ltd.

| Weapon | Material | Characteristics |
|---|---|---|
| No 4 | Plastic | Press, blast |

# Israel

## Israel Military Industries (aka TAAS)

| Weapon | Material | Characteristics |
|---|---|---|
| No 10 | Plastic | Press, blast |
| No. 12 (M12A1) | | Trip, frag, bound |

# Italy

## Fiat Group
### BPD Difesa e Spazio srl (formerly Misar)

| Weapon | Material | Characteristics |
|---|---|---|
| SB-33 | Plastic | Press, blast, anti-disturb |
| P-25 | Plastic | Trip, frag |
| P-40 | Plastic | Bound, frag, jump |

## Valsella Meccanotecnica SpA

| Weapon | Material | Characteristics |
|---|---|---|
| VS-50 | Plastic | Press, blast |
| VS-50 AR | | Anti-dist., press, blast |
| VS-Mk 2 | Non-metal | Press, blast |
| Valmara 69 | Plastic | Bound, jump, frag |
| VS-APFM1 | Plastic | Bound, trip, jump, self-de |
| VS-ER-83 | Metal | Stake, frag |
| Valmara | Metal or plastic | Bound, frag |
| Valmara 59 | Metal | Bound, frag |
| VS-Mk 2-E | Non-metal | Blast, anti-lift |
| VS-JAP | | Jumping, frag, trip. |
| VS-DAFMI | Plastic | Clay, dir, frag., plastic, trip or remote |
| VS-MK2-EL | Plastic | Press, anti-lift, self-deact or self-dest, |

## Not known

| Weapon | Material | Characteristics |
|---|---|---|
| Maus-1 | | Press, blast |
| R | Wood | Frag |
| AUPS | Plastic | Blast, frag |
| AUS 50/5 | Plastic | Bound, frag, press or trip |
| B 4 | Metal | Blast, trip |
| ICM | | Frag |
| IT-S-AP | | Blast |
| LORY | plastic & rubber | Blast, press |
| M 51 | | Bound, frag |
| M-59 | Metal | Bound, frag |
| Maus | Metal & Plastic | |
| Minelba Type A | Plastic | Blast, press |
| Minelba Type B | Plastic | Blast, press |
| Model R | Wood | Blast, frag |
| Model V | Metal | Frag, trip |
| Picket Mine | Metal | Blast, trip |

## Italy

**Not known**

### Tecnovar Italiana SpA

| Weapon | Material | Characteristics |
|---|---|---|
| TS-50 | Plastic | Blast |
| VAR/40 | Plastic | Press, blast |
| VAR/100 | Plastic | Press, blast |
| VAR/100/SP | Metal | Frag |
| BM/85 | Plastic | Press, trip, frag, bound |

## Japan

### Ishikawa Siesakusho Limited

| Weapon | Material | Characteristics |
|---|---|---|
| FFV013 | | Clay, dir, frag |

**Not known**

| Weapon | Material | Characteristics |
|---|---|---|
| M-67 | | |

## Korea, North

### North Korean state arsenals

| Weapon | Material | Characteristics |
|---|---|---|
| Model 15 | Metal | Press, blast |
| Shrapnel A/P | Metal | Frag |
| PMD Mortar Mine | Wood | Blast |
| Wooden AP | Wood | Blast |

## Korea, South

### Daewoo Corporation

| Weapon | Material | Characteristics |
|---|---|---|
| K440 | | Clay, dir, frag |

### Korea Explosives Company Ltd.

| Weapon | Material | Characteristics |
|---|---|---|
| M18A1 | | Clay, dir, frag |

## Korea, South

### Korea Explosives Company Ltd.

#### Not known

| Weapon | Material | Characteristics |
|--------|----------|-----------------|
| KM16A2 | | |

## Mexico

### Not known

| Weapon | Material | Characteristics |
|--------|----------|-----------------|
| Min AP NM AE T1 | Plastic | Blast |

## Netherlands

### EUROMETAAL

| Weapon | Material | Characteristics |
|--------|----------|-----------------|
| AP 23 | Metal | Bound, frag |

#### Not known

| Weapon | Material | Characteristics |
|--------|----------|-----------------|
| Model 15 | Non-metal | Press, blast |
| Model 22 | Plastic | Press |

## Nicaragua

### Not known

| Weapon | Material | Characteristics |
|--------|----------|-----------------|
| TAP-4 | | EM-1, electric detonators |

## Pakistan

### Pakistan Ordnance Factories

| Weapon | Material | Characteristics |
|--------|----------|-----------------|
| P2 Mk2 | | Blast |
| P-7 | | Bound; blast or frag; press or trip |
| P5 Mark 1 | | Clay, dir, frag |
| P4 Mk1 | Plastic | Blast |

## Peru

### Servicios Industirales de la Marina (SIMA)
#### Centro de Fabricacion de Armas

| Weapon | Material | Characteristics |
|--------|----------|-----------------|
| MGP-30 | Non-metal | |

## Poland

### Not known

| Weapon | Material | Characteristics |
|--------|----------|-----------------|
| Plastic A/P | Plastic | Frag |

## Portugal

### Explosivos da Trafaria, S.A.R.L.

| Weapon | Material | Characteristics |
|--------|----------|-----------------|
| MAPS | Non-metal | Press, blast |

### Not known

| Weapon | Material | Characteristics |
|--------|----------|-----------------|
| M/966, Frag | | Frag, trip |
| M/966 | | Frag, bound |
| M954 | "Non-metal" | |
| M412 | "Non-metal" | |

### Sociedade Portuguesa de Explosivos, S.A.R.L.

| Weapon | Material | Characteristics |
|--------|----------|-----------------|
| M432 | Metal | Bound, frag |
| M411 | | Blast |
| BPD SB-33 | Plastic | |

## Romania

### Romanian State Factories

| Weapon | Material | Characteristics |
|--------|----------|-----------------|
| Lightweight AP | | Press, blast |
| MS-3 Ambush M. | | Press |
| Directional | | Frag |

## Singapore

### Chartered Industries of Singapore

| Weapon | Material | Characteristics |
|---|---|---|
| VS-50<br>VS-69<br>SPM-1 | Plastic | Press, blast<br>Bound, jump, frag |

## South Africa

### Denel (Pty) Ltd. (Successor to Armscor)

| Weapon | Material | Characteristics |
|---|---|---|
| No. 69<br>A/P HE or R2M1<br>Shrapnel M No. 2<br>Claymore M18A1<br>Type 72 | Plastic<br><br><br><br>Plastic | Bound, jump, frag<br>Press, blast<br>Clay, dir, frag<br>Clay, dir, frag<br>Blast, press |

## Spain

### Explosivos Alaveses SA

| Weapon | Material | Characteristics |
|---|---|---|
| BPD SB-33<br>P-S-1<br>P-4-A<br>P-4<br>P-4-B | Metal<br>Plastic<br>Plastic<br>"Non-metal" | Bound, Frag<br>Press, blast<br>Press, blast |

### Not known

| Weapon | Material | Characteristics |
|---|---|---|
| FAMA<br>H-1<br>M45B | Plastic | Blast |

# Sweden

## Celsius AB

| Weapon | Material | Characteristics |
|---|---|---|
| Airfield | Wood | Blast |
| AP 12 | | Dir, frag, elctr or trip |
| M-11 | Metal | Bound, frag |
| M-12 | | Frag, electr or trip |
| M-46 | Cardboard | Blast |
| M/41 | Wood | Blast |
| M/43 | Cardboard | Blast |
| M/43T | Cardboard | Blast |
| M/48 | Metal | Frag |
| M/49 | Cardboard | Blast |
| M/49B | Cardboard | Blast |
| M43 (47MM) | | Frag |
| M43 (80mm) | | Frag |
| M43T (10CM) | | Frag |
| Model 43 and 43(T) | Concrete & Metal | Frag |
| Truppmina 9 | Metal | Frag |

### Bofors

| Weapon | Material | Characteristics |
|---|---|---|
| FFV 013 | | Clay, dir, frag |
| FFV 013R | | Clay, dir, frag |
| Mina 5 | | |

### Lindesbergs Industrier AB

| Weapon | Material | Characteristics |
|---|---|---|
| LI-11 (Truppmina 10) | Plastic & rubber | Blast, press |
| LI-12 | | Dir, frag |

# Switzerland

## Not known

| Weapon | Material | Characteristics |
|---|---|---|
| P59 | | Press |
| Model 49 | | Frag, press |
| M3 | Plastic, nylon | Blast |
| P 59 | Plastic | Blast |
| Plastic AP Mine | Plastic | Blast |

## Taiwan

### Hsing Hua

| Weapon | Material | Characteristics |
|---|---|---|
| M16A1 | | |
| M18A1 | | Clay, dir, frag |
| M2A4 | | |
| M3 | | Frag |

## U.S.S.R. (ex)

### ELECTRONINTORG Ltd.

| Weapon | Material | Characteristics |
|---|---|---|
| OZM-72 | | Frag, bound; com, pull, or press. |

### Soviet State Factories

| Weapon | Material | Characteristics |
|---|---|---|
| PMN | Plastic | Press, blast |
| PMN-2 | | Blast |
| POMZ-2 | | Stake frag trip |
| PMD-6 | Wood | Press, blast, MUV series |
| PMD-7 | Wood | Press, blast |
| PMD-57 | Wood | Blast |
| MON-50 | | Clay, dir, frag |
| MON-90 | | Clay, dir, frag |
| MON-100 | Metal | Dir, frag |
| MON-200 | Metal | Dir, frag |
| PFM-1 | Metal | Blast |
| OZM-160 | Metal | Com, Frag, bound |
| KhF-1 | | Bound, chem, com |
| KhF-2 | Metal | Chem |
| MS-3 | | |
| MZ | Metal | Frag |
| OZM-72 | Metal | Bound, frag |
| PMD-56 | Wood | Blast |
| PMD-7ts | Wood | Blast |
| PMK-40 | Cardboard | Blast |
| PMM-3 | Metal | Blast |
| PMM-5 | Metal | Blast, frag |
| PMP | Metal | Integral fuze |
| PMP 71/1 | Plastic | Blast, frag |
| PMZ-4 | | Bound, frag |
| POM 2S | Metal | Frag |
| Unknown | | Chem |
| OZM | Metal | Bound, frag |
| PMD-6M | | AP, blast, MUV series |
| POMZ-2m | | Stake frag trip |

# United Kingdom

## British Aerospace
### Royal Ordnance

| Weapon | Material | Characteristics |
|--------|----------|-----------------|
| No. 6 | Plastic | Blast |

## Not known

| Weapon | Material | Characteristics |
|--------|----------|-----------------|
| DORIS | Plastic | |
| Mark 1 "Dingbat" No. 7 | | Blast |
| Mark 2 | Metal | Bound, frag |
| No. 5 | Cardboard | Blast |
| No. 7 | Metal | Blast |
| Ointment Box | | |
| PADMINE | | Frag, trip or electr, dir |

## Thorn/EMI Electronics
### Defense Systems Division

| Weapon | Material | Characteristics |
|--------|----------|-----------------|
| L10 Ranger | | Blast |

# United States

## Accudyne Corporation

| Weapon | Material | Characteristics |
|--------|----------|-----------------|
| BLU-92/B [Gator] | Metal | Electr, frag, anti-dist, self-dest |

## Aerojet Ordnance Co.

| Weapon | Material | Characteristics |
|--------|----------|-----------------|
| BLU-92/B [Gator] | Metal | Electr, self-dest |

## Alliant Techsystems
### (Formerly Honeywell Defense Systems)

| Weapon | Material | Characteristics |
|--------|----------|-----------------|
| M86 PDM | Metal | Bound, frag, self-dest |
| M74 | Metal | Blast, frag, anti-dist |
| BLU-92/B [Gator] | Metal | Electr, frag, anti-dist, self-dest |

# United States

### Day and Zimmerman
#### Lone Star Army Ammunition Plant

| Weapon | Material | Characteristics |
|---|---|---|
| Claymore M18A1 | | Clay, dir, frag |

## EMCO Inc.

| Weapon | Material | Characteristics |
|---|---|---|
| BLU-92/B [Gator] | Metal | Electr, self-dest |

### Gencorp
#### Aerojet Ordnance

| Weapon | Material | Characteristics |
|---|---|---|
| M77 | | |
| BLU-92/B [Gator] | Metal | Electr, self-dest |

## Hughes Aircraft Company

| Weapon | Material | Characteristics |
|---|---|---|
| MOPMS | | |

## International Signal and Control Group PLC

| Weapon | Material | Characteristics |
|---|---|---|
| Claymore M18A1 (detonator | | Clay, dir, frag |

## Lockheed Corporation

| Weapon | Material | Characteristics |
|---|---|---|
| M74 | Metal | Blast, frag |
| BLU-92/B [Gator] | Metal | Electr, self-dest |

## Magnavox

| Weapon | Material | Characteristics |
|---|---|---|
| BLU-92/B [Gator] | Metal | Electr, self-dest |

# United States

## Mason-Hanger
### Iowa Army Ammunition Plant

| Weapon | Material | Characteristics |
|--------|----------|-----------------|
| Claymore M18A1 | | Clay, dir, frag |

## Mohawk Electrical Systems Inc.

| Weapon | Material | Characteristics |
|--------|----------|-----------------|
| Claymore M18A1 | | Clay, dir, frag |

## Multiple manufacturers or not given

| Weapon | Material | Characteristics |
|--------|----------|-----------------|
| M26 | Metal | Bound, frag, press or trip |
| M16 | Metal | Bound, press, trip |
| M16A1 | Metal | Bound, press, trip |
| M16A2 | Metal | Bound, press, trip |
| M14 | Plastic | Press |
| M2A4 | | Bound, frag, press or trip |
| M1 1 Gallon Chem. | | Chem |
| M23 Chemical Agent Mine | | Chem |
| BLU 42 | Metal | Bound, frag |
| BLU 43 (Short Dragon Tooth) | | Blast |
| BLU 61A/B Bomblet | Metal | Frag |
| BLU 63/B & 86/B Bomblet | Metal | Frag |
| BLU-54 | | Blast, frag |
| Deneye | | Frag |
| M25 | Metal & Plastic | Dir, blast |
| M2A3B2 | | |
| M3 | Metal | Frag |
| MDH C-40 | Metal | Dir, frag |
| MLU/54-E | Metal | Frag |
| XM-37 | | |
| XM-55 | | |
| XM-131 | | Frag |
| XM-27 | | |
| XM-65 | | |
| BLU 31/B | Metal | Blast, frag |
| M7A2 | Metal | Blast |
| BLU 44 (Long Dragon Tooth | | |
| XM-90 | | |
| M510 Minimore | | Frag |
| M2 | | |
| M2A1 | | |

## United States

### Quantic

| Weapon | Material | Characteristics |
|--------|----------|-----------------|
| M74 | Metal | Blast, frag |

### RCA
#### Solid State Division

| Weapon | Material | Characteristics |
|--------|----------|-----------------|
| BLU-92/B [Gator] | Metal | Electr, self-dest |

### Southern Ordnance Industries

| Weapon | Material | Characteristics |
|--------|----------|-----------------|
| MOPMS | | |

### Thiokol Corp.
#### Ordnance Marketing

| Weapon | Material | Characteristics |
|--------|----------|-----------------|
| Claymore M18A1<br>M86 PDM | | Clay, dir, frag |

## Venezuela

### Not known

| Weapon | Material | Characteristics |
|--------|----------|-----------------|
| M 6 | | Blast |

# Vietnam

## State Factories

| Weapon | Material | Characteristics |
|---|---|---|
| DH-10 | Metal | Dir, frag |
| DH-3 | Metal | Dir, frag |
| DH-3 (Rectangular) | Metal | Dir, frag |
| DH-5 | Metal | Dir, frag |
| MDH | Metal | Dir, frag |
| MDH-10K | Metal | Dir, frag |
| MDH-2 | Metal | Dir, frag |
| MDH-4K | Metal | Dir, frag |
| MDH-6K | Metal | Dir, frag |
| MDH-7 | Metal | Dir, frag |
| MDH-8K | Metal | Dir, frag |
| MIN | Metal | Frag |
| MD 82B | | Blast |
| MN-79 | | Blast |
| NOMZ 2b | | Blast |
| P40 "ball mine" | | Frag |
| MBV 78A2 | | Frag |
| POMZ-2B | | Bound, frag |

# Yugoslavia (ex)

## Federal Directorate of Supply & Procurement (SDPR)

| Weapon | Material | Characteristics |
|---|---|---|
| UDARFuel-Air Explosive | | Com |
| PMA-3 | Plastic | Press, blast, "anti-magnetic" |
| PMA-2 | Plastic | Press, "anti-magnetic", weight |
| PROM-1 | | Bound, press or trip, frag |
| PMR-2A | Cast steel | Stake, trip, frag |
| MRUD | | Clay, dir, frag |
| PMR-1 | Metal | Frag |
| PMA-1A | Plastic | Blast, "anti-magnetic", .4 kg. |
| PMD-1 | Wood | Blast |
| PMR-2 | Metal & Concrete | Frag |
| PMR-3 | | |
| PMA-1 | Non-metal | Press, blast |
| PMRS | Metal | Frag |
| PP-56 | Plastic | |
| Rocochel | Metal | Press, frag |

# Zimbabwe

## Zimbabwe Defence Industries

| Weapon | Material | Characteristics |
|---|---|---|
| RAP-1 | | Blast, frag, press |
| RAP-2 | | Blast, frag, press |

## Zimbabwe (pre-indep. only)

### Various companies

| Weapon | Material | Characteristics |
|--------|----------|-----------------|
| 'Ploughshare' | | Dir, frag, trip |

# Key to: Antipersonnel Landmine Types and Producers

**Weapon** column lists most commonly reported designation.
Some mines (esp. Chinese and former East Bloc products) have been encountered with more than one designation.

**Material** column lists mines as "plastic" or "non-metallic" only if they contain too little metal to be detected with currently available equipment. (Many "plastic" mines do contain minute amounts of metal — usually under one gram.)

**Mine characteristics include:**

### Activation and detonation methods:
**Electr:** Electronic detonation
**Press:** pressure-activated
**Pull:** pull-activated
**Trip:** tripwire-activated
**Com:** command detonated (mechanical or electric)

### Advanced features:
**Anti-lift**
**Anti-disturb**
**Anti-handle**
**Delay:** Delayed detonation
**Self-dest:** self-destructing
**Self-neut:** self-neutralizing

### "Kill" mechanisms:
**Blast:** blast
**Frag:** fragmentation
**Chem:** chemical weapons (all listed
as "scheduled for destruction")

### Other characteristics:
**Bounce:** Bouncing
**Bound:** bounding
**Circular**
**Clay:** Claymore-type
**Dir:** Directional
**Jump:** Jumping
**Stake**

**Source:** Arms Project Landmines Database. Note that the complete database contains considerably more information on all listed mines. For detailed discussion of sources used in compiling the database, see Chapter 3.

# BIBLIOGRAPHY

# BIBLIOGRAPHY

## Books

Adams, James, *The Unnatural Alliance: Israel and South Africa* (London: Quartet, 1984).

Anthony, Ian (ed.), *Arms Export Regulations* (SIPRI) (New York: Oxford University Press, 1991).

Beck, A., Bortz, A., Lynch, C., Mayo, L., and Weld, R., *The Corps of Engineers: The War Against Germany* (1984).

Brzoska, Michael and Lock, Peter (eds.), *Restructuring of Arms Production in Western Europe* (New York: Oxford University Press, 1992).

Cawthra, Gavin, *Brutal Force: the war machine* (London: International Defense and Aid Fund For South Africa, 1986).

Cockburn, Andrew and Leslie, *Dangerous Liaison,* (New York: Harper Collins, 1991).

Cole, B., *The Elite: Rhodesian Special Air Service Pictorial* (Transkei: Three Knights).

Courtney-Green, Lieutenant Colonel P.R., *Ammunition for the Land Battle* (London: Brassey's UK, 1991).

Davies, Paul and Dunlop, Nic, *The War of the Mines* (London: Pluto Press, forthcoming, April 1994).

Diagram Group, *Weapons: an international encyclopedia from 5000 BC to 2000 AD* (New York: St. Martin's Press, 1980).

Dod, Karl C., *The Corps of Engineers: The War Against Japan* (1966).

Friedman, Alan, *Agnelli and the network of Italian power* (London: Harrap, 1988).

Gander, Terry, *Guerrilla Warfare Weapons: The modern underground fighters' amoury* (New York: Sterling Publishing Co., 1990).

Geissler, E. (ed.), *Biological and Toxin Weapons Today* (New York: Oxford U. Press, 1986).

Geuss, M.J.M., *Theorie de L'Art du Mineur* (1776).

Gill, R. Bates, *Chinese Arms Transfers: Purposes, Patterns, and Prospects in the New World Order* (Westport: Praeger, 1992).

Heitman, Helmoed-Römer, *South African Armed Forces* (Cape Town: Buffalo Publications, 1990).

_____, *South African Arms and Armour* (Cape Town: Struik Publishers, 1988).

Hussain, Nazir, *Defence Production in the Muslim World* (Karachi: Royal Book Company, 1989).

Jefferson, Paul, *Warsaw Pact Mines* (Basildon U.K.: Miltra Engineering Ltd., 1992).

Jeshurun, Chandan (ed.), *Arms and Defense in Southeast Asia* (Singapore: Institute of Southeast Asian Studies, 1989).

King, Fiona, *Landmine Injury in Cambodia: A Case Study*, (London School of Hygiene and Tropical Medicine, U.K., Sept. 1991) (unpublished manuscript).

Landgren, Signe, *Embargo Disimplemented: South Africa's military industry* (New York: Oxford University Press, 1989).

Marwick, C., *Your Right to Government Information, An American Civil Liberties Handbook* (New York: Bantam, 1985).

McWilliams, James P., *Armscor: South Africa's Arms Merchant* (London: Brassey's UK, 1989).

Meyer, Michael A. (ed.), *Armed Conflict and the New Law: Aspects of the 1977 Geneva Protocols and the 1981 Weapons Convention* (London: British Institute of International and Comparative Law, 1980).

Owen, J.I.H. (ed.), *Brassey's Infantry Weapons of the World: 1950-75.* (New York: Bonanza Books, 1975).

Peri, Dr. Yoram and Neubach, Amnon, *The Military-Industrial Complex in Israel: A Pilot Study* (Tel Aviv: International Center for Peace in the Middle East, 1985).

Reiser, Stewart, *The Israeli Arms Industry: foreign policy, arms transfers, and military doctrine of a small state* (New York: Holmes & Meier, 1989).

Roberts, A., and Guelff, R. (eds.), *Documents on the Laws of War* (New York: Oxford University Press, 1982).

Sanders, Ralph, *Arms Industries: New Suppliers and Regional Security* (Washington: National Defense University, 1990).

Shapley, Deborah, *Promise and Power: The Life and Times of Robert McNamara* (Boston: Little Brown and Co., Jan. 1993).

Sloan, Lt. Col. C.E.E., (RE), *Mine Warfare on Land* 1 (1986).

Sohr, Raul, *La Industria Militair Chilena*, (Santiago: South American Commission of Peace, undated).

Strauss, David Levi and Adams, Bobby Neel, *The Mines Project* (working title), (to be published in 1994-5).

Vines, A. and Wilson, K. (eds.), *War in Mozambique: Local Perspectives* (to be published in 1994).

Westing, Arthur H. (ed.), *Explosive Remnants of War: Mitigating the Environmental Effects* (London: Taylor and Francis, 1985).

## Articles

Alexander, Paul, untitled *Associated Press* wire story on demining in Somalia, May 30, 1993.

Arkin, William M., "Military Technology and the Banning of Land Mines," *Non-Governmental Organizations Conference on Antipersonnel Mines* (London, May 24, 1993) (unpublished paper).

Baron, N., "The Struggle Continues: Diary of a Kidnapping in Mozambique by Robert Rosskamp: An Analysis" (a translation and commentary; original in German) in Vines, A. and Wilson, K. (eds.), *War in Mozambique: Local Perspectives* (n.p., to be published in 1994).

Carnahan, Lieutenant B., "The Law of Land Mine Warfare: Protocol II to the United Nations Convention on Certain Conventional Weapons," 105 *Military L. Rev.* 73 (1984).

Coupland, R. and Korver, A., "Injuries from antipersonnel mines: the experience of the International Committee of the Red Cross," 303 *British Medical Journal* 1509, Dec. 14, 1991.

Danon, L.D., Nili, E., and El Dolev, "Primary treatment of battle casualties in the Lebanon war," *Israeli Journal of Medical Sciences*, 1978.

*Disarmament Times* (NY), "Breakthrough on Openness for Conventional Arms," Vol. XIV, No. 8, December 16, 1991.

Doswald-Beck, Louise, "The Value of the 1977 Geneva Protocols for the Protection of Civilians," in Meyer, Michael (ed.), *Armed Conflict and the New Law: Aspects of the 1977 Geneva Protocols and the 1981 Weapons Convention* (London: British Institute of International and Comparative Law, 1980).

*Engineering Week*, "Company of the Year: Armscor," reprinted in *Foreign Broadcast Information Service* (Sub-Saharan African Supplement), March 19, 1990, pp. 21–22.

Eshaya, Chauvin B. and Coupland, R.M., "Transfusion requirements for the management of war wounded: the experience of the International Committee of the Red Cross," 68 *B.J. Anaes.* 221 (1992).

Fasol, R., Irvine, S., and Zilla, P., "Vascular injuries caused by antipersonnel mines," 30 *J. Cardiovascular Surgery* 467 (1989).

Fetter, Gregory, (lead article) *World Weapons Review*, Sept. 23, 1993.

Fowler, William, "The Devil's Seed," *Defence*, Aug. 1992, pp. 11–19.

488

Hanley, Charles J., "Lethal Leftovers," *AP Newswire*, Oct. 10, 1993.

Hardaway, R.M., "Vietnam wound analysis," *18 Journal of Trauma 635* (1978).

Johnson, D.E., Panijayanond, P., Lumjiak, S., Crum, J.W., and Boonkrapu, P., "Epidemiology of combat casualties in Thailand," 21 *J. Trauma* (1981).

Kalshoven, Frits, "Conventional Weaponry: The Law from St. Petersburg to Lucerne and Beyond" in Meyers, Michael (ed.), *Armed Conflict and the New Law: Aspects of the 1977 Geneva Protocols and the 1981 Weapons Convention* (London: British Institute of International and Comparative Law, 1980).

Laurence, Edward, "The U.N. Register of Conventional Arms," 16 *Washington Quarterly* No. 2 (Spring 1993).

Leahy, Senator Patrick, "Landmine Moratorium: A Strategy for Stronger International Limits," *Arms Control Today*, Jan.-Feb. 1993, p. 11.

Lewis, Flora, "Make a Misstep and You're Dead," *New York Times*, May 4, 1992, p. A17.

Matheson, Michael J., "The United States Position on the Relation of Customary International Law to the 1977 Protocols Additional to the 1949 Geneva Conventions," in 2 *Am. U.J. Int'l L. and Pol.* 419 (1987) (Proceedings of the Sixth Annual American Red Cross—Washington College of Law Conference on Int'l Humanitarian Law: A Workshop on Customary Int'l Law and the 1977 Protocols Additional to the 1949 Geneva Conventions).

McClellan, D., "New Limbs for Viet amputees," *San Francisco Examiner*, May 12, 1991, p. A1.

McGrath, Rae, "Mine Warfare: An Aid Issue," *RPN* (Refugee Studies Program, Oxford), August 1990.

_____, and Stover, Eric, "Injuries from Landmines," 303 *British Medical Journal*, Dec. 14, 1991.

Milling, James S. "Mines and Booby Traps," *Infantry*, Jan-Feb. 1969.

Muradian, Vago, "U.S. Mine Firms Hit Foreign Ban," *Defense News*, July 19-25, 1993, p. 36.

*Newsday*, "After the Blast," March 21, 1993.

North, James, "War Without End," *In These Times*, Sept. 6–19, 1993, p. 16.

Ottinger, "Landmine and Countermine Warfare, North Africa, 1940–1943," 13 *ETO General Board Report 73: Engineer Technical Policies.*

Perani, Giulio and Pianta, Mario, "The slow restructing of the Italian arms industry," in Brzoska, Michael and Lock, Peter (eds.),

*Restructuring of Arms Production in Western Europe* (Oxford: Oxford University Press, 1992), pp. 140-54.

*Press Association Newsfile*, "Indian Poacher Kills 22 Pursuers with Landmine," April 10, 1993.

Rafique, Najam and Husain, Tariq A., *Indian Armed Forces, Islamabad Papers No. 12* (The Institute of Strategic Studies, Sector F-5/2, Box 1173, Islamabad, 1988).

Rautio, J. and Paavolainen, P., "Afghan war wounded: experience with 200 cases," *28 J. Trauma 523* (1988).

*Reuter Library Report*, "Landmines, Cambodia's Deadly Harvest," Mar. 23, 1993.

Roy, David V., "Anti-personnel Mines: Historical and Current Battlefield Roles," May 1993 (unpublished paper on file at the Arms Project).

Schneck, William C., "After Action Report, Operations Desert Shield and Desert Storm," Fort Belvoir Research, Development and Engineering Center, November 12, 1991, pp. C-1 and C-2.

Schneck, William, Visser, Malcolm and Leigh, Stuart, "Advances in Mine Warfare: An Overview," *Engineer*, April 1993, p. 2.

Scott, R., "Unnecessary Suffering?—A Medical View" in Meyers, Michael (ed.), *Armed Conflict and the New Law: Aspects of the 1977 Geneva Protocols and the 1981 Weapons Convention* (London: British Institute of International and Comparative Law, 1980).

Sgaier, Khairi, "Explosive Remnants of World War II in Libya: Impact on Agricultural Development," in Westing, Arthur H. (ed.), *Explosive Remants of War: Mitigating the Environmental Effects* (London: Taylor and Francis, 1985), pp. 33-37.

Singh, Bilveer and Guan, Kwa Chong, "The Singapore Defense Industries: Motivations, Organization and Impact," in Jeshurun, Chandran (ed.), *Arms and Defense in Southeast Asia* (Singapore: Institute of Southeast Asian Studies, 1989), pp. 96–124.

Stover, E. and Charles, D., "The Killing Minefields of Cambodia," *New Scientist*, October 19, 1991, p. 27.

Taub, Stephen, "Smart Money Loves Alliant (Alliant Techsystems)," *Financial World*, Jan. 19, 1993.

Traverso, L.W., Fleming A., Johnson, D.E., and Wongrukmitr, B., "Combat Casualties in Northern Thailand: emphasis on land mines and levels of amputation," 146 Milit. Med 682 (1981).

Wagenmakers, H., "The UN Register of Conventional Arms: A New Instrument for Cooperative Security," 23 *Arms Control Today* No. 3 (April 1993).

490

Weinschenk, Andrew, "Land Mines May be Somali Conflict's Most Lethal Legacy," *Defense Week*, Volume 14, Number 36, Sept. 13, 1993.

Wurst, Jim, "Ten Million Tragedies, One Step at a Time," *The Bulletin of the Atomic Scientists*, July/August 1993.

## Reports

Africa Watch, *Landmines in Angola* (New York: Africa Watch, January 1993).

Aldrich, George, Report of the United States Delegation to the United Nations Conference on Prohibitions or Restrictions of Use of Certain Conventional Weapons which may be deemed to be excessively injurious or to have indiscriminate effects—Second Session (1981) (Report to the U.S. Secretary of State).

Aldrich, George, Report of the United States Delegation to the United Nations Conference on Prohibitions or Restrictions of Use of Certain Conventional Weapons Which may be Deemed to be Excessively Injurious or to Have Indiscriminate Effects—First Session (1979) (Report to the U.S. Secretary of State).

American Defense Preparedness Association, *Symposium and Exhibition on Mines, Countermine & Demolitions*, Asheville, North Carolina, Sept. 7–9, 1993 (advance texts and charts of certain presentations are contained in a bound volume):

Boedec, Maj. Andre, "French Mine Warfare."

Chu, Mrs. Julie C., "Mines and Louisiana Maneuvers."

Gardner, Charles C., "Countermine Systems Development," Briefing."

Gowdey, David, "Uncleared Landmines: The Scope of the Problem."

Gros, Lt. Col. Jean Francois, "De-Mining Cambodia."

Guilmain, Michelle I., "Shallow Water MCM Overview."

Hafer, Dr. Thomas A., "ARPA Current and Future Tech Base Countermine Programs."

Heberlein, Dr. David C., "Countermine Top Level Demonstration."

Moreo, Dominick, "Mine Tech Base."

Rosamilia, John A., "Mine Programs."

Stewart, Ronald L., "Early Entry Lethality and Survivability."

Suart, Robert D., PhD, "Applications of Explosives for Combat Engineers — Recent Developments at DRES."

Thompson, John J. (Presenter) and Gauthier, Lt. Col. J.C.M., "De-Mining Yugoslavia."

Thompson, Col. William F. (Presenter) and Vaughn, David A., "Countermine: Engine for Mobility/Survivability."

Wagner, Richard Q., "Demolitions — Past, Present and Future."

Wilson, Col. Alasdair, "The U.K. Perspective."

Americas Watch, *Landmines in El Salvador and Nicaragua: The Civilian Victims* (New York: Americas Watch, December 1986).

Asia Watch and Physicians for Human Rights, *Land Mines in Cambodia: The Cowards' War* (New York: Human Rights Watch and Physicians for Human Rights, September 1991).

Board on Army Science and Technology, Commission on Engineering and Technical Systems, National Research Council, *STAR 21: Strategic technologies for the army of the twenty-first century* (Washington: National Academy Press, 1992), p. 21.

British American Security Information Council, *Basic Reports*, No. 33, September 17, 1993.

Cambodian Mine Action Centre, *Progress Report on the Implementation and Funding Situation of the Short Term Plan of Operations*, November 1992–June 1993.

Defense Marketing Services, *DMS Market Intelligence Report: Ordnance* (Washington: Jane's Information Group, 1989).

Engineer Agency for Resource Inventories, *Landmines and Countermine Warfare: Vietnam Lessons Learned, 1965-1968*, Washington, D.C., July 1973.

_____, *Landmine and Countermine Warfare: Western Europe, WWII*, Washington, D.C., July 1973.

Forecast International/DMS Market Intelligence Report, *Ordnance & Munitions Forecast, Landmines Section* (three parts: U.S., Europe, and International), March 1993.

_____, *Market Intelligence Reports, XM93 Wide Area Mine*, December, 1992.

_____, *Italy* (Country Survey), July 1992.

Handicap International, *La Guerre des Lâches* (French translation of Asia Watch and Physicians for Human Rights, *Land Mines in Cambodia: The Coward's War*), (Paris: Handicap International, May 1992).

492

Hirschhorn, N., Haviland, L., and Salvo, J., *Critical Needs Assessment in Cambodia: The Humanitarian Issues*, a Report to the U.S. Agency for International Development, April 1991, p.8.

*Jane's Military Vehicles and Logistics 1992-93*, (Surrey: Janes Information Group Limited, 1992).

Jederlund, Lars, "Svesnka minor - och dess offer," Svenska Freds (Swedish Peace and Arbitration Society), November 1992.

Medical Educational Trust, *Indiscriminate Weapons: Landmines* (London: MET Reports, June 1992).

_____, *Indiscriminate Weapons: Landmines* (London: MET Reports, March 1993).

Middle East Watch, *Hidden Death: Land Mines and Civilian Casualties in Iraqi Kurdistan* (New York: Human Rights Watch, October 1992).

Mines Advisory Group, *Report of the Afghanistan Mines Survey*, 1991.

Minty, Abdul, *South Africa's Defense Strategy* (London, The Anti-Apartheid Movement, 1969) (Pamphlet).

Physicians for Human Rights, *Hidden Enemies: Land Mines in Northern Somalia* (Boston: Physicians for Human Rights, November 1992).

Sohr, Raul, *La Industria Militair Chilena* (Santiago: South American Commission of Peace, undated).

## Government Documents

Department of the Army, *Army Countermine Modernization Plan*, April 21, 1992.

Department of the Army, *Field Manual 20–32: Mine/Countermine Operations*, 30 September 1992.

Government of India, Ministry of Defense, *Annual Report: 1990-91*.

Italy, Ministero del Commerciacon l'Estero, "Elenco delle autorizzaioni rilasciate dal 1980 alla Valsella Meccanotecnica per esportazioni di materiale di armamento verso tutti i peasi" (undated).

National Security Council, "Memorandum for Robert C. McFarlane," by Oliver R. North, May 1, 1985 (Declassified).

United Kingdom, Foreign and Commonwealth Office, Letter from the Minister of State to Chris Mullin MP, Jan. 22, 1993.

UNPROFOR, *Mine Data Handbook*, 16 October 1992.

U.S. Agency for International Development and U.S. Dept. of Public Health and Human Services, *Planning for Improved Orthotic Programs in Uganda and Mozambique*, June 26, 1989.

U.S. Army, *Anti-Personnel Mine M18A1 and M18 (Claymore) — Department of Army Field Manual* (Washington: Department of the Army, 1966).

_____, *Information Paper—Anti-Personnel Land Mine Procurement and Production*, 1992.

U.S. Army Armament, Munitions, and Chemical Command, "Lousiana Army Ammunition Plant," August 1987.

_____, Letter to the Arms Project, Aug. 25, 1993, and attached statistical tables on Foreign Military Sales of Landmines 1969–92 and shipments of mines for use in Southwest Asia (Operation Desert Storm).

_____, "Estimated Expenditures" (mines shipped for use in Operation Desert Storm), undated.

U.S. Army Countermine Systems Directorate, Fort Belvoir Research, Development and Engineering Center, *Sapper Countermine Guide*, BRDEC Pamphlet 350-4, Nov. 30, 1990.

_____, *Worldwide Informational Mine Guide*, 1993 (Electronic database) (USRDE).

U.S. Army Engineer Center, *Desert Shield Mine Recognition and Warfare Handbook* (Missouri: Fort Leonard Wood, November 1990).

U.S. Army Intelligence Agency — U.S. Army Foreign Science and Technology Center, *Operation Desert Shield Special Report: Iraqi Combat Engineer Capabilities*, 30 November 1990. AST-266OZ-131-90. (USAIA)

_____, *Operation Desert Shield Special Report: Iraqi Combat Engineer Capabilities, Supplement 2: Barriers and Fortification Protection*. 30 November 1990. AST-266OZ-131-90-SUP 2. (USAIA-2)

_____, *Somalia Handbook: Foreign Ground Weapons and Health Issues*, (U), DST-1100H-107-92, FSTC: Charlottesville, VA: December, 1992.

U.S. Army, Intelligence and Threat Analysis Center of the U.S. Intelligency and Security Command, *Restore Hope—Socaliinta Rajada Soldier Handbook*, ATC-RM-1100-065-93, December 1992.

U.S. Central Intelligence Agency, Directorate of Intelligence, *The Defence Industries of the Newly Independent States of Eurasia* (OSE 93-10001, Springfield, VA: National Technical Information Service, January 1993).

U.S. Defense Intelligence Agency and U.S. Army Foreign Science and Technology Center, *Landmine Warfare—Trends & Projections*, December 1992, DST-116OS-019-92.

494

U.S. Department of Defense, Defense Security Assistance Administration, *Land Mines Purchased under the Foreign Military Sales Program as of July 15, 1992* (US-DSAA).

_____, Congressional notifications of proposed letters of offer (various dates, 1979-90) provided to the Arms Project under FOIA request of April 28, 1993 and U.S. Defense Department response letter of June 1, 1993.

_____, *Foreign Military Sales of Anti-Personnel Mines for the period FY 1983-1993 to date*, JF171 as of 8/11/93. (US-DSAA 1993.)

_____, Office of Assistant Secretary of Defense (Public Affairs), Press Release—Contract Awards (various dates).

U.S. Department of State, *Hidden Killers: The Global Problem with Uncleared Landmines* (Washington, D.C.: U.S. Department of State Political—Military Affairs Bureau, Office of International Security Operations, July 1993).

_____, Letter to Vietnam Veterans of America Foundation, June 18, 1992.

_____, Undersecretary of State for Security Assistance, Lynn E. Davis, response to "Question for the Record Submitted by Senator Leahy," Senate Appropriations Subcommittee on Foreign Operations, May 12, 1993.

_____, *Dispatch*, Vol. 4, No. 12, March 22, 1993.


## Legislative Materials

The Arms Export Control Act (Pub. L. No. 90-629, as amended).

*Congressional Record*, July 22, 1993, p. S9291 (introduction of the Landmine Moratorium Extension Act of 1993).

*Congressional Record*, Sept. 10, 1993, pp. S11376-77, S11391-95, and S11452-3 (debate and amendment of the proposed Landmine Moratorium Extension Act of 1993).

*Congressional Record*, Sept. 14, 1993, p. S11616 (vote on the Landmine Moratorium Extension Act of 1993).

Congressional Research Service, *Report to Sen. Patrick Leahy on Anti-personnel Landmines*, Jan. 13, 1993.

Congressional Research Service, *U.S. Military Sales and Assistance Programs: Laws, Regulations, and Procedures*, prepared for the U.S. House Committee on Foreign Affairs, July 23, 1985.

*Federal Register*, Vol, 57, p. 228, Nov. 25, 1992; "Suspension of Transfers of Anti-Personnel Mines" (regulations implementing the Landmine Moratorium Act).

The Foreign Assistance Act of 1961 (Pub. L. No. 87-195, as amended).

The Landmine Moratorium Extension Act of 1993, introduced July 22, 1993 as S.1276 and H.R. 2706.

Liberal, Democratic and Reformist Group, European Parliament, "Motion for a Resolution on the Havoc Caused by Mines," Strasbourg, Dec. 14, 1992.

"Moratorium on the Export of Landmines," an early day motion introduced in the House of Commons, United Kingdom.

National Defense Authorization Act for Fiscal Year 1993, Pub. L. No. 102-484, sec. 1365 (The Landmines Moratorium Act).

"Petition on Land Mines in Cambodia" (presented to the House of Representatives of Australia), *Weekly House Hansard*, Feb. 27, 1992, p. 301.

Senate Appropriations Subcommittee on Foreign Operations, Transcript from hearing, March 30, 1993.

## International Treaties

The Additional Protocols of June 8, 1977 to the Geneva Conventions of August 12, 1949 (Additional Protocol I Relating to the Protection of Victims of International Armed Conflicts, and Additional Protocol II Relating to the Protection of Victims of Non-International Armed Conflicts, respectively). U.N.G.A. Doc. A/32/144, Anns. I and II, August 15, 1977; 16 *Int'l Legal Materials* 1391 (1977).

Convention on the Prohibition of the Development, Production and Stockpiling of Bacteriological (Biological) and Toxin Weapons and on their Destruction, April 10, 1972; in Geissler, E. (ed.), *Biological and Toxin Weapons Today* (New York: Oxford U. Press, 1986), p. 135.

The Declaration concerning asphyxiating gases, The Hague, July 29, 1899; reprinted in Roberts, A. and Guelff, R. (eds.), *Documents on the Laws of War* (New York: Oxford U. Press, 1982), pp. 36–37.

The Declaration concerning expanding bullets, the Hague, July 29, 1899; reprinted in *International Law Concerning the Conduct of Hostilities*, (Geneva: ICRC, 1989).

The Declaration Renouncing the Use, in Time of War, of Explosive Projectiles under 400 Grammes Weight, December 11, 1868; reprinted in ICRC, *International Law Concerning the Conduct of Hostilities*, (Geneva: ICRC, 1989), p. 165.

1925 Geneva Protocol for the Prohibition of the Use in War of Asphyxiating, Poisonous or other Gases, of Bacteriological Methods of Warfare, June 17, 1925; reprinted in ICRC, *International Law Concerning the Conduct of Hostilities* (Geneva: ICRC, 1989), p. 174.

Protocol on Prohibitions or Restrictions on the Use of Mines, Booby Traps and Other Devices (Protocol II) annexed to the U.N. Convention on Prohibitions or Restrictions on the Use of Certain Conventional Weapons Which May be Deemed to be Excessively Injurious and to Have Indiscriminate Effects. U.N.G.A. Doc. A/Conf. 95/15 and Corr 1-5; 19 *Int'l Legal Materials* 1534 (1980).

Regulations respecting the laws and customs of war on land annexed to the Convention respecting the laws and customs of war on land, the Hague, October 18, 1907; reprinted in ICRC, *International Law Concerning the Conduct of Hostilities* (Geneva: ICRC, 1989), p. 167.

**United Nations Documents**

Register of Conventional Arms—Annex, U.N. Doc. A/RES/46/36, December 9, 1991.

Conference Resolution 22 (IV), *Follow-up Regarding Prohibition of Restriction of the Use of Certain Conventional Weapons*, 1 Official Records of the Diplomatic Conference on the Reaffirmation and Development of International Humanitarian Law Applicable in Armed Conflicts 52; U.N.G.A. Res. 32/152, December 19, 1977.

Final Report of the United Nations Conference on Prohibitions or Restrictions of the Use of Certain Conventional Weapons Which may be Deemed to be Excessively Injurious or to have Indiscriminate Effects,___U.N. GAOR___; U.N. Doc. A/CONF. 95/15 and Corr 1–5 (Oct. 27, 1980); 19 *Int'l Legal Materials* 1534 (1980).

Report of the Ad Hoc Committee on Conventional Weapons, 16 Official Records of the Diplomatic Conference on the Reaffirmation and Development of International Humanitarian Law Applicable in Armed Conflicts (1978).

Report of the Committee of the Whole on Prohibitions Or Restrictions of Use of Certain Conventional Weapons Which May be Deemed to be Excessively Injurious or to have Indiscriminate Effects, __ U.N. GAOR__; U.N. Doc. A/CONF.95/11 (1980).

Report of the Conference to the General Assembly on Prohibitions Or Restrictions of Use of Certain Conventional Weapons Which May be Deemed to be Excessively Injurious or to have Indiscriminate Effects, __U.N. GAOR__; U.N. Doc. A/CONF. 95/8 (1979).

Report of the Preparatory Conference for the United Nations Conference on Prohibitions or Restrictions of the Use of Certain Conventional Weapons Which May be Deemed to be Excessively Injurious or to have Indiscriminate Effects,__ U.N. GAOR __; U.N. Doc. A/CONF. 95/3 (May 25, 1979).

Report of the Secretary-General on the United Nations Conference on Prohibitions or Restrictions of the Use of Certain Conventional Weapons Which May be Deemed to be Excessively Injurious or to have Indiscriminate Effects, U.N. Doc. A/37/199, October 5, 1982.

Report of the Working Group on Landmines and Booby Traps, __U.N. GAOR__; U.N. Doc. A/CONF./CW/7 (1980).

Study on ways and means of promoting transparency in international transfers of conventional arms: Report of the Secretary-General, U.N. Doc. A/46/301 (September 1991).

Summary Records of the Ad Hoc Committee on Conventional Weapons, 16 Official Records of the Diplomatic Conference on the Reaffirmation and Development of International Humanitarian Law Applicable in Armed Conflicts (1978).

U.N. Commission on Human Rights Resolution 1993/83, "Consequences of Armed Conflicts on Children Lives," adopted March 10, 1993.

U.N. Department of Humanitarian Affairs, "Informal paper on the subject of land mines," prepared by Under-Secretary-General Jan Eliasson, April 7, 1993.

U.N. Disarmament Yearbook, Vol. 5: 1980, pp. 305-306.

U.N. Focus, "The Scourge of Land Mines," by Susan Ruel (New York: U.N. Department of Public Information, October 1993).

U.N. General Assembly, 35th Session: Verbatim Record of the 37th Meeting of the First Committee, __U.N. GAOR __; U.N. Doc. A/C.1/35/PV.37 (Nov. 21, 1980).

U.N. General Assembly Draft Resolution A/48/L.5, "Assistance in Mine Clearance," October 8, 1993.

U.N. General Assembly Resolution 46/36L, "Transparency in Armaments," December 9, 1991.

U.N. General Assembly Resolution 2444, "Respect for Human Rights in Armed Conflicts," adopted January 13, 1969.

U.N. General Assembly Resolution 3571, "Problem of Remnants of War," adopted December 5, 1980.


## ICRC Documents

Aubert, Maurice, "The International Committee of The Red Cross and the problem of excessively injurious or indiscriminate weapons, " *International Review of the Red Cross* (Nov.–Dec. 1990), pp. 477–497.

Doswald-Beck, Louise and Cauderay, Gérald C., "The Development of New Anti-personnel Weapons," *International Reviw of the Red Cross* (Nov.–Dec. 1990), pp. 565–577.

ICRC, *International Law Concerning the Conduct of Hostilities* (Geneva: ICRC, 1989).

_____, *Mines: A Perverse Use of Technology* (Geneva: ICRC, 1992).

_____, *Report on the Conference of Government Experts on the Use of Certain Weapons: Lucerne 1974* (Geneva: ICRC, 1975).

_____, *Report on the Conference of Government Experts on the Use of Certain Conventional Weapons: Lugano 1976* (Geneva: ICRC, 1976).

_____, *Report on the Reaffirmation and Development of the Laws and Customs Applicable in Armed Conflicts,* submitted to the Twenty-first International Conference of the Red Cross (Istanbul, 1969).

_____, *Report of the Symposium on Anti-personnel Mines: Montreux 1993* (Geneva: ICRC, 1993).

Anderson, Kenneth, "Overview of the problem of anti-personnel mines," p. 13.

Blagden, Patrick M., "Summary of United Nations demining," p. 117.

Chabasse, Philippe, "The proliferation of anti-personnel landmines in developing countries: considerable damage in

Rollo, Lt. Col. N. Hamish, "The military use of anti-personnel mines," p. 211.

Williams, Jody, "Social consequences of widespread use of landmines," p. 69.

_____, *Statement on the 1980 Weapons Convention to the First Committee of the U.N. General Assembly* (47th Session, Oct. 27, 1992).

_____, *Weapons that May Cause Unnecessary Suffering or Have Indiscriminate Effects: Report on the Work of the Experts* (Geneva: ICRC, 1973).

_____, Training video on landmine amputations for Surgeons, Switzerland (1992).

Kalshoven, Frits, *Constraints on the Waging of War* (Geneva: ICRC, 1987).

Sandoz, Yves, Swinarski, Christophe, and Zimmerman, Bruno (eds.), ICRC, *Commentary on the Additional Protocols of 8 June 1977 to the Geneva Conventions of 12 August 1949* (Geneva: Martinus Nijhoff Publishers, 1987).

Sandoz, Yves, "Prohibitions or Restrictions on the Use of Certain Conventional Weapons," *International Review of the Red Cross* (Jan.–Feb. 1981).

Varas, Augusto and Fuentes, Claudio, "La Industria de Bienes de USO Militair en Chile," Augusto Varas & Claudio Fuentes, June 1993.

Williams, Jody, "Social Consequences of Widespread Use of Landmines," paper prepared for the ICRC Symposium on Landmines, April 1993.

## Speeches and Presentations

Digney, Charles E., Deputy Project Manager, U.S. Army, Mines, Countermine and Demolitions, "Program Opportunities," presentation to American Defense Preparedness Association, *Mines, Countermine and Demolitions Symposium*, Asheville, North Carolina, Sept. 7–9, 1993.

Eliasson, Jan, "Keynote Address," given at the *Consultation of the International Negotiation Network*, at the Carter Centre Atlanta, Feb. 17, 1993.

Gardner, Charles, Office of the Project Manager for Mines, Coutermine and Demolitions, U.S. Army, "Countermine Systems Development," presentation to American Defense Preparedness Association, *Mines, Countermine and Demolitions Symposium*, Asheville, North Carolina, Sept 7–9, 1993.

Gray, Gen. Alfred M. Jr. (Ret.), former Commandant, United States Marine Corps, address to American Defense Preparedness Association, *Mines, Countermine and Demolitions Symposium*, Asheville, North Carolina, Sept. 7–9, 1993.

Gros, Lt. Col. Jean Francois, French Army Corps of Engineers, "De-Mining Cambodia," presentation to American Defense Preparedness Association, *Mines, Countermine and Demolitions Symposium*, Asheville, North Carolina, Sept 7–9, 1993.

Hafer, Dr. Thomas A., Acting Assistant Director, Advance Land Systems, Advance Systems Technology Office, Advance Research Projects Agency, "ARPA Current and Future Tech Base Countermine Programs," presentation to American Defense Preparedness Association, *Mines, Countermine and Demolitions Symposium*, Asheville, North Carolina, Sept 7–9, 1993.

Kuebler, Mst. Sgt. Mark C., Munitions and Demolitions Project Officer, U.S. Army Special Operations Command Combat Development Division, presentation to American Defense Preparedness Association, *Mines, Countermine and Demolitions Symposium*, Asheville, North Carolina, Sept. 7–9, 1993.

McDonough, Col. William C., Chief, Intelligence Division, Inter-American Defense Board, presentation to American Defense Preparedness Association, *Mines, Countermine and Demolitions Symposium*, Asheville, North Carolina, Sept 7–9, 1993.

McGrath, Rae, "Collateral Damage: Anti-Personnel Mines: A Human Rights Perspective," talk given at *Handicap International*, Brussels, March 6, 1992.

Ragano, Maj. Gen. (Ret.) Frank P., President and CEO, CMS, Inc., presentation to American Defense Preparedness Association, *Mines, Countermine and Demolitions Symposium*, Asheville, North Carolina, Sept 7–9, 1993.

Reeder, Thomas S., Senior Mine Warfare Analyst, U.S. Army Foreign Science and Technology Center, "DOD Scientific and Technical Intelligence (S&TI) Support to International Mineclearing Programs," briefing, *Foreign Science and Technology Center*, Charlottesville, VA.

_____, Presentation at American Defense Preparedness Association, *Mines, Countermine and Demolitions Symposium*, Asheville, North Carolina, Sept. 7–9, 1993.

Rosamilia, John A., Chief, Mines Division, Project Manager for Mines, Countermine and Demolitions, U.S. Army, "Mine Programs," presentation to American Defense Preparedness Association, *Mines, Countermine and Demolitions Symposium*, Asheville, North Carolina, Sept 7–9, 1993.

Thompson, (Can.) Major John, "Demining Yugoslavia," presentation to American Defense Preparedness Association, *Mines, Countermine and Demolitions Symposium*, Asheville, North Carolina, Sept 7–9, 1993.


## Public Declarations

Center for Security Policy, "Should Germany's M.B.B. be permitted to reap what it 'sowed' in the Gulf?," 1 page press release, July 31, 1991.

Dole, Elizabeth, "Statement of the American Red Cross on the Use of Antipersonnel Mines", April 21, 1993.

Grundmann, William, Director for Combat Support, Defense Intelligence Agency, *Statement for the Record to the Joint Economic Committee of Congress*, June 11, 1993.

Handicap International, Human Rights Watch, Medico International, Mines Advisory Group, Physicians for Human Rights, and Vietnam Veterans of America Foundation, "A Joint Call to Ban Antipersonnel Landmines," 1993.

International Federation Terres des Hommes, Oral Intervention Presented to the Commission on Human Rights, 49th Session, Agenda Item 12, Feb. 1993.

Lutheran World Federation Council, "Statement on the Banning of Landmines," in Minutes of the Meeting of the Lutheran World Federation Council, Madras, India, Sept. 13–23, 1992.

Swedish Peace and Arbitration Society (SPAS), "Memorandum to the European Network Against Arms Trade," November 1992.


## Selected List of Interviews

Alliant Techsystems, April 22, 1993.

Blagden, Brigadier (Ret.) Patrick, demining expert, *United Nations*, telephone interview, Feb. 17, 1993.

Brackenreed-Johnston, Maurice, *Rimfire International Ltd*, (April 8, 1993).

Brown, James, *Halo Trust*, Pursat, June 9, 1993.

503

Davis, Terry, Compliance Division, Office of Defense Trade Controls, *U.S. Department of State*, telephone interview, May 3, 1993.

Flanagan, Major John, Chief Information Officer, *Cambodian Mine Action Centre*, Phnom Penh, June 5, 1992.

Geolotti, Dr. Mark, Lecturer, International History, *University of Keele*, England; telephone interview, July 19, 1993.

Gowdey, David, Office of International Security Operations, Bureau of Political Military Affairs, *U.S. Department of State*, numerous interviews and conversations.

Hartley, Steve, Defense Procurement Officer, *Embassy of United Kingdom*; telephone interview, Washington, D.C., April 29, 1993.

Jederlund, Lars, *Swedish Peace and Arbitration Society*; telephone interview, Aug. 31, 1993.

Johnson, Col. Richard, Project Manager, Mines, Countermine and Demolitions, Picatinny Arsenal, *U.S. Army*, New Jersey, June 15, 1993.

Jun, Lt. Col. Jong-Bun, Foreign Military Sales officer, *Embassy of the Republic of Korea*, Washington, D.C., April 23, 1993.

Lappin, Donald, Director, Legal Department, U.S. Army Armament, Munitions and Chemical Command, *U.S. Army*; telephone interview, July 16, 1993.

Moon, Chris, *Halo Trust*, Pursat, June 13, 1993.

Nee, Lawrence J., Chief, Countermine Development and Engineering Division and Jacobs, Pamela M., Chief, Data Analysis Team, *U.S. Army, Countermine Systems Directorate*, Ft. Belvoir, VA, Apr. 23, 1993.

Sherr, Dr. James, Lecturer, International Relations, *Lincoln College*, Oxford; telephone interview, July 21, 1993.

Taffe, John C., *Explosive Ordnance Disposal World Services Inc.*, Sept. 7, 1993, and Sept. 30, 1993.

Various interviews with industry and military officials at American Defense Preparedness Association, *Mines, Countermine and Demolitions Symposium*, Asheville, North Carolina, Sept. 7–8, 1993.

Verderkuijl, Major Cees, Air Force Defence Materials officer, military section, *Embassy of Netherlands*; telephone interview, Washington, D.C., April 29, 1993.

Wilkerson, Jody, Manager, Market Development, *Alliant Techsystems, Inc.*, interviewed by Jody Williams, April 9, 1993.

## Correspondence

Beer, Angelika, Medico International, Memorandum to the Arms Project, April 4, 1993.

Letter from French Foreign Minister Alain Juppe to Philippe Chabasse, Director of Handicap International, July 26, 1993.

Letter from Jimmy Carter to Jody Williams, Vietnam Veterans of America Foundation, August 28, 1993.

Letter from Bilge Ogun-Bassani, Deputy Director of the Geneva office of UNICEF to Stuart Maslen of the Vietnam Veterans of America Foundation, Aug. 16, 1993.


## Business Publications and Brochures

Alliant Techsystems, "Family of Scatterable Mines" (Sales brochure), February 1991.

_____, "Current Potential Fascam Overseas Markets" (chart), 1993.

_____, "Product and Capability Profile," 1992.

_____, "AP Mine Moratorium," April 1993.

_____, "Anti-personnel Mine Moratorium Bulletin," June 1993.

_____, "Moratorium on Sale of Anti-Personnel Mines," September 23, 1992.

Bofors AB, Letter to the Swedish Peace and Arbitration Society, November 18, 1992.

Chartered Industries of Singapore, company profile (undated).

Federal Directorate of Supply and Procurement (SDPR), Beograd, Yugoslavia, "Engineer Equipment," (undated sales brochure).

Ferranti Weapons Equipment, sales brochure for mines and fuzes (undated).

Fiat Group, *1991 Annual Report* (Turin: Fiat S.p.A., 1992).

_____, Memorandum on Moratorium on Sale of Anti-Personnel Mines (2 pages), September 23, 1992.

Motorola Inc., "Government Electronics Group, Fuze Systems Office," sales brochure for XM84 Wide Area Side Penetrating Mine, undated.

Pakistan Ordnance Factories, "Provide Force to the Forces," sales brochure (Wah: 1991).

_____, Technical Specifications for Mine Anti-Personnel (P4 MK2)

Rheinmetall GmbH, *Mine Systems* — "Rheinmetall Defence Technology" (sales brochure), Dusseldorf, Germany, September 1990.

Sherwood International, undated brochure for Claymore M18-A1 and accessories, manufactured by Mohawk Electrical Systems.

SNC Industrial Technologies Inc., "Mine, anti-personnel, non-metallic, C3A1" (sales brochure), Le Gardeur Québec, Aug. 1991.

Swedish Ordnance/FFV (Bofors subsidiary), undated sales brochure for FFV013 and FFV013R A/P mines.

_____, "Swedish Ordnance Mine to Switzerland," press release, December 16, 1991.

Unicorn International (a subsidiary of Chartered Industries of Singapore), Company Profile (undated).

Valsella Meccanotecnica, company profile and product brochure (undated, probably issued in 1992).

_____, Product description brochures for VS-50, VS-MK2, Valmara 69, VS-APFM1, VS-MD H helicopter scatter-drop system, Istrice land mine scattering system and other mine-related products (1990).


## Periodicals, News Services, and Electronic Data Services

ABC Color (Paraguay)
Aerospace Daily
American University Journal of International Law and Policy
The Argus (Johannesburg)
Armada International
Armed Forces Journal International
Arms Control Today
Arms Trade News
Arms Transfers News
Army Times
Associated Press
Barron's
Boston Globe
British Journal of Anaesthesiology
British Medical Journal
Business Day (Johannesburg)
Defence
Defense Daily

Defense News
Defence Today
Disclosure
Disarmament Times
Engineer
Engineering Week
The Federal Register
Financial World
Forbes
Foreign Broadcast Information Service
Guardian (London)
Infantry
Intelligence Newsletter
International Defense Intelligence
International Defense Review
International Legal Materials
International Observer
Inter Press Service
In These Times
Israeli Journal of Medical Sciences
Jane's Defense Weekly
Jane's Intelligence Review
Jane's Soviet Intelligence Review
Journal of Trauma
Military Law Review
Military Technology
New Scientist
Newsday
New York Times
The Observer (London)
Press Association Newsfile
Pretoria Daily News
Refugee Policy News
Reuters
Sunday Star (Johannesburg)
Times of India
United Press International
U.S. News and World Report
Wall Street Journal
Washington Quarterly

Weekly Mail (Johannesburg)
World Weapons Review
Xinhua (China)

# ACKNOWLEDGMENTS

This book was written by staff and consultants to the Arms Project of Human Rights Watch (the Arms Project) and Physicians for Human Rights (PHR).

Its executive editors were Kenneth Anderson, director of the Arms Project; Stephen D. Goose, Washington director of the Arms Project; Monica Schurtman, counsel to the Arms Project; and Eric Stover, executive director of PHR. It was reviewed by Holly Burkhalter, Washington Director of Human Rights Watch (HRW), and Aryeh Neier, formerly executive director of HRW and currently president of the Open Society Fund.

Mr. Anderson wrote the introduction (Chapter 1) and the chapter on Transparency (Chapter 4). Mr. Goose wrote the Country Studies (Chapter 6), drawing on reports written by various divisions of HRW and PHR; he also wrote the chapters on Mine Clearance (Chapter 7) and the Future of Landmines (Chapter 10). Ms. Schurtman wrote the chapters on International Law Governing Landmines (Chapter 8), Initiatives to Control Landmines (Chapter 9), and the Conclusion (Chapter 11). Mr. Stover wrote the chapters on the the Development and Use of Landmines (Chapter 2) and the Overview of Medical and Social Consequences of Landmines (Chapter 5). The chapter on Production and Trade in Landmines (Chapter 3) was written and researched by Steve Askin, a journalist and consultant to the Arms Project. Mr. Askin also contributed substantially to the book as a whole, through his writing and research and, particularly, to Chapters 2, 7, and 10.

The book was prepared for publication by Barbara Baker, New York staff associate of the Arms Project. Addditional production assistance was given by Cesar Bolaños, New York staff associate of the Arms Project. Kathleen Bleakley, Washington staff associate of the Arms Project, provided research, editorial, and production support. Maps were made by Michael S. Miller, a New York geographer. Drawings were made by Pamela Blotner, a Boston artist. Copy editing was provided by Ezra Field. The Arms Project and PHR are grateful to Handicap International, the International Committee of the Red Cross, Medico International, and Mines Advisory Group for providing photos. The Arms Project and PHR thank the many staff members of HRW and PHR who have worked on landmines issues in past years, producing important country reports on landmines; their work figures heavily in this book.

The Arms Project and PHR especially thank Senator Patrick J. Leahy for writing the Preface. They are grateful for the unwavering support that he and Representative Lane Evans have given to the campaign to ban landmines. In addition, the Arms Project and PHR thank Tim Rieser, staff member to Senator Leahy, and Tom O'Donnell, staff member to Representative Evans, for their invaluable assistance. *Arms Control Today*, a publication of the Arms Control Association, Washington, D.C., has kindly given permission to reproduce Senator Leahy's article "Landmine Moratorium: A Strategy for Stronger International Limits" as an appendix to this book.

Many individuals have given generously of their time and expertise to this book. They include Jody Williams and Bobby Muller of the Vietnam Veterans of America Foundation (VVAF), Rae McGrath of the Mines Advisory Group (United Kingdom), Philippe Chabasse and Tim Carstairs of Handicap International (France), Angelika Beer and Ronald Ofteringer of Medico International (Germany), and Louise Doswald-Beck and Robin Coupland of the International Committee of the Red Cross (Switzerland). The Arms Project and PHR are grateful for the cooperation of David Gowdey of the State Department and other State Department and Defense Department personnel. The Arms Project and PHR thank William Arkin, Patrick Blagden, Ed Cairns, Thomas Cardemone, Terry Gander, Jose Gonzales, Francoise Hampson, Nicolene Hengen, Lars Jederlund, Richard Knight, Karel Koster, Lucy Mathiak, Aryeh Neier, Ferruccio F. Petracco, David Roy, Renee Simar, James Wurst, and the staffs of the United States Army Countermine Systems Directorate, Fort Belvoir and the Office of the Project Manager, Mines, Countermine and Demolitions, Picatinny Arsenal, United States Army.

This book has benefitted greatly from informal comments and background papers presented at a conference of experts organized by the International Committee of the Red Cross at Montreux, Switzerland on April 21-23, 1993, and at the London Conference of Nongovernmental Organizations in Support of a Ban on Antipersonnel Landmines on May 24-26, 1993. The co-sponsors of the London NGO Conference were the Arms Project, PHR, VVAF, Handicap International (France), Medico International (Germany), and Mines Advisory Group (United Kingdom).

The views and contents of this book are solely the responsibility of the Arms Project and Physicians for Human Rights.